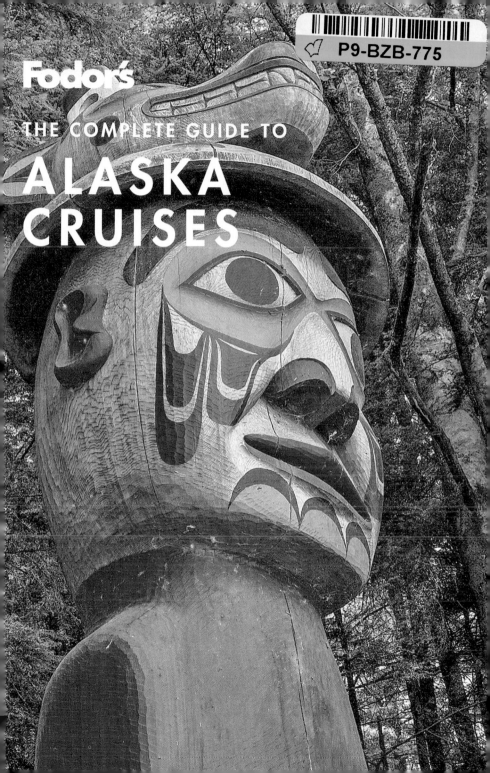

P9-BZB-775

Fodor's
THE COMPLETE GUIDE TO
ALASKA CRUISES

Welcome to Alaska Cruising

For lovers of nature, few places exhilarate like Alaska, and the easiest way to see America's last frontier is on a cruise ship. Traveling past the lush rain forests of the Inside Passage and the forested slopes of the Kenai Peninsula, ships sail near sights such as calving glaciers and jagged sea cliffs, offering views of the Northern Lights and more. Activities on land and sea can include kayaking to icebergs, fishing for salmon, flightseeing over soaring mountain peaks, riding the Alaska Railroad, and viewing the region's wildlife, from bears to whales.

TOP REASONS TO GO

★ **Glaciers:** Nothing beats the panoramic views from a cruise in Glacier Bay.

★ **Bears:** When the salmon run, the brown bears of Kodiak spring into action.

★ **Art:** Aleut weaving and Inupiaq ivory carvings evoke native Alaskan traditions.

★ **Outdoor Adventures:** Fishing the Kenai and hiking Mendenhall Glacier are just a start.

★ **Denali:** A side trip to this national park to see North America's tallest peak is a must.

★ **Ketchikan:** Totem poles and Gold Rush history make this one of the state's top ports.

Contents

MAPS

Chapter 1

EXPERIENCE AN ALASKA CRUISE

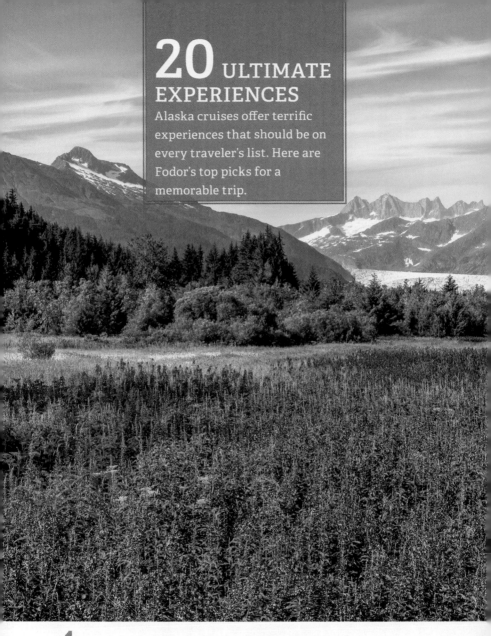

20 ULTIMATE EXPERIENCES

Alaska cruises offer terrific experiences that should be on every traveler's list. Here are Fodor's top picks for a memorable trip.

1 Juneau and Mendenhall Glacier

Alaska's capital city has a vibrant downtown filled with charming shops, restaurants, and bars, but it's also known for its proximity to the most easily accessible glacier in the state, Mendenhall Glacier. *(Ch. 5)*

2 Bear Spotting

Magnificent brown bears can be found all over southern Alaska, but Kodiak Island is one of the most popular spots for a sighting, especially late in the cruise season. *(Ch. 5)*

3 Cruising Through Glacier Bay

In this stunning national park and preserve in Southeast Alaska, you'll witness calving glaciers and abundant wildlife right from the deck of your cruise ship. *(Ch. 5)*

4 Kayaking and Rafting

With 365,000 miles of streams and rivers, there are plenty of opportunities for water adventures, whether it's calm kayaking or class IV white-water rafting. *(Ch. 5)*

5 Gold Rush History

The discovery of gold created modern Alaska, bringing thousands north to establish towns like Skagway and Dawson City, which still offer gold-panning tours today. *(Ch. 5, 6)*

6 Whale Watching

A variety of cetaceans, from gray whales to humpbacks to orcas, are found in Alaskan waters. Prince William Sound and the Inside Passage are prime spots for watching. *(Ch. 4, 5)*

7 Anchorage

Alaska's most populous city is also its most thriving urban center, with impressive cuisine and nightlife, not to mention gorgeous urban trails for hiking and biking. *(Ch. 4)*

8 Denali National Park

Home to North America's tallest mountain, Denali is Alaska's most famous park, and yet remains surprisingly pristine, with plenty of moose, bears, caribou, and wolves. *(Ch. 6)*

9 Native Culture

With 229 federally recognized tribes, Alaska has a thriving Native culture, from Anchorage's Alaska Native Heritage Center to Ketchikan's Saxman Totem Park. *(Ch. 4, 5)*

10 Flightseeing Tours

When you're on land, take a flightseeing excursion—small bush planes offer amazing views and unparalleled access to some of the state's most wondrous spots. *(Ch. 5)*

11 Fishing

From Ketchikan to Homer, Alaska is perhaps the best place for fishing in the world. Try your hand at nabbing a salmon or halibut via a chartered boat or fly-fishing. *(Ch. 5)*

12 The Midnight Sun

In summer, some Alaskan regions see nearly 24 hours of sunlight. Take advantage by going to a midnight baseball game in Fairbanks or attending various festivals. *(Ch. 6)*

13 Fairbanks

Home to the University of Alaska, the state's second largest city is a young, hip college town with plenty of art, culture, breweries, and outdoor activities. *(Ch. 6)*

14 Glacier Trekking

Alaska is home to nearly 100,000 glaciers like Mendenhall and Matanuska, and a guided glacier trek is the perfect way to explore these otherworldly giants up close. *(Ch. 5)*

15 Dogsledding

Mushing is one of Alaska's most popular sports, thanks to the famed Iditarod race from Anchorage to Nome. In the off-season, you can visit dogsled camps across the state. *(Ch. 5, 6)*

16 Seafood

Dining in Alaska is all about the freshly caught seafood, from Copper River red salmon and halibut cheeks to Dungeness and king crabs. *(Ch. 4, 5)*

17 Wildlife

Wildlife abounds all over Alaska, from bears, moose, caribou, and wolves in Denali to bison, bald eagles, and Dall sheep in various parks and reserves. *(Ch. 4, 5, 6)*

18 Ketchikan

Experience the frontier spirit of Alaska in this port of call, home to Saxman Totem Park and the colorful houses of Creek Street. *(Ch. 5)*

19 The Northern Lights

Seeing the stunning greens, purples, and reds of the Aurora Borealis is possible during a cruise. Plan a trip in the late season (September) for your best chance. *(Ch. 6)*

20 Alaska's Railroads

Adding a train ride before or after your cruise on the famed White Pass and Yukon Railway is a great way to see Alaska's towering mountains. *(Ch. 6)*

WHAT'S WHERE

1 Southeast Alaska. Southeast Alaska ("the Panhandle" or "Southeast") includes the Inside Passage. Only Haines and Skagway have roads to "the Outside." Juneau, the state capital, and Sitka, the former Russian hub, are here. At Glacier Bay National Park you can get close to massive tidewater glaciers, and the Alaska Chilkat Bald Eagle Preserve draws more than 4,000 of these birds to the Haines area. Long fjords snake between the mountains, timbered slopes plunge to the rocky shores, and marine life abounds. You're almost certain to spend at least some time here on your cruise.

2 Anchorage. With nearly half the state's population, Anchorage is Alaska's biggest city and a common arrival or departure point for cruisers—even if you'll likely be traveling to either Seward or Whittier where your ship is docked. The restaurants, art and history museums, copious espresso stands, and performing arts have earned the city the sobriquet "Seattle of the North." Alaskans often deride the place as "Los Anchorage," but the occasional moose am-

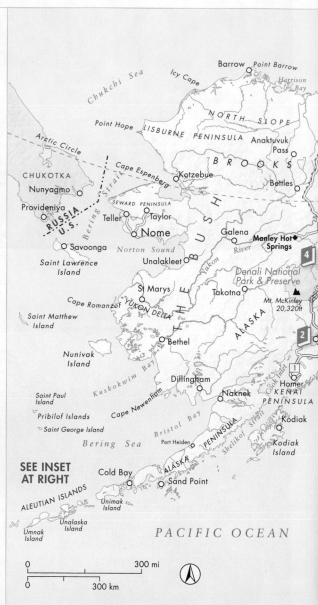

bling down a bike trail hints at the nearby wilderness.

3 Southcentral Alaska. This is the place for great fishing, hiking, rafting, and wildlife viewing. Prince William Sound is a top destination for these activities and is a common cruise stop. Your ship might call at Seward or Homer on the Kenai Peninsula, two laid-back towns with great museums. Kodiak is a lesser-called-at port known for its green-carpeted mountains and Kodiak brown bears; if you're one of the lucky few who visits, charter outfits can take you to remote wilderness spots.

4 Denali National Park. Home to the "Great One"—the highest peak in North America—Denali National Park and Preserve comprises 6 million acres of Alaska's best wildlife, scenery, and adventures. If you do one land extension before or after your cruise, make it this one.

5 The Interior. Bound by the Brooks Range to the north and the Alaska Range to the south, the interior is home to Denali National Park and Preserve. The region's major city is Fairbanks; Canada's Yukon Territory is within striking distance.

What to Eat and Drink in Alaska

BLACK COD
Black cod may be overshadowed by more famous Alaskan seafood like salmon and halibut, but it's still one of the most delicious fresh fishes you can sample here. So oily it's also known as butterfish, black cod is a rich and succulent choice found on many menus throughout the state.

BLUEBERRIES
Berry picking here is a serious business. People compete with each other for the best spots during the short growing season for the chance to sample fresh, sweet berries. If you can't go berry picking, look for options like gooseberry pie, wild berry cobbler, and blueberry French toast on menus.

BEER
The craft beer craze has made it to Alaska, and now dozens of microbreweries scattered across the state provide ample tasting opportunities for beer-lovers. Try creations that make use of the native bounty, like beers brewed with spruce tips, an Alaskan specialty since Captain Cook made his first voyage here.

SALMON
Sampling salmon, perhaps Alaska's most famous food, is an essential experience. Throughout the summer, five types of salmon (king, coho, sockeye, chum, and pink) fill Alaska's rivers, beckoning commercial and amateur fishers alike. Many consider Copper River salmon to be some of the best in the world, and there's nothing like trying it fresh. Have it grilled simply and alongside fresh local vegetables. Or try smoked salmon, a quintessential Alaskan snack.

BAKED ALASKA
Complete with parading waiters and flaming meringue, Baked Alaska has long been a festive cruise-ship tradition. Presented with a flourish, it's a staple that Holland America raises to new heights by serving it sprinkled with edible gold.

HALIBUT CHEEKS
Another favorite of amateur fishers (Ketchikan in particular has some excellent waters for halibut fishing), fresh-caught halibut should also be on your must-eat list, and halibut cheeks are a delicate, sweet treat. Cut from the head of the fish, the cheeks are small, oval-shaped, and often compared to scallops in appearance and texture. Try them breaded or sautéed with garlic and butter.

Traditional Alaskan smoked salmon

REINDEER
These domesticated cousins of caribou were first brought over from Siberia and have since become a popular Alaskan protein. Reindeer store their fat on the outside of their muscles, which results in a lean cut free from the marbling found in other red meats. Pair a side of reindeer sausage with breakfast or savor reindeer meatloaf or burgers at dinner.

SOURDOUGH BREAD
A favorite of those who came to Alaska in search of riches during the Klondike Gold Rush, sourdough bread is created with naturally occurring fermentation instead of baker's yeast. During the Gold Rush, yeast and baking soda were difficult to find, and so a legend was born (sourdough also keeps a lot longer than regular bread). Today items like sourdough pancakes and pastries help keep the Gold Rush spirit alive on menus throughout the state.

KELP
Kelp has been on the menu for Native people along Alaska's southern coast for centuries. Luckily for gourmands, interest has been sparked again and local companies like Barnacle Foods are harvesting and selling it in a variety of forms, including kelp pickles, salsa, and spice mix. Pick some up from an Alaskan grocery store.

CRABS
Whether it's Dungeness, snow, or king, you'll find crab in any seaside Alaskan town, freshly caught from places like the Aleutian Islands. Get ready to crack open a crab leg and dip the succulent meat in melted butter, one of the most memorable, and tastiest, Alaskan culinary experiences.

What to Buy in Alaska

ULU KNIFE
Originally made from rock, slate, or jade with a wooden or bone handle, the ulu is a curved, all-purpose knife originally used by Alaska Natives for everything from making clothes to cutting food to building boats. Today, it's a fun gift with an interesting history as well as a great kitchen tool, often paired with a bowl for dicing and mincing.

HAND-CRAFTED BOWLS
Birch logs that arrive at the Great Alaskan Bowl Company undergo a 22-step process of shaping, sanding, oiling, and drying until they turn into beautiful objets d'art that ripple with streaks of dark and light grain unique to each piece.

XTRATUFS
These dependable rubber boots are quintessential Alaska, owned by nearly every local in a coastal town. Preferred because of their comfort and ability to withstand brutal Alaskan weather, Xtratufs have become a veritable rite-of-passage for Alaskans. In recent years, the boot-maker has paired with Alaskan company Salmon Sisters, releasing more fashionable Xtratufs with colorful, patterned interiors.

QUIVET HATS
Alaskans excel at inventing ways to keep warm, and the quivet hat is one of their most beloved creations. Quivet is the undercoat of a musk ox that yields a yarn finer than cashmere and eight times warmer than wool. Find hand-knit hats in places like the Oomingmak Musk Ox Co-op.

JADE
Alaska's state gem, jade has long been used by Native people for tools, jewelry, and weapons. There's lots of it to go around—including an entire jade mountain on Alaska's Seward Peninsula—so jade carvings and jewelry can be found in gift shops across the state.

SMOKED SALMON
You can't head home without bringing back some of Alaska's most famous seafood. Caught fresh and then filleted, brined, and smoked with a variety of methods, smoked salmon is especially delicious when paired with crackers and/or cheese. It often needs to be kept refrigerated, so be sure to check the package before you put it in your luggage.

Kobuk Tea Company in Anchorage

TEA

Alaskans can get pretty experimental with their tea. Popular varieties include wild rose and tea made from chaga, an antioxidant-packed fungus that grows on birch trees throughout the north. The Anchorage-based Kobuk Tea Company has been leading this tea brigade for more than 50 years, and at their eclectic downtown store, you can buy all manner of local and international goods; be sure to take home some of their signature Samovar Tea.

GOLD

Alaska's other most famous precious metal is what sent thousands careening north during the Yukon Gold Rush. Today, you can easily buy this prized Alaskan gold or find some yourself on a gold-panning tour. Once you get home, you'll be able to relive the thrill of those first Klondikers as you show off your Alaskan gold.

CHRISTMAS DECORATIONS

It may be July, but that won't stop shoppers from buying Christmas ornaments at the Santa Claus House in North Pole, Alaska. Fifteen minutes south of Fairbanks, the town is decorated for the holidays year-round and offers plenty of items to put you in the holiday spirit. You can even tell your kids that their gifts really did come from the North Pole.

ALASKA NATIVE CRAFTS

Alaska's Native culture is reflected in its abundance of craft traditions, from totem poles to intricate baskets and detailed carvings. Many of these reflect traditions passed down across countless generations. Each of Alaska's Native groups is noted for particular skills and visual-art styles.

Best Wildlife Experiences in Alaska

BALD EAGLES IN HAINES
These majestic birds can be found all over the state, lounging everywhere from the docks of Juneau to the northern villages of the Bush. But the world's largest gathering of bald eagles occurs in southeast Alaska each winter, along the Chilkat River near Haines. Here they build the biggest nests in the world, the largest one to date weighing almost 3 tons.

THE BIG 5 IN DENALI NATIONAL PARK
Denali gives you the best chance to spot the "Big 5" of Alaskan animals. Bears, moose, wolves, caribou, and Dall sheep all live throughout the park in various regions, and sightings happen often. Always be on the lookout (even if you're on a bus tour), and be sure to keep your distance.

OTTERS AND SEALS IN GLACIER BAY
Whether you're sailing through Glacier Bay National Park on a large cruise ship or kayaking on a guided tour, keep your eyes out for the many animals that inhabit this area. Otters and harbor seals are often found on the rocky shores, hanging out on ice floes, or swimming in the waters.

HUMPBACK AND ORCA WHALES IN JUNEAU
Whale-watching tours are offered from many coastal towns, but the best leave from Juneau. Here huge humpback whales move in pods, traveling and feeding together. The finale occurs when every whale rockets to the surface for air. You can also often spot majestic orcas traveling with their young.

IDITAROD SLED DOG RACE

The original Iditarod was a relay of dog teams getting medication to Nome during a diphtheria outbreak in 1925. Today the Iditarod commemorates the history and culture of dog mushing in Alaska. The race begins in early March in Anchorage with the top runners reaching Nome eight to ten days later.

SALMON IN KETCHIKAN

The southeast town of Ketchikan is often referred to as the salmon capital of the world. Head out on a fishing boat to try your luck catching one yourself. Every summer, salmon return to where they were born to spawn and die; seeing them fill the rivers is morbid, but part of the Alaskan circle of life.

BROWN BEARS ON KODIAK ISLAND

Brown bears, or grizzlies, are found throughout the state, from Admiralty Island near Wrangell to Katmai National Park. But one the most accessible places is Kodiak National Wildlife Refuge. Spot them most easily in July and August, feeding along the salmon-filled streams.

BELUGA WHALES AND DOLPHINS IN TURNAGAIN ARM

Turnagain Arm, a waterway in the north-western part of the Gulf of Alaska, is known for its large tidal ranges (it has the second-highest tides in North America). Driving along it through the Cook Inlet is one of the most scenic road trips in the country. As you head from Anchorage to the Kenai Peninsula, be on constant look-out for the beluga whales and dolphins that regularly swim through these waters; Beluga Point is a popular stop for a photo-op.

HORNED PUFFINS IN KENAI FJORDS

Not far from Seward, Kenai Fjords National Park is a prime spot to see horned puffins, favorites among birders. Named for the black, fleshy projec-tions above each eye, these diving seabirds are expert swimmers, using their wings to "fly" underwater and their webbed feet as rudders. You can also spot them in Glacier Bay National Park and Preserve.

Best Shore Excursions in Alaska

SNORKELING IN KETCHIKAN
With a wet suit and guide, you can spend an hour spying on the cool marine species—including sunflower and blood starfish, sea urchins, and sea cucumbers—that inhabit the calm tide pools and submerged rock walls around Mountain Point.

HELICOPTER GLACIER TREKKING IN JUNEAU
The Juneau Icefield is home to massive glaciers with awesome bright blue crevasses, and can be your landing pad when you take a scenic helicopter tour from Juneau. No experience is required, but you'll need to be in decent physical condition as you strap on mountaineering spikes and other glacier gear and explore two miles or more of steep, uneven, and visually surreal terrain. Some treks even teach you the basics of ice-wall climbing.

ROCK CLIMBING IN SKAGWAY
If you're looking for a physical challenge in the remote Alaskan wilderness, the Klondike Rock Climbing and Rappelling Adventure in Skagway definitely qualifies. After a short hike to the base of granite cliffs in the region's renowned White Pass, you'll learn the proper techniques of rock climbing and rappelling from experienced guides. There are multiple climbing routes to choose from—from easy to very difficult. The payoff is twofold: the awesome views of the Skagway River and surrounding wilderness as well as the exhilaration of rappelling back down to the base.

FISHING IN SITKA
If you love to fish, Sitka is the place to go, thanks to its location on the open ocean; anglers can catch any of five species of Pacific salmon, including prized king salmon, as well as halibut. Opt for a half-day excursion focused on trolling or mooching for salmon or book a full day to also anchor and jig for halibut. Any fish you catch can be processed, frozen, and shipped home for you to enjoy.

ATV TOUR IN KETCHIKAN
Keep your foot on the gas pedal and your eyes on the trail as you navigate an ATV over 10 miles of backcountry rain forest. There's a chance to spot local wildlife—from eagles to deer and bears—as you race over rugged terrain. Enjoy the adrenaline rush of navigating sharp curves, then swap the steering wheel for the passenger seat and enjoy the views of Tongass National Forest (the largest in the country), Behm Canal, and the Inside Passage where your ship is docked.

WHALE-WATCHING IN THE ICY STRAIT
Humpbacks or orcas—do you have a favorite? It doesn't really matter, because during a whale-watching excursion in the Icy Strait, you're likely to see both. How many and how close depends on the month, the weather, and however the whales are feeling that day. But spending three or four hours watching these magnificent creatures

Glacier trekking on the Juneau Icefield

surface, splash, spout, bubble-feed, and even breach out of the water from any distance is pretty amazing. Sea lions, dolphins, and even bears are bonus species you might see, so bring your binoculars and have your camera ready.

MISTY FJORDS FLIGHT-SEEING TOUR IN KETCHIKAN

During a Misty Fjords Flightseeing tour, you'll soar above the huge granite cliffs, cascading waterfalls, and unspoiled wilderness of this two million-acre national monument area located on postcard-perfect Rudyerd Bay. Depending on the tour you book, you might even land on a secluded lake where you can soak in the serenity by stepping onto the pontoon.

DOG SLEDDING ON MENDENHALL GLACIER IN JUNEAU

If you've always wanted to get behind a sled of ready-to-run Alaskan huskies and yell mush, book an authentic dogsled adventure—even in the middle of summer—by helicoptering from Juneau to a dog sled camp on the icy-blue Mendenhall Glacier. There, you'll meet dozens of resident canines who love to run (as well as their irresistibly cute puppies) and even take the reins yourself to guide your dog team on an exhilarating sled adventure across the snow pack.

WHITE PASS TRAIN AND MOUNTAIN BIKING IN SKAGWAY

Don't let the sedate train ride from Skagway on the vintage White Pass & Yukon Route Railroad fool you. Once you've enjoyed the stunning scenery of the Skagway Valley and arrive at White Pass Summit, it will be time to put on your helmet, straddle your mountain bike, and ride back down—descending almost 3,000 thrilling feet over 15 miles along the Klondike Highway.

BEAR WATCHING AND FLIGHTSEEING IN KETCHIKAN

Soar high above the wild landscape around Ketchikan in a float plane before landing on a lake at one of several locations where Alaskan black bears (and occasionally brown bears) congregate: Neets Bay (home to the highest black bear population per square mile in North America), Prince of Wales Island (the third-largest island in the U.S. and a known bear habitat), or Misty Fjords.

Best Bets

BEST CRUISE LINE: MAINSTREAM

■ **Carnival Cruise Line.** With its adults-only Serenity area, water park–style slides, and Vegas-style entertainment (not to mention all the other activities), the line's ships are designed to appeal to the widest range of travelers.

■ **Norwegian Cruise Line.** Noted for their family-friendly accommodations, specialty dining, and outstanding entertainment, the line gets high marks from passengers of all ages.

■ **Royal Caribbean International.** The line appeals to families with its high-energy entertainment, extensive sports facilities, youth programs, and even nurseries for toddlers and babies.

BEST CRUISE LINE: PREMIUM

■ **Princess Cruises.** Sophisticated styling includes piazza-style atriums, specialty restaurants, and quiet enclaves. Spas are noted for their facilities and service.

■ **Holland America Line.** Traditional cruise enthusiasts find that HAL hits the right note with gracious, art-filled ships that also include all the latest high-tech gadgets.

■ **Celebrity Cruises.** For sheer beauty and innovative cuisine, Celebrity ships deliver a quality experience in modern surroundings.

BEST CRUISE LINE: LUXURY

■ **Silversea Cruises.** Butlers assigned to every suite add an extra level of pampering on luxuriously appointed vessels.

■ **Regent Seven Seas Cruises.** In the luxury segment Regent offers the most all-inclusive cruises, even including all shore excursions in the fare.

BEST CRUISE SHIP: LARGE

■ *Celebrity Solstice*, **Celebrity Cruises.** This ship offers a dozen places to dine, with half of them included in the fare, and a serene atmosphere for total relaxation.

■ *Royal Princess*, **Princess Cruises.** *Royal Princess* incorporates all the line's signature elements, including a stunning atrium with a sidewalk café atmosphere.

■ *Norwegian Bliss*, **Norwegian Cruise Line.** This ship was designed especially for cruising in Alaska and offers more than a dozen dining options along with nonstop activities.

BEST CRUISE SHIP: MEDIUM

■ *Seven Seas Mariner*, **Regent Seven Seas Cruises.** With complimentary gourmet specialty restaurants and shore excursions, this ship is a stylish choice for discerning travelers.

■ *Oceania Regatta*, **Oceania Cruises.** With only 684 passengers onboard, Regatta scores high marks for its country club casual ambience in intimate spaces with beautifully appointed accommodations, unobtrusive service, and fine dining.

■ *Eurodam*, **Holland America Line.** Accommodations filled with amenities are some of the most comfortable at sea, and the alcoholic beverage and specialty dining charges are the most reasonable you will find without sacrificing quality.

BEST CRUISE SHIP: SMALL

■ *Safari Endeavour*, **UnCruise Adventures.** The luxury adventure yachts offer a nearly all-inclusive experience on vessels with well-appointed public areas and accommodations.

■ *Silver Muse*, **Silversea Cruises.** High-end specialty restaurants, expansive decks and lounges, and a theater for superior entertainment are just some of the luxury features aboard *Silver Muse*.

BEST REGULAR OUTSIDE CABINS

■ *Coral Princess*, **Princess Cruises.** All cabins feature niceties such as a refrigerator and generous storage for even the largest wardrobe.

■ *Eurodam*, Holland America Line. Comfort is key, and all cabins have flat-screen televisions, lighted magnifying makeup mirrors, and comfortable bedding.

BEST INSIDE CABINS

■ *Amsterdam*, Holland America Line. The largest inside cabin category measures in at a whopping 293 square feet—some of the most spacious inside accommodations at sea.

■ *Disney Wonder*, Disney Cruise Line. Designed with families in mind, *Disney Wonder*'s inside cabins have all the space needed for a comfortable cruise.

BEST REGULAR DINING ROOM CUISINE

■ Holland America Line. Under the leadership of Master Chef Rudi Sodamin, the culinary staff of Holland America Line creates dishes high in quality and taste.

■ Regent Seven Seas Cruises. Creative dishes and wines chosen to complement all menus are a hallmark of Regent Seven Seas.

■ Silversea Cruises. A true gourmet meal is hard to come by on land, let alone at sea, but Silversea chefs accomplish just such a feat with dishes prepared à la minute.

BEST SHIPS FOR FAMILIES

■ *Carnival Legend*, Carnival Cruise Line. Pools and the disco are elaborate, and even picky kids should find the active programs enticing.

■ *Ovation of the Seas*, Royal Caribbean International. Well-conceived areas for children and teens, plus facilities that invite family members to play together, are bonuses for parents who want to spend quality family time with the kids.

■ *Disney Wonder*, Disney Cruise Line. Designed from the keel up with family fun in mind, *Disney Wonder* delivers fun for all with entertainment and age-appropriate activities and facilities.

BEST SHIPS FOR SPA LOVERS

■ *Celebrity Solstice*, Celebrity Cruises. Tranquil decor and a full complement of wraps, massages, and deluxe treatments are features of the AquaSpa. The expansive Persian Garden thermal suite includes cold and hot rooms as well as a Turkish hammam.

■ *Eurodam*, Holland America Line. Massages and facials take a back seat to the soothing whirlpool and indoor relaxation areas worthy of a fine European spa resort.

■ *Celebrity Millennium*, Celebrity Cruises. In addition to offering a wide range of massages and spa treatments, the decadent spa on this ship has a complimentary hydrotherapy pool and café.

BEST SHIPS FOR TRAVELERS WITH DISABILITIES

■ *Celebrity Solstice*, Celebrity Cruises. Although accommodations designed for accessibility are some of the best at sea, equally as desirable are the line's "easy" shore excursion options.

■ *Amsterdam*, Holland America Line. This ship has a variety of services for passengers with mobility, sight, and breathing impairments. All shore tenders are equipped with wheelchair-accessible platforms.

■ *Royal Princess*, Princess Cruises. Not only are accessible staterooms and suites available in a wide range of categories but there is also shore-side wheelchair access to appropriate tours on vehicles equipped with lifts.

BEST SHIPS FOR SERVICE

■ *Seven Seas Mariner*, Regent Seven Seas Cruises. Staff efforts almost go unnoticed, yet even out-of-the-ordinary requests are handled with ease. Butlers provide personalized service to guests in the top-category suites.

■ *Silver Muse*, Silversea Cruises. Butlers assigned to every suite fulfill even the most unusual requests.

BEST ENRICHMENT PROGRAMS

■ UnCruise Adventures. Naturalists and expedition guides are knowledgeable about the history, cultures, and wildlife of Alaska.

■ Holland America Line. Guest lecturers cover a wide range of topics and the Culinary Arts Center offers hands-on cooking classes, gourmet food presentations, and tasting events.

Chapter 2

PLANNING YOUR ALASKA CRUISE

Updated by
Linda Coffman

Alaska is one of cruising's showcase destinations. Itineraries give passengers more choices than ever before—from traditional loop cruises of the Inside Passage, to round-trips from Vancouver or Seattle, to one-way Inside Passage–Gulf of Alaska cruises.

Though Alaska cruises have generally attracted an older-passenger demographic, more young people and families were among the nearly 1.2 million passengers who set sail for the 49th state in 2018, and children are a common sight aboard ship. Cruise lines have responded with youth programs and shore excursions that appeal to youngsters and their parents. Shore excursions have become more active, too, often incorporating activities families can enjoy together, such as bicycling, kayaking, and hiking. Many lines also offer pre- or post-cruise land tours as an optional package trip, and onboard entertainment and learning programs are extensive. Most also hire naturalists, historians, or local experts to lead discussions stimulated by the local environment.

Cruise ships may seem like floating resorts, but you can't check out and go elsewhere if you don't like your ship. The one you choose will be your home—it determines the type of accommodations you have, the kind of food you eat, the style of entertainment you see, and even the destinations you visit. If you don't enjoy your ship, you probably won't enjoy your cruise. That is why the most important choice you'll make when booking a cruise is the combined selection of cruise line and cruise ship.

Choosing Your Cruise

Which cruise is right for you depends on numerous factors, notably your budget, the size and style of ship you choose, and the itinerary.

Itineraries

Cruise ships typically follow one of two itineraries in Alaska: round-trip Inside Passage loops and one-way Inside Passage–Gulf of Alaska cruises. Itineraries are usually seven days, though some lines offer longer trips. ■TIP→ Keep in mind that the landscape along the Inside Passage changes dramatically over the course of the summer cruise season. In May and June, you'll see snowcapped mountains and dramatic waterfalls from snowmelt cascading down the cliff faces, but by July and August most of the snow and some waterfalls will be gone.

The most popular Alaskan ports of call are Haines, Juneau, Skagway, Ketchikan, and Sitka. Lesser-known ports in British Columbia, such as Victoria and the charming fishing port of Prince Rupert, have begun to see more cruise traffic.

Small ships typically sail within Alaska, setting sail from Juneau or other Alaskan ports, stopping at the popular ports as well as smaller, less visited villages. Some expedition vessels focus on remote beaches and fjords, with few, if any, port calls.

ROUND-TRIP INSIDE PASSAGE LOOPS

A seven-day cruise typically starts and finishes in Vancouver, British Columbia, or Seattle, Washington. The first and last days are spent at sea, traveling to and from Alaska along the mountainous coast of British Columbia. Once in Alaska waters, most ships call at a different port on each of four days, and reserve one day for cruising in or near Glacier Bay National Park or another glacier-rich fjord.

ONE-WAY INSIDE PASSAGE– GULF OF ALASKA ITINERARIES

These cruises depart from Vancouver, Seattle, or, occasionally, San Francisco or Los Angeles (these are often repositioning cruises, so they happen only once a season), and finish at Seward or Whittier, the seaports for Anchorage (or vice versa). They're a good choice if you want to explore Alaska by land, either before or after your cruise. For this itinerary, you'll need to fly into and out of different cities (into Vancouver and out of Anchorage, for example), which can be pricier than round-trip airfare to and from the same city.

SMALL-SHIP ALASKA-ONLY ITINERARIES

Most small ships and yachts home port in Juneau or other Alaskan ports and offer a variety of one-way and round-trip cruises entirely within Alaska. A typical small-ship cruise is a seven-day, one-way or round-trip from Juneau, stopping at several Inside Passage ports—including smaller ports skipped by large cruise ships.

SMALL-SHIP INSIDE PASSAGE REPOSITIONING CRUISES

Alaska's small cruise ships and yachts are based in Juneau or other Alaskan ports throughout the summer. In September they sail back to their winter homes in the Pacific Northwest; in May they return to Alaska via the Inside Passage. These repositioning trips are usually about 11 days and are sometimes discounted because they take place during the shoulder season.

OTHER ITINERARIES

Although mainstream lines stick to the popular seven-day Alaskan itineraries, some smaller luxury or excursion lines add more exotic options. For example, you may find an occasional voyage across the Bering Sea to Japan, Russia, and Asia. You can also create your own itinerary by taking Alaska Marine Highway System ferries to ports of your choosing.

FERRY TRAVEL IN ALASKA

The cruise-ship season is over by October, but for independent, off-season ferry travel, November is the best month. After the stormy month of October, it's still relatively warm on the Inside Passage (temperatures will average about 40°F), and it's a good month for wildlife watching. In particular, humpback whales are abundant off Sitka, and bald eagles congregate by the thousands near Haines.

Inland Cruise Tours

Most cruise lines offer the option of independent, hosted, or fully escorted land tours before or after your cruise. Independent tours give you a preplanned itinerary with confirmed hotel and transportation arrangements, but you're free to follow your interests in each town. Hosted tours are similar, but tour-company representatives are available along the route for assistance. On fully escorted tours you travel with a group, led by a tour director. Activities are preplanned (and typically prepaid), so you have a good idea of how much your trip will cost (not counting some meals and incidentals) before departure. Most lines offer cruise-tour itineraries that include a ride aboard the Alaska Railroad.

Running between Anchorage, Denali National Park, and Fairbanks are Holland America Line's *McKinley Explorer,* Princess Tours' *Denali Express* and *McKinley Express,* and Royal Caribbean's *Wilderness Express,* which offer unobstructed views of the passing terrain and wildlife from private glass-dome railcars. Princess Cruises and Holland America Line have the most extensive Alaska cruise tours, owning and operating their own coaches, railcars, and lodges.

In addition to rail trips to Denali, Holland America offers tours into the Yukon, as well as river cruises on the Yukon River. Princess's cruise tours include trips to the Yukon and the Kenai Peninsula. Both lines offer land excursions across the Arctic Circle to Prudhoe Bay. Several cruise lines also offer pre- and post-cruise tours of the Canadian Rockies. Of the traditional cruise-ship fleets, Carnival Cruise Lines, Oceania Cruises, and Disney Cruise Line do not offer cruise-tour packages in Alaska at this writing. Many cruise lines also offer pre- or post-cruise hotel and sightseeing packages in Vancouver, Seattle, or Anchorage lasting one to three days.

SMALL-SHIP LINES
Most small-ship lines offer hotel add-ons, but not land tours.

DO-IT-YOURSELF LAND SEGMENTS
Independent travel by rental car or RV before or after a cruise is another option. Passengers who wish to do so generally begin or end their cruise in Anchorage, the most practical port city to use as a base for exploring Alaska. Almost any type of car or recreational vehicle can be rented here.

When to Go

Cruise season runs from mid-May to late September. The most popular sailing dates are from late June through August, when warm days are apt to be most plentiful. In spring, wildflowers are abundant, and you'll likely see more wildlife along the shore because the animals haven't yet migrated to higher elevations. May and June are traditionally drier than July and August. Alaska's early fall brings the splendor of autumn hues and the first snowfalls in the mountains. Animals return to low ground, and shorter days bring the possibility of seeing the northern lights. Daytime temperatures in May, June, and September are in the 50s and 60s. July and August averages are in the 60s and 70s, with occasional days in the 80s. Cruising in the low and shoulder seasons provides other advantages besides discounted fares: availability of ships and particular cabins is greater, and ports are almost completely free of tourists.

Cruise Costs

Average fares for Alaskan itineraries vary dramatically depending on when you sail, which ship and grade of cabin you choose, and when you book. Published rates are highest during June, July, and August; you'll pay less—and have more space on ship and ashore—if you sail in May or September.

Whenever you choose to sail, remember that the brochure price is the highest fare the line can charge for a given cruise. Most lines offer early-booking discounts. Although these vary tremendously, many lines will offer at least 10% off if you book ahead of time, usually by the end of January for a summer cruise. Sometimes you can book a discounted last-minute cruise if the ship hasn't filled all its cabins, but you won't get your pick of ships, cabins, or sailing dates.

Recommended Gratuities by Cruise Line

Each cruise line has a different tipping policy. Some allow you to add tips to your shipboard account, and others expect you to dole out the dollars in cash on the last night of the cruise. Here are the suggested tipping amounts for each line covered in this book. Gratuity recommendations are often higher if you're staying in a suite with extra services, such as a butler.

- Alaskan Dream Cruises: $15 per person per day

- Alaska Marine Highway: No tipping allowed

- American Cruise Line: $125 per person per week

- Carnival Cruise Lines: $12.95-$13.95 per person per day

- Celebrity Cruises: $14.50-$18 per person per day

- Crystal Cruises: No tipping expected

- Disney Cruise Line: $12 per person per day

- Holland America Line: $13.50-$15 per person per day

- Lindblad Expeditions: $12-$15 per person per day

- Norwegian Cruise Line: $14.50-$17.50 per person per day

- Oceania Cruises: $16-$23 per person per day

- Princess Cruises: $13.50-$15.50 per person per day

- Regent Seven Seas Cruises: No tipping expected

- Royal Caribbean International: $14.50-$17.50 per person per day

- Seabourn: No tipping expected

- Silversea Cruises: No tipping expected

- UnCruise Adventures: 10% of the fare

- Viking Ocean Cruises: $15 per person per day

- Windstar Cruises: $13.50 per person per day

However, if your fare drops after you've paid your deposit and before you make your final payment, your travel agent may be able to negotiate to get the lower fare for you, obtain an onboard credit for the difference, or arrange an upgrade in your accommodations—for instance, from an ocean-view cabin to one with a balcony. Your travel agent should be your advocate in such instances.

TIPS

One of the most delicate—yet frequently debated—topics of conversation among cruise passengers involves the matter of tipping. Whom do you tip? How much? What's "customary" and "recommended"? Should parents tip the full amount for children, or is just half adequate? Why do you have to tip at all?

When transfers to and from your ship are a part of your air-and-sea program, gratuities are generally included for luggage handling. In that case, do not worry about the interim tipping. However, if you take a taxi to the pier and hand over your bags to a stevedore, be sure to tip him. Treat him with respect and pass along at least $5.

During your cruise, room-service waiters generally receive a cash tip of $1 to $3 per delivery. A 15% to 18% gratuity will automatically be added to each bar bill during the cruise. If you use salon and spa services, a similar percentage might be added to the bills there as well. If you dine in a specialty restaurant, you may be asked to provide a one-time gratuity for the service staff.

Nowadays, tips for cruise staff generally add up to about $12 to $23 per person per day, depending on the category of your accommodations. You tip the same amount for each person who shares the cabin, including children, unless otherwise indicated. Most cruise lines now either automatically add gratuities to passengers' onboard charge accounts or offer the option.

EXTRAS

Cruise fares typically include accommodation, onboard meals and snacks, and most onboard activities. Not normally included are airfare, shore excursions, tips, soft drinks, alcoholic drinks, or spa treatments. Some lines now add a room service fee, for instance Norwegian Cruise Line charges a $7.95 fee for all room service, with the exception of suites, and Royal Caribbean adds a $3.95 fee for late-night orders. Port fees, fuel surcharges, and sales taxes are generally added to your fare at booking.

Cabins

In years gone by, cabins were almost an afterthought. The general attitude of both passengers and the cruise lines used to be that a cabin is a cabin and is used only for changing clothes and sleeping. That's why the cabins on most older cruise ships are skimpy in size and short on amenities.

Most cabin layouts on a ship are identical or nearly so, but cabins with a commanding view fetch higher fares. But you should know that they are also more susceptible to side-to-side movement; in rough seas you could find yourself tossed right out of bed. On lower decks, you'll pay less and find more stability, particularly in the middle of the ship, but even upper-level cabins in the middle of the ship are more steady than others.

Some forward cabins have a tendency to be oddly shaped, as they follow the contour of the bow. They are also likely to be noisy; when the ship's anchor drops, you won't need a wake-up call. In rough seas you can feel the ship's pitch (its upward and downward motion) more in the front.

Should you go for the stern location instead? You're more likely to hear engine and machinery noise there, but you may also feel the pitch and possibly some vibration. However, many passengers feel the view of the ship's wake (the ripples it leaves behind as its massive engines move it forward) is worth any noise or vibration they might encounter there.

Above all, don't be confused by all the categories listed in cruise-line brochures—the categories more accurately reflect price levels based on location than any physical differences in the cabins themselves (keep repeating: prefabricated). Shipboard accommodations fall into four basic configurations: inside cabins, outside cabins, balcony cabins, and suites.

INSIDE CABINS

An inside cabin has no window or porthole. These are always the least expensive cabins and are ideal for passengers who would rather spend their vacation funds on excursions or other incidentals than on upgraded accommodations. Inside cabins are generally just as spacious as the lowest category of outside cabins, and decor and amenities are similar. Parents sometimes book an inside cabin for their older children and teens, while their own cabin is an outside across the hall with a window or balcony.

OUTSIDE CABINS

A standard outside cabin has either a picture window or porthole. To give the illusion of more space, these cabins might also rely on the generous use of mirrors for an even airier feeling. Two twin beds can be joined together to create one large bed. Going one step further, standard and larger outside staterooms on modern ships are often outfitted with a small sofa or loveseat with a cocktail table or small side table. Some larger cabins may have a combination bathtub–shower instead of just a shower.

BALCONY CABINS

A balcony—or veranda—cabin is an outside cabin with floor-to-ceiling glass doors that open onto a private deck. Although the cabin may have large expanses of glass, the balcony is sometimes cut out of the cabin's square footage (depending on the ship). Balconies are usually furnished with two chairs and a table for lounging and casual dining outdoors. However, you should be aware that balconies are not always completely private; sometimes your balcony is visible from balconies next door and also from balconies above. The furnishings and amenities of balcony cabins are otherwise much like those in standard outside cabins.

SUITES

Suites are the most lavish accommodations afloat, and although suites are always larger than regular cabins, they do not always have separate rooms for sleeping. Suites almost always have amenities that standard cabins do not have. Depending on the cruise line, you may find a small refrigerator or minibar stocked with complimentary soft drinks, bottled water, and the alcoholic beverages of your choice. Top suites on some ships include complimentary laundry service and complex entertainment centers with large flat-screen TVs, and DVD players. An added bonus to the suite life is the extra level of services many ships offer. Little extras might include afternoon tea and evening canapés delivered to you and served by a white-gloved butler.

Although minisuites on most contemporary ships have separate sitting areas with a sofa, chair, and cocktail table, don't let the marketing skill of the cruise lines fool you: so-called minisuites are usually little more than slightly larger versions of standard balcony cabins and seldom include the extra services and elaborate amenities you can get in regular suites. They're still generally a good value for the price if space matters.

ACCESSIBILITY ISSUES

All major cruise lines offer a limited number of staterooms designed to be wheelchair- and scooter-accessible. Booking a newer vessel will generally assure more choices. On newer ships, public rooms are usually more accessible, and more facilities have been planned with wheelchair users in mind. Auxiliary aids, such as flashers for the hearing impaired and buzzers for visually impaired passengers, as well as lifts for swimming pools and hot tubs, are sometimes available. However, more than the usual amount of preplanning is necessary for smooth sailing if you have special needs.

For example, when a ship is unable to dock—as is the case in Sitka—passengers are taken ashore on tenders that are sometimes problematic even for the able-bodied to negotiate. Some people with limited mobility may find it difficult to embark or disembark the ship when docked because of the steep angle of the gangways during high or low tide at certain times of day. In some situations, crew members may offer assistance that involves carrying guests, but if the sea is choppy when tendering is a necessity, that might not be an option.

Passengers who require continuous oxygen or have service animals have further hurdles to overcome. You can bring both aboard a cruise ship, but you should be prepared to present up-to-date records for your service animal if they are requested.

DECIPHER YOUR DECK PLAN

LIDO DECK

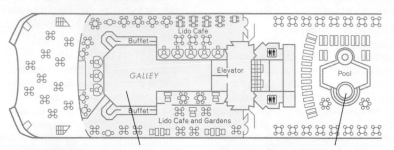

The Lido Deck is a potential source of noise—deck chairs are set out early in the morning and put away late at night; the sound of chairs scraping on the floor of the Lido buffet can be an annoyance.

Music performances by poolside bands can often be heard on upper-deck balconies located immediately below.

UPPER DECK AFT

Take note of where lifeboats are located—views from some outside cabins can be partially, or entirely, obstructed by the boats.

Upper-deck cabins, as well as those far forward and far aft, are usually more susceptible to motion than those in the middle of the ship on a low deck.

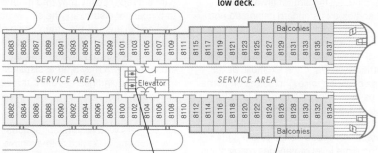

Cabins near elevators or stairs are a double-edged sword. Being close by is a convenience; however, although the elevators aren't necessarily noisy, the traffic they attract can be.

Balcony cabins are indicated by a rectangle split into two sections. The small box is the balcony.

MAIN PUBLIC DECK

Cabins immediately below restaurants and dining rooms can be noisy. Late sleepers might be bothered by early breakfast noise, early sleepers by late diners.

Theaters and dining rooms are often located on middle or lower decks.

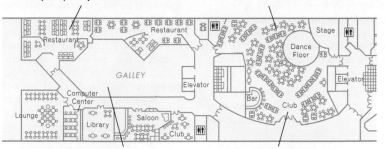

The ship's galley isn't usually labeled on deck plans, but you can figure out where it is by locating a large blank space near the dining room. Cabins beneath it can be very noisy.

Locate the ship's show lounge, disco, children's playroom, and teen center and avoid booking a cabin directly above or below them for obvious reasons.

LOWER DECK AFT

Cabins designated for passengers with disabilities are often situated near elevators.

Interior cabins have no windows and are the least expensive on board.

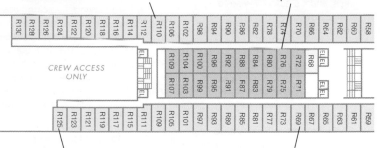

Lower-deck cabins, particularly those far aft, can be plagued by mechanical noises and vibration.

Ocean-view cabins are generally located on lower decks.

Booking Your Cruise

As a rule, the majority of cruisers plan their trips four to six months ahead of time. It follows, then, that a four- to six-month window should give you the pick of sailing dates, ships, itineraries, cabins, and flights to the port city. If you're looking for a standard itinerary and aren't choosy about the vessel or dates, you could wait for a last-minute discount, but they are rare and more difficult to find than in the past.

If particular shore excursions are important to you, consider booking them when you book your cruise to avoid disappointment later.

Using a Travel Agent

Whether it is your first or 50th sailing, your best friend in booking a cruise is a knowledgeable travel agent. The last thing you want when considering a costly cruise vacation is an agent who has never been on a cruise, calls a cruise ship "the boat," or—worse still—quotes brochure rates. The most important steps in cruise-travel planning are research, research, and more research; your partner in this process is an experienced travel agent. Booking a cruise is a complex process, and it's seldom wise to try to go it alone, particularly the first time. But how do you find a cruise travel agent you can trust?

The most experienced and reliable agent will be certified as an Accredited Cruise Counselor (ACC), Master Cruise Counselor (MCC), or Elite Cruise Counselor (ECC) by CLIA (the Cruise Lines International Association). These agents have completed demanding training programs, including touring or sailing on a specific number of ships. Your agent should also belong to a professional trade organization. In North America, membership in the American Society of Travel Agents (ASTA) indicates that an agency has

pledged to follow the code of ethics set forth by the world's largest association for travel professionals. In the best of all worlds, your travel agent is affiliated with both ASTA and CLIA.

Contrary to what conventional wisdom might suggest, cutting out the travel agent and booking directly with a cruise line won't necessarily get you the lowest price. Approximately 70% of all cruise bookings are still handled through travel agents. In fact, cruise-line reservation systems simply are not capable of dealing with tens of thousands of direct calls from potential passengers. Without an agent working on your behalf, you're on your own. Do not rely solely on Internet message boards for authoritative responses to your questions—that is a service more accurately provided by your travel agent.

TRAVEL AGENT PROFESSIONAL ORGANIZATION American Society of Travel Agents (*ASTA*) ☎ *703/739–2782, 800/965–2782 (24-hr hotline)* ⊕ *www.travelsense.org.*

CRUISE LINE ORGANIZATIONS Cruise Lines International Association (*CLIA*) ☎ *202/759–9370* ⊕ *www.cruising.org.*

Booking Your Cruise Online

In addition to local travel agencies, there are many hardworking, dedicated travel professionals working for websites. Both big-name travel sellers and mom-and-pop agencies compete for the attention of cyber-savvy clients, and it never hurts to compare prices from a variety of these sources. Some cruise lines even allow you to book directly with them through their websites.

As a rule, Web-based and toll-free brokers will do a decent job for you. They often offer discounted fares, though not always the lowest, so it pays to check around. If you know precisely what you want and how much you should pay to get a real bargain—and you don't mind

Before You Book

If you've decided to use a travel agent, ask yourself these 10 simple questions, and you'll be better prepared to help the agent do his or her job.

1. Who will be going on the cruise?

2. What can you afford to spend for the entire trip?

3. Where would you like to go?

4. How much vacation time do you have?

5. When can you get away?

6. What are your interests?

7. Do you prefer a casual or structured vacation?

8. What kind of accommodations do you want?

9. What are your dining preferences?

10. How will you get to the embarkation port?

dealing with an anonymous voice on the phone—by all means make your reservations when the price is right. Just don't expect the personal service you get from an agent you know. Also, be prepared to spend a lot of time and effort on the phone if something goes wrong.

Before You Go

To expedite your preboarding paperwork, most cruise lines have convenient forms on their websites. As long as you have your reservation number, you can provide the required immigration information (usually your citizenship information and passport number), reserve shore excursions, and even indicate any special requests from the comfort of your home. A few less-wired cruise lines still mail preboarding paperwork to you or your travel agent for completion after you make your final payment and request that you return the forms by mail or fax. No matter how you submit them, be sure to make hard copies of any forms you fill out and bring them with you to the pier to smooth the embarkation process.

What to Pack

Don't forget your valid passport or passport card; American and Canadian citizens are now required to provide proof of citizenship regardless of whether their Alaska cruise is crossing international boundaries. If you are flying into or connecting through Vancouver, you must have a valid passport; a passport card will not do. Although disposable and small digital cameras are very handy for candid shots, they are not much good for catching wildlife from afar. A good zoom lens can be heavy, but can make all the difference. Even if you have a high-quality camera, pack binoculars for everyone unless your cruise line provides them. Be sure to take bug spray during the summer months, as the mosquitoes are large, plentiful, and fierce.

What to Wear

When preparing for your Alaska cruise, remember this first rule of Alaskan thumb: be an onion. Never leave the ship without dressing in layers. Your first layer should be thin and airy so that if it gets warm, your skin can breathe. Every layer over that, however, should aim to keep you warm and dry. In Alaska it is quite common for a hot and sunny day to change abruptly. For onboard dress, follow your cruise line's suggestions about what to bring for the evening or two you might need to wear something formal to dinner.

Insurance

It's a good idea to purchase travel insurance, which covers a variety of possible hazards and mishaps, when you book a cruise. Any policy should insure you for travel and luggage delays. A travel policy will ensure that you can get to the next port of call should you miss your ship, or replace delayed necessities secure in the knowledge that you will be reimbursed for those unexpected expenditures. Save your receipts for all out-of-pocket expenses to file your claim, and be sure to get an incident report from the airline at fault.

Insurance should also cover you for unexpected injuries and illnesses. The medical insurance program you depend on at home might not extend coverage beyond the borders of the United States (many Alaska cruises stop in Canada). Medicare assuredly will not cover you if you are hurt or sick while abroad. It is worth noting that all ships of foreign registry are considered to be "outside the United States" by Medicare.

Nearly all cruise lines offer their own line of insurance. Compare the coverage and rates to determine which is best for you. Keep in mind that insurance purchased from an independent carrier is more likely to include coverage if the cruise line goes out of business before or during your cruise. Although it is a rare and unlikely occurrence, you do want to be insured in the event that it happens.

U.S. TRAVEL INSURERS Allianz Travel Insurance ☎ *866/884–3556* ⊕ *www. allianztravelinsurance.com.* **CSA Travel Protection** ☎ *877/243–4135* ⊕ *www. csatravelprotection.com.* **HTH Worldwide** ☎ *610/254–8700, 888/243–2358* ⊕ *www. hthworldwide.com.* **Travelex Insurance** ☎ *800/228–9792* ⊕ *www.travelexinsurance.com.* **Travel Guard International** ☎ *715/345–0505, 800/826–4919* ⊕ *www. travelguard.com.* **Travel Insured International** ☎ *800/243–3174* ⊕ *www.travelinsured.com.*

Arriving and Embarking

Most cruise-ship passengers fly to the port of embarkation. If you book your cruise far enough in advance, you'll be given the opportunity to purchase an air-and-sea package, which may—or may not—save you money on your flight. You might get a lower fare by booking your air independently or get considerably more convenient flight times, so it's a good idea to check for the best fare and most convenient flights available. Independent air arrangements might save you enough to cover the cost of a hotel room in your embarkation port so you can arrive early. It's not a bad idea to arrive a day early to overcome any jet lag and avoid the possibility of delayed flights.

If you buy an air-and-sea package from your cruise line, a uniformed cruise-line agent will meet you at baggage claim to smooth your way from airport to pier. You will need to claim your own bags and give them to the transfer driver so they can be loaded onto the bus. On arrival at the pier, luggage is automatically transferred to the ship for delivery to your cabin. The cruise-line ground transfer system can also be available to independent fliers. However, be sure to ask your travel agent how much it costs; you may find that a taxi or shuttle service is less expensive and more convenient.

Getting to the Port

Even if you opt to purchase your own airfare without an air-and-sea package, you can usually still access the cruise's transfer service, but it might cost more than a cab or shuttle.

Boarding

The lines at check-in can be long (up to an hour of wait time) if you are boarding a large cruise ship. You'll be issued a boarding card that doubles as your stateroom key and shipboard charge card. Either before you enter the check-in area or before proceeding to the ship, you and your hand luggage will pass through a security checkpoint. Once you're onboard, you'll produce your boarding card once more before heading to your cabin. On a small-ship cruise, embarkation is much more relaxed and relatively line-free.

Onboard

Check out your cabin to make sure that everything is in order. Try the plumbing and set the thermostat to the temperature you prefer. Your cabin may feel warm while docked but will cool off when the ship is underway. You should find a copy of the ship's daily schedule in the cabin. Take a few moments to look it over—you will want to know what time the lifeboat (or muster) drill takes place (a placard on the back of your cabin door will indicate directions to your emergency station), as well as meal hours and the schedule for various activities and entertainments.

Rented tuxedos are either hanging in the closet or will be delivered sometime during the afternoon; bon voyage gifts sent by your friends or travel agent should appear as well. Be patient if you are expecting deliveries, particularly on megaships. Cabin stewards participate in

the ship's turnaround and are extremely busy, although yours will no doubt introduce himself at the first available opportunity. It will also be awhile before your checked luggage arrives, so your initial order of business is usually the buffet, if you haven't already had lunch. Bring along the daily schedule to check over while you eat.

While making your way to the Lido buffet, no doubt you'll notice bar waiters offering trays of colorful bon voyage drinks, often in souvenir glasses that you can keep. Beware—they are not complimentary! If you choose one, you will be asked to sign for it. You are under no obligation to purchase.

Do your plans for the cruise include booking shore excursions and indulging in spa treatments? The most popular tours sometimes sell out, and spas can be busy during sea days, so your next stops should be the Shore Excursion Desk to book tours and the spa to make appointments if you didn't already book your spa visits and excursions in advance.

Dining room seating arrangements are another matter for consideration. If you aren't happy with your assigned dinner seating, speak to the maître d'. The employees at the reception desk can tell you where and when to meet with him. If you plan to dine in the ship's specialty restaurant, make those reservations as soon as possible to avoid disappointment.

Paying for Things Onboard

Because cashless society prevails on cruise ships, during check-in an imprint is made of your credit card, or you must make a cash deposit for use against your onboard charges. Most onboard expenditures are charged to your shipboard account (via a swipe of your key card) with your signature as verification, with the exception of some casino gaming.

Fodor's Cruise Preparation Time Line

4–6 Months Before Sailing

■ Check with your travel agent or the State Department for the identification required for your cruise.

■ Gather the necessary identification you need. If you need to replace a lost birth certificate, apply for a new passport, or renew one that's about to expire, start the paperwork now. Doing it at the last minute is stressful and often costly.

60–75 Days Before Sailing

■ Make the final payment on your cruise fare. Though the dates vary, your travel agent should remind you when the payment date draws near. Failure to submit the balance on time can result in the cancellation of your reservation.

■ Make a packing list for each person you'll be packing for.

■ Begin your wardrobe planning now. Try things on to make sure they fit and are in good repair (it's amazing how stains can magically appear months after something has been dry cleaned). Set things aside.

■ If you need to shop, get started so you have time to find just the right thing (and perhaps to return or exchange just the right thing).

■ Make kennel reservations for your pets. (If you're traveling during a holiday period, you may need to do this even earlier.)

■ Arrange for a house sitter.

If you're cruising, but your kids are staying home:

■ Make childcare arrangements.

■ Go over children's schedules to make sure they'll have everything they need while you're gone (gift for a birthday party, supplies for a school project, permission slip for a field trip).

30 Days Before Sailing

■ If you purchased an air-and-sea package, call your travel agent for the details of your airline schedule. Request seat assignments.

■ If your children are sailing with you, check their wardrobes now (do it too early and the really little kids may actually grow out of garments).

■ Make appointments for any personal services you wish to have before your cruise (for example, a haircut or manicure).

■ Get out your luggage and check the locks and zippers. Check for anything that might have spilled inside on a previous trip.

■ If you need new luggage or want an extra piece to bring home souvenirs, purchase it now.

2–4 Weeks Before Sailing

■ Receive your cruise documents through the travel agent or print them from the cruise line's website.

■ Examine the documents for accuracy (correct cabin number, sailing date, and dining arrangements); make sure names are spelled correctly. If there's something you do not understand, ask now.

■ Read all the literature in your document package for suggestions specific to your cruise. Most cruise lines include helpful information.

■ Pay any routine bills that may be due while you're gone.

■ Go over your personalized packing list again. Finish shopping.

1 Week Before Sailing

■ Finalize your packing list and continue organizing everything in one area.

■ Buy film or digital media and check the batteries in your camera.

■ Refill prescription medications with an adequate supply.

■ Make two photocopies of your passport or ID and credit cards. Leave one copy with a friend and carry the other copy separately from the originals.

■ Get cash. Get a supply of one-dollar bills for tipping baggage handlers (at the airport, hotel, pier, etc.).

■ You may also want to put valuables and jewelry that you won't be taking with you in the safety deposit box while you're at the bank.

■ Arrange to have your mail held at the post office or ask a neighbor to pick it up.

■ Stop newspaper delivery or ask a neighbor to bring it in for you.

■ Arrange for lawn and houseplant care or snow removal during your absence (if necessary).

■ Leave your itinerary, the ship's telephone number (plus the name of your ship and your stateroom number), and a house key with a relative or friend.

■ If traveling with young children, purchase small games or toys to keep them occupied while en route to your embarkation port.

3 Days Before Sailing

■ Confirm your airline flights; departure times are sometimes subject to change.

■ Put a card with your name, address, telephone number, and itinerary inside each suitcase.

■ Fill out the luggage tags that came with your document packet, and follow the instructions regarding when and how to attach them.

■ Complete any other paperwork that the cruise line included with your documents, either hard copy or online (foreign customs and immigration forms, onboard charge application, etc.). Do not wait until you're standing in the pier check-in line to fill them in!

■ Do last-minute laundry and tidy up the house.

■ Pull out the luggage and begin packing.

The Day Before Sailing

■ Take pets to the kennel.

■ Water houseplants and lawn (if necessary).

■ Dispose of any perishable food in the refrigerator.

■ Mail any last-minute bills.

■ Set timers for indoor lights.

■ Reorganize your wallet. Remove anything you will not need (local affinity cards, department store or gas credit cards, etc.), and put them in an envelope.

■ Finish packing and lock your suitcases.

Departure Day

■ Adjust the thermostat and double-check the door locks.

■ Turn off the water if there's danger of frozen pipes while you're away.

■ Arrange to be at the airport a minimum of two hours before your departure time (follow the airline's instructions).

■ Have government-issued photo ID and/or your passport ready for airport check-in.

■ Slip your car keys, parking claim checks, and airline tickets into your carry-on luggage. Never pack these items in checked luggage.

You'll get an itemized bill listing your purchases at the end of the voyage, and any discrepancies can be discussed at the purser's desk. To save time, check the balance of your shipboard account before the last day by requesting an interim printout of your bill from the purser to ensure accuracy. On some ships you can even access your account on your stateroom television.

Dining

All food, all the time? Not quite, but it is possible to literally eat away the day and most of the night on a cruise. A popular cruise directors' joke is, "You came on as passengers, and you will be leaving as cargo." Although it is meant in fun, it does contain a ring of truth. Food—tasty and plentiful—is available 24 hours a day on most cruise ships, and the dining experience at sea has reached almost mythic proportions. Perhaps it has something to do with legendary midnight buffets and the absence of menu prices, or maybe it's the vast selection and availability.

RESTAURANTS

Every ship has at least one main restaurant and a Lido, or casual, buffet alternative. Increasingly important are specialty restaurants. Meals in the primary and buffet restaurants are included in the cruise fare, as are round-the-clock room service, midday tea and snacks, and late-night buffets. Most mainstream cruise lines levy a surcharge for dining in alternative restaurants that may also include a gratuity, although there generally is no additional charge on luxury cruise lines.

You may also find a pizzeria or a specialty coffee bar on your ship—increasingly popular favorites cropping up on ships old and new. Although pizza is usually complimentary (though on some ships it is not), expect an additional charge for specialty coffees at the coffee bar and, quite likely, in the dining room as well.

You will also likely be charged for sodas and drinks other than iced tea, regular coffee, tap water, and fruit juice during meals.

There is often a direct relationship between the cost of a cruise and the quality of its cuisine. The food is sophisticated on some (mostly expensive) lines, among them Regent Seven Seas, Seabourn, Crystal Cruises, and Silversea. In the more moderate price range, Celebrity Cruises has always been known for its fine cuisine, and Oceania Cruises scores high marks as well. The trend toward featuring specialty dishes and even entire menus designed by acclaimed chefs has spread throughout the cruise industry; however, on most mainstream cruise lines the food is of the quality that you would find in any good hotel banquet—perfectly acceptable but certainly not great.

DINNER SEATINGS

If your cruise ship has traditional seatings for dinner, the one decision that may set the tone for your entire cruise is your dinner seating. Which is best? Early dinner seating is generally scheduled between 6 and 6:30 pm, and late seating can begin from 8:15 to 8:45 pm.

Families with young children and older passengers often choose an early seating. Early-seating diners are encouraged not to linger too long over dessert and coffee, because the dining room has to be readied for late seating. Late seating is viewed by some passengers as more romantic and less rushed.

Cruise lines understand that strict schedules no longer satisfy the desires of all modern cruise passengers. Almost all cruise lines now offer alternatives to the set schedules in the dining room, including casual dinner menus in their buffet facilities where more flexibility is allowed in dress and mealtimes. Open seating is the norm on more upscale lines; it allows passengers the flexibility to dine any time

Onboard Extras

As you budget for your trip, keep these likely additional costs in mind.

Cocktails: $8–$15

Wine by the glass: $8–$15

Beer: $6–$8

Bottled water: $2.50–$5

Soft drinks: $2.50–$3

Specialty ice cream and coffee: $5–$7

Laundry: $2–$11 per piece (where self-launder facilities are unavailable)

Spa treatments: $145–$265

Salon services: $30–$149

Casino gambling: 1¢ to $10 for slot machines; $5 and up for table games

Bingo: $5–$15 per card for multiple games in each session

during restaurant hours and be seated with whomever they please.

However, most contemporary and premium cruise lines now offer adaptations of open seating for variety and a more personalized experience for their passengers.

SPECIALTY RESTAURANTS
Sophisticated specialty restaurants that require reservations and frequently charge a fee have become increasingly popular in shipboard dining and are known to have some of the best food onboard. From as little as $30 per person for a complete steak dinner to $200 per person for an elaborate gourmet meal including fine wines paired with each course, specialty restaurants offer a refined dining option that cannot be duplicated in your ship's main restaurants. If you anticipate dining in your ship's intimate specialty restaurant, make reservations as soon as possible to avoid disappointment.

SPECIAL DIETS
Cruise lines make every possible attempt to ensure dining satisfaction. If you have special dietary considerations—such as low-salt, kosher, or food allergies—be sure to indicate them well ahead of time and check to be certain your needs are known by your waiter once onboard.

In addition to the usual menu items, so-called "spa," gluten-free or vegetarian selections, as well as children's menus, are usually available. Requests for dishes not featured on the menu can often be granted if you ask in advance.

ALCOHOL
On all but the most upscale lines, you pay for alcohol aboard the ship, including wine with dinner. Wine typically costs about what you would expect to pay at a nice lounge or restaurant in a resort or in a major city. Wine by the bottle is a more economical choice at dinner than ordering it by the glass. Any wine you don't finish will be kept for you and served the next night. Gifts of wine or champagne ordered from the cruise line (either by you, a friend, or your travel agent) can be taken to the dining room. Wine from any other source will incur a corkage fee of approximately $10 to $25 per bottle. Some (though not all) lines will allow you to carry wine aboard when you embark for the first time; almost no line allows you to carry other alcohol onboard.

Entertainment

It's hard to imagine, but in the early years of cruise travel, shipboard entertainment consisted of little more than poetry readings and passenger talent shows.

Drinking and Gambling Ages

Many underage passengers have learned to their chagrin that the rules that apply on land are also adhered to at sea. On most mainstream cruise ships you must be 21 to imbibe alcoholic beverages. There are exceptions—for instance, on cruises departing from countries where the legal drinking age is typically lower than 21. On some cruise lines, a parent who is sailing with his or her son(s) and/or daughter(s) who is between the ages of 18 and 20 may sign a waiver allowing the 18- to 20-year-old to consume alcoholic beverages, generally limited to beer and wine. However, by and large, if you haven't achieved the magic age of 21, your shipboard charge card will be coded as booze-free, and bartenders won't risk their jobs to sell you alcohol.

Gambling is a bit looser, and 18-year-olds can try their luck on cruise lines such as Carnival, Celebrity, Holland America, Norwegian, Royal Caribbean, and Silversea; most other cruise lines adhere to the age-21 minimum.

Those days are long gone. These days, seven-night cruises usually include two original production shows. One of these might be a Las Vegas–style extravaganza and the other a best-of-Broadway show featuring old and new favorites from the Great White Way. Other shows highlight the talents of individual singers, dancers, magicians, comedians, and even acrobats.

Real treats are the folkloric shows or other entertainments arranged to take place while cruise ships are in port. Local performers come aboard, usually shortly before the ship sails, to present traditional songs and dances. It's an excellent way to get a glimpse of their performing arts.

Most ships also have a movie theater or offer in-cabin movies, or you may be able to rent or borrow movies to watch on your in-cabin DVD player, if you have one. The latest twist in video programming can be found on Princess, Disney, Carnival and other lines with large cruise ships—huge outdoor LED screens where movies, music video concerts, news channels, and even the ship's activities are broadcast for passengers lounging poolside.

Enrichment programs have also become a popular pastime at sea. It may come as a surprise that port lecturers on many large contemporary cruise ships offer more information on shore tours and shopping than insight into the ports of call. If more cerebral presentations are important to you, consider a cruise on a line that features stimulating enrichment programs and seminars at sea. Speakers can include destination-oriented historians, popular authors, business leaders, radio or television personalities, and even movie stars.

LOUNGES AND NIGHTCLUBS

You'll often find live entertainment in the ship lounges after dinner (and even sometimes before dinner). If you want to unleash your inner American Idol, look for karaoke. Singing along in a lively piano bar is another shipboard favorite for would-be crooners.

Other lounges might feature easy-listening or jazz performances or live music for pre- and post-dinner social dancing. Later in the evening, lounges pick up the pace with music from the 1950s and '60s; clubs aimed at a younger crowd usually have more contemporary dance music during the late-night hours.

Will I Get Seasick?

Many first-time passengers are anxious about whether they'll be stricken by seasickness, but there is no way to tell until you actually sail. Modern vessels are equipped with stabilizers that eliminate much of the motion responsible for seasickness. On an Alaska cruise you will spend most of your time in calm, sheltered waters, so unless your cruise includes time out in the open sea (say, between San Francisco and Vancouver), you may not even feel the ship's movement—particularly if your ship is a megaliner. You may feel slightly more movement on a small ship, but not by much, as these ships ply remote bays and coves that are even more sheltered than those traveled by regular cruise ships.

If you have a history of seasickness, don't book an inside cabin. For the terminally seasick, it will begin to resemble a movable coffin in short order. If you do become seasick, you can use common drugs such as Dramamine and Bonine. Some people find anti-seasickness wristbands helpful; these apply gentle pressure to the wrist in lieu of drugs. Worn behind the ear, the Transderm Scop patch dispenses a continuous metered dose of medication, which is absorbed into the skin and enters the bloodstream. Apply the patch four hours before sailing and it will continue to be effective for three days.

CASINOS

On most ships, lavish casinos pulsate with activity. On ships that feature them, the rationale for locating casinos where most passengers must pass either through or alongside them is obvious—the unspoken allure of winning. In addition to slot machines in a variety of denominations, cruise ship casinos usually have table games. Casino hours vary based on the itinerary or location of the ship; most are required to close while in port, whereas others may be able to offer 24-hour slot machines and simply close table games. Every casino has a cashier, and you may be able to charge a cash advance to your onboard account, for a fee.

Sports and Fitness

Onboard sports facilities might include a court for basketball, volleyball, tennis—or all three—a jogging track, or even an ice skating rink. Some ships are even offering innovative and unexpected features, such as rock-climbing walls, bungee trampolines, and surfing pools on some Royal Caribbean ships. For the less adventurous, there's always table tennis and shuffleboard.

Naturally, you will find at least one swimming pool, and possibly several. Cruise-ship pools are generally on the small side—more appropriate for cooling off than doing laps—and the majority contain filtered saltwater. But some are elaborate affairs, with waterslides and interactive water play areas for family fun. Some Princess and Windstar ships have challenging "swim against the current" pools for swimming enthusiasts who want to get their low-impact exercise while onboard.

Shipboard fitness centers have become ever more elaborate, offering state-of-the-art exercise machines, treadmills, and stair steppers, not to mention weights and weight machines. As a bonus, many fitness centers with floor-to-ceiling windows have the world's most inspiring

Safety at Sea

Safety begins with you, the passenger. Once settled into your cabin, locate your life vests if they are stored there, and review the posted emergency instructions. Make sure the vests are in good condition, and learn how to secure them properly. Make certain the ship's purser knows if you have a physical infirmity that may hamper a speedy exit from your cabin, so that in an emergency he or she can quickly dispatch a crew member to assist you. If you're traveling with children, be sure that child-size life jackets are placed in your cabin.

Before your ship leaves the embarkation port, you'll be required to attend a mandatory lifeboat drill. Do so and listen carefully. If you're unsure about how to use your vest, now is the time to ask. Some cruise lines no longer require you to bring your vest to the muster drill and instead store them near the muster station, but crew members are more than willing to assist if you have questions. Only in the most extreme circumstances will you need to abandon ship—but it has happened. The time you spend learning the procedure may serve you well in a mishap.

In actuality, the greatest danger facing cruise-ship passengers is fire. All cruise lines must meet international standards for fire safety, which require sprinkler systems, smoke detectors, and other safety features. Fires on cruise ships are not common, but they do happen, and these rules have made ships much safer. You can do your part by *not* using an iron in your cabin, taking care to properly extinguish smoking materials, and *not* leaving fabric items, such as towels, on your balcony. Never throw a lighted cigarette overboard—it could be blown back into an opening in the ship and start a fire.

sea views. Most ships offer complimentary fitness classes, but you might also find classes in Pilates, spinning, or yoga (usually for a fee). Personal trainers are usually onboard to get you off on the right foot, also for a fee.

On small-ship lines in Alaska you are likely to find fitness equipment outside on the top deck where your ship may also have a hot tub, but you'll rarely, if ever, find a swimming pool. Treks ashore and kayaking are often the preferred exercise options.

Spas

With all the usual pampering and service in luxurious surroundings, simply being on a cruise can be a stress-reducing experience. Add to that the menu of spa and salon services at your fingertips and you have a recipe for total relaxation. Spas have also become among the most popular of shipboard areas. While high-end Canyon Ranch has made inroads with the cruise industry by opening spas on an increasing number of ships, Steiner Leisure is still the largest spa and salon operator at sea (the company also operates the Mandara and the Greenhouse spa brands), with facilities on more than 100 cruise ships worldwide.

In addition to facials, manicures, pedicures, massages, and sensual body treatments, other hallmarks of Steiner Leisure are salon services and products for hair and skin. Founded in 1901 by Henry Steiner of London, a single salon prospered when Steiner's son joined the business in 1926 and was granted a Royal Warrant as hairdresser to Her

Majesty Queen Mary in 1937. In 1956 Steiner won its first cruise-ship contract to operate the salon onboard the ships of the Cunard Line. By the mid-1990s Steiner Leisure began taking an active role in creating shipboard spas offering a wide variety of wellness therapies and beauty programs for both women and men.

Other Shipboard Services

COMMUNICATIONS

Just because you are out to sea does not mean you have to be out of touch. However, ship-to-shore telephone calls can cost $2 to $15 a minute, so it makes more economic sense to use email to remain in contact with your home or office. Most ships have basic computer systems, and some newer vessels offer more high-tech connectivity—even in-cabin hookups or wireless connections for mobile devices and either your own laptop computer or one you can rent onboard. Expect to pay an activation fee and subsequent charges in the 75¢- to $1-per-minute range for the use of these Internet services. Ships usually offer a variety of packages so that you get a reduced per-minute price if you pay a set fee up front.

The ability to use your own mobile phone for calls from the high seas is an alternative that is gaining in popularity. It's usually cheaper than using a cabin phone if your ship offers the service; however, it can still cost $2.50 to $5 a minute. A rather ingenious concept, the ship acts as a cell "tower" in international waters—you use your own cell phone and your own number when roaming at sea, and you can even send and receive text messages and email with some smartphones (albeit with a surcharge in addition to any roaming fees). Before leaving home, ask your cell-phone service provider to activate international roaming on your account. When in port, depending on the type of cell phone you own and the agreements your mobile

service-provider has established, you may be able to connect to local networks in Alaska. Most GSM phones are also usable in Canada. Rates for using the maritime service, as well as any roaming charges from Alaskan and Canadian cities, are established by your mobile service carrier and are worth checking into before your trip. To avoid excessive charges, it's a good idea to turn off your phone's data roaming option while at sea.

LAUNDRY AND DRY CLEANING

Most cruise ships offer valet laundry and pressing (and some also offer dry-cleaning) service. Expenses can add up fast, especially for laundry, since charges are per item and the rates are similar to those charged in hotels, unless your ship offers a fixed-price laundry deal (all you can stuff into a bag they provide for a single fee). If doing laundry is important to you and you do not want to send it out to be done, some cruise ships have a self-service laundry room (which usually features an iron and ironing board in addition to washers and dryers). If you book one of the top-dollar suites, laundry service may be included for no additional cost. Upscale ships such as those in the Regent Seven Seas Cruises, Seabourn, and Silversea Cruises fleets have complimentary self-service launderettes. On other cruise lines, such as Disney Cruise Line, Princess Cruises, Oceania Cruises, Carnival Cruise Lines, and Holland America Line (except Vista-class and Signature-class ships), you can do your own laundry for about $5 or less per load. None of the vessels in the Norwegian, Royal Caribbean, or Celebrity Cruises fleets has self-service laundry facilities.

Disembarkation

All cruises come to an end eventually, and the disembarkation process actually begins the day before you arrive at your ship's final port. During that day your cabin steward delivers special luggage

Crime on Ships

Crime aboard cruise ships has occasionally become headline news, thanks in large part to a few well-publicized cases. Most people never have any type of problem, but you should exercise the same precautions aboard a ship that you would at home. Keep your valuables out of sight—on big ships virtually every cabin has a small safe. Don't carry too much cash ashore, use your credit card whenever possible, and keep your money in a secure place, such as a front pocket that's harder to pick. Single women traveling with friends should stick together, especially when returning to their cabins late at night. When assaults occur, it often comes to light that excessive drinking of alcohol is a factor. Be careful about whom you befriend, as you would anywhere, whether it's a fellow passenger or a member of the crew. Don't be paranoid, but do be prudent.

Your cruise is a wonderful opportunity to leave everyday responsibilities behind, but don't neglect to pack your common sense. After a few drinks it might seem like a good idea to sit on a railing or lean over the rail to get a better view of the ship's wake. Passengers have been known to fall. "Man overboard" is more likely to be the result of carelessness than criminal intent.

tags to your stateroom, along with customs forms and instructions on some itineraries.

The night before you disembark, you'll need to set aside clothing to wear the next morning when you leave the ship. Many people dress in whatever casual outfits they wear for the final dinner onboard, or change into travel clothes after dinner. Also, do not forget to put your passport or other proof of citizenship, airline tickets, and medications in your hand luggage. The luggage tags go onto your larger bags, which are placed outside your stateroom door for pickup during the hours indicated. Your cruise line may offer self-assist debarkation, and in that case, you do not have to put your luggage outside your stateroom the night before departure and may leave the ship early if you can take all your luggage with you.

A statement itemizing your onboard charges is delivered before you arise on disembarkation morning. Plan to get up early enough to check it over for accuracy, finish packing your personal belongings, and vacate your stateroom by the appointed hour. Any discrepancies in your onboard account should be taken care of before leaving the ship, usually at the reception desk. Breakfast is served in the main restaurant as well as the buffet on the last morning, but room service usually isn't available. Disembarkation procedures vary by cruise line, but you'll probably have to wait in a lounge or on deck for your tag color or number to be called.

Then you take a taxi, bus, or other transportation to your post-cruise hotel or to the airport for your flight home. If you are flying out the day your cruise ends, leave plenty of time to go through the usual check-in, passport control/immigration, and security procedures at the airport.

Customs and Duties

U.S. CUSTOMS

If your cruise includes a stop in Canada, each individual or family must fill out a customs declaration form, which will be provided before your ship docks. Be sure to keep receipts for all purchases made outside the United States; you may also be asked to show officials what you've bought. After showing your passport to Canadian immigration officials upon debarkation, you must collect your luggage from the dock. If your ship sails round-trip from Vancouver, you will not go through U.S. Customs and Immigration until you reach the Vancouver airport. Once you've completed the process there, you will board what is essentially a "domestic" flight to the United States with no further U.S. Customs and Immigration procedure upon arrival.

You're always allowed to bring goods of a certain value back home without having to pay any duty or import tax. But there's a limit on the amount of tobacco and liquor you can bring back duty-free. The values of so-called "duty-free" goods are included in these amounts. When you shop abroad, save all your receipts, as customs inspectors may ask to see them as well as the items you purchased. If the total value of your goods is more than the duty-free limit, you'll have to pay a tax (most often a flat percentage) on the value of everything beyond that limit. For U.S. citizens who have been out of the country for at least 48 hours, the duty-free exemption is $800. For visits of less than 48 hours, the allowance is only $200. But the duty-free exemption includes only one carton of 200 cigarettes, 100 cigars, and 1 liter of alcohol (this includes wine); above these limits, you have to pay duties, even if you didn't spend more than the limit allowed.

Alaska Cruise Ships and Itineraries

SHIP	EMBARKATION PORT	DURATION IN NIGHTS	ITINERARY AND PORTS OF CALL
Alaskan Dream Cruises			
Alaskan Dream	Ketchikan	8	Northbound: Metlakatla and Misty Fjords, Kasaan and Thorne Bay, Wrangell, Petersburg, Windham Bay, Sawyer Glacier, Juneau and Orca Point Lodge, Glacier Bay, Sitka
	Sitka	8	Southbound: Glacier Bay, Orca Point Lodge and Juneau, Sawyer Glacier, Windham Bay, Petersburg, Wrangell, Kasaan and Thorne Bay, Misty Fjords and Metlakatla, Ketchikan
Alaskan Dream	Sitka	10	Southbound: Glacier Bay, Skagway, Haines, Juneau and Orca Point Lodge, Sawyer Glacier, Windham Bay, Petersburg, Wrangell, Thorne Bay and Kasaan, Misty Fjords, Metlakatla, Ketchikan
	Ketchikan	10	Northbound: Misty Fjords, Metlakatla, Thorne Bay and Kasaan, Wrangell, Petersburg, Windham Bay, Sawyer Glacier Juneau and Orca Point Lodge, Haine, Skagway, Glacier Bay, Sitka
Misty Fjord	Sitka	7	Northbound: Baranof Island, Tenakee Inlet, Icy Strait, Port Frederick, Sawyer Glacier, Frederick Sound, Juneau
	Juneau	7	Southbound; Tenakee Inlet, Icy Strait, Port Frederick, Sawyer Glacier, Frederick Sound, Sitka
Chichagof Dream	Sitka	7	Northbound: Petersburg. Sawyer Glacier, Glacier Bay (2 days), Juneau

Alaska Cruise Ships and Itineraries

SHIP	EMBARKATION PORT	DURATION IN NIGHTS	ITINERARY AND PORTS OF CALL
	Sitka	7	Northbound: Glacier Bay, Saginaw Bay, Petersburg, Sawyer Glacier, Fords Terror, Frederick Sound and Kake, Orca Point Lodge, Juneau
	Juneau	7	Southbound: Glacier Bay, Saginaw Bay, Petersburg, Sawyer Glacier, Fords Terror, Frederick Sound and Kake, Orca Point Lodge, Sitka
American Cruise Lines			
American Constellation	Juneau	7	Round-trip: Skagway, Glacier Bay, Haines, Petersburg, Sawyer Glacier
	Seattle	11	Northbound: Anacortes, WA; Friday Harbor, WA; Ketchikan; Wrangell; Haines; Skagway; Petersburg; Sawyer Glacier; Juneau
	Juneau	11	Southbound: Ketchikan; Wrangell; Petersburg; Sawyer Glacier; Anacortes, WA; Friday Harbor, WA; Seattle
Carnival Cruise Line			
Carnival Legend	Seattle	7	Northbound: Juneau, Skagway, Ketchikan, Victoria, Sawyer Glacier, Vancouver
	Vancouver	7	Southbound: Juneau, Skagway, Ketchikan, Glacier Bay or Sawyer Glacier, Victoria, Seattle
	Seattle	7	Round-trip: Juneau, Skagway, Ketchikan, Victoria, Sawyer Glacier, Vancouver
	Seattle	7	Round-trip: Skagway, Ketchikan, Victoria, Icy Strait Point, Glacier Bay
	Seattle	7	Round-trip: Juneau, Skagway, Ketchikan, Victoria, Sawyer Glacier
Celebrity Cruises			
Celebrity Solstice	Seattle	7	Round-trip: Ketchikan, Juneau, Skagway, Victoria, Sawyer Glacier
	Vancouver	7	Southbound: Juneau, Skagway, Ketchikan, Sawyer Glacier, Victoria, Seattle
Celebrity Eclipse	Vancouver	7	Round-trip: Ketchikan, Juneau, Icy Strait Point or Sitka, Hubbard Glacier
Celebrity Millennium	Vancouver	10	Northbound: Skagway, Juneau, Ketchikan, Icy Strait Point, Hubbard Glacier, Seward
	Seward	7	Southbound: Skagway, Juneau, Ketchikan, Icy Strait Point, Hubbard Glacier, Vancouver
Crystal Cruises			
Crystal Symphony	Vancouver	7	Round-trip: Ketchikan, Juneau, Skagway, Sawyer Glacier or Glacier Bay
	Vancouver	10	Northbound: Ketchikan, Juneau, Skagway, Sitka, Haines, Sawyer Glacier, Hoonah, Hubbard Glacier, Seward
	Seward	11	Southbound: Hubbard Glacier, Hoonah, Ketchikan, Juneau, Skagway, Sawyer Glacier, Sitka, Wrangell, Victoria, Vancouver

Alaska Cruise Ships and Itineraries

SHIP	EMBARKATION PORT	DURATION IN NIGHTS	ITINERARY AND PORTS OF CALL
	Vancouver	7	Northbound: Ketchikan, Juneau, Skagway, Sawyer Glacier, Hubbard Glacier, Whittier
	Whittier	7	Southbound: Hubbard Glacier, Sitka, Ketchikan, Juneau, Skagway, Vancouver
	Vancouver	11	Round-trip: Ketchikan, Juneau, Skagway, Sawyer Glacier, Hubbard Glacier, Sitka, Prince Rupert, BC, Victoria
	Vancouver	10	Round-trip: Ketchikan, Juneau, Sitka, Haines, Hoonah, Sawyer Glacier, Victoria
	Vancouver	7	Northbound: Ketchikan, Juneau, Skagway, Sitka, Hubbard Glacier, Seward
	Seward	7	Southbound: Hubbard Glacier, Ketchikan, Juneau, Skagway, Sawyer Glacier, Vancouver
	Vancouver	11	Southbound: Ketchikan, Juneau, Sitka, Glacier Bay, San Francisco, Santa Barbara, Los Angeles
Disney Cruise Line			
Disney Wonder	Vancouver	5	Round-trip: Ketchikan, Juneau, Skagway, Sawyer Glacier
	Vancouver	9	Round-trip: Hubbard Glacier, Ketchikan, Juneau, Skagway or Sitka, Icy Strait Point, Victoria
Holland America Line			
Amsterdam	Seattle	14	Round-trip: Ketchikan, Sawyer Glacier, Hubbard Glacier, Sitka, Icy Strait Point, Anchorage, Homer; Kodiak, Victoria
	Seattle	7	Round-trip: Juneau, Skagway, Ketchikan, Sawyer Glacier, Victoria
Westerdam	Vancouver	7	Northbound: Juneau, Ketchikan, Skagway, Glacier Bay, Seward
	Seward	7	Southbound: Glacier Bay, Haines, Juneau, Ketchikan, Vancouver
Maasdam	San Francisco	21	Round-trip: Juneau, Ketchikan, Sawyer Glacier, Hubbard Glacier, Sitka, Homer, Kodiak, Victoria, Valdez, College Fjord, Haines, Wrangell, Vancouver, Port Alberni, BC, Astoria, OR
Volendam, Noordam, Nieuw Amsterdam	Vancouver	7	Round-trip: Skagway, Juneau, Ketchikan, Glacier Bay
Eurodam	Seattle	7	Round-trip: Juneau, Sitka, Ketchikan, Victoria, Glacier Bay
Oosterdam	Seattle	7	Round-trip: Skagway, Juneau, Hubbard Glacier, Sitka, Victoria
Lindblad Expeditions			
National Geographic Sea Bird and *Sea Lion* and *National Geographic Venture* and *Quest*	Sitka	7	Northbound: Icy Strait, Glacier Bay or Dundas Bay (Sea Lion), Petersburg, Frederick Sound, Dawes or Sawyer Glacier, Juneau

Alaska Cruise Ships and Itineraries

SHIP	EMBARKATION PORT	DURATION IN NIGHTS	ITINERARY AND PORTS OF CALL
	Juneau	7	Southbound: Dawes or Sawyer Glacier, Petersburg, Frederick Sound, Glacier Bay or Dundas Bay (SeaLion), Icy Strait, Sitka
National Geographic Sea Bird	Sitka	5	Northbound: Baranof Or Chichagof Islands, Icy Strait, Haines, Sawyer or Dawes Glacier, Juneau
	Juneau	5	Southbound: Baranof Or Chichagof Islands, Icy Strait, Haines, Sawyer or Dawes Glacier, Sitka
National Geographic Sea Bird	Sitka	10	Northbound: Misty Fiords, Behm Canal, Petersburg, Sawyer or Dawes Glacier, Haines, Glacier Bay, Icy Strait, Baranof or Chichagof Islands, Ketchikan
	Ketchikan	10	Southbound: Misty Fiords, Behm Canal, Petersburg, Sawyer or Dawes Glacier, Haines, Glacier Bay, Icy Strait, Baranof or Chichagof Islands, Sitka
National Geographic Sea Bird and *Sea Lion*	Seattle	14	Northbound: Gulf Islands, Johnstone Strait, Alert Bay, Haida Gwaii, Misty Fiords, Petersburg, Dawes or Sawyer Glacier, Glacier Bay, Icy Strait, Sitka
	Sitka	14	Southbound: Gulf Islands, Johnstone Strait, Alert Bay, Haida Gwaii, Misty Fiords, Petersburg, Dawes or Sawyer Glacier, Glacier Bay, Icy Strait, Seattle
National Geographic Venture and *Quest*	Sitka	7	Northbound: Sitka, Glacier Bay, Petersburg, Frederick Sound, Icy Strait, Dawes or Sawyer Glacier, Juneau
	Juneau	7	Southbound: Dawes or Sawyer Glacier, Petersburg, Frederick Sound, Icy Strait, Glacier Bay, Sitka
National Geographic Venture and *Quest*	Sitka	13	Southbound: San Juan Islands, Washington, Victoria, BC, Gulf Islands, Alert Bay And Johnstone Strait, Misty Fiords, Petersburg. Dawes or Sawyer Glacier, Glacier Bay, Inian Islands, Icy Strait, Chichagof Island, Seattle
	Seattle	13	Northbound: San Juan Islands, Washington,Victoria, BC, Gulf Islands, Alert Bay And Johnstone Strait, Misty Fiords, Petersburg. Dawes or Sawyer Glacier, Glacier Bay, Inian Islands, Icy Strait, Chichagof Island, Sitka
Norwegian Cruise Line			
Norwegian Pearl, Norwegian Bliss	Seattle	7	Round-trip: Juneau, Skagway, Ketchikan, Victoria, Glacier Bay
Norwegian Jewel	Seward	7	Southbound: Icy Strait Point, Juneau, Skagway, Ketchikan, Sawyer Glacier, Vancouver
	Vancouver	7	Northbound: Ketchikan, Juneau, Skagway, Glacier Bay, Seward
Oceania Cruises			
Regatta	San Francisco	10	Northbound: Astoria, Ketchikan, Juneau, Sitka, Hubbard Glacier, Wrangell, Vancouver
	Vancouver	14	Southbound: Sitka, Ketchikan, Hubbard Glacier, Icy Strait Point, Wrangell, Seward, Kodiak, Skagway, Prince Rupert, BC, Victoria, Seattle
	Seattle	7	Round-trip: Ketchikan, Sitka, Juneau, Victoria

Alaska Cruise Ships and Itineraries

SHIP	EMBARKATION PORT	DURATION IN NIGHTS	ITINERARY AND PORTS OF CALL
	Seattle	10	Round-trip: Ketchikan, Skagway, Juneau, Sitka, Victoria, Hubbard Glacier
	Seattle	9	Northbound: Ketchikan, Juneau, Hubbard Glacier, Skagway, Sitka, Victoria, Vancouver
	Seattle	11	Northbound: Ketchikan; Juneau; Hubbard Glacier, Icy Strait Point, Skagway, Sitka, Prince Rupert, BC, Victoria, Vancouver
	Seattle	10	Northbound: Ketchikan, Skagway, Sitka, Hubbard Glacier, Wrangell, Juneau, Victoria, Vancouver
	Vancouver	11	Southbound: Ketchikan; Juneau; Sitka; Hubbard Glacier; Prince Rupert, BC, Victoria; Astoria, OR; San Francisco
Princess Cruises			
Golden Princess	Vancouver	4	Round-trip: Ketchikan
Island Princess	Vancouver	4	Round-trip: Ketchikan, Juneau
Star Princess	Vancouver	7	Southbound: Ketchikan, Juneau, Skagway, Sawyer Glacier, Victoria, Seattle
Ruby Princess	Seattle	7	Round-trip: Ketchikan, Juneau, Skagway, Glacier Bay, Victoria
Star Princess	Seattle	7	Round-trip: Juneau, Skagway, Ketchikan, Sawyer Glacier, Victoria
Grand Princess	San Francisco	10	Round-trip: Juneau, Skagway, Ketchikan, Victoria, Sawyer Glacier
Island Princess	Vancouver	7	Northbound: Icy Strait Point, Juneau, Skagway, Glacier Bay, College Fjord, Whittier
Island Princess, Royal Princess, Coral, Golden Princess	Whittier	7	Southbound: Ketchikan, Juneau, Skagway, Glacier Bay, Hubbard Glacier, Vancouver
Royal Princess, Golden Princess, Coral Princess	Vancouver	7	Northbound: Juneau, Skagway, Ketchikan, Glacier Bay, College Fjord, Whittier
Ruby Princess	Seattle	7	Northbound: Ketchikan, Juneau, Skagway, Glacier Bay, Victoria, Vancouver
Island Princess, Golden Princess, Coral Princess	Vancouver	7	Round-trip: Juneau, Skagway, Ketchikan, Glacier Bay
Golden Princess	San Francisco	10	Round-trip: Juneau, Skagway, Glacier Bay, Ketchikan, Victoria
	San Francisco	10	Round-trip: Juneau, Hubbard Glacier, Haines, Ketchikan, Victoria
	San Francisco	10	Round-trip: Juneau, Sawyer Glacier, Skagway, Ketchikan, Victoria
	San Francisco	10	Round-trip: Juneau, Sitka, Haines, Sawyer Glacier, Victoria

Alaska Cruise Ships and Itineraries

SHIP	EMBARKATION PORT	DURATION IN NIGHTS	ITINERARY AND PORTS OF CALL
Ruby Princess, Star Princess, Royal Princess	Los Angeles	12	Round-trip: Juneau, Skagway, Glacier Bay, Ketchikan, Victoria
Regent Seven Seas Cruises			
Seven Seas Mariner	Vancouver	7	Northbound: Sitka, Juneau, Skagway, Ketchikan, Hubbard Glacier, Seward
	Seward	7	Southbound: Sitka, Juneau, Skagway, Ketchikan, Hubbard Glacier, Vancouver
	Vancouver	10	Northbound: Skagway; Ketchikan; Juneau; Wrangell; Sitka; Hubbard Glacier; Icy Strait Point, Homer, Seward
	Seward	10	Southbound: Hubbard Glacier; Icy Strait Point, Juneau, Skagway, Sitka, Ketchikan, Prince Rupert, BC, Victoria, Vancouver
	Vancouver	11	Round-trip: Skagway; Ketchikan; Juneau; Wrangell; Sitka; Hubbard Glacier; Icy Strait Point, Victoria
	Vancouver	12	Southbound: Sitka; Ketchikan; Juneau; Hubbard Glacier; Victoria; Astoria, OR; San Francisco, Los Angeles
Royal Caribbean International			
Radiance of the Seas	Vancouver	7	Northbound: Ketchikan, Juneau, Skagway, Icy Strait Point, Hubbard Glacier, Seward
	Seward	7	Southbound: Ketchikan, Juneau, Skagway, Icy Strait Point, Hubbard Glacier, Vancouver
	Vancouver	4	Round-trip: Ketchikan
Ovation of the Seas	Seattle	7	Round-trip: Juneau, Skagway, Victoria, Sawyer or Hawes Glacier
	Seattle	7	Northbound: Juneau, Skagway, Victoria, Sawyer or Hawes Glacier, Vancouver
Seabourn			
Seabourn Sojourn	Vancouver	11	Northbound: Ketchikan, Wrangell, Sitka, Sawyer Glacier, Haines, Juneau, Icy Strait Point, Seward
	Seward	14	Southbound: Holgate Glacier, Aialik Glacier, Juneau, Haines, Icy Strait Point, Sawyer Glacier, Sitka, Wrangell, Ketchikan, Prince Rupert, BC, Klemtu, BC, Vancouver
	Vancouver	12	Round-trip: Wrangell, Sitka, Icy Strait Point, Juneau, Sawyer Glacier, Ketchikan, Prince Rupert, BC, Klemtu, BC
	Vancouver	20	Southbound: Ketchikan, Sitka, Icy Strait Point, Juneau, Sawyer Glacier, Wrangell, Prince Rupert, BC, Klemtu, BC, Victoria, Seattle, San Francisco, Monterey, Santa Barbara, Los Angeles

Alaska Cruise Ships and Itineraries

SHIP	EMBARKATION PORT	DURATION IN NIGHTS	ITINERARY AND PORTS OF CALL
Silversea Cruises			
Silver Explorer	Seward	11	Southbound: College Fjord, Columbia Glacier, Hubbard Glacier, Ketchikan, Walker Cove, Elfin Cove, Idaho Inlet, Brothers Islands, Little Prybus Bay, Misty Fjords, Metlaktla, Nanaimo, BC, Vancouver
	Vancouver	13	Northbound: Metlakatla, Misty Fjords, Walker Cove, Ketchikan, Petersburg, Sail Island, Endicott Arm, Juneau, Inian Islands, Elfin Cove, Hubbard Glacier, Kukak Bay, Geographic Harbor, Kodiak, The Triplets, Chiswell Islands, Holgate Glacier, Seward
Silver Muse	Vancouver	7	Northbound: Ketchikan, Juneau, Skagway, Sitka, Wrangell, Prince Rupert, BC, Seward
	Seward	7	Southbound: Ketchikan, Juneau, Haines, Sitka, Hubbard Glacier, Vancouver
	Seward	10	Southbound: Ketchikan, Juneau, Haines, Sitka, Sawyer Glacier, Wrangell, Prince Rupert, BC, Vancouver
	Vancouver	11	Round-trip: Ketchikan, Sitka, Haines, Sawyer Glacier, Juneau, Wrangell, Prince Rupert, BC
	Vancouver	10	Round-trip: Ketchikan, Sitka, Haines, Juneau, Wrangell, Walker Cove, Misty Fjords, Prince Rupert, BC
	Vancouver	7	Northbound: Ketchikan, Juneau, Skagway, Sitka, Hubbard Glacier, Seward
UnCruise Adventures			
Wilderness Discoverer, Wilderness Explorer	Ketchikan	7	Northbound: Endicott Arm, Dawes Glacier, Fords Terror, Stephens Passage, Thomas Bay, Wrangell Narrows, Wrangell, Behm Canal, Misty Fjords, Juneau
	Juneau	7	Southbound: Dawes Glacier, Endicott Arm, Fords Terror, Stephens Passage, Thomas Bay, Wrangell Narrows, Wrangell, Behm Canal, Misty Fiords, Ketchikan
Wilderness Discoverer, Wilderness Explorer, Wilderness Adventurer	Sitka	7	Northbound: Glacier Bay (2 days), Icy Strait Point, Chichagof and Kuiu Islands, Peril Strait, Sergius Narrows, Lynn Canal or Chatham Strait, Juneau
	Juneau	7	Southbound: Glacier Bay (2 days), Icy Strait Point, Chichagof and Kuiu Islands, Peril Strait, Sergius Narrows, Neva Strait, Krestof and Nakwasina Straits, Sitka
	Juneau	7	Southbound: Prince of Wales Island, Frederick Sound, Chatham Strait, Stephens Passage, Sawyer Glacier, Ketchikan
	Ketchikan	7	Northbound: Prince of Wales Island, Frederick Sound, Chatham Strait, Stephens Passage, Sawyer Glacier, Juneau
Safari Endeavour	Sitka	7	Northbound: Krestof Sound, N ekwasina Sound, Icy Strait, Glacier Bay, Chichagof Island, Lynn Canal, Haines, Juneau

Alaska Cruise Ships and Itineraries

SHIP	EMBARKATION PORT	DURATION IN NIGHTS	ITINERARY AND PORTS OF CALL
Safari Quest	Petersburg	8	Round-trip: Kake, Keku Islands, Tebenkof Bay Wilderness, South Baranof Wilderness, Chatham Strait, Frederick Sound, Admiralty Island, Stikine-Le Conte Wilderness
Wilderness Adventurer	Juneau	7	Round-trip: Glacier Bay (2 days), Chatham Strait, Kuiu Island, Frederick Sound, Endicott Arm, Dawes Glacier
Wilderness Adventurer, Wilderness Explorer	Juneau	7	Round-trip: Glacier Bay (2 days), Cross Sound, Lynn Canal, Haines, Icy Strait Point
Safari Endeavour, Safari Explorer, SS Legacy	Juneau	14	Round-trip: Haines, Sitka, Kake, Glacier Bay, Tracy Arm, Stephens Passage, Lynn Canal, Sergius Narrows, Icy Strait, Ideal Cove, Thomas Bay, Baranof and Chichagof Islands, Peril and Neva Straits, Frederick Sound, Krestof and Nakwasina Sounds
Wilderness Discoverer, Wilderness Explorer	Sitka	14	Southbound: Juneau, Wrangell, Krestof and Nakwasina Sounds, Sergius Narrows, Neva, Peril and Icy Straits, Chichagof Island, Glacier Bay, Endicott Arm, Fords Terror, Stephens Passage, Thomas Bay, Wrangell Narrows, Behm Canal, Misty Fjords, Ketchikan
	Ketchikan	14	Northbound: Juneau, Wrangell, Krestof and Nakwasina Sounds, Sergius Narrows, Neva, Peril and Icy Straits, Chichagof Island, Glacier Bay, Endicott Arm, Fords Terror, Stephens Passage, Thomas Bay, Wrangell Narrows, Behm Canal, Misty Fjords, Sitka
Safari Endeavour, Wilderness Discoverer, SS Legacy	Seattle	14	Northbound: Olympic National Park, San Juan Islands, Salish Sea, Ketchikan, Misty Fjords, Behm Canal, Ernest Sound, Petersburg, Frederick Sound, Chatham Strait, Chichagof Island, Glacier Bay, Icy Strait, Haines, Juneau
	Juneau	143	Southbound: Olympic National Park, San Juan Islands, Salish Sea, Ketchikan, Misty Fjords, Behm Canal, Ernest Sound, Petersburg, Frederick Sound, Chatham Strait, Chichagof Island, Glacier Bay, Icy Strait, Haines, Seattle
Viking Ocean Cruises			
Viking Orion	Vancouver	11	Northbound: Ketchikan, Sitka, Juneau, Skagway, Icy Strait Point, Hubbard Glacier, Valdez, Seward
	Seward	11	Southbound: Ketchikan, Sitka, Juneau, Skagway, Icy Strait Point, Hubbard Glacier, Valdez, Vancouver
Windstar Cruises			
Star Legend	Seward	12	Southbound: Icy Strait Point, Haines, Juneau, Sawyer Glacier, Wrangell, Ketchikan or Prince Rupert, BC, Vancouver
	Seward	11	Southbound: Juneau, Sawyer Glacier, Haines, Wrangell, Ketchikan, Sitka, Vancouver
	Vancouver	11	Northbound: Haines, Juneau, Sitka, Sawyer Glacier, Wrangell, Ketchikan, Seward

Chapter 3

CRUISE LINES AND CRUISE SHIPS

3

Updated by
Linda Coffman

After the Caribbean and Europe, more ships sail in Alaska than in any other region of the world, offering passengers a wide range of choices, from mainstream to luxury, from large megaliners to small yachtlike vessels.

The size of the ship will in part dictate where it can go and how passengers will enjoy their vacation. So just as with other popular cruise destinations, picking the right cruise ship is the most important decision you will make in choosing your cruise, particularly if you stick with a large ship.

Make no mistake about it: cruise ships have distinct personalities. Norwegian's lack of formality and range of dining choices and entertainment makes these ships the favorites of some and the bane of others. Even those belonging to the same class and nearly indistinguishable from one another have certain traits that make them stand out.

That is why the most important choice you'll make when booking a cruise is the combined selection of cruise line and cruise ship. Cruise lines set the tone for their fleets, but since the cruise industry is relatively fluid, some new features introduced on one ship may not be found on all the ships owned by the same cruise line. For instance, you'll find ice-skating rinks only on the biggest Royal Caribbean ships. However, most cruise lines attempt to standardize the overall experience throughout their fleets (for example, you'll find a rock-climbing wall on *every* Royal Caribbean ship).

About the Cruise Lines

Just as cruise ships differ by size and style, so do the cruise lines themselves, and finding a cruise line that matches your personality is as important as finding the right ship. Some cruise lines cater to families, others to couples, active singles, and even food and wine aficionados. Selecting the right one can mean the difference between struggling with unmet expectations and enjoying the vacation of a lifetime. Although some of the differences are subtle, most of today's cruise lines still fall into three basic categories: Mainstream, Premium, and Luxury.

Mainstream Lines

Mainstream cruise lines usually have a little something for everyone: Ships tend to be the big, bigger, and biggest at sea, carrying the highest number of passengers per available space. Cabins can be basic or fancy since most mainstream lines also offer more upscale accommodations categories, including suites. Some mainstream lines still offer traditional dining, with two assigned seatings in the main restaurant for dinner. But following the popular trend, all mainstream cruise lines have introduced variations of open seating dining and alternative restaurant options that allow passengers to dine when and with whom they please, though almost all alternative restaurants carry an extra charge.

Premium Lines

Premium lines usually offer a more subdued atmosphere and refined style: Ships tend to be newer midsize to large vessels that carry fewer passengers than mainstream ships and have a more spacious feel. Staterooms still range from more basic to more upscale, but even the basic accommodations tend to have more style and space. Cuisine on these ships tends to be a bit better, and most of these ships have à la carte options for more upscale dining for an extra charge, often higher than those on mainstream lines. There are still extra charges on the ship.

Luxury Lines

The air on these deluxe vessels is as rarefied as the champagne and caviar: Ships range from megayachts for only a hundred or so privileged guests to midsize vessels, which are considered large for this category. Space is so abundant that you might wonder where the other passengers are hiding. Spacious staterooms are frequently all suites; at the least, they are the equivalent to higher-grade accommodations on mainstream and premium ships. Open seating is the norm, and guests dine where and with whom they please during dinner hours. There are relatively few extra charges on these ships, except for premium wines by the bottle, spa services, and excursions, but some lines even include excursions and airfare in their prices.

Small-Ship Lines

A casual, relaxed atmosphere in intimate spaces prevails on these yachtlike vessels for fewer than a hundred passengers. Emphasis is placed on unique and flexible itineraries to off-the-beaten-path destinations with exploration leaders guiding the way to insightful encounters ashore. Accommodations are proportionately small, but basic amenities are provided. Meals often feature fresh local ingredients and are served in open seating, buffet, or family style. The dress code is always comfortable casual, and evenings onboard may include a lecture, but socializing with other passengers is the most common activity. Exercise equipment is usually found onboard, but kayaking and nature hikes are offered for a more adventurous workout.

About the Ships
Large Cruise Ships

Large cruise lines account for the majority of passengers sailing to Alaska. These typically have large cruise ships in their fleets with plentiful deck space and, often, a promenade deck that allows you to stroll around the ship's perimeter. In the newest vessels, traditional meets trendy with resort-style innovations; however, they still feature cruise-ship classics such as afternoon tea, and most offer complimentary room service. The smallest cruise ships in the major cruise lines' fleets carry as few as 400 passengers, whereas the biggest can accommodate between 1,500 and 3,000 passengers—enough people to outnumber the residents of many Alaskan port towns. Large ships are a good choice if you're looking for nonstop activity and lots of options; they're especially appealing for groups and families with older kids. If you prefer

Small-Ship Cruises

We cover the most recognized small-ship lines sailing in Alaska, but that is by no means exhaustive. Other great small ships sail the Inside Passage.

Fantasy Cruises Fantasy Cruises' Island Spirit is owned and operated by Captain Jeff Behrens. Captain Behrens is committed to rapport-building with and respect for the area's smallest communities; as a result, 32-passenger Island Spirit can make off-the-beaten-path port calls like Tenakee Springs, Five Finger Lighthouse, and Baranof Warm Springs, in addition to scenic anchorages like Fords Terror that only small ships can access. Charters and photography-focused cruises are also offered. ☎800/234–3861 ⊕ www. smallalaskaship.com.

Alaska Sea Adventures Alaska Sea Adventures focuses on charters and single-theme cruises on wildlife photography, birding, research, archaeology, whale migration, or fish spawning. Its 84-foot expedition yacht, *Northern Song*, can accommodate up to nine passengers. ☎ *888/772–8588, 907/772–4700* ⊕ *www. yachtalaska.com.*

a gentler pace and a chance to get to know your shipmates, try a smaller ship.

Small Ships

Compact expedition-type vessels bring you right up to the shoreline to skirt the face of a glacier and pull through narrow channels where big ships don't fit. These cruises focus on Alaska, and you'll see more wildlife and call into smaller ports, as well as some of the better-known towns. Enrichment talks—conducted by naturalists, Native Alaskans, and other experts in the state's natural history and Native cultures—are the norm. Cabins on expedition ships can be tiny, sometimes with no phone or TV, and bathrooms are often no bigger than cubbyholes. The dining room and lounge are usually the only public areas on these vessels; however, some are luxurious with cushy cabins, comfy lounges and libraries, and hot tubs. You won't find much nightlife aboard, but what you trade for space and onboard diversions is a unique and unforgettable glimpse of Alaska.

Many small ships are based in Juneau or another Alaska port and sail entirely within Alaska. Twice annually, some offer an Inside Passage cruise as the ships reposition to and from their winter homes elsewhere.

Small-ship cruising can be pricey, as fares tend to be inclusive (except for airfare), but there are few onboard charges, and, given the size of ship and style of cruise, fewer opportunities to spend onboard.

About these Reviews

For each cruise line described, ships that regularly cruise in Alaska are grouped by class or similar configuration. Some ships owned by the cruise lines listed do not include regularly scheduled Alaska cruises on their published itineraries as of this writing and are not reviewed in this book.

⇨ *For a complete listing of the ships and the itineraries they are scheduled to follow in the 2019 cruising season, see the chart in Chapter 2.*

Many ships are designed with an eye to less-than-perfect weather. For that reason, you're likely to find indoor swimming pools featured on their deck plans. Except in rare cases, these are usually dual-purpose pools that can be covered when necessary by a sliding roof or magrodome to create an indoor-swimming environment. Our reviews indicate the total number of swimming pools found on each ship, with such permanently or temporarily covered pools included in the total and also noted as "# indoors" in parentheses.

When ships belong to the same class—or are basically similar—they're listed together in the subhead under the name of the class; the year each was introduced is also given in the same order in the statistics section. Capacity figures are based on double occupancy, but when maximum capacity numbers are available (the number of passengers a ship holds when all possible berths are filled), those are listed in parentheses.

Many larger ships have three- and four-berth cabins that can substantially increase the total number of passengers onboard when all berths are booked.

Unlike other cruise guides, we not only describe the features but also list the cabin dimensions for each accommodation category available on the ships reviewed. Dimensions should be considered approximate and used for comparison purposes, since they sometimes vary depending on the actual location of the cabin. For instance, although staterooms are largely prefabricated and consistent in size and configuration, those at the front of some ships may be oddly curved to conform to the shape of the bow.

When you're armed with all the right information, we're sure you'll be able to find one that not only fits your style but also offers you the service and value you expect.

ALASKAN DREAM CRUISES

Founded by Alaskans who pioneered Alaska day boat tours more than 40 years ago to explore the Inside Passage, Alaskan Dream Cruises now offers multiday cruises aboard their yachtlike vessels. With shallow drafts and agile maneuverability, they offer up-

Alaskan Dream Cruises

close views of glaciers and the wildlife abundant in the region. Varied itineraries of 4 to 13 days throughout Southeast Alaska, departing from Sitka or Ketchikan, focus on natural wonders and native villages off the beaten track as well as some of the more well-known ports, including Juneau.

☎ *855/747–8100*
⊕ *www.alaskandream-cruises.com*
☞ *Cruise Style: Small-ship.*

The ships are small, offering an experience that is casual, personal, and intimate. Itineraries are designed to explore the Alaska where big ships cannot venture. Included are visits to the line's exclusive wilderness lodges, Orca Point Lodge and Windham Bay Lodge. A full day in Glacier Bay gets you as close as you can get to the glaciers. Provided for use during the cruise are high-powered binoculars and "Alaska" gear, including rain jackets, pants, and boots. Alaska-crafted products and food are featured onboard. There's also a full library of books on the region on each ship.

Cruises are enhanced by an all-American crew, knowledgeable expedition leaders, and an open-bridge policy. Educational lectures are presented by cultural and scientific expedition leaders who also guide excursions and kayaking, hiking, and watercraft exploration. Basic excursions and airport or hotel transfers are included in the fare, and alternative tours are available at additional cost, as are pre- or post-cruise fishing adventures.

FOOD
After a social hour accompanied by hors d'oeuvres and drinks, chef-inspired cuisine is served in the open seating dining room. Dinner menus include several selections usually with a seafood or meat entrée and

are prepared with primarily fresh, organic, and locally produced ingredients. Locally caught Alaskan seafood is a specialty of Alaskan Dream Cruises, and a complimentary glass of beer or wine is served with dinner. A continental buffet breakfast is served for early risers, while other mealtimes vary depending on the day's activities. Coffee, tea, and hot chocolate are available at all times in the dining room and forward viewing lounges. A king crab/salmon feast is held at Orca Point Lodge or Windham Bay Lodge during every sailing longer than four days. Special diets or meal requests can be accommodated in most cases with 60 days' advance notice.

ENTERTAINMENT

Don't expect much in the way of organized entertainment on these small vessels. TVs are located in public areas, but most passengers prefer to attend a nightly social hour, when a recap of the day is presented prior to dinner in the forward viewing lounges and expedition leaders offer a preview of the next day's activities.

FITNESS AND RECREATION

There are no fitness facilities onboard, but passengers can count on getting plenty of exercise during walks ashore with expedition leaders. Kayaking and hiking offer more-adventurous workouts.

YOUR SHIPMATES

Typically, passengers tend to be active, well-traveled mature couples and families with an adventurous spirit. Physical conditions aboard the vessels such as stairs, raised thresholds, a lack of an elevator, and narrow doorways or passageways may restrict access to some areas aboard the vessels for mobility-challenged passengers.

DRESS CODE

Dress is always casual onboard and ashore. While "Alaska" gear is provided, it is recommended that guests pack waterproof jackets and other layered clothing options, as well as a warm hat and gloves and comfortable waterproof or all-terrain footwear. There are no laundry facilities onboard.

JUNIOR CRUISERS

Alaskan Dream Cruises does not discourage families from cruising together, but there are no dedicated facilities or activities for kids and no in-cabin TVs. Additionally, there is no Wi-Fi, and cell phone accessibility is limited. Inquisitive children and teens who don't require organized activities should find the itineraries educational and stimulating.

Top: A Vista View cabin on *Alaskan Dream*
Middle: The dining room on *Alaskan Dream.*
Bottom: A cabin on *Baranot Dream*

SERVICE

With the services of an American crew, your needs will be satisfied in a friendly manner without a language barrier.

TIPPING

There is no tipping required; however, you may reward crew members at a suggested rate of $15 per person per day.

SHIPS OF THE LINE

Admiralty Dream. With its spacious bow area and partially covered sundeck, *Admiralty Dream* offers plenty of space to view fjords and glaciers and gather around the bar in the Forward Lounge to attend lectures and socialize. The open seating dining room seats all passengers for meals. All cabins have picture windows, hair dryers, and fans. Bathrooms with showers are stocked with Alaska-crafted soaps and shampoo. Both the Owner's Suite and Deluxe cabins (135 and 134 square feet) have a queen bed and a sitting area. AAA cabins (122 square feet) have either a queen bed or two singles; a few can accommodate a third guest. Categories AA (93 square feet) and A (95 square feet) have two twin beds. All beds are dressed with duvets.

Alaskan Dream. A streamlined catamaran style allows *Alaskan Dream* to navigate narrow channels, affording its passengers a close look ashore from the bow-viewing area, covered open aft deck, and partially covered observation area. The Vista View Lounge is a forward-facing gathering spot. The dining room seats all passengers for meals in open seating style. All cabins have picture windows, hair dryers, and fans. Bathrooms with showers are stocked with Alaska-crafted soaps and shampoo. The Owner's Cabin (208 square feet) has a queen bed, a sitting area, and bathroom with shower. Vista View cabins (147 square feet) have a forward view, queen bed, and sitting area. AA and A cabins (120 square feet) have either a queen bed or two twin beds. A few cabins can accommodate a third or fourth guest. All beds are dressed with duvets.

CHOOSE THIS LINE IF...

■ What you see from aboard the vessel is more important than the ship itself.

■ Your idea of an entertaining evening is quiet conversation.

■ You want something a bit more active than a traditional sightseeing cruise.

Baranof Dream. Its shallow draft allows *Baranof Dream's* 49 guests to explore intimate coves and enjoy prime viewing spots from the bow, sundeck, or Explorer's Lounge. The dining room seats all passengers for meals in open seating. Cabins have picture windows, hair dryers, and fans. Bathrooms with showers are stocked with Alaska-crafted toiletries. The Deluxe Suite (210 square feet) has a queen bed and a sitting area with chairs, which can be replaced with a twin bed or bunk beds to accommodate a third or fourth guest. Deluxe cabins (110 square feet) and AAA cabins (116 square feet) have a queen bed and a sitting area with chairs or a twin for a third guest. AA cabins (109 square feet) have a queen bed and a twin bed, and A (105 square feet) have two twin beds. All beds have duvets.

Misty Fjord. The intimate *Misty Fjord* expedition vessel's hull, which is based on the design of Alaska commercial fishing boats to offer stability while sailing the Inside Passage, was built for wilderness exploration. Plush interiors feature teak finishes in a spacious aft salon and a dining area that seats all guests. The outer deck was engineered for optimal viewing. Five yacht-style cabins have hair dryers and fans. Bathrooms with showers are stocked with Alaska-crafted soaps and shampoo, and beds are dressed with duvets.

Chichagof Dream. With a hull optimized for comfort in Alaskan waters, *Chichagof Dream* features viewing areas on the bow and aft decks. Forward-facing windows in the lounge extend from floor to ceiling, offering panoramic views off the bow. The 37 cabins are outfitted with hair dryers, fans, binoculars, Alaska-crafted toiletries, and bathrooms with showers. All cabins have either a queen bed or two twins dressed with duvets and picture windows or portholes in Category A. Each Deluxe Suite (218 square feet) features two bathrooms. Chairs can be replaced with one twin bed or twin bunk beds to accommodate third and fourth passengers. Deluxe Cabins are 155 square feet; AAA and AA are 109 square feet; and A are 105 square feet.

HELPFUL HINTS

■ Shore excursions are all included in the fare, as is ground transportation before and after the cruise.

■ There are no elevators on the small vessels, and guests requiring a wheelchair must provide their own.

■ Don't expect room service; however, coffee, tea, and hot chocolate are always available.

■ Recreational equipment is provided for use during visits to Windham Bay Lodge.

■ Cabins are fairly spacious, but you should limit yourself to two pieces of luggage.

DON'T CHOOSE THIS LINE IF...

■ You need cell phone and Wi-Fi access at all times; these cruises visit isolated areas without modern communications.

■ You require a wheelchair for mobility. These vessels are not wheelchair accessible.

■ You must smoke when and where you please. Smoking is allowed only on outside decks in designated areas.

ALASKA MARINE HIGHWAY

From its humble beginnings in 1948, when three men from Haines—Steve Homer and Ray and Gustav Gelotte—had a dream to provide marine transportation between territorial Alaska's coastal communities, the Alaska Marine Highway System has grown from one ex-

Alaska Marine Highway

U.S. Navy landing craft to today's fleet of 10 ferries (with more in the works). When Alaska became a state in 1959, the Alaska legislature approved the Alaska Ferry Transportation Act and in 1963 the Alaska Marine Highway System was formally founded.

☎ 800/642–0066
⊕ www.dot.state.
ak.us/amhs
☞ Cruise Style:
Small-ship.

Today's system has grown to cover 3,500 miles from the Aleutian Islands to Washington State and calls in 35 port communities. Its 10 vessels carry an average of 330,000 passengers and 110,000 vehicles a year.

While not exactly a cruise, the Alaska Marine Highway System vessels travel through some of the world's most breathtaking scenery, making the ferries an ideal option for independent visitors who wish to chart their own course. Travelers can walk onboard, drive a vehicle, ride a bicycle, or even bring along a kayak. Cabins are available to book on some vessels, but you can also simply pitch a tent on deck. Along the way you will see vivid blue glaciers, snowcapped mountains, active volcanoes, majestic fjords, lush green forests, and abundant wildlife.

Inexpensive, casual, and laid back, the ferries are the way many Alaskans travel through their state and offer an excellent way to reach areas off the beaten path. For backpackers and campers who plan to walk on and off the ferries at their whim, passenger space is usually available anytime. To bring a car or get a cabin, you'll need to make a reservation, either directly through the Alaska Marine Highway System or through a travel agent.

FOOD

With the exception of the *Lituya,* all vessels offer food and beverage service. Hot and cold items, including Alaska seafood, salads, sandwiches, and beverage service are available throughout the day in self-service dining areas. Vending machines are found on each vessel for quick snacks. The M/Vs *Columbia* and *Tustumena* have full-service dining rooms that feature entrées of fresh Alaskan seafood. Passengers can also bring their own food and beverages onboard. All vessels have microwaves, and some have coin-operated ice machines.

ENTERTAINMENT

Some vessels have theater areas that show general-interest films and documentaries featuring Alaska and the outdoors. Additionally, some vessels have card rooms, reading rooms, small video game arcades, and toddler play areas.

FITNESS AND RECREATION

None of the vessels of the Alaska Marine Highway System has a gym, but passengers can take the opportunity to get in a walk or jog during port stops.

YOUR SHIPMATES

onboard you will find a wide variety of passengers—local Alaska residents, backpackers, independently minded travelers of all ages, and even pets.

DRESS CODE

Dress is all casual all the time as long as it suits the weather. Comfortable walking shoes, a hat, gloves, light rainwear, and an umbrella are suggested.

JUNIOR CRUISERS

Inquisitive children and teens who don't require organized activities should find the experience educational and stimulating, but there are no TVs in cabins and no Wi-Fi, and cell phone service is limited. Children under age 6 travel free, and children ages 6–11 travel for approximately half price.

SERVICE

The crew is all-American, and cabin service is usually limited to trash removal.

TIPPING

State of Alaska employees crew are not allowed to accept gratuities.

KNOWN FOR

■ **Casual Environment:** There is no need to pack any dressy attire. Fellow passengers are likely to show up for meals in the clothing they wore all day.

■ **Pay As You Go:** The ferries are an inexpensive way to see Alaska. Only transportation and a cabin, if required, are included in the fare. There is a charge for all food and beverages.

■ **No Cabin Required:** Recliner lounges serve as popular sleeping areas with space to roll out a sleeping bag, and covered solariums located on the upper decks of each vessel are also popular sleeping areas.

■ **Camping on the Water:** Passengers with a spirit of adventure may set up small tents on the outside upper decks. All vessels have public bathrooms and, except on *Lituya, Chenega, and Fairweather,* public showers are available.

■ **Transportation:** The Alaska Marine Highway System is the 49th state's "Interstate" highway and you'll find many local residents onboard its vessels.

Top: Passengers in the solarium
Middle: Ashore in Juneau
Bottom: Departing Juneau Harbor

SHIPS OF THE LINE

Aurora. With a passenger capacity of 300 on its short runs, *Aurora* does not have cabins. You will find food service and a solarium.

Chenega. A fast ferry, *Chenega* has no cabins, but interior seating, consisting of reclining airplane-style seats and small tables (suitable for working on a laptop or dining), is provided for 150 in the observation lounge and 109 midship. In addition, there is seating in the outdoor solarium. A full-service snack bar sells food and beverages.

Columbia. Usually operating round-trip from Bellingham, Washington, the *Columbia* has 103 cabins as well as a dining room, snack bar, gift shop, theater, and video arcade. Two lounges located forward offer panoramic vistas. Of the 59 two-berth cabins, 3 are suitable for wheelchairs. Additionally, there are 44 four-berth cabins, 5 of which include a sitting area. The only cabin service is daily trash collection; fresh linens, pillows, and blankets are available for a fee. Toiletries are not provided.

Fairweather. Another fast ferry, *Fairweather* has no cabins, but interior seating, consisting of reclining airplane-style seats and small tables (suitable for working on a laptop or dining), is provided for 150 in the observation lounge and 109 midship. Additional seating is in the outdoor solarium. A full-service snack bar sells food and beverages.

Kennicott. *Kennicott* is designed to serve as a command center during oil spills or natural disasters. Observation lounges and a heated solarium are favorite spots to enjoy Alaska's scenic beauty. There is a theater, and food and beverage services are available. Accommodations include 56 two-berth cabins (2 are designated ADA-compliant) and 48 four-berth cabins (3 designated ADA-compliant). The only cabin service is daily trash collection; fresh linens, pillows, and blankets are available for a fee. Toiletries are not provided.

CHOOSE THIS LINE IF...

■ You want to avoid the typical cruise ship experience and prefer to travel like a local.

■ You are independent and want to set your own pace.

■ You consider yourself a traveler, not a tourist.

LeConte. Although it can carry 300 passengers on its short runs, *LeConte* has no cabins. However, in addition to its lounge and deck space, passengers will find a solarium and food service.

Lituya. Suitable for the truly adventurous, the Alaska Marine Highway's *Lituya* carries only 149 passengers and has no cabins or food and beverage service except vending machines.

Malaspina. The *Malaspina*'s 499 passengers enjoy a forward observation lounge, theater, solarium, gift shop, and cafeteria. The 73 cabins include 26 with two berths and 46 with four berths. An additional two-berth cabin is wheelchair accessible. Trash is collected daily, and fresh linens, pillows, and blankets are available for a fee. Toiletries are not provided.

Matanuska. Capable of carrying 499 passengers, *Matanuska* operates in winter months from Bellingham, Washington, when *Columbia* is out of service. It has a forward observation lounge, theater, solarium, gift shop, and cafeteria. The 108 cabins include 80 with two berths, 23 with three berths, and 4 with four berths. In addition, 1 two-berth cabin is wheelchair-accessible. Trash is collected daily, and fresh linens, pillows, and blankets are available for a fee. Toiletries are not provided.

Tustumena. Usually operating from Homer and Kodiak, *Tustumena* ventures all the way out to Unalaska and Dutch Harbor. Services onboard for 174 passengers include a solarium, forward observation lounge, and cafeteria. There are also 26 cabins (18 with two berths, 1 of which is wheelchair-accessible, and 8 with four berths). Only daily trash collection is provided; fresh linens, pillows, and blankets are available for a fee. Toiletries are not provided.

HELPFUL HINTS

■ Reservations can be made on the Alaska Marine Highway website or through a travel agent.

■ The Alaska Marine Highway website contains a wealth of information, including schedules for all vessels and suggested itineraries for a cruiselike experience.

■ Cabins are sold per trip, not per person, and fill up quickly. Reservations should be made well in advance to avoid being put on a wait list.

■ It takes time to load vehicles on the ferries, so take heed of the arrival time when driving to port.

■ Research your destinations carefully to determine the time you will have ashore in each port in order to make arrangements ahead of time for any sightseeing you want to do.

DON'T CHOOSE THIS LINE IF...

■ You require a structured schedule of daily activities; this is not a traditional cruise.

■ You can't handle surprises along the way; this is the wilderness, and you have to go with the flow.

■ Your enjoyment depends on being pampered and entertained; there's none of that on these ships.

AMERICAN CRUISE LINES

American Cruise Lines specializes in a unique style of small-ship cruising along the inland waterways and rivers of the United States. Typical itineraries for its All-American fleet include the Pacific Northwest, New England, and the Mississippi River. The line's coastal

American Spirit at sea

cruiser, *American Constellation*, is designed for cruising the Pacific Northwest and Alaska's Inside Passage. With no more than 175 passengers onboard, the small ship allows passengers to experience each port of call up close and personal.

☎ 800/460–4518
⊕ www.american-cruiselines.com
☞ Cruise Style: Small-ship.

American Cruise Lines offers round-trip Inside Passage cruises from Juneau and 11-night repositioning cruises between Seattle and Juneau at the beginning of the season—and from Juneau to Seattle at season's end. Itineraries are designed to explore some of Alaska's most popular ports, such as Skagway, Haines, and Glacier Bay, as well as remote wilderness areas.

To enhance the cruise experience, American Cruise Lines invites carefully selected experts to join each voyage. Through informal lectures, open discussions, and activities, they bring local history, nature, and culture alive with their knowledge and passion for American heritage. These naturalists and historians also lead shore excursions while in port to give you behind-the-scenes tours of some of Alaska's best-kept secrets and favorite treasures. Basic shore excursions are included in the fare in Alaska, and alternative tours are available for purchase.

FOOD

Using the freshest ingredients available, menus are inspired by regional and local specialties and take advantage of fresh meats and seafood and in-season fruits and vegetables. Special menus are available to passengers on restricted diets. Every evening before dinner, a complimentary cocktail hour is hosted with a bar setup and hors d'oeuvres. Dinner is served with complimentary wine and beer.

ENTERTAINMENT

American Cruise Lines provides unique, regional entertainment on its cruises, so don't look for splashy entertainers or a casino onboard. Activities are designed to highlight the areas through which you are sailing, including local musicians, demonstrations, minor theatrical performances, and games. Activities and lectures are as rich in history and culture as the ports themselves.

FITNESS AND RECREATION

Exercise equipment and a putting green to hone your game are featured onboard. Walks ashore led by the ship's naturalist offer a more rigorous workout. There is no spa or salon, but the reception desk may be able to recommend possibilities to you in ports.

YOUR SHIPMATES

Typical passengers are older, well-traveled individuals looking for a destination-focused adventure where they will have the opportunity to explore the history, culture, natural scenery, and wildlife of the unique areas visited.

DRESS CODE

Casual sportswear is suggested during the day. Attire should include clothing for layering when the weather turns cool. Comfortable walking shoes, a windbreaker, and light rainwear are also recommended items. Evening attire is always country club casual.

JUNIOR CRUISERS

Families are more than welcome, but it is rare to see children onboard. There are no youth facilities; however, the cruise director will plan appropriate activities when children are sailing.

SERVICE

With the services of an American crew, your needs will be satisfied in an attentive, if not overly polished, manner and without a language barrier.

TIPPING

Tips are entirely at your personal discretion and generally average about $125 per person on a seven-night cruise.

PAST PASSENGERS

After your first cruise you will receive an invitation to join the Eagle Society in the mail. If you are already a past passenger and would like to join, you can do so onboard your next cruise or by calling a cruise specialist

---

KNOWN FOR

■ **All-American:** The large fleet of American-built, flagged, and crewed small ships is also environmentally friendly, and smoking is allowed only in designated areas.

■ **Budget-Conscious Beverage Policy:** Although not all alcoholic beverages are included in the fare, your own alcohol is welcome onboard, and a complimentary cocktail hour is hosted every evening. Wine and beer are served with lunch and dinner at no additional charge.

■ **Accessibility:** With elevator service to all decks, the ships are accessible to the mobility impaired.

■ **United States Passenger Advantage:** All departure ports and ports of call are located in the United States; a passport is recommended for Alaska cruises but not usually required.

3

AMERICAN CRUISE LINES

Whale-watching

Top: Shopping for crafts
Middle: View from the bridge
Bottom: Dinner on informal night

and requesting an invitation. Past-passenger benefits include complimentary standard shore excursions after having taken three cruises—after your third cruise you will never have to pay for standard shore excursions again; special gifts on subsequent cruises; a complimentary 11th cruise after you complete 10 cruises; invitations to Eagle Society cruises and select sailings; Eagle Society luggage tags and name tags; and members-only savings and promotions. In addition, when a ship is in port near a member's hometown, American Cruise Lines extends an invitation to come aboard for lunch or dinner and when in port during a sailing, members may invite friends or family aboard for a tour of the ship or to join them for meals.

SHIPS OF THE LINE

American Cruise Lines offers small-ship cruises along the inland waterways and rivers of the United States, from the Mississippi River to New England, and Alaska.

American Constellation. Built to provide maximum relaxation and amenities that are often unexpected on ships this size, the casual and inviting public areas of American Cruise Line's 175-passenger *American Constellation* reflect the company's American heritage in spaces that are comfortable and stylish.

Outside you'll find plenty of space on the ship's partially covered sundeck to view the passing scenery, either at the rail or from a deck chair. You won't miss Alaska's scenic wonders from inside the ship either—both the main lounge and dining salon feature walls of windows that bring the outside in. Lounges, sundecks, and dining salons are accessible by wheelchairs or other walking aid devices. Wheelchairs, walkers, and shower chairs are available for loan, by prearrangement. The ship is also equipped with an elevator for ease of movement between decks. Wireless Internet access is available shipwide, but you'll have to be close to shore to receive a signal for cell phone use.

CHOOSE THIS LINE IF...

■ You are a discriminating traveler looking for the intimacy of a small ship.

■ You appreciate learning about the history and culture of the ports you visit.

■ You prefer a relaxed and casual atmosphere.

Each evening before dinner you are invited to mingle with your fellow passengers to share the day's adventures over complimentary cocktails and hors d'oeuvres.

Meals are served in the open seating dining salon, which is large enough to accommodate all passengers at once. The day's menu is announced in advance, and special menus are available to passengers on restricted diets. Breakfast is prepared to order on most mornings, and lunches are light and casual. Coffee, nonalcoholic beverages, and snacks are available 24 hours a day, and there is breakfast room service upon request.

The most spacious cabins in the fleet feature flat-screen televisions with DVD players, a sitting area, and more than half have a balcony. While storage space is plentiful in the cabin itself, it is somewhat tight in the bathroom. Bedding configurations are either king or two twin beds. Cabins without a balcony have large picture windows that open to the sea air. Amenities include hair dryers as well as basic toiletries. Ideal for solo travelers, single staterooms with a private balcony feature a twin bed, sliding glass door, and full-size bathrooms. Slightly smaller single staterooms with a large picture window have a twin bed and sizable bathroom. Two cabins are designated as wheelchair accessible.

HELPFUL HINTS

■ Each ship has a large resource library, including books and videos, as well as naturalists and historians onboard for each sailing.

■ Complimentary guided walking tours are offered on port days, and optional shore excursions are reasonably priced.

■ The main lounge has panoramic windows to view the scenery when the weather is not ideal, but the observation deck is also partially covered.

■ It's a good idea to arrive in the embarkation port a day before sailing as cruises leave early in the day. Departures are at 1:30 pm (sometimes earlier if all passengers have arrived), and embarkation begins at 10 am. Passengers need to be onboard by 12:30.

3

DON'T CHOOSE THIS LINE IF...

■ You must be entertained with splashy production shows and nonstop activity.

■ Your daily routine includes a fully equipped gym—there are none on these ships.

■ You would rather spend time in a casino than attend an evening lecture.

CARNIVAL CRUISE LINE

The world's largest cruise line—and one of the most widely recognized—originated its "Fun Ship" concept in 1972 and has been launching party-packed superliners with signature red funnels ever since. The line's ever-growing fleet features entertainment and

Lobby Bar on board *Carnival Fantasy*

activities designed for passengers of all ages, from game shows and lip sync competitions to twisting waterslides and mini golf. These ships are a reliable choice for families as well as young singles and couples who want a vacation that won't break the bank.

☎ 305/599–2600, 800/227–6482

⊕ www.carnival.com

☞ Cruise Style: Mainstream.

Nearly all onboard dining options are included in the fare, as are comedy and production shows, children's programs, and use of state-of-the-art fitness centers. With some of the most comfortable accommodations at sea, large new ships are continuously added to the fleet and rarely deviate from a successful pattern, while older vessels are updated with popular features, such as the poolside BlueIguana Tequila Bar with an adjacent burrito cantina, the Red Frog Rum Bar that also serves Carnival's own brand of Thirsty Frog Red beer, and Guy's Burger Joint, created with Food Network star Guy Fieri.

FOOD

Carnival ships have both flexible dining options as well as casual alternative restaurants. Although the tradition of two set mealtimes for dinner prevails on Carnival ships, the line's open seating concept—Your Time Dining—is available fleet-wide.

Choices are numerous, and the skill of Carnival's chefs has elevated the line's menus to an unexpected level. Although the waiters still sing and dance, the good-to-excellent dining room food appeals to American tastes. Upscale steak houses on certain ships serve cuisine comparable to the best midrange steak houses ashore.

Carnival serves the best food of the mainstream cruise lines. In addition to the regular menu, vegetarian, low-calorie, low-carbohydrate, low-salt, and no-sugar selections are available. A children's menu includes such favorites as macaroni and cheese, chicken fingers, and peanut-butter-and-jelly sandwiches. If you don't feel like dressing up for dinner, the Lido buffet serves full meals, including sandwiches, a salad bar, rotisserie chicken, Asian stir-fry, and excellent pizza.

ENTERTAINMENT

More high-energy than cerebral, the entertainment consists of lavish Las Vegas–style revues presented in main show lounges by a company of singers and dancers. Other performers might include magicians, jugglers, acrobats, passengers performing in the talent show, or karaoke. Live bands play a wide range of musical styles for dancing and every ship has a nightclub, piano bar, and a comedy club. Adult activities, particularly the competitive ones, tend to be silly and hilarious and play to full houses. With Carnival's branding initiative, look for Hasbro, The Game Show, and performances created by Playlist Productions.

FITNESS AND RECREATION

Manned by staff members trained to keep passengers in shipshape form, Carnival's trademark spas and fitness centers are some of the largest and best equipped at sea. Spas and salons are operated by Steiner Leisure, and treatments include a variety of massages, body wraps, and facials; salons offer hair and nail services and even tooth whitening. Fitness centers have state-of-the-art cardio and strength-training equipment, a jogging track, and basic exercise classes at no charge. There's a fee for personal training, body composition analysis, and specialized classes such as yoga and Pilates.

YOUR SHIPMATES

Carnival's passengers are predominantly active Americans, mostly couples in their mid-thirties to mid-fifties. Many families enjoy Carnival cruises in the Caribbean year-round. Holidays and school vacation periods are very popular with families, and you'll see a lot of kids in summer. More than 700,000 children sail on Carnival ships every year.

DRESS CODE

Two "cruise elegant" nights are standard on seven-night cruises; one is the norm on shorter sailings. Although men should feel free to wear tuxedos, dark suits (or sport coats) and ties are more prevalent. All other evenings are "cruise casual," with nice jeans and dress

Carnival Victory dining room

Top: *Carnival Triumph*
walking and jogging track
Middle: *Carnival Elation*
at sea
Bottom: *Carnival Destiny*
penthouse suite

shorts permitted in the dining rooms. All ships request that no short-shorts or cutoffs be worn after 6 pm, but that policy is often ignored.

JUNIOR CRUISERS

Camp Carnival, run year-round by professionals, earns high marks for keeping young cruisers busy and content. Dedicated children's areas include great playrooms with separate splash pools. Toddlers from two to five years are treated to puppet shows, sponge painting, face painting, coloring, drawing, and crafts. As long as diapers and supplies are provided, staff will change toddlers. Activities for ages six to eight include arts and crafts, pizza parties, computer time, T-shirt painting, a talent show, and fitness programs. Nine- to 11-year-olds can play Ping-Pong, take dance lessons, play video games, and participate in swim parties, scavenger hunts, and sports. Tweens ages 12 to 14 appreciate the social events, parties, contests, and sports in Circle C. Every night they have access to the ships' discos, followed by late-night movies, karaoke, or pizza.

Club O2 is geared toward teens 15 to 17. Program directors play host at the spacious teen clubs, where kicking back is the order of the day between scheduled activities. The fleet-wide spa program for older teens offers a high level of pampering. Staff members also accompany teens on shore excursions designed just for them.

Daytime group babysitting for infants two and under allows parents the freedom to explore ports of call without the kids until noon. Parents can also pursue leisurely adults-only evenings from 10 pm to 3 am, when slumber party–style group babysitting is available for children from ages 6 months to 11 years. Babysitting is available for a fee.

SERVICE

Service on Carnival ships is friendly but not polished. Stateroom attendants are not only recognized for their attention to cleanliness but also for their expertise in creating towel animals—cute critters fashioned from

CHOOSE THIS LINE IF...

■ You want an action-packed casino with a choice of table games and rows upon rows of clanging slot machines.

■ You don't mind standing in line—these are big ships with a lot of passengers, and lines are not uncommon.

■ You don't mind hearing announcements over the public-address system reminding you of what's next on the schedule.

bath towels that appear during nightly turndown service. They've become so popular that Carnival publishes an instruction book on how to create them yourself.

TIPPING

A gratuity of $12.95 per person per day for passengers in standard accommodations and $13.95 per passenger per day for those booked in suites is automatically added to passenger accounts, and gratuities are distributed to stewards and waitstaff. Passengers may adjust the amount based on the level of service experienced. All beverage tabs at bars get an automatic 15% addition.

PAST PASSENGERS

After sailing on one Carnival cruise, you'll receive a complimentary subscription to the company email magazine, and access to your past sailing history on the Carnival website. You are recognized on subsequent cruises with color-coded key cards determined by points or the number of days you've sailed—Red (starting on your second cruise), Gold (when you've accumulated 25–74 points); Platinum (75–199 points); and Diamond (200+ points)—which serve as your entrée to a by-invitation-only cocktail reception. Platinum and Diamond members are eligible for benefits including priority embarkation and debarkation, priority dining assignments, supper club and spa reservations, a logo item gift, and limited complimentary laundry service.

DON'T CHOOSE THIS LINE IF...

■ You want an intimate, sedate atmosphere. Carnival's ships are big and bold.

■ You want elaborate accommodations. Carnival suites are spacious but not as feature-filled as the term "suite" may suggest.

■ You're turned off by men in tank tops. Casual on these ships means casual indeed.

SPIRIT-CLASS
Carnival Spirit, Carnival Pride, Carnival Legend, Carnival Miracle

CREW MEMBERS	930
ENTERED SERVICE	2001, 2001, 2002, 2004
700 ft. **GROSS TONS**	88,500
LENGTH	960 feet
500 ft. **NUMBER OF CABINS**	1,062
PASSENGER CAPACITY	2,124 (2,667 max)
300 ft. **WIDTH**	105.7 feet

Spirit-class vessels may have seemed like throwbacks in size when they launched, but these sleek ships have the advantage of fitting through the Panama Canal's original locks and, with their additional length, include all the trademark characteristics of their larger fleetmates. They're also racehorses with the speed to reach far-flung destinations. *Carnival Spirit*—for which the class is named—makes its home port in Australia, primarily serving the Australian and New Zealand markets.

A rosy red skylight in the front bulkhead of the funnel—which houses the reservations-only upscale steak house—caps a soaring, 11-deck atrium. Lovely chapels are available for weddings, either upon embarkation or while in a port of call, and are also used for occasional shipboard religious services.

The upper and lower interior promenade decks are unhampered by a mid-ship restaurant or galley, which means that passenger flow throughout the ships is much improved over earlier, and even subsequent, designs.

CABINS
Layout: Cabins on Carnival ships are spacious, and these are no exception. Nearly 80% have an ocean view and, of those, more than 80% have balconies. Suites and some ocean-view cabins have private balconies outfitted with chairs and tables; some cabins have balconies at least 50% larger than average. Every cabin has adequate closet and drawer/shelf storage, as well as bathroom shelves. High-thread-count linens and plush pillows and duvets are a luxurious touch in all accommodations. Suites also have a whirlpool tub and walk-in closet. Decks 5, 6, and 7 each have a pair of balcony staterooms that connect to adjoining interior staterooms that are ideal for families because of their close proximity to children and teen areas.

Decor: Light-wood cabinetry, soft pastels, mirrored accents, a small refrigerator, a personal safe, a hair dryer, and a seating area with sofa, chair, and table are typical for ocean-view cabins and suites. Inside cabins have ample room but no seating area.

Bathrooms: Extras include shampoo and bath gel provided in shower-mounted dispensers, as well as fluffy

Top: *Carnival Legend* at sea Bottom: Spirit-class balcony stateroom

towels and a wall-mounted magnifying mirror. Bathrobes for use during the cruise are provided for all.

Accessibility: Sixteen staterooms are designed for wheelchair accessibility.

RESTAURANTS

One formal restaurant serves open seating breakfast and lunch and adds a brunch on sea days; it also serves dinner in two traditional assigned evening seatings or an open seating option. The casual Lido buffet with stations offers a variety of food choices (including a deli, salad bar, dessert station, and different daily regional cuisines); at night it serves casual dinners. A pizzeria and poolside Guy's Burger Joint, for burgers and fries, and BlueIguana Cantina, serving burritos, tacos, and all the trimmings, round out casual options. There's also an upscale steak house and a sushi restaurant that require reservations and an additional charge. A specialty coffee bar and patisserie and sushi bar have per-item charges. Taste Bar serves complimentary appetizers before dinner and light snacks during the day; room service operates round the clock with a limited menu of breakfast selections, sandwiches, and snacks.

SPAS

Steiner Leisure operates the 14,500-square-foot spas that offer an indoor therapy pool as well as such indulgences as a variety of massages, body wraps, and facials for adults and teens. Complimentary steam rooms and saunas in men's and women's changing rooms feature glass walls for sea views. Salons offer tooth whitening in addition to hair and nail services.

BARS AND ENTERTAINMENT

All ships have received newly branded bars and comedy clubs, and all offer high-energy shows by resident singers and dancers or guest performers in the main show room. Spirited piano bars, nightclubs featuring music for dancing and listening and karaoke, and deck parties add to the fun after dark.

PROS AND CONS

Pros: the enclosed space located forward on the promenade deck is quiet and good for reading; for relaxation, his-and-hers saunas and steam rooms have glass walls and sea views; complimentary self-serve ice cream dispensers are on the Lido deck.

Cons: these are long ships, and some cabins are quite far from elevators; connecting staterooms are relatively scarce; the video arcade is almost hidden at the forward end of the ship.

Cabin Type	Size (sq. ft.)
Penthouse Suite	370 sq. ft. (average)
Suite	275 sq. ft.
Ocean View	185 sq. ft.
Interior	185 sq. ft.

3

FAST FACTS

- 12 passenger decks
- specialty restaurant, dining room, buffet, ice cream parlor, pizzeria
- Wi-Fi, safe, refrigerator
- 3 pools (1 indoor), children's pool
- fitness classes, gym, hot tubs, sauna, spa, steam room
- 7 bars, casino, 2 dance clubs, library, show room, video game room
- children's programs
- laundry facilities, laundry service
- Internet terminal
- no-smoking cabins

Carnival Miracle Gatsby's Garden

82

CELEBRITY CRUISES

Since it was founded in 1989, Celebrity Cruises has grown from a single refurbished ocean liner into a fleet of premium, sophisticated cruise ships that have a reputation for professional service, fine food, and some of the best design in the industry. Signature amenities

Swim-up bar under the stars

have grown with the fleet, including gourmet specialty restaurants that carry an additional fee, large staterooms with generous storage, fully equipped spas, and butler service for guests in the top accommodations categories. Valuable art collections grace the stylish modern luxury ship interiors.

☎ *800/647–2251*
⊕ *www.celebritycruis-es.com*
☞ *Cruise Style: Premium.*

Although spacious accommodations in every category are a Celebrity standard, Concierge-class, an upscale element on all ships, makes certain premium ocean-view and balcony staterooms almost the equivalent of suites in terms of service. A Concierge-class stateroom includes numerous extras, such as chilled champagne, fresh fruit, and flowers upon arrival; exclusive room-service menus; evening canapés; luxury bedding, pillows, and linens; upgraded balcony furnishings; priority boarding and luggage service; and other VIP perks. At the touch of a single telephone button, a Concierge-class desk representative is at hand to offer assistance. Suites are still the ultimate, though, and include the services of a butler to assist with unpacking, booking spa services and dining reservations, shining shoes, and even replacing a popped button.

FOOD
Aside from the sophisticated ambience of its restaurants, the cuisine has always been a highlight of a Celebrity cruise. Happily, every ship in the fleet has a highly experienced team headed by executive chefs and food and beverage managers who have developed their skills in some of the world's finest restaurants and hotels.

Alternative restaurants throughout the fleet offer fine dining and a variety of international cuisines in splendid surroundings. A less formal evening alternative is offered in Lido restaurants, where you'll find made-to-order sushi, stir-fry, pasta, pizza, and curry stations, as well as a carving station, an array of vegetables, "loaded" baked potatoes, and desserts. The spa cafés serve light and healthy cuisine from breakfast until evening. Cafés serve a variety of coffees, teas, and pastries that carry an additional charge. Late-night treats served by white-gloved waiters in public rooms throughout the ships can include mini–beef Wellingtons and crispy tempura.

To further complement the food, Celebrity's extensive wine collection features more than 500 choices, including vintages from every major wine-producing region.

ENTERTAINMENT

Entertainment has never been a primary focus of Celebrity Cruises, although every ship offers a lineup of lavish production shows. In addition, ships have guest entertainers and music for dancing and listening, and you'll find lectures on every Celebrity cruise. Presentations may range from financial strategies, astronomy, wine appreciation, photography tips, and politics to the food, history, and culture of ports of call. Culinary demonstrations, bingo, and art auctions are additional diversions throughout the fleet. There are plenty of activities outlined in the daily program of events. There are no public-address announcements for bingo or hawking of gold-by-the-inch sales. You can still play and buy, but you won't be reminded repeatedly.

FITNESS AND RECREATION

Celebrity's Canyon Ranch SpaClub and fitness centers are some of the most tranquil and nicely equipped at sea, with complimentary access to thalassotherapy pools on Millennium-class ships. Spa services are operated by Canyon Ranch, one of the world's leading spa and wellness brands, and treatments include a variety of massages, body wraps, and facials and a menu of options just for teens. Trendy and traditional hair and nail services are offered in the salons.

State-of-the-art exercise equipment, a jogging track, and basic fitness classes are available at no charge. There's a fee for personal training, body composition analysis, and specialized classes such as yoga and Pilates. Golf pros offer hands-on instruction, and game simulators allow passengers to play world-famous courses. Each

3

Top: The Millennium AquaSpa
Bottom: Millennium-class cinema and conference center

Top: *Century* Rendezvous Lounge
Middle: Lounge in climate-controlled comfort
Bottom: Lounging on deck

ship also has an Acupuncture at Sea treatment area staffed by licensed practitioners of Oriental medicine.

YOUR SHIPMATES

Celebrity caters to American cruise passengers, primarily couples from their mid-thirties to mid-fifties. Many families enjoy cruising on Celebrity's fleet during summer months and holiday periods, particularly in the Caribbean. Lengthier cruises and exotic itineraries attract passengers in the over-sixty age group.

DRESS CODE

Two dressy "evening chic" nights are standard on seven-night cruises. Men are encouraged to wear tuxedos, but dark suits or sport coats and ties are more prevalent. Other evenings are designated "smart casual and above." Although jeans are discouraged in formal restaurants, they are appropriate for casual dining venues after 6 pm. The line requests that no shorts be worn in public areas after 6 pm, and most people observe the dress code of the evening, unlike on some other cruise lines.

JUNIOR CRUISERS

Each Celebrity vessel has a dedicated playroom and offers a four-tier program of age-appropriate games and activities designed for children ages 3 to 5, 6 to 8, and 9 to 11. Younger children must be toilet-trained to participate in the programs and use the facilities; however, families are welcome to borrow toys for their non-toilet-trained kids. A fee may be assessed for participation in children's dinner parties, the Late-Night Slumber Party, and Afternoon Get-Togethers while parents are ashore in ports of call. Evening group babysitting is available for a fee. All ships have teen centers, where tweens and teenagers (ages 12 to 17) can hang out and attend mocktail and pizza parties.

SERVICE

Service on Celebrity ships is unobtrusive and polished. Concierge-class adds an unexpected level of service and amenities that are usually reserved for luxury ships

CHOOSE THIS LINE IF...

- You want an upscale atmosphere at a relatively reasonable fare.

- You don't mind paying extra for exceptional specialty dining experiences.

- You want to dine amid elegant surroundings in some of the best restaurants at sea.

or passengers in top-category suites on other premium cruise lines.

TIPPING

Gratuities are automatically added daily to onboard accounts in the following amounts (which may be adjusted at your discretion): $14.50 per person per day for passengers in stateroom categories; $15 per person per day for Concierge-class and Aqua-class staterooms; and $18 per person per day for suites. An automatic gratuity of 15% is added to all beverage tabs, minibar purchases, and salon and spa services.

PAST PASSENGERS

Once you've sailed with Celebrity, you become a member of the Captain's Club and receive benefits commensurate with the number of cruises you've taken, with more benefits added at each level. Classic members have been on at least one Celebrity cruise and receive exclusive onboard premium offers. Select members have sailed at least six cruises and get perks such as discounted Internet and laundry service specials. After 10 cruises you become an Elite member and are also invited to a complimentary cocktail hour. Elite Plus members are also recognized with beverage and specialty dining discounts, complimentary specialty coffees, and 240 free Internet minutes. Zenith members are additionally offered access to Michael's Club Concierge Lounge, receive a complimentary beverage package, free laundry, and unlimited Internet minutes.

HELPFUL HINTS

■ Wine/dining packages are a comparative bargain since fees for specialty restaurants are so high, but they are offered only in limited numbers; book them early.

■ The line offers stateroom bar setups and flat-rate beverage packages to help you avoid per-drink charges.

■ Ship's photographers will cover individual special events if asked.

■ Service animals are welcome onboard all ships, including those sailing to the United Kingdom if they are in compliance with DEFRA regulations.

■ Celebrity's private shore excursions (in 50 ports) offer personalized travel in the comfort of a private car or van.

DON'T CHOOSE THIS LINE IF...

■ You need to be reminded of when activities are scheduled. Announcements are kept to a minimum.

■ You look forward to boisterous pool games and wacky contests. These cruises are fairly quiet and sophisticated.

■ You think funky avant-garde art is weird. Abstract modernism abounds in the art collections.

MILLENNIUM-CLASS
Millennium, Summit, Infinity, Constellation

CREW MEMBERS	
	999
ENTERED SERVICE	
	2000, 2001, 2001, 2002
700 ft. **GROSS TONS**	
	91,000
LENGTH	
	965 feet
500 ft. **NUMBER OF CABINS**	
	1069, 1079, 1085, 1085
PASSENGER CAPACITY	
	2,138, 2,158, 2,170, 2,170
300 ft. **WIDTH**	
	105 feet

Millennium-class ships are among the largest and most feature-filled in the Celebrity fleet. The ships include show lounges reminiscent of splendid opera houses, and an alternative restaurant with a classic ocean liner theme. The spas are immense and house a complimentary hydrotherapy pool and café. These ships have a lot to offer families, with some of the most expansive children's facilities in the Celebrity fleet. Upgrades have introduced more accommodation categories and dining venues similar to those found on Solstice-class ships.

Rich fabrics in jewel tones mix elegantly with the abundant use of marble and wood accents throughout public areas. The atmosphere is not unlike a luxurious European hotel filled with grand spaces that flow nicely from one to the other.

CABINS

Layout: As on most Celebrity ships, cabins are thoughtfully designed, with ample closet and drawer/shelf storage, as well as bathroom shelves. Some ocean-view cabins and suites have balconies. Penthouse suites also have guest bathrooms. Most staterooms and suites have convertible sofa beds, and many can accommodate third and fourth occupants. Connecting staterooms are also widely available. Family staterooms have huge balconies, and some have two sofa beds. Aqua-class accommodations with direct spa access are a relatively new addition.

Amenities: A small refrigerator, personal safe, hair dryer, and a seating area with sofa, chair, and table are typical standard amenities. Extras include bathroom toiletries (shampoo, soaps, and lotion) and bathrobes. Suite luxuries vary, but most include a whirlpool tub, a DVD player, an Internet-connected computer, and a walk-in closet, while all have butler service, personalized stationery, and a logo tote bag. Penthouse and Royal suites have outdoor whirlpool tubs on the balconies.

Accessibility: Twenty-six staterooms are designed for wheelchair accessibility.

RESTAURANTS

The formal two-deck restaurant serves open seating breakfast and lunch, while dinner is served in two assigned seatings or open seating. The casual Lido buffet offers breakfast and lunch; for dinner, it has

Top: Qsine restaurant on *Celebrity Infinity*
Bottom: *Celebrity Infinity* solarium

made-to-order entrées, a carving station, and an array of side dishes. A poolside grill offers fast food, while a spa café serves lighter fare. Each ship has upscale alternative restaurants that serve Italian cuisine and modern American dishes (reservation and cover charge). Each also has a café that offers sushi and other light items (cover charge), and an extra-charge specialty coffee, tea, and gelato bar. All ships feature a second specialty restaurant reserved for passengers in suites and Aqua-class accommodations. Pizza delivery and 24-hour room service augment dining choices.

SPAS

The Canyon Ranch SpaClub is one of the most nicely equipped at sea with spa services operated by high-end Canyon Ranch. In addition to treatments that include a variety of massages, body wraps, and facials, each ship also has an acupuncture treatment area and offers Medi-Spa Cosmetic services. A relaxation room and thermal suite with a dry sauna, aromatherapy steam room, and a Turkish bath are available to Aqua-class passengers and those who have booked a treatment or purchased a pass. Changing rooms for men and women have complimentary saunas, and a large hydrotherapy pool is available to all adults at no charge.

BARS AND ENTERTAINMENT

Production companies and guest entertainers perform in the show lounges. Bars and lounges are designed as unique destinations onboard with drink menus with both classic and also "signature" and trendier cocktails. Some drinks are a reflection of the regions you are visiting. Live bands or DJs provide music for listening and dancing.

PROS AND CONS

Pros: stylishly appointed Grand Foyers have sweeping staircases; there's no charge for use of the thalassotherapy pool in the Solarium; the spa Café serves complimentary light and healthy selections.

Cons: these ships just have too many passengers to offer truly personal service; wines in the specialty restaurants are pricey; there are no self-service laundries.

Cabin Type	Size (sq. ft.)
Penthouse Suite	1,432 sq. ft.
Royal Suite	538 sq. ft.
Celebrity Suite	467 sq. ft.
Sky Suite	251 sq. ft.
Family Ocean View	271 sq. ft.
Concierge-Class	191 sq. ft.
Ocean View/ Interior	170 sq. ft.

FAST FACTS

- 11 passenger decks
- 3 specialty restaurants, dining room, buffet, ice cream parlor, pizzeria
- Internet (*Constellation*), Wi-Fi, safe, refrigerator, DVD (some)
- 3 pools (1 indoor), children's pool
- fitness classes, gym, hot tubs, sauna, spa, steam room
- 7 bars, casino, dance club, library, showroom, video game room
- children's programs
- dry cleaning, laundry service
- no-smoking cabins

Celebrity Infinity stateroom

SOLSTICE-CLASS
Solstice, Equinox, Eclipse, Silhouette, Reflection

CREW MEMBERS	1,253
ENTERED SERVICE	2008, 2009, 2010, 2011, 2012
700 ft. **GROSS TONS**	122,000, 122,000, 122,000, 122,400, 126,000
LENGTH	1,033 ft., 1,041 ft., 1,041 ft., 1,047 ft., 1,047 ft.
500 ft. **NUMBER OF CABINS**	1,425, 1,425, 1,425, 1,425, 1,515
300 ft. **PASSENGER CAPACITY**	2,850, 2,850, 2,850, 2,886, 3,046
WIDTH	121 ft., 121 ft., 121 ft., 123 ft., 123 ft.

While Solstice-class ships are contemporary in design—even a bit edgy for Celebrity—the line included enough spaces with old-world ambience to satisfy traditionalists. The atmosphere is not unlike a hip boutique hotel filled with grand spaces as well as intimate nooks and crannies. *Celebrity Reflection* adds an additional deck for more high-end suite accommodations.

The Lawn Club, a half acre of real grass on deck 15, is where you can play genteel games of croquet, practice golf putting, indulge in lawn games and picnics, or simply take barefoot strolls. In a nearby open-air "theater" on *Solstice, Eclipse,* and *Equinox,* artisans demonstrate glassmaking in the Hot Glass Show. A similar space on *Silhouette* and *Reflection* houses an outdoor grill restaurant, and those ships, along with *Solstice* also have private cabanas in the Lawn Club (for a fee). These ships have a lot to offer families, with a family pool and the most extensive children's facilities in the Celebrity fleet.

CABINS

Layout: Although cabins are larger than those on other Celebrity ships, closet and drawer storage is barely adequate. On the other hand, bathrooms are generous and have plentiful storage space. An impressive 85% of all outside accommodations have balconies. With sofa–trundle beds, many categories are capable of accommodating third and fourth occupants. Connecting staterooms are also available. Family staterooms have a second bedroom with bunk beds.

Suites: Most suites have a whirlpool tub, DVD player, and walk-in closet, while all have butler service, personalized stationery, and a logo tote bag. Penthouse suites have guest powder rooms; Penthouse and Royal suites have whirlpool tubs on the balconies. *Celebrity Reflection* introduces several additional suite categories.

Amenities: A refrigerator, TV, personal safe, hair dryer, seating area with sofa and table, bathroom toiletries (shampoo, soaps, and lotion), and bathrobes for use during the cruise are standard.

Accessibility: Thirty staterooms are designed for wheelchair accessibility.

Top: Blu, the AquaClass specialty restaurant
Bottom: Lawn bowling

RESTAURANTS

The main restaurant serves open seating breakfast and lunch; dinner is served in two traditional assigned seatings or an open seating option. Additional dining rooms on each ship are reserved for suite and Aqua-class passengers. There are also a casual Lido buffet, pizza, the spa Café with healthy selections, a luncheon grill, a café that offers sushi (cover charge), and specialty coffee, tea, and gelato bar (extra charge). Three upscale alternative restaurants require dinner reservations and charge extra for contemporary French, Asian fusion, and Italian. *Eclipse, Silhouette,* and *Reflection* replaced the Asian restaurant with one serving modern American food. Additionally, *Silhouette* and *Reflection* feature the Lawn Club Grill for evening alfresco dining (cover charge) and the Porch for light breakfast and lunch fare (cover charge). Available 24 hours, room service rounds out the dining choices.

SPAS

The Canyon Ranch SpaClub is one of the most tranquil at sea with spa services operated by world famous Canyon Ranch. In addition to treatments that include a variety of massages, body wraps, and facials, each ship also has an acupuncture treatment area and Medi-Spa Cosmetic services. A relaxation room and thermal suite with dry and aromatherapy steam rooms and a hot Turkish bath are available to Aqua-class passengers and those who have booked a treatment or purchased a pass. Changing rooms for men and women have complimentary saunas.

BARS AND ENTERTAINMENT

Production companies and guest entertainers perform in the show lounges. Bars and lounges are designed as unique destinations onboard with drink menus offering not only a selection of classics, but also "signature" and trendier cocktails. Some drinks are a reflection of the regions you are visiting. Live bands or DJs provide music for listening and dancing.

PROS AND CONS

Pros: an interactive TV system allows you to book shore excursions and order room service; Aqua-class has its own staircase direct to the spa; a Hospitality Director oversees restaurant reservations.

Cons: closet space is skimpy in standard cabins; there are no self-service laundries; dining choices are plentiful, but pricey.

Cabin Type	Size (sq. ft.)
Penthouse/Reflection Suite	1,291–1,636 sq. ft.
Royal Suites	590 sq. ft.
Celebrity/Signature Suites	394–441 sq. ft.
Sky/Aqua-Class Suites	300 sq. ft.
Family Ocean-View Balcony	575 sq. ft.
Ocean-View Balcony	194 sq. ft.
Sunset Veranda	194 sq. ft.
Ocean View	177 sq. ft.
Inside	183–200 sq. ft.

FAST FACTS

- 13 passenger decks (14 *Celebrity Reflection*)
- 4 specialty restaurants (5 *Celebrity Reflection*), 3 dining rooms, buffet, ice cream parlor, pizzeria
- Wi-Fi, safe, refrigerator, DVD (some)
- 3 pools (1 indoor)
- fitness classes, gym, hot tubs, sauna, spa
- 11 bars, casino, dance club, library, showroom, video game room
- children's programs
- dry cleaning, laundry service
- Internet terminal
- no-smoking cabins

The solarium on *Solstice*

CRYSTAL CRUISES

Winner of accolades and too many hospitality industry awards to count, Crystal Cruises offers a taste of the grandeur of the past along with all the modern touches discerning passengers demand today. Founded in 1990 in Japan, Crystal has large ships, unlike other

Crystal Symphony

luxury vessels, that carry upward of 900 passengers. What makes them distinctive are superior service, a variety of dining options, spacious accommodations, and some of the highest ratios of space per passenger of any cruise ship.

☎ 888/799–4625, 310/785–9300
⊕ *www.crystalcruises. com*
☞ *Cruise Style: Luxury.*

Beginning with ship designs based on the principles of feng shui, the Eastern art of arranging your surroundings to attract positive energy, no detail is overlooked to provide passengers with the best imaginable experience. Just mention a preference for a certain food or beverage and your waiter will have it available whenever you request it.

Afternoon tea in the Palm Court is a delightful daily ritual. You're greeted by staff members in 18th-century Viennese brocade and velvet costumes for Mozart Tea; traditional scones and clotted cream are served during English Colonial Tea; and American Tea is a summertime classic created by Crystal culinary artists.

The line's Ambassador Host Program brings cultured gentlemen on each cruise to dine, socialize, and dance with unaccompanied ladies who wish to participate.

FOOD

The food alone is reason enough to book a Crystal cruise. Dining in the main restaurants is an event starring a Continental-inspired menu of dishes served by European-trained waiters. Off-menu item requests are honored when possible, and special dietary considerations are handled with ease. Full-course vegetarian menus are among the best at sea. Themed to the region you are sailing, lavish luncheon buffets take place on deck on select days at sea. Casual poolside dining beneath the stars is offered on some evenings in a relaxed, no-reservations option. A variety of hot-and-cold hors d'oeuvres are served in bars and lounges every evening before dinner and again during the wee hours in The Bistro.

But the specialty restaurants really shine. Contemporary Japanese-Peruvian cuisine is served in Umi Uma, featuring the signature dishes of Nobu Matsuhisa. Both ships also have Prego, which serves Northern Italian cuisine. In the evening the Churrascaria serves Brazilian steakhouse favorites in the Lido Marketplace, and Silk offers Chinese-inspired alfresco dining on deck at lunch and dinner.

Exclusive Wine & Champagne Makers dinners are hosted in the Vintage Room. On select evenings, casual poolside theme dinners are served under the stars.

Complimentary wines are poured with meals from Crystal's extensive wine list, as is common on other luxury cruise lines. You won't pay extra for any alcoholic beverages, bottled water, soft drinks, and specialty coffees; all are included in your basic fare.

ENTERTAINMENT

The complete roster of entertainment and activities includes production shows, but where Crystal really excels is in the variety of enrichment and educational programs. Passengers can participate in the hands-on Computer University@Sea, interactive Creative Learning Institute classes, or attend lectures featuring top experts in their fields: keyboard lessons with Yamaha, language classes by Berlitz, wellness lectures with the Cleveland Clinic, and an introduction to tai chi with the Tai Chi Cultural Center. Professional ACBL Bridge instructors are on every cruise, and dance instructors offer lessons in contemporary and social dance styles. Each ship has a large theater where movies are screened.

FITNESS AND RECREATION

Large spas offer innovative pampering therapies, body wraps, and exotic Asian-inspired treatments by Steiner Leisure. Feng shui principles were scrupulously adhered to in their creation, to assure the spas and salons remain havens of tranquility.

Fitness centers have a range of exercise and weight-training equipment and workout areas for aerobics

Top: Crystal penthouse on *Crystal Symphony*
Bottom: Lido deck

3

CRYSTAL CRUISES

Top: Umi Uma restaurant
Middle: Seahorse pool
Bottom: Prego restaurant

classes, plus complimentary yoga and Pilates instruction. In addition, golfers enjoy extensive shipboard facilities, including a driving range practice cage and putting green. Passengers can leave their bags at home and rent top-quality TaylorMade clubs for use ashore. The line's resident golf pros offer complimentary lessons and group clinics.

YOUR SHIPMATES

Affluent, well-traveled couples, from their late-thirties and up, are attracted to Crystal's destination-rich itineraries, shipboard enrichment programs, and elegant ambience. The average age of passengers is noticeably older on longer itineraries.

DRESS CODE

Formal attire is required on at least two Black Tie Optional designated evenings, depending on the length of the cruise. Men are encouraged to wear tuxedos, and many do, although dark suits are also acceptable. Other evenings are informal or resort casual; the number of each is based on the number of sea days. The line requests that dress codes be observed in public areas after 6 pm, and few, if any, passengers disregard the suggestion. Most, in fact, dress up just a notch from guidelines.

JUNIOR CRUISERS

Although these ships are decidedly adult-oriented, Crystal welcomes children but limits the number of children under age three on any given cruise. Children under six months are not allowed without a signed waiver by parents.

Dedicated facilities for children and teens ages 3 to 17 are staffed by counselors during holiday periods, select summer sailings, and when warranted by the number of children booked. The program is three-tiered for 3- to 7-year-olds, 8- to 12-year-olds, and 13- to 17-year-olds. Activities—including games, computer time, scavenger hunts, and arts and crafts—usually have an eye toward the educational. Teenagers can play complimentary

CHOOSE THIS LINE IF...

■ You crave peace and quiet. Announcements are kept to a bare minimum, and the ambience is sedate.

■ You prefer to plan ahead. You can make spa, restaurant, shore excursion, and class reservations when you book your cruise.

■ You love sushi and other Asian delights—Crystal ships serve some of the best at sea.

video games to their hearts' content in Waves, the arcade dedicated for their use. Babysitting can be arranged with staff members for a fee. Baby food, high chairs, and booster seats are available upon request.

SERVICE

Crystal's European-trained staff members provide gracious service in an unobtrusive manner.

TIPPING

Housekeeping and dining gratuities are included in the fare. Gratuity is suggested for spa and salon services.

PAST PASSENGERS

You're automatically enrolled in the Crystal Society on completion of your first Crystal cruise and are entitled to special savings and members-only events. Membership benefits increase with each completed Crystal cruise and include such perks as stateroom upgrades, shipboard spending credits, special events, gifts, air upgrades, and even free cruises. Society members also receive Crystal Cruises' complimentary quarterly magazine, which shares up-to-date information on itineraries, destinations, special offers, and society news.

HELPFUL HINTS

■ Before sailing, each passenger receives a personal email address.

■ Ambassador Hosts on Crystal cruises interact with female passengers.

■ Each ship has complimentary self-service laundry rooms.

■ Specialty restaurants can fill up quickly; make reservations immediately after booking.

■ Wi-Fi is totally free and unlimited for all your devices.

3

CRYSTAL CRUISES

DON'T CHOOSE THIS LINE IF...

■ You don't want to follow the dress code. Everyone does, and you'll stand out—and not in a good way—if you rebel.

■ You want a smoke-free environment. Smoking is allowed in designated areas of public rooms and decks.

■ You want a less structured cruise. Even with open seating dining, Crystal is a bit more regimented than other luxury lines.

CRYSTAL SERENITY
Crystal Serenity

CREW MEMBERS	655
ENTERED SERVICE	2003
GROSS TONS	68,000
LENGTH	820 feet
NUMBER OF CABINS	544
PASSENGER CAPACITY	980
WIDTH	106 feet

700 ft.

500 ft.

300 ft.

Crystal Serenity was introduced in 2003, the line's first new ship since 1995. Although more than a third larger than Crystal's earlier ships, it's similar in layout and follows the successful formula of creating intimate spaces in understated yet sophisticated surroundings. Stylish public rooms, uncrowded and uncluttered, are clubby in the tradition of elegantly proportioned drawing rooms (even the main show lounge is on a single level).

Muted colors and warm woods create a soft atmosphere conducive to socializing in the refined environment. The Palm Court could be mistaken for the kind of British colonial–era lounge you might have seen in Hong Kong or India in the 19th century. A thoughtful touch is an entirely separate room for scrutinizing the art pieces available for auction. The understatement even continues into the casino, although it contains plenty of slot machines and gaming tables.

CABINS

Cabins: *Crystal Serenity* has no inside cabins. Although suites are generous in size, lesser categories are somewhat smaller than industry standard at this level. All accommodations are designed with ample closet and drawer/shelf storage, as well as bathroom shelves and twin sinks. An impressive 85% of all cabins have private balconies furnished with chairs and tables. Most suites and penthouses have walk-in closets. Crystal Penthouse suites have private workout areas, pantries, and guest powder rooms. There are 50 connecting staterooms and 134 staterooms with a third berth for families.

Amenities: All cabins have a refrigerator with complimentary water and soft drinks, a personal safe, two hair dryers, broadband connection, a flat-screen TV with a DVD player, Aveda bath products, slippers, Frette bathrobes, and an umbrella. A seating area with sofa, chair, and table are typical standard features of all cabins. Most suites and penthouses also have CD players; all have butler service, personalized stationery, and a complimentary fully stocked minibar upon embarkation.

Accessibility: Eight staterooms are designed for wheelchair accessibility.

RESTAURANTS

The formal restaurant serves open seating breakfast and lunch and offers international cuisine in two traditional

Top: Palm Court, *Crystal Serenity*
Bottom: Seabreeze penthouse, *Crystal Serenity*

early and late assigned dinner seatings; Open Dining by Reservation is also available. There's no additional charge for the intimate Asian- and Italian-specialty restaurants, but reservations are required. Theme luncheons and dinners are sometimes held poolside; special wine dinners are held in the Vintage Room. Tastes, a casual café, serves breakfast, lunch, and dinner; the Lido buffet has breakfast and lunch; a poolside grill serves casual lunch and snacks; The Bistro, a specialty coffee and wine bar, also offers snacks; and there's an ice cream bar. Afternoon tea is served in the Palm Court. Room service is available 24 hours, and during dinner hours selections can be delivered from the formal restaurant menu. Suite passengers also have the option of ordering dinner from the specialty restaurants, to be served by their butlers.

SPAS

Inspired by the principles of feng shui, the Crystal Spa is a tranquil haven where such services as aroma stone therapy, a Japanese silk booster facial, and well-being massage are offered. A private, canopied relaxation area on the spa's aft deck is available before or after a treatment. Facilities for men and women include saunas and changing areas featuring showers with multiple head and side body jets, fiber-optic lighting, and a selection of rain and mist functions.

BARS/ENTERTAINMENT

With the open-bar policy setting a convivial tone, Crystal's lounges are the ships' social centers. Every lounge has a different atmosphere, ranging from the signature cocktail and piano bar known for its intimate "clubby" feel to the cigar lounge that is ideal for after-dinner drinks and conversation. After a production show or concert in the main show room, dance aficionados can find musical styles that range from big band to contemporary.

PROS AND CONS

Pros: alternative restaurants are yours to enjoy at no additional cost; every bathroom has a full-size tub; a wide teak promenade deck encircles the ship.

Cons: few staterooms have a third berth for families; reservations for specialty restaurants can be hard to secure; the clubbiness of repeat passengers can be off-putting to people new to Crystal.

Cabin Type	Size (sq. ft.)
Crystal Penthouse	1,345 sq. ft.
Penthouse Suites	538 sq. ft.
Regular Penthouses	403 sq. ft.

FAST FACTS

- 9 passenger decks
- 2 specialty restaurants, dining room, buffet, ice cream parlor
- Wi-Fi, safe, refrigerator, DVD
- 2 pools (1 indoor)
- fitness classes, gym, hot tubs, sauna, spa
- steam room
- 6 bars, casino, 2 dance clubs, library, show room, video game room
- children's programs
- dry cleaning, laundry facilities, laundry service
- Internet terminal
- no kids under 6 months

3

CRYSTAL CRUISES

CRYSTAL SYMPHONY
Crystal Symphony

CREW MEMBERS	566
ENTERED SERVICE	1995
GROSS TONS	51,044
LENGTH	781 feet
NUMBER OF CABINS	424
PASSENGER CAPACITY	848
WIDTH	99 feet

700 ft.

500 ft.

300 ft.

Although large, *Crystal Symphony* is noteworthy in the luxury market for creating intimate spaces in understated, yet sophisticated, surroundings. Generous per-passenger space ratios have become a Crystal trademark, along with forward-facing observation decks, a Palm Court lounge, and a wide teak promenade encircling the ship. A refurbishment in 2017 transformed the Marketplace Lido Café and reduced passenger capacity by converting standard staterooms to penthouse accommodations.

Accented by a lovely waterfall, the focal point of the central two-deck atrium is a sculpture of two ballet dancers created especially for the space. Crystal Cove, the lobby lounge, is the spot to meet for cocktails as you make your way to the nearby dining room. Throughout the ship, public rooms shine with low-key contemporary style and flow easily from one to the next.

CABINS

Cabins: There are no inside cabins on *Crystal Symphony,* but staterooms are relatively small, with boutique-hotel-style decor. All cabins have ample closet and drawer/shelf storage, as well as bathroom shelves. Many have private balconies furnished with chairs and tables. Most suites and penthouses have a walk-in closet. Penthouse suites have guest powder rooms.

Amenities: A small refrigerator with complimentary bottled water and soft drinks, a safe, two hair dryers, a flat-screen TV with DVD player, and a seating area with sofa, chair, and table are typical standard features in all cabins. Suite and penthouse extras vary, but all have a DVD player, butler service, personalized stationery, and fully stocked minibar.

Bathrooms: Every bathroom has oval glass sinks, granite counters, a full-size tub, Aveda toiletries, plush towels, and bathrobes for use during the cruise. Many suites and penthouses have a whirlpool tub and separate shower.

Accessibility: Five staterooms are wheelchair accessible.

Top: Spa

RESTAURANTS

The formal restaurant serves open seating breakfast, lunch, and dinner. Although there's no additional charge for your first reservation in the intimate Asian- and

Italian-specialty restaurants, there is a service charge if you can obtain additional reservations. Other dining choices include the Marketplace buffet for breakfast and lunch, which transforms to the Churrascaria Brazilian steakhouse at dinner; Silk, Chinese-inspired alfresco dining on deck at lunch and dinner; The Bistro, a specialty coffee and wine bar offering snacks all day and evening; and an ice cream bar. Afternoon tea is served in the Palm Court. Room service, with an extensive menu, is available 24 hours, and during dinner hours selections can be delivered from the formal restaurant menu. Suite passengers can also order from the specialty restaurants, to be served by their butlers.

SPAS

The Crystal Spa is a tranquil haven where such services as aroma stone therapy, Japanese silk booster facial, and well-being massage are offered. A private, canopied relaxation area on the spa's aft deck is available before or after a treatment. Changing areas have elaborate showers with fiber optic lighting and a selection of rain and mist functions as well as saunas.

BARS/ENTERTAINMENT

With the open bar policy setting a convivial tone, Crystal's lounges are the ship's social hubs. Lounges feature unique styles ranging from the signature cocktail and piano bar known for its intimate "clubby" atmosphere to the clublike cigar lounge, ideal for after-dinner drinks and conversation. After a production show or concert in the main show room, dance aficionados can find musical styles that range from classic to contemporary.

PROS AND CONS

Pros: the professionalism of the ships' staff sets them apart; the large theater has ample seating and free popcorn; casual dining areas have more than enough seating indoors and outside.

Cons: few staterooms can accommodate families; while large, the solitary pool and hot tub can feel crowded at times; lower-category staterooms can feel cramped for a luxury ship.

Cabin Type	Size (sq. ft.)
Penthouse Suite	982 sq. ft.
Penthouse	367-491 sq. ft.
Ocean View with Balcony	246 sq. ft.
Ocean View	206 sq. ft.

FAST FACTS

- 8 passenger decks
- 2 specialty restaurants, dining room, buffet, ice cream parlor
- Wi-Fi, safe, refrigerator, DVD
- 1 pool
- fitness classes, gym, hot tub, sauna, spa, steam room
- 5 bars, casino, dance club, library, show room, video game room
- children's programs
- dry cleaning, laundry facilities, laundry service
- Internet terminal
- no kids under 6 months

DISNEY CRUISE LINE

With the launch of Disney Cruise Line in 1998, families were offered yet another reason to take a cruise. The magic of a Walt Disney resort vacation plus the romance of a sea voyage are a tempting combination, especially for adults who discovered Disney movies

Disney ships have a classic style

and the Mickey Mouse Club as children. Mixed with traditional shipboard activities, who can resist scheduled opportunities for the young and young-at-heart to interact with their favorite Disney characters?

☎ *407/566–3500, 888/325–2500*
⊕ *www.disneycruise. com*
☞ *Cruise Style: Mainstream.*

Although Disney Cruise Line voyages stuck to tried-and-true Bahamas and Caribbean itineraries in their formative years, and sailed exclusively from Port Canaveral, Florida, where a terminal was designed especially for Disney ships, the line has branched out to other regions, including Alaska and Europe.

FOOD

Don't expect top chefs and gourmet food. This is Disney, and the fare in each ship's casual restaurants is all-American for the most part. A third restaurant is a bit fancier, with French-inspired dishes on the menus. Naturally, all have children's menus with an array of favorite sandwiches and entrées. Vegetarian and healthy selections are also available in all restaurants. A bonus is complimentary soft drinks, lemonade, and iced tea throughout the sailing. A beverage station in the buffet area is always open; however, there is a charge for soft drinks ordered from the bars and room service.

Palo, the adults-only restaurant serving Northern Italian cuisine, requires reservations for a romantic evening of fine dining. Although there's a cover charge for dinner, it's a steal and reservations go fast. A brunch also commands a surcharge. More upscale and pricey, Remy on *Disney Dream* and *Disney Fantasy* serves French cuisine in an elegant atmosphere.

ENTERTAINMENT

Shipboard entertainment leans heavily on popular Disney themes and characters. Parents are actively involved in the audience with their children at production shows, movies, live character meetings, deck parties, and dancing in the family nightclub. Teens have a supervised, no-adults-allowed club space in the forward fake funnel, where they gather for activities and parties. For adults, there are traditional no-kids-allowed bars and lounges with live music, dancing, theme parties, and late-night comedy, as well as daytime wine-tasting sessions, game shows, culinary arts and home entertaining demonstrations, and behind-the-scenes lectures on animation and filmmaking. This is Disney, so there are no casinos.

A giant LED screen is affixed to the forward funnels of both the original ships and their newer fleetmates. Passengers can watch movies and special broadcasts while lounging in the family pool area.

FITNESS AND RECREATION

Three swimming pool areas are designated for different groups: children (Mickey's Pool, which has a waterslide and requires a parent to be present); families (Goofy Pool); and adults (Quiet Cove). Young children who aren't potty trained can't swim in the pools but are invited to splash about in the fountain play area near Mickey's Pool. Be sure to bring their swim diapers.

The salon and spa feature a complete menu of hair- and nail-care services as well as facials and massages. The Tropical Rainforest is a soothing coed thermal suite with heated tile lounges. It's complimentary for the day if you book a spa treatment or available on a daily or cruise-long basis for a fee. SpaVillas are indoor–outdoor treatment suites that feature a veranda with a hot tub and an open-air shower. In addition to a nicely equipped fitness center and aerobics studio are a jogging track and basketball court.

YOUR SHIPMATES

Disney Cruises appeal to kids of all ages—the young and not so young, singles, couples, and families. Multigeneration family groups are the core audience for these ships, and the facilities are ideal for family gatherings. What you might not expect are the numerous newlywed couples celebrating their honeymoons onboard.

KNOWN FOR

- **Character Interaction:** Disney characters make frequent appearances.

- **Classic Ships:** Classic ship design (Disney's are the first passenger ships since the 1950s to have two funnels).

- **Entertainment:** Some of the best entertainment at sea for guests of all ages.

- **Fireworks:** Among the few ships that are allowed to host fireworks at sea.

- **Kid Stuff:** Excellent facilities for children and teens.

3

DISNEY CRUISE LINE

Top: Dining in Palo, the adults-only restaurant
Bottom: Relax in a Mickey-approved spa

Top: Sweet treats await you on board
Middle: Enjoy a quarter-mile track for walking or jogging
Bottom: *Disney Magic* and *Disney Wonder* at sea

DRESS CODE

One-week cruises schedule a semiformal evening and a formal night, during which men are encouraged to wear suits, but sport coats and ties are acceptable for both. Resort casual is the evening dress code for dinner in the more laid-back dining rooms. A sport coat is appropriate for the restaurants designated as fancier, as well as the adults-only specialty restaurants, where a jacket is required at Remy and optional for Palo.

JUNIOR CRUISERS

As expected, Disney ships have extensive programs for children and teens, including shore excursions designed for families to enjoy together. Parents are issued a pager for peace of mind while their children are participating in onboard activities and to alert them when their offspring need them. Complimentary age-appropriate activities are scheduled from 9 am to midnight in the Oceaneer Club and Oceaneer Lab for ages 3 to 12. While some activities are recommended for certain age groups, participation is based on the child's interest level and maturity. Activities include arts projects, contests, computer games, pool parties, interactive lab stations, and opportunities for individual and group play. The emphasis is on fun over education, but subtle educational themes are certainly there. Coffeehouse-style tween (ages 11–14) and teen (ages 14–17) clubs offer music, a dance floor, big-screen TV, and Internet café for the younger set. Scheduled activities include challenging games, photography lessons, sporting contests, beach events, and parties, but they are also great places to just hang out with new friends in an adult-free zone.

An hourly fee is charged for childcare in Flounder's Reef Nursery, which is open during select hours for infants as young as three months through three years. Supply your own diapers, and nursery attendants will change them. Private, in-cabin babysitting is not available.

CHOOSE THIS LINE IF...

■ You want to cruise with the entire family—Mom, Dad, the kids, and grandparents.

■ You enjoy having kids around. (There are adults-only areas to retreat to when the fun wears off.)

■ Your family enjoys Disney's theme parks and can't get enough wholesome entertainment.

SERVICE

Friendly service is extended to all passengers, with particular importance placed on treating children with the same courtesy extended to adults.

TIPPING

Suggested gratuity amounts are calculated on a per-person per-cruise rather than per-night basis and can be added to onboard accounts or offered in cash on the last night of the cruise. Guidelines include gratuities for your dining-room server, assistant server, head server, and stateroom host/hostess on the basis of $12 per night. Tips for room-service delivery, spa services, and the dining manager are at the passenger's discretion. An automatic 15% gratuity is added to all bar tabs.

PAST PASSENGERS

Castaway Club membership is automatic after completing a Disney cruise. Benefits include a complimentary gift (such as a tote bag or beach towel), communication about special offers, priority check-in, invitations to shipboard cocktail parties during subsequent cruises, and a special toll-free reservation telephone number (*800/449-3380*) for convenience.

HELPFUL HINTS

■ There are hidden Mickeys all over the ships, just as in the theme parks.

■ Consider buying pins and autograph books at a Disney store before your cruise.

■ You can reserve many services and make dinner reservations prior to sailing.

■ Roomier than average standard cabins can easily handle four occupants.

■ Alcohol may be brought onboard but must be hand-carried on embarkation by an adult, age 21 or older, and cannot be consumed in lounges and other public areas.

3

DISNEY CRUISE LINE

DON'T CHOOSE THIS LINE IF...

■ You want to spend a lot of quality time bonding with your kids. Your kids may not want to leave the fun activities.

■ You want to dine in peace and quiet. The dining rooms and buffet can be boisterous.

■ You want to gamble. There are no casinos, so you'll have to settle for bingo.

DISNEY MAGIC/WONDER
Disney Magic, Disney Wonder

CREW MEMBERS	950
ENTERED SERVICE	1998, 1999
GROSS TONS	83,000
LENGTH	964 feet
NUMBER OF CABINS	877
PASSENGER CAPACITY	1,754 (2,400 max)
WIDTH	106 feet

700 ft.

500 ft.

300 ft.

Reminiscent of classic ocean liners, Disney vessels have two funnels (the forward one is nonfunctional) and high-tech interiors behind their art deco and art nouveau styling. Whimsical design accents cleverly incorporate images of Mickey Mouse and his friends without overpowering the warm and elegant decor. Artwork showcases the creativity of Disney artists and animators. The atmosphere is never stuffy.

More than 15,000 square feet—nearly an entire deck—are devoted to children's activity centers, outdoor activity areas, and swimming pools. Theaters cater to family entertainment with large-scale production shows, movies, dances, lively game shows, and even 3-D movies.

Adults-only hideaways include an avenue of theme bars and lounges tucked into the area just forward of the lobby atrium; the Promenade Lounge, near the aft elevator lobby; and Cove Café, a quiet spot adjacent to the adult pool to relax with coffee or a cocktail, surf the Internet, or read.

CABINS

Layout: Designed for families, Disney ships have some of the roomiest, most functional staterooms at sea. Natural woods, imported tiles, and a nautical flavor add to the decor, which even includes the touch of Disney-inspired artwork on the walls. Most cabins can accommodate at least three people and have a seating area and unique bath-and-a-half arrangement. Three-quarters of all accommodations are outside cabins, and 44% of those include private balconies with kid-proof door handles and higher-than-usual railings for safety. All cabins have adequate closet and drawer/shelf storage, as well as bathroom shelves.

Suites: Suites are truly expansive, with master bedrooms separated from the living areas for privacy. All suites have walk-in closets, a dining table and chairs, a wet bar, a DVD player, and a large balcony.

Amenities: Though not luxurious, Disney cabins are comfortably furnished. Each has a flat-screen TV, a small refrigerator, a personal safe, and a hair dryer; bathrobes are provided for use during the cruise in the top-category staterooms. All suites have concierge service.

Accessibility: Sixteen cabins are wheelchair accessible.

Top: Friendships are forged on a cruise
Bottom: Dreams come true on a Disney cruise

RESTAURANTS

In a novel approach to dining, passengers (and their waiters) rotate through the three main dining rooms in assigned seatings. Tiana's Place (*Disney Wonder*), Carioca's (*Disney Magic*), and Animator's Palate are casual, while Triton's (*Disney Wonder*) and Lumière's (*Disney Magic*) are a bit fancier. Palo is a beautifully appointed Northern Italian restaurant for adults only that requires reservations for brunch, dinner, or tea and carries an extra charge. Breakfast and lunch are open seating in dining rooms. Disney characters make an appearance at a character breakfast on seven-night cruises. Breakfast, lunch, and dinner are also offered in the casual pool-deck buffet, while poolside pizzerias, snack bars, grills, and ice cream bars serve everything from pizza, burgers, and hot dogs to fresh fruit, wraps, and frozen treats during the day. Specialty coffees are available in the adults-only Cove Café for an extra charge. Room service is available around the clock.

SPAS

Spas feature a complete menu of facials and massages. The Tropical Rainforest is a soothing coed thermal suite with heated tile lounges and is complimentary for the day if you book a spa treatment; it's available on a daily or cruise-long basis for a fee. SpaVillas, indoor–outdoor treatment suites, each have a veranda with a hot tub and an open-air shower.

BARS AND ENTERTAINMENT

After the energetic production shows, deck parties, and activities designed for the entire family, adults can slip off to bars and lounges reserved for them after dark, including a sports bar or nightclub where the entertainment staff offers activities such as karaoke or themed dance parties. For quiet conversation and a drink under the stars, there's a cozy bar alongside the adult pool.

PROS AND CONS

Pros: there are plenty of connecting cabins that fit up to seven; soft drinks at meals and beverage stations are complimentary; for adults, each ship has a piano bar/jazz club.

Cons: only the splash play areas are available for youngsters who wear swim diapers; although a Disney cruise isn't all Disney all the time, it can get tiring if you aren't really into the atmosphere; there's no library onboard.

Cabin Type	Size (sq. ft.)
Royal Suite	1,029 sq. ft.
Two-Bedroom Suite	945 sq. ft.
One-Bedroom Suite	614 sq. ft.
Deluxe Family Balcony	304 sq. ft.
Deluxe Balcony	268 sq. ft.
Ocean View	226 sq. ft.
Deluxe Inside	214 sq. ft.
Standard Inside	184 sq. ft.

FAST FACTS

■ 11 passenger decks

■ specialty restaurant, 3 dining rooms, buffet, ice cream parlor, pizzeria

■ Wi-Fi, safe, refrigerator, DVD (some)

■ 2 pools, children's pool

■ fitness classes, gym, hot tubs, sauna, spa

■ 6 bars, dance club, 2 showrooms, video game room

■ children's programs

■ dry cleaning, laundry facilities, laundry service

■ Internet terminal

■ no kids under 12 weeks, no-smoking cabins

Goofy touches up the paint on *Disney Magic*

HOLLAND AMERICA LINE

Holland America Line has enjoyed a distinguished record of traditional cruises, world exploration, and transatlantic crossings since 1873—all facets of its history that are reflected in the fleet's multimillion-dollar shipboard art and antiques collections. Even the ships'

A day on the Lido Deck

names follow a pattern set long ago: all end in the suffix dam and are either derived from the names of various dams that cross Holland's rivers, important Dutch landmarks, or points of the compass. The names are even recycled when vessels are retired, and some are in their fifth and sixth generation of use.

☎ *206/281–3535,*
800/577–1728
⊕ *www.hollandameri-ca.com*
☞ *Cruise Style:*
Premium.

Noted for focusing on passenger comfort, Holland America Line cruises are classic in design and style, and with an infusion of younger adults and families onboard, they remain refined without being stuffy or stodgy. Following a basic design theme, returning passengers feel as at home on the newest Holland America vessels as they do on older ones.

FOOD

Holland America Line chefs, led by Master Chef Rudi Sodamin, utilize more than 500 different food items on a typical weeklong cruise to create the modern Continental cuisine and traditional favorites served to their passengers. Vegetarian options as well as health-conscious cuisine are available, and special dietary requests can be handled with advance notice. The food quality, taste, and selection have greatly improved in recent years. A case in point is the reservations-required Pinnacle Grill alternative restaurants, where fresh seafood and premium cuts of sustainably raised beef from Washington State's Double R Ranch are used to prepare creative specialty dishes. The $35 per person charge for dinner would be worth it for the Dungeness crab cakes starter and dessert alone. Other delicious traditions are afternoon tea, a Dutch Chocolate Extravaganza, and Holland America Line's signature bread pudding.

Flexible scheduling allows for early or late seatings in the two-deck, formal restaurants. An open seating option from 5:15 to 9 has been introduced fleetwide.

ENTERTAINMENT

Entertainment tends to be more Broadway-stylish than Las Vegas–brash. Colorful revues are presented in main show lounges by the ships' companies of singers and dancers. Other performances might include a range of cabaret acts: comedians, magicians, jugglers, and acrobats. Live bands play a wide range of musical styles for dancing and listening in smaller lounges and piano bars. Movies are shown daily in cinemas that double as the Culinary Arts Centers.

Holland America Line may never be considered cutting-edge, but their innovative Signature of Excellence concept sets it apart from other premium cruise lines. An interactive Culinary Arts Center offers cooking demonstrations and wine-tasting sessions; Explorations Café (powered by the *New York Times*) is a coffeehouse, library, and Internet center; the Explorations Guest Speakers Series is supported by in-cabin televised programming on flat-screen TVs in all cabins; the traditional Crow's Nest observation lounge has a nightclub-disco layout, video wall, and sound-and-light systems; and facilities for children and teens have been greatly expanded.

FITNESS AND RECREATION

Well-equipped and fully staffed fitness facilities contain state-of-the-art exercise equipment; basic fitness classes are available at no charge. There's a fee for personal training, body composition analysis, and specialized classes such as yoga and Pilates.

Treatments in the Greenhouse Spa include a variety of massages, body wraps, and facials. Hair styling and nail services are offered in the salons. All ships have a jogging track, multiple swimming pools, and sports courts; some have hydrotherapy pools and soothing thermal suites.

YOUR SHIPMATES

No longer just your grandparents' cruise line, today's Holland America sailings attract families and couples, mostly from their late thirties on up. Holidays and summer months are peak periods when you'll find more children in the mix. Retirees are often still in the majority, particularly on longer cruises. Families cruising together

KNOWN FOR

■ **Comfort:** Ships in the fleet are noted for their cozy and warm atmosphere.

■ **Consistency:** From afternoon tea to the chimes that announce dinner, each ship in the fleet delivers the expected experience.

■ **The Promenade:** A trademark of each ship is its wraparound promenade deck for walking, jogging, or stretching out in the shade on a padded steamer chair.

■ **Service:** It's not unusual for crew members to remember passengers' names, even if they haven't seen them for years.

■ **Tradition Rules:** Holland America Line is one of the most traditional cruise lines, and the line's history is an important part of the experience.

Top: Casino action
Bottom: Stay fit or stay loose

3

HOLLAND AMERICA LINE

who book five or more cabins receive perks such as a fountain-soda package for each family member, a family photo for each stateroom, and complimentary water toys at Half Moon Cay (for Caribbean itineraries that call at the private island). If the group is larger than 10 cabins, the Head-of-Family is recognized with an upgrade from outside stateroom to a veranda cabin. It's the best family deal at sea, and there's no extra charge.

DRESS CODE

Evenings on Holland America Line cruises fall into two categories: smart casual and formal. For the two formal nights standard on seven-night cruises, men are encouraged to wear tuxedos, but dark suits or sport coats and ties are acceptable, and you'll certainly see them. On smart-casual nights, expect the type of attire you'd see at a country club or upscale resort. It's requested that no T-shirts, jeans, swimsuits, tank tops, or shorts be worn in public areas after 6 pm.

JUNIOR CRUISERS

Club HAL is Holland America Line's professionally staffed youth and teen program. Age-appropriate activities planned for children ages 3 to 7 include storytelling, arts and crafts, ice cream or pizza parties, and games; for children ages 8 to 12 there are arcade games, Sony PlayStations, theme parties, on-deck sports events, and scavenger hunts. Club HAL After Hours offers late-night activities from 10 pm until midnight for an hourly fee. Baby food, diapers, cribs, high chairs, and booster seats may be requested in advance of boarding. Private in-cabin babysitting is sometimes available if a staff member is willing.

Teens ages 13 to 17 have their own lounge, with activities including dance contests, arcade games, sports tournaments, movies, and an exclusive sundeck on some ships.

Top: Soak up some sun on the outdoor deck
Middle: Production showtime Bottom: Spa relaxation

CHOOSE THIS LINE IF...

■ You crave relaxation. Grab a padded steamer chair on the teak promenade deck and watch the sea pass by.

■ You like to go to the movies, especially when the popcorn is free.

■ You want to bring the kids. Areas designed exclusively for children and teens are hot features on all ships.

SERVICE

Professional, unobtrusive service is a fleet-wide standard on Holland America Line. Crew members are trained in Indonesia at a custom-built facility called the MS *Nieuw Jakarta,* where employees polish their English-language skills and learn housekeeping in mock cabins.

TIPPING

Gratuities of $13.50 per passenger per day, or $15 per passenger per day for suite passengers, are automatically added to shipboard accounts, and distributed to stewards and waitstaff. Passengers may adjust the amount based on the level of service experienced. Room-service tips are usually given in cash (it's at the passenger's discretion here). Gratuities for spa and salon services can be added to the bill or offered in cash. An automatic 15% gratuity is added to bar-service tabs.

PAST PASSENGERS

All passengers who sail with Holland America Line are automatically enrolled in the Mariner Society and receive special offers on upcoming cruises, as well as insider information concerning new ships and product enhancements. Mariner Society benefits also include preferred pricing on many cruises; Mariner baggage tags and buttons that identify you as a member during embarkation; an invitation to the Mariner Society Champagne reception and awards party hosted by the captain; lapel pins and medallions acknowledging your history of Holland America sailings; a special collectible gift delivered to your cabin; and a subscription to *Mariner,* the full-color magazine featuring news and Mariner Society savings.

HELPFUL HINTS

■ Charges for specialty dining on Holland America Line ships are some of the most reasonable at sea.

■ All passengers are presented with a complimentary tote bag imprinted with the line's logo.

■ Narrated iPod art tours of the ships' art collections can be borrowed from the library on each vessel.

■ A wide variety of shore excursions that fit lifestyles ranging from easygoing to active adventure can be booked before sailing.

■ A reservation may be canceled for any reason whatsoever up to 24 hours prior to departure and a refund of 80% to 90% of eligible amounts will be paid with the Cancellation Protection Plan.

3

HOLLAND AMERICA LINE

DON'T CHOOSE THIS LINE IF...

■ You want to party hard. Most of the action on these ships ends relatively early.

■ Dressing for dinner isn't your thing. Passengers tend to ramp up the dress code most evenings.

■ You have an aversion to extending tips. The line's "tipping not required" policy has been dropped.

ROTTERDAM, AMSTERDAM
Rotterdam, Amsterdam

CREW MEMBERS	600, 615
ENTERED SERVICE	1997, 2000
GROSS TONS	61,859, 62,735
LENGTH	780 feet
NUMBER OF CABINS	702, 690
PASSENGER CAPACITY	1,404, 1,380
WIDTH	106 feet

700 ft.

500 ft.

300 ft.

The most traditional ships in the fleet, the interiors of sister ships *Amsterdam* and *Rotterdam* display abundant wood appointments in the public areas on promenade and lower promenade decks and priceless works of art throughout.

The Ocean Bar, Explorer's Lounge, Wajang Theater, and Crow's Nest are familiar lounges to longtime Holland American passengers. Newer additions include the spa's thermal suite, a culinary-arts demonstration center in the theater, Explorations Café, and expansive areas for children and teens. Multimillion-dollar collections of art and artifacts are showcased throughout both vessels. In addition to works commissioned specifically for each ship, Holland America Line celebrates its heritage by featuring antiques and artworks that reflect the theme of worldwide Dutch seafaring history.

CABINS

Layout: Staterooms are spacious and comfortable, although fewer have private balconies than newer fleetmates. Lanai cabins were added during *Rotterdam*'s latest upgrade. Every cabin has adequate closet and drawer/shelf storage, as well as bathroom shelves. Some suites also have a whirlpool tub, powder room, and walk-in closet. Connecting cabins are available in a range of categories, as well as a number of triple and a few quad cabins.

Suites: Extras include duvets on beds, a fully stocked minibar, and personalized stationery. Penthouse and Deluxe Verandah suites have exclusive use of the Neptune Lounge, concierge service, canapés before dinner, binoculars and umbrellas for use during the cruise, an invitation to a VIP party with the captain, and complimentary laundry, pressing, and dry-cleaning services.

Amenities: All staterooms and suites are appointed with pillow-top mattresses, 250-thread-count cotton bed linens, magnifying halo-lighted mirrors, hair dryers, a fruit basket, flat-panel TVs, and DVD players. Bathrooms have Egyptian cotton towels, nice toiletries, plus deluxe bathrobes to use during the cruise.

Accessibility: Twenty-one staterooms are designed for wheelchair accessibility on *Amsterdam,* 22 on *Rotterdam.*

Top: Pinnacle Grill dining
Bottom: *Rotterdam* at sea

RESTAURANTS

The formal dining room offers open seating breakfast and lunch, as well as two assigned seatings or open seating for dinner. Pinnacle Grill (reservation, cover charge) serves lunch and dinner. A casual Lido restaurant serves buffet breakfast and lunch; at dinner, the Lido offers combination buffet/table service. Italian fare is served in the adjacent Canaletto Restaurant (reservation, cover charge). Poolside lunch at the Dive-In Grill includes fast food and sandwiches. The extra-charge Explorations Café offers specialty coffees and pastries. There's daily afternoon tea service. Complimentary hors d'oeuvres are served by waiters during cocktail hour, hand-dipped chocolates are offered after dinner in the Explorer's Lounge, and a late-night buffet and chocolate extravaganza is served in the Lido restaurant during every cruise. Room service is available 24 hours.

SPAS

Treatments in the Greenhouse Spa include a variety of massages, body wraps, and facials, as well as acupuncture and tooth-whitening services. A thermal suite with heated ceramic lounges for relaxation and dry sauna and steam rooms is available for a fee or complimentary when a spa appointment is booked. Changing rooms for men and women have complimentary saunas.

BARS AND ENTERTAINMENT

Popular spots before dinner are the Ocean Club and Explorer's Lounge, where servers pass through with canapés. Later, those bars are quiet spots for drinks and conversation. For livelier action aboard *Amsterdam*, there's a Sports and Piano Bar; on *Rotterdam*, try Mix—where champagne, martinis, ales, and spirits are served near the piano. The late-night dance spot on both is the Crow's Nest.

PROS AND CONS

Pros: *Rotterdam* has the Retreat, a resort-style pool on the aft Lido deck; as the line's flagships, *Rotterdam* and *Amsterdam* have the fleet's most elegant interior decor; realistic landscapes with surreal touches accent walls in *Amsterdam*'s Pinnacle Grill.

Cons: one-way window glass in outside cabins on lower promenade deck does not offer occupants complete privacy; there is little shipboard nightlife more than an hour after dinner; despite excellent facilities designed for kids and teens, family cabins are limited.

Cabin Type	Size (sq. ft.)
Penthouse Suite	1,159 sq. ft.
Deluxe Verandah Suite	556 sq. ft.
Verandah Suite	292 sq. ft.
Lanai	197 (Rotterdam only) sq. ft.
Ocean View	197 sq. ft.
Inside	182 sq. ft.

FAST FACTS

- 9 passenger decks
- specialty restaurant, dining room, buffet
- Wi-Fi, safe, refrigerator, DVD
- 2 pools (1 indoor), 2 children's pools
- fitness classes, gym, hot tubs, sauna, spa
- 6 bars, casino, dance club, library, showroom, video game room
- children's programs
- dry cleaning, laundry facilities, laundry service
- Internet terminal
- no-smoking cabins

A brisk walk starts the day

3

HOLLAND AMERICA LINE

SIGNATURE-CLASS
Eurodam, Nieuw Amsterdam

CREW MEMBERS	929
ENTERED SERVICE	2008, 2010
GROSS TONS	86,273, 86,700
LENGTH	936 feet
NUMBER OF CABINS	1,052, 1,053
PASSENGER CAPACITY	2,104, 2,106
WIDTH	106 feet

700 ft.

500 ft.

300 ft.

Signature-class vessels were so named because they are the first ships in the fleet to be launched fully integrated with all the so-called Signature of Excellence features. Larger than the other midsize ships in the fleet, they are pure Holland America, with all the traditional amenities and services plus some added bonuses. You'll find familiar public spaces as well as a second specialty restaurant and adjacent lounge, a new bar that anchors the Explorer's Lounge, and an Italian eatery tucked into a corner of the Lido.

No-smoking Spa staterooms near the Greenhouse Spa feature Asian-inspired decor and spa amenities. Poolside are private, draped cabanas, and one deck up the tented Retreat cabanas are filled with amenities that include the use of handheld fans, an Evian spray mister, iPods with music preloaded, chilled water, special refreshments, and afternoon champagne. Cabanas are reserved by the day or by the cruise (for an extra fee).

CABINS
Layout: Warm wood tones, burnished nickel fixtures, and punches of color complement the drapery, carpeting, and bedspreads in all categories. Eighty-five percent have an ocean view, and 79% of outside staterooms and suites offer a private veranda with attractive furnishings.

Suites: Penthouse suites have separate living-room, dining-room, and bedroom areas. A veranda with hot tub, walk-in closets, bathroom with whirlpool tub, double sinks, separate guest powder room, and butler's pantry complete the features. Deluxe and Superior Verandah suites have large verandas, dressing areas, and generous sitting areas; the bathrooms also have double sinks, a whirlpool tub, and a separate shower. Suite occupants can use the private Neptune Lounge and personal concierge service.

Amenities: All categories are outfitted with plush pillow-top mattresses, bathrobes, Egyptian cotton towels, flat-panel TVs, lighted makeup mirrors, hair dryers, massaging showerheads, personal safes, refrigerators, and closets configured for hanging and/or drop-down shelves.

Accessibility: Thirty cabins are designed for wheelchair accessibility.

Pinnacle Bar on *Eurodam*

RESTAURANTS

The formal restaurant offers open seating for breakfast and lunch, with dinner in two traditional assigned dinner seatings or open seating. The Pinnacle Grill (reservation, cover charge) serves lunch and dinner. Tamarind (reservation, cover charge for dinner only) offers Pan-Asian fare. For casual dining, the Lido restaurant serves buffet breakfast and lunch; for dinner there is combination buffet/table service, and a section becomes Canaletto, serving Italian fare (reservation, cover charge). A poolside grill, Dive-In, features hamburgers and hot dogs with all the trimmings. The Explorations Café offers extra-charge specialty coffees and free pastries. Daily afternoon tea service is offered, hors d'oeuvres are served by waiters before dinner, chocolates are offered after dinner, and a chocolate extravaganza buffet is held once during every cruise. Room service is available 24 hours.

SPAS

Treatments in the Greenhouse Spa include a variety of massages, body wraps, and facials, as well as acupuncture services and tooth-whitening treatments. A hydrotherapy pool and thermal suite with heated ceramic loungers for relaxation as well as dry saunas and steam rooms can be used for a fee (one-time or for the cruise); it's complimentary for the day when a spa appointment is booked.

BARS AND ENTERTAINMENT

Popular spots before dinner are the Ocean Club and Explorer's Lounge, where servers pass through with appetizers. After dinner and a show or concert, those bars are quiet spots for drinks and conversation. For livelier action, there's the Music Walk, with B.B. King's Blues Club for late-night dancing.

PROS AND CONS

Pros: spa staterooms and suites can be completely no-smoking; with sea views and intimate seating alcoves, the Silk Den Lounge is one of the prettiest in the fleet; guests love culinary presentations in the demonstration kitchen.

Cons: shelves are okay, but drawer space is inadequate in standard cabins; some spa cabins have only unusable Juliet balconies; teens areas aren't as good as on other Holland America ships.

Cabin Type	Size (sq. ft.)
Penthouse Suite	1,318 sq. ft.
Verandah Suite	510–700 sq. ft.
Superior Verandah	398 sq. ft.
Deluxe Verandah	254 sq. ft.
Ocean View	185 sq. ft.
Inside	170–200 sq. ft.

FAST FACTS

- 11 passenger decks
- 3 specialty restaurants, dining room, buffet, pizzeria
- Wi-Fi, safe, refrigerator, DVD
- 2 pools
- fitness classes, gym, hot tubs, spa
- 11 bars, casino, 2 dance clubs, library, showroom, video game room
- children's programs
- dry cleaning, laundry service
- Internet terminal
- no-smoking cabins

Pinnacle Grill, *Eurodam*

STATENDAM-CLASS
Statendam, Maasdam, Veendam

CREW MEMBERS	580
ENTERED SERVICE	1993, 1993, 1996
GROSS TONS	55,819, 55,575, 57,092
LENGTH	720 feet
NUMBER OF CABINS	630, 658, 630, 675
PASSENGER CAPACITY	1,260, 1,258, 1,350
WIDTH	101 feet

700 ft.

500 ft.

300 ft.

The sister ships included in the S- or Statendam-class retain the most classic and traditional characteristics of Holland America Line vessels. Routinely updated with innovative features, including Signature of Excellence upgrades, they combine all the advantages of intimate, midsize vessels with high-tech and stylish details.

At the heart of the ships, triple-deck atriums graced by suspended glass sculptures open onto three so-called promenade decks; the lowest contains staterooms encircled by a wide, teak outdoor deck furnished with padded steamer chairs, while interior, art-filled passage-ways flow past lounges and public rooms on the two decks above. Either reach the lower dining room floor via the aft elevator, or enter one deck above and make a grand entrance down the sweeping staircase.

CABINS
Layout: Staterooms are spacious and comfortable, although fewer of them have private balconies than on newer ships. Lanai cabins, with a door that directly accesses the promenade deck, were added to *Maasdam* and *Veendam* during the ships' latest upgrades. Every cabin has adequate closet and drawer/shelf storage, as well as bathroom shelves. Connecting cabins are featured in a range of categories.

Suites: Suites have duvets on beds, a fully stocked minibar, and personalized stationery. Penthouse Verandah and Deluxe Verandah suites have exclusive use of the private Neptune Lounge, personal concierge service, canapés before dinner on request, binoculars and umbrellas for use during the cruise, an invitation to a VIP party with the captain, and complimentary laundry, pressing, and dry-cleaning services.

Amenities: All staterooms and suites are now appointed with pillow-top mattresses, 250-thread-count cotton bed linens, magnifying lighted mirrors, hair dryers, a fruit basket, and flat-panel TVs. Bathroom extras include Egyptian cotton towels, shampoo, body lotion, and bath gel, plus deluxe bathrobes to use during the cruise. Accommodations near the spa offer extras such as a yoga mat and iPod docking station.

Accessibility: Nine cabins on each ship are modified with ramps although doors are standard width.

Top: Enjoy a Vegas-style show
Bottom: Deluxe veranda suite

RESTAURANTS

The formal dining room offers open seating breakfast and lunch, as well as both assigned and open seating dinner. Pinnacle Grill (reservation, cover charge) serves lunch and dinner. A casual Lido restaurant serves buffet breakfast and lunch; at dinner the Lido offers combination buffet/table service; Italian fare is served in the adjacent Canaletto Restaurant (reservation, cover charge). Poolside lunch is served at Dive In at the Terrace Grill; on *Veendam* the pizzeria is in the aft pool Retreat area. The Explorations Café offers specialty coffees for an extra charge and free pastries. Daily afternoon tea service is elevated to Royal Dutch High Tea once per cruise. Complimentary hors d'oeuvres are served by waiters during cocktail hour, hand-dipped chocolates are offered after dinner in the Explorer's Lounge, and a late-night buffet and chocolate extravaganza is served in the Lido restaurant during every cruise. Room service is available 24 hours.

SPAS

Treatments in the Greenhouse Spa include a variety of massages, body wraps, and facials, as well as acupuncture services and tooth-whitening treatments. A thermal suite with heated ceramic loungers for relaxation as well as dry saunas and steam rooms can be used by anyone for a fee or is complimentary when a spa appointment is booked.

BARS AND ENTERTAINMENT

Popular before-dinner spots are the Ocean Club and Explorer's Lounge, where servers pass through with appetizers. After dinner and a show, a movie, or concert, those bars are quiet spots for drinks and conversation. For livelier action, try Mix—where champagne, martinis, ales, and spirits are served near the piano. The late-night spot for a nightcap is still the Crow's Nest.

PROS AND CONS

Pros: Statendam-class ships have some of the fleet's most trendy bars; the Ocean Bar hits the right balance for socializing with the after-dinner crowd; movie theaters double as Culinary Arts Centers.

Cons: railings on the balcony level of the main show lounge obstruct the view of the stage; Club HAL can feel empty on some cruises; the addition of Explorations Café means no more free coffee bar.

Cabin Type	Size (sq. ft.)
Penthouse Suite	1,159 sq. ft.
Deluxe Verandah Suite	556 sq. ft.
Verandah Suite	292 sq. ft.
Lanai	197 sq. ft.
Ocean View	197 sq. ft.
Inside	182 sq. ft.

FAST FACTS

- 10 passenger decks
- specialty restaurant, dining room, buffet, pizzeria
- Wi-Fi, safe, refrigerator, DVD
- 2 pools (1 indoor), 2 children's pools
- fitness classes, gym, hot tubs, spa
- 9 bars, casino, dance club, library, showroom, video game room
- children's programs
- dry cleaning, laundry facilities, laundry service
- Internet terminal
- no-smoking cabins

Share a sunset

VISTA-CLASS
Zuiderdam, Oosterdam, Westerdam, Noordam

CREW MEMBERS	817, 817, 817, 820
ENTERED SERVICE	2002, 2003, 2004, 2006
GROSS TONS	82,305
LENGTH	936 feet
NUMBER OF CABINS	958, 958, 958, 959
PASSENGER CAPACITY	1,916, 1,916, 1,916, 1,924
WIDTH	106 feet

700 ft.

500 ft.

300 ft.

Vista-class vessels integrate new, youthful, and family-friendly elements into Holland America Line's classic fleet. Exquisite Waterford-crystal sculptures adorn triple-deck atriums and reflect vivid, almost daring color schemes throughout. Although all the public rooms carry the traditional Holland America names (Ocean Bar, Explorer's Lounge, Crow's Nest) and aren't much different in atmosphere, their louder decor (toned down a bit since the introduction of the *Zuiderdam*) may make them unfamiliar to returning passengers.

Veterans of cruises on older Holland America ships will find the layout of public spaces somewhat different; still, everyone's favorite Crow's Nest lounges continue to offer those commanding views.

CABINS
Layout: Comfortable and roomy, 85% of all Vista-class accommodations have an ocean view, and almost 80% of those also have the luxury of a private balcony furnished with chairs, loungers, and tables. Every cabin has adequate closet and drawer/shelf storage, as well as bathroom shelves. Some suites have a whirlpool tub, powder room, and walk-in closet.

Suites: Suites include duvets on beds and a fully stocked minibar; some also have a whirlpool tub, powder room, and walk-in closet. Penthouse and Deluxe Verandah suites have exclusive use of the private Neptune Lounge, personal concierge service, canapés before dinner, and complimentary laundry, pressing, and dry-cleaning services.

Amenities: All staterooms and suites are appointed with pillow-top mattresses, 250-thread-count cotton bed linens, magnifying halogen-lighted makeup mirrors, hair dryers, a fruit basket, and flat-panel TVs. Bathroom extras include Egyptian cotton towels, shampoo, body lotion, and bath gel, plus deluxe bathrobes to use during the cruise.

Accessibility: Twenty-eight staterooms are wheelchair accessible.

RESTAURANTS
The formal dining room offers open seating breakfast and lunch, with a choice at dinner between two assigned seatings or open seating. The Pinnacle Grill (reservation, cover charge) serves lunch and dinner.

Top: Oosterdam hydropool
Bottom: Vista-class Ocean-View stateroom

A casual Lido restaurant serves buffet breakfast and lunch; at dinner the Lido offers a combination buffet/table service with entrées from both the Lido and main dining room menus, and Italian fare is served in the adjacent Canaletto Restaurant (reservation, cover charge). Poolside lunch at Dive In at the Terrace Grill includes hamburgers, and hot dogs with all the trimmings. The Explorations Café offers extra-charge specialty coffees and free pastries. Daily afternoon tea service is elevated to Royal Dutch High Tea once per cruise. Complimentary hors d'oeuvres are served by waiters during cocktail hour, hand-dipped chocolates are offered after dinner in the Explorer's Lounge, and a late-night buffet and chocolate extravaganza is served in the Lido restaurant during every cruise. Room service is available 24 hours.

SPAS

The Greenhouse Spa treatments include a variety of massages, body wraps, and facials, as well as acupuncture and tooth-whitening services. A hydrotherapy pool and thermal suite with heated ceramic lounges for relaxation and dry sauna and steam rooms are free to use when a spa appointment is booked and available for a fee to all other passengers.

BARS AND ENTERTAINMENT

Before dinner, the Ocean Club and Explorer's Lounge are popular spots where servers pass through with appetizers. After dinner and a show or concert, those bars are quiet spots for drinks and conversation. For livelier action, there's B.B. King's Blues Club or the Crow's Nest for late-night dancing.

PROS AND CONS

Pros: next to the Crow's Nest, an outdoor seating area is a quiet hideaway; exterior panoramic elevators offer an elevated view of the seascape; you can borrow iPod shipboard art tours.

Cons: Vista-class ships do not have self-service laundry rooms; murals in Pinnacle Grill restaurants look out of place alongside priceless art found throughout the rest of the ships; some chairs in Pinnacle Grill are so heavy that they barely budge without effort.

Cabin Type	Size (sq. ft.)
Penthouse Suite	1,318 sq. ft.
Deluxe Verandah Suite	510–700 sq. ft.
Superior Verandah Suite	398 sq. ft.
Deluxe Ocean View	254 sq. ft.
Standard Ocean View	185 sq. ft.
Inside	170–200 sq. ft.

FAST FACTS

- 11 passenger decks
- specialty restaurant, dining room, buffet, pizzeria
- Wi-Fi, safe, refrigerator, DVD
- 2 pools (1 indoor)
- fitness classes, gym, hot tubs, spa
- 9 bars, casino, 2 dance clubs, library, showroom, video game room
- children's programs
- dry cleaning, laundry service
- Internet terminal
- no-smoking cabins

3

HOLLAND AMERICA LINE

Westerdam at sea

VOLENDAM, ZAANDAM
Volendam, Zaandam

CREW MEMBERS	615
ENTERED SERVICE	1999, 2000
GROSS TONS	61,214, 61,396
LENGTH	781 feet
NUMBER OF CABINS	716
PASSENGER CAPACITY	1,432
WIDTH	106 feet

700 ft.

500 ft.

300 ft.

Similar to Statendam-class vessels, these slightly larger sister ships have more playful design elements than Holland America Line's classic vessels. Triple-deck atriums have a fantastic—and fiber-optic-lighted—Murano-glass sculpture (*Volendam*) or an almost scary towering pipe organ (*Zaandam*).

The interior decor and much of the artwork found in each vessel has a predominant theme—*Volendam* centers on flowers and *Zaandam* around music. Look for *Zaandam*'s collection of guitars autographed by the Rolling Stones and a saxophone signed by President Bill Clinton. The extra space in these ships allows for a larger specialty restaurant and a roomier feel throughout.

CABINS
Layout: Staterooms are spacious and comfortable with a few more balconies than Statendam-class. Every cabin has adequate closet and drawer/shelf storage, as well as bathroom shelves. Connecting cabins are featured in a range of categories. However, although the number of triple cabins is generous, there are not many that accommodate four.

Suites: Suite amenities include duvets on beds, a fully stocked minibar, and personalized stationery. Penthouse Verandah and Deluxe Verandah suites have exclusive use of the private Neptune Lounge, personal concierge service, canapés before dinner, binoculars and umbrellas for use during the cruise, an invitation to a captain's VIP party, and complimentary laundry, pressing, and dry cleaning.

Amenities: All staterooms and suites are appointed with pillow-top mattresses, 250-thread-count cotton bed linens, magnifying halo-lighted mirrors, hair dryers, a fruit basket, and flat-panel TVs. Bathrooms have Egyptian cotton towels, shampoo, body lotion, and bath gel, plus deluxe bathrobes to use during the cruise.

Accessibility: Twenty-two staterooms are designed for wheelchair accessibility.

RESTAURANTS
The formal dining room offers open seating breakfast and lunch and a choice between two traditional assigned dinner seatings or open seating. The upscale Pinnacle Grill alternative restaurant serves lunch and dinner, requires reservations, and has a cover charge.

Top: Celebrate a special occasion.
Bottom: Deluxe Verandah suite

A casual Lido restaurant serves buffet breakfast and lunch; at dinner the Lido offers combination buffet/table service featuring entrées from both the Lido and main dining room menus. Canaletto Restaurant, adjacent to the Lido restaurant dining area, serves classic Italian fare with table-side service for dinners only (reservation, cover charge). Poolside lunch at Dive In at the Terrace Grill offers hamburgers, hot dogs, sandwiches, and gourmet sausages. The Explorations Café offers specialty coffees for an extra charge and free pastries. Daily afternoon tea service is elevated to Royal Dutch High Tea once per cruise. Complimentary hors d'oeuvres are served by waiters during cocktail hour, hand-dipped chocolates are offered after dinner in the Explorer's Lounge, and a late-night buffet and chocolate extravaganza is served in the Lido restaurant during every cruise. Room service is available 24 hours.

SPAS

Treatments in the Greenhouse Spa include a variety of massages, body wraps, and facials, as well as acupuncture and tooth-whitening. A thermal suite with heated ceramic loungers as well as sauna and steam rooms can be used by everyone for a fee or free whenever a spa appointment is booked. Changing rooms for men and women have free saunas.

BARS AND ENTERTAINMENT

Popular spots before dinner are the Ocean Club and Explorer's Lounge, where servers pass through with appetizers. After dinner and a show or concert, those bars are quiet spots for drinks and conversation. For livelier action, there's a Piano Bar or the Crow's Nest for late-night dancing.

PROS AND CONS

Pros: ship movie theaters are also home to the Culinary Arts Centers; waiters serve made-to-order entrées in the Lido restaurant at dinner; an evening poolside barbecue buffet is usually scheduled during each cruise.

Cons: expanded spa facilities make the gym area somewhat tight; there are no longer complimentary men's and women's steam rooms; sandwiched between the Lido pool and Lido bar, the children's wading pool area can become quite boisterous.

Cabin Type	Size (sq. ft.)
Penthouse Suite	1,126 sq. ft.
Deluxe Verandah Suite	563 sq. ft.
Verandah Suite	284 sq. ft.
Ocean View	197 sq. ft.
Inside	182 sq. ft.

FAST FACTS

- 10 passenger decks
- specialty restaurant, dining room, buffet
- Wi-Fi, safe, refrigerator, DVD
- 2 pools (1 indoor), 2 children's pools
- fitness classes, gym, hot tubs, sauna, spa
- 6 bars, casino, dance club, library, showroom, video game room
- children's programs
- dry cleaning, laundry facilities, laundry service
- Internet terminal
- no-smoking cabins

3

HOLLAND AMERICA LINE

Zaandam atrium organ

LINDBLAD EXPEDITIONS

Designed with curious, intelligent people in mind, Lindblad Expeditions' cruises are educational, focusing on soft adventure and environmentally conscientious travel. Founded in 1979 by Sven-Olof Lindblad, the line partners with National Geographic to enhance

National Geographic Sea Lion in Southeast Alaska

the cruise experience by including experts and photographers onboard to lead discussions and hold workshops. They're especially good at balancing "must-see" destinations and less traveled spots, taking passengers on active excursions that get them up-close-and-personal with nature.

☎ 212/765–7740, 800/397–3348
⊕ www.expeditions. com
☞ Cruise Style: Small-ship.

Beginning in 2008, National Geographic Expeditions began working exclusively with Lindblad Expeditions. The multifaceted strategic partnership that Lindblad Expeditions has with the National Geographic Society enables Lindblad travelers to participate in the world of natural and cultural history as engaged, active explorers who care about the planet.

The ships of Lindblad Expeditions spend time looking for wildlife, exploring out-of-the-way inlets, and making Zodiac landings at isolated beaches. Itineraries are flexible, so as to take maximum advantage of reported wildlife sightings and weather conditions. Each ship has a fleet of kayaks as well as a video-microphone: a hydrophone (underwater microphone) is combined with an underwater camera so passengers can listen to whale songs and watch live video of what's going on beneath the waves. In the evening the ship's naturalist recaps the day's sights and adventures over cocktails in the lounge. An "open bridge" policy provides passengers the opportunity to meet the captain and his officers and learn the intricacies of navigation or simply observe.

All activities and shore excursions, from guided walks and hikes to museum entrance fees to water activities like kayaking and snorkeling, are included in the cost.

FOOD

Appetizers are often served on deck as you sail from port, while regional specialties are served in the dining room. Lindblad prides itself on serving fresh Alaska seafood, including Dungeness crab, halibut, and Alaska king salmon, but there are also plenty of meat and vegetarian options. The "Seafood for Thought" program ensures that sustainable seafood is served.

ENTERTAINMENT

Lindblad clientele should not expect shuffleboard and glitzy Broadway shows or a casino, but it's more likely they prefer reflective moments gazing at constellations, speaking about maritime navigation with the ship's captain, or watching a video slideshow about biodiversity anyway. Expect to have the most fun boarding a Zodiac for remote shore visits or snorkeling surrounded by spectacular marine wildlife.

FITNESS AND RECREATION

Ships carry exercise equipment on deck and offer a holistic Tonic of Wellness program that might include activities such as kayaking and hiking, fitness activities like yoga and Pilates, or massage therapy and other body treatments. The fitness staff provides expertise in massage therapy and relaxation, water sports and aerobic hikes, stretching classes, and personalized guidance with the fitness equipment.

YOUR SHIPMATES

Lindblad attracts active, adventurous, well-traveled over-forties, and quite a few singles, as the line charges one of the industry's lowest single supplements. However, the line has made a successful push to be more family-friendly by adding cruises aimed specifically at families. To that end, staff members have undergone extensive training designed by several of Lindblad's family travel experts with years of experience in childhood and environmental education to tailor activities toward children. Some family expeditions are offered during the Alaska season, which follow the same itinerary as Lindblad's other trips but include a crew member dedicated to running educational programs for school-age kids. All Lindblad cruises offer substantial discounts for young people up to age 21 traveling with their parents.

DRESS CODE

Casual and comfortable attire is always appropriate. Recommendations are based on practicality and the likely weather conditions in the region you're exploring. Good walking shoes are essential.

Enjoying the view from the top deck

Top: Informal yet elegant dining
Bottom: Kayaking

JUNIOR CRUISERS

Although there are no dedicated children's facilities onboard, families are welcome on all Lindblad itineraries. The National Geographic Global Explorers program, developed in conjunction with National Geographic Education to help children develop the skills of an explorer, was launched in Alaska in 2018. Children and teens can participate in fun activities and benefit from National Geographic certified field educators.

SERVICE

Service is friendly and helpful, if not overly polished.

TIPPING

Although gratuities are at your discretion, tips of $12–$15 per person per day are suggested; these are pooled among the crew at journey's end. Tip the massage therapist individually following a treatment.

SHIPS OF THE LINE

Lindblad currently sails 13 vessels for adventure cruising around the world. Ships are comfortable, outfitted with modern amenities, offer top-notch cuisine, and afford both quiet refuge and social interaction.

National Geographic Sea Bird, Sea Lion, Venture, Quest. These pairs of identical expedition ships each carry 62 guests in 31 outside cabins on *National Geographic Sea Bird* and *Sea Lion* and 100 guests in 50 cabins on *National Geographic Venture* and *Quest*. Ideally suited for exploring Alaskan waters, the small, shallow-draft ships can reach nooks and crannies that bigger ships can't. An open-top sundeck, a forward observation lounge, and a viewing deck at the bow on each ship offer plenty of room to take in the scenery. The ships are also equipped with bowcams (underwater cameras that monitor activity), and you can navigate the camera using a joystick to observe sea life. Additional expedition equipment includes a hydrophone for eavesdropping on marine mammals and an underwater video "splash" camera to record the passing undersea scenery. The smaller ships' Internet kiosks provide email access, and

CHOOSE THIS LINE IF...

■ You want to be an ecologically responsible traveler.

■ You consider travel a learning experience.

■ What you see from the ship and landings is more important than the vessel itself.

there is Wi-Fi access on the larger sister ships. Fitness equipment is set up on the bridge deck of the smaller ships, and the wellness room offers massages, body treatments, and a morning stretching program on deck. The larger vessels have a small spa and gym.

All meals are served open seating during scheduled times in a single dining room. Breakfast is buffet-style, although you may order eggs and omelets from the kitchen, and lunch is served family-style. Afternoon tea includes sandwiches and sweets; hors d'oeuvres are served during the nightly cocktail hour. The open seating dinner typically consists of two entrée choices. Special dietary restrictions can be accommodated with advance notice. Room service is restricted to ill passengers confined to cabins.

National Geographic Sea Bird and *Sea Lion* are comfortable, but cabins are small and basic in decor (there are no TVs, for example). All staterooms are outside, and some have picture windows that open; the lowest-category cabins on main deck have portholes that admit light, but do not open or afford a view. Most cabins have single beds that can convert to a double, and a few on the upper deck have pull-out beds to accommodate a third person. Cabins aboard *National Geographic Venture* and *Quest* are larger and are efficiently designed. Twenty-two of the 50 cabins feature small balconies with floor-to-ceiling sliding doors and 12 cabins connect via internal doorway access. All suites accommodate a third person on a convertible sofa bed. Accommodations also have Wi-Fi access. Every room has electrical and USB outlets. No accommodations are designated accessible, and only *National Geographic Venture* and *Quest* feature an elevator.

HELPFUL HINTS

- Although fares are rather expensive, wine and cocktails are not included; nonalcoholic beverages are.

- All shore excursions except flightseeing are included, as are transfers to and from airports.

- Extensive pre-trip information, including recommended reading, photography guidelines, and what to pack, will arrive with your documents.

- There is no elevator onboard, nor are there accessible features for the mobility impaired.

- Don't expect round-the-clock availability of food; room service is available only if you are sick and confined to your cabin.

DON'T CHOOSE THIS LINE IF...

- You are mobility-impaired. The ships are not accessible, and Zodiacs are used to reach shore for certain explorations.

- Your happiness depends on being entertained. Other than enrichment programs, there is no formal entertainment.

- You consider TV essential. There are none in the staterooms.

NORWEGIAN CRUISE LINE

Norwegian Cruise Line set sail in 1966 with an entirely new concept—regularly scheduled Caribbean cruises from the then-obscure port of Miami. Good food and friendly service combined with value fares established the line as a winner for active adults and

Norwegian Bliss Ketchikan

families. Innovative and forward-looking, Norwegian has been a cruise-industry leader for decades, and its fleet is as much at home worldwide as in the Caribbean. Several of the line's ships cruise Alaska's Inside Passage, including one of its newest, *Norwegian Bliss.*

☎ *305/436–4000, 800/327–7030*
⊕ *www.ncl.com*
☞ *Cruise Style: Mainstream.*

Noted for top-quality entertainment, Norwegian combines action and high-energy activities as well as a variety of dining options in a casual, free-flowing atmosphere. Norwegian's freestyle cruising signaled an end to rigid dining schedules and dress codes. Norwegian ships now offer a host of flexible dining options that allow passengers to eat in the main dining rooms or any of a number of à la carte and specialty restaurants at any time and with whom they please. The ships' accommodations include some of the largest suites at sea, studio cabins for solo travelers, and a private ship-within-a-ship complex called The Haven, a more luxurious area with personalized service.

From a distance, most cruise ships look so similar that it's often difficult to tell them apart, but Norwegian's largest, modern ships stand out with their distinctive use of hull art. Each new ship is distinguished by murals extending from bow to midship.

FOOD
Main dining rooms serve what is traditionally deemed Continental fare, although it's about what you would expect at a really good hotel banquet. Health-conscious menu selections are nicely prepared, and vegetarian choices are always available. Where Norwegian

really shines is the specialty restaurants, especially the French-Mediterranean Le Bistro (on all ships), the pan-Asian restaurants, and steak houses (on the newer ships). As a rule of thumb, the newer the ship, the wider the variety, because new ships were purpose-built with as many as 10 or more places to eat. You may find Spanish tapas, an Italian trattoria, a steak house, a pub, and a pan-Asian restaurant complete with a sushi and sashimi bar and teppanyaki room. Most carry a cover charge or are priced à la carte and require reservations. A Norwegian staple, the late-night Chocoholic Buffet continues to be a favorite event. A charge of $7.95 per order has been instituted for room service; however, continental breakfast and coffee are still free.

ENTERTAINMENT

More high jinks than highbrow, entertainment after dark features extravagant Las Vegas–style revues presented in main show lounges by lavishly costumed singers and dancers. Other performers might include comedians, magicians, jugglers, and acrobats. Entertainment varies by ship depending on facilities; the newest ships—*Norwegian Bliss* and *Norwegian Escape*, for example—have the most appealing options, such as Broadway shows. Passengers can get into the act by stepping up to the karaoke microphone or singing along in a piano bar. Live bands play for dancing and listening in smaller lounges, and each ship has a lively dance club.

Casinos, bingo sessions, and art auctions are well attended. Adult games, particularly the competitive ones, are fun to participate in and provide laughs for audience members. Goofy pool games are a Norwegian staple, and the ships' bands or DJs crank up the volume during afternoon and evening deck parties.

FITNESS AND RECREATION

Mandara Spa offers exotic spa treatments fleet-wide on Norwegian, although facilities vary widely. Spa treatments include a long menu of massages, body wraps, and facials, and current trends in hair and nail services are offered in the salons. The latest addition on board is a Medi-Spa physician, who can create individualized treatment plans using nonsurgical treatments such as Botox Cosmetic. State-of-the-art exercise equipment, jogging tracks, and basic fitness classes are available at no charge. There's a fee for personal training, body composition analysis, and specialized classes such as yoga and Pilates.

KNOWN FOR

■ **Casual Atmosphere:** With no dress code, Norwegian's ships have shed the "stuffy" reputation of cruises in the past.

■ **Dining Options:** Norwegian Cruise Line is an industry innovator in onboard dining, from open seating dining rooms to specialty restaurants.

■ **Entertainment:** Their partnership with widely recognized acts and shows has made Norwegian a leader in entertainment at sea.

■ **Family-Friendliness:** Numerous connecting staterooms and suites on Norwegian's ships can be combined to create multicabin accommodations ideal for families.

■ **Itineraries:** With some exceptions, Norwegian's sailings don't stray far from the tried-and-true one-week length.

3

NORWEGIAN CRUISE LINE

Norwegian Joy Manhattan Dining Room

Top: Norwegian Bliss
Ocean Loops
Middle: Family Suite
Bottom: *Norwegian Bliss*
The Haven Restaurant

YOUR SHIPMATES

Norwegian's mostly American cruise passengers are active couples ranging from their mid-thirties to mid-fifties. Many families enjoy cruising on Norwegian ships during holidays and summer months. Longer cruises and more exotic itineraries attract passengers in the over-55 age group.

DRESS CODE

Resort casual attire is appropriate at all times; the option of one formal evening is available on all cruises of seven nights and longer. Most passengers actually raise the casual dress code a notch to what could be called casual chic attire.

JUNIOR CRUISERS

For children and teens, each Norwegian vessel offers a Splash Academy program of supervised entertainment for young cruisers ages 3 to 12. Younger children are split into three groups, ages 3 to 5, 6 to 9, and 10 to 12; activities range from storytelling, games, and arts and crafts to dinner with counselors, pajama parties, and treasure hunts. The program now also offers activities for kids from six months to three years old. "Guppies" offers their parents the opportunity to engage in a variety of sensory-based programs with them, including baby art, storytelling, and a parent and baby mini-workout.

Group Port Play is available in the children's area to accommodate parents booked on shore excursions. Evening babysitting services are available for a fee. Parents whose children are not toilet-trained are issued a beeper to alert them when diaper changing is necessary. Reduced fares are charged for third and fourth guests in the same stateroom, including all children. Infants under six months of age cannot travel on Norwegian ships.

For teens ages 13 to 17, options in the Entourage program include sports, pool parties, teen disco, movies,

CHOOSE THIS LINE IF...

■ Doing your own thing is your idea of a real vacation. You could almost remove your watch and just go with the flow.

■ You want to leave your formal dress-up wardrobe at home.

■ You're competitive. There's always a pickup game in progress on the sports courts.

and video games. Some ships have their own cool clubs where teens hang out in adult-free zones.

SERVICE
Somewhat inconsistent, service is nonetheless congenial.

TIPPING
A fixed service charge of $14.50 per person per day for passengers three years of age and older is added to shipboard accounts for staterooms and minisuites; for suites and The Haven the service charge is $17.50. An automatic 15% gratuity is added to bar tabs. Staff members may also accept cash gratuities. Passengers in suites who have access to concierge and butler services are asked to offer a cash gratuity at their own discretion.

PAST PASSENGERS
On completion of your first Norwegian cruise you're automatically enrolled in Latitudes, the club for repeat passengers. Membership benefits accrue based on the number of cruise nights sailed: Bronze (1 through 29), Silver (30 through 54), Gold (55 through 79), Platinum (80 through 174), Platinum Plus (175-699), and Ambassador (700 or more). Everyone receives *Latitudes*, Norwegian's e-magazine, Latitudes pricing, Latitudes check-in at the pier, a bottle of sparkling wine, and access to a special customer service desk, and discounts in onboard shops. Higher tiers—depending on level—receive such amenities as an invitation to the captain's cocktail party, dinner in a specialty restaurant, free Internet minutes, free laundry, discounts on shore excursions, and priority for check-in, tender tickets, and disembarkation.

NORWEGIAN CRUISE LINE 3

DON'T CHOOSE THIS LINE IF...

■ You don't like to pay extra for food on a ship. All the best specialty restaurants have extra charges.

■ You don't want to stand in line. There are lines for nearly everything.

■ You don't want to hear announcements. They're frequent on these ships—and loud.

NORWEGIAN SKY/SUN
Norwegian Sky, Norwegian Sun

CREW MEMBERS	
	917,916
ENTERED SERVICE	
	1999, 2001
700 ft. **GROSS TONS**	
	77,104, 78,309
LENGTH	
	853 feet
500 ft. **NUMBER OF CABINS**	
	1,002, 968
PASSENGER CAPACITY	
	2,004, 1,936
300 ft. **WIDTH**	
	105 feet

Norwegian Cruise Line hadn't introduced many new ships in awhile at the time *Norwegian Sky* was launched and *Norwegian Sun* was on the drawing board, but it didn't take long before they got the hang of it. With Freestyle cruising growing in popularity, the vessels moved into the forefront of the fleet with multiple restaurant choices, expansive casino, trendy spas, and more family- and kid-friendly facilities.

Rich wood tones and fabric colors prevail throughout. The Observation Lounge is a subdued spot for afternoon tea in a light, tropical setting with nothing to distract attention from the expansive views beyond the floor-to-ceiling windows.

The Internet café is large, and the nearby coffee bar is a delight. Sunshine pours into the atrium through an overhead skylight by day; at night it's the ship's glamorous hub of activity.

CABINS

Layout: Staterooms are a bit more generous in size than on the previous vessels in the Norwegian fleet and contain adequate closet and drawer space for a one-week cruise. More than two-thirds have an ocean view, and nearly two-thirds of those have a private balcony. All have a sitting area with sofa, chair, and table. Clever use of primary colors and strategically placed mirrors achieves an open feeling. Connecting staterooms are available in several categories, including those with balconies. Oddly sandwiched in between decks 6 and 7 forward is deck 6A, which has no direct elevator access.

Suites: Suites have walk-in closets as well as whirlpool tubs and entertainment centers. Butlers and a concierge are at the service of suite occupants.

Amenities: Light-wood cabinetry, mirrored accents, a small refrigerator, a tea/coffeemaker, a personal safe, broadband Internet connections, duvets on beds, a wall-mounted hair dryer over the dressing table, and bathrobes for use during the cruise are typical standard amenities. Bathrooms have shampoo and bath gel in shower-mounted dispensers, as well as limited storage.

Accessibility: Sixteen cabins are wheelchair accessible.

Top: Las Ramblas Tapas Bar & Restaurant
Bottom: *Norwegian Sun* at sea

RESTAURANTS

Two complimentary dining rooms serve open seating breakfast, lunch, and dinner. Specialty restaurants on both ships that carry varying cover charges and require reservations include Norwegian's signature French restaurant Le Bistro, steak houses, and Italian eateries; *Norwegian Sun* also has an extra-charge Japanese restaurant, sushi bar, and teppanyaki room, Brazilian steak house, bakery, and a complimentary tapas bar. Screens located throughout the ship illustrate the status (full to empty) and waiting time you can expect for each restaurant. Casual choices are the Lido buffet for breakfast, lunch, and dinner; the poolside grill for lunch; a pizzeria; and an ice cream bar. A coffee bar serves specialty coffees and pastries priced by item. Room service is available 24 hours with an extra charge per order except for continental breakfast and coffee.

SPAS

Although the facilities aren't as extensive as on newer ships, Mandara Spa offers a lengthy menu of massages, body wraps, and facials. A Medi-Spa physician is on hand to create individualized therapies. Each ship has saunas and steam rooms that are available to all at no extra charge.

BARS AND ENTERTAINMENT

You'll find a nice selection of bars and lounges where musicians or DJs provide dance tunes; the entertainment staff hosts Norwegian's signature late-night parties after performances by the production company; other nights, comedians or other entertainers perform in the main theater. Each ship has a top-deck lounge ideal for an intimate nightcap (*Norwegian Sky*) or complimentary tapas (*Norwegian Sun*).

PROS AND CONS

Pros: many of the elements found in newer fleetmates have been added to these older ships; there is a hot tub exclusively for kids; *Norwegian Sun* has separate steam rooms and saunas for men and women.

Cons: the main restaurant is not on a direct route from the main atrium; these are sister ships but not twins, and dining facilities vary; standard accommodations are somewhat tight for more than two people.

Cabin Type	Size (sq. ft.)
Owner's Suite	828 sq. ft.
Penthouse and Romance Suite	504 sq. ft.
Minisuite	332 sq. ft.
Ocean View with Balcony	221 sq. ft.
Deluxe Interior	172 sq. ft.
Interior	145 sq. ft.
Ocean View	145 sq. ft.

FAST FACTS

- 11 passenger decks
- 4 specialty restaurants, 2 dining rooms, buffet, ice cream parlor, pizzeria
- Wi-Fi, safe, refrigerator (some), DVD (some)
- 2 pools, children's pool
- fitness classes, gym, hot tubs, sauna, spa, steam room
- 8 bars, casino, dance club, library, showroom, video game room
- children's programs
- dry-cleaning, laundry service
- Internet terminal
- no-smoking cabins

3

NORWEGIAN CRUISE LINE

Balcony stateroom

JEWEL-CLASS
Norwegian Jewel, Norwegian Jade, Norwegian Pearl, Norwegian Gem

CREW MEMBERS	1,081, 1,075, 1,084, 1,092
ENTERED SERVICE	2005, 2006, 2006, 2007
GROSS TONS	93,502, 93,558, 93,530, 93,530
LENGTH	965 feet
NUMBER OF CABINS	1,188, 1,201, 1,197, 1,197
PASSENGER CAPACITY	2,376, 2,402, 2,394, 2,394
WIDTH	105 feet

700 ft.

500 ft.

300 ft.

Jewel-class ships were designed as the next step in the continuing evolution of Freestyle ship design: the interior location of some public rooms and restaurants has been tweaked since the introduction of Freestyle cruising vessels, and new categories of deluxe accommodations have been added.

These ships have more than a dozen dining alternatives, a variety of entertainment options, and expansive areas reserved for children and teens. Pools have waterslides and a plethora of lounge chairs, although when your ship is full, it can be difficult to find one in a prime location. *Norwegian Pearl* and *Norwegian Gem* introduced the line's first rock-climbing walls, as well as Bliss Lounge, which has trendy South Beach decor, and the first full-size 10-pin bowling alleys on modern cruise ships.

CABINS
Layout: Norwegian ships are not noted for large staterooms, but all have a small sitting area with sofa, chair, and table. Every cabin has adequate closet and drawer/shelf storage, as well as limited bathroom storage. Suites have walk-in closets. Some staterooms interconnect in most categories.

Garden and Courtyard Villas: The Garden Villas, located in a private complex called The Haven, have three bedrooms, a living-dining room, and private deck garden with a spa tub, and are among the largest suites at sea. Courtyard Villas—not as large as Garden Villas—have an exclusive concierge lounge and a shared private courtyard with pool, hot tub, sundeck, and small gym.

Amenities: A small refrigerator, tea/coffeemaker, personal safe, broadband Internet connection, duvets on beds, a wall-mounted hair dryer, and bathrobes are standard. Bathrooms have a shampoo/bath-gel dispenser on the shower wall and a magnifying mirror. Suites have a whirlpool tub, an entertainment center, and concierge and butler service.

Accessibility: Twenty-seven staterooms are wheelchair accessible.

RESTAURANTS
Two main complimentary dining rooms serve open seating breakfast, lunch, and dinner. Specialty restaurants, including Norwegian's signature French restaurant Le Bistro, Cagney's Steakhouse, an Asian restaurant, sushi

Top: *Norwegian Jewel's* Azura restaurant
Bottom: Hydropool in the spa

bar, teppanyaki room, tapas and salsa eatery, a Brazilian steak house, and an Italian trattoria–style restaurant carry varying cover charges and require reservations. Screens located throughout the ship illustrate the status (full, moderately busy, empty) and waiting time you can expect for each restaurant on board. Casual choices are the Lido buffet for breakfast, lunch, and dinner; O'Sheehan's Bar & Grill for soup, sandwiches, and snacks around the clock; and the poolside grill for lunch. Java Café serves specialty coffees and the bakery features pastries for an additional charge. Although the 24-hour room-service menu has expanded along with the new $7.95 charge per order, suite occupants may order from any restaurant on the ship.

SPAS
The Mandara Spa's treatments include a long menu of massages, body wraps, and facials and include the services of a Medi-Spa physician. Spa facilities include an enormous thermal suite with hydrotherapy pool, heated lounges, steam rooms, and saunas for which there is a charge.

BARS AND ENTERTAINMENT
Your evening might start with a high-energy production show, a comedy performance, or a show by a featured entertainer, then continue in the bar complex that includes a beer and whiskey bar, martini bar, and a champagne bar. You'll find music for dancing, signature Norwegian parties, and even a cigar lounge. The perfect spot to end the night is the Star Bar with its pianist and views of the pool deck and the sea.

PROS AND CONS
Pros: there are themed parties galore with no cover charge; the ship's tranquil library offers a quiet escape with a sea view; Courtyard Villa accommodations are like a ship within a ship and have a private pool area.

Cons: there is a fee for use of the thermal suites in the spa; Freestyle dining doesn't mean you get to eat precisely when you want to; for such a large ship, the Internet center is tiny.

Cabin Type	Size (sq. ft.)
Garden Villa	4,390 sq. ft.
Deluxe Owner's Suite*	928 sq. ft.
Owner's Suite	823 sq. ft.
Penthouse Suite	575 sq. ft.
Courtyard Villa	574 sq. ft.
Minisuite	284 sq. ft.
Ocean View with Balcony	205–243 sq. ft.
Ocean View	161 sq. ft.
Inside	143 sq. ft.

*Deluxe Owner's Suites on *Norwegian Pearl* and *Norwegian Gem* only.

FAST FACTS

- 15 passenger decks
- 7 restaurants, 2 dining rooms, buffet, ice cream parlor, pizzeria
- Internet, Wi-Fi, safe, refrigerator, DVD (some)
- 2 pools, children's pool
- fitness classes, gym, hot tubs, spa
- 9 bars, casino, dance club, library, showroom, video game room
- children's programs
- dry-cleaning, laundry service
- Internet terminal
- no-smoking cabins

The sports deck

NORWEGIAN BREAKAWAY-PLUS
Norwegian Bliss, Norwegian Joy

CREW MEMBERS	1,821
ENTERED SERVICE	2017
GROSS TONS	167,725
LENGTH	1,094
NUMBER OF CABINS	2,002
PASSENGER CAPACITY	3,802
WIDTH	136 ft.

700 ft.
500 ft.
300 ft.

Along with its sister ship *Norwegian Joy, Norwegian Bliss,* is an expanded Breakaway-Plus version of the Breakaway-Class. Although it is a slightly larger vessel, it carries fewer passengers and, like its Breakaway-Class sister ships, it has three main dining rooms and numerous specialty restaurants, some of which offer outdoor dining. You can check restaurant wait times and make reservations on digital screens throughout the ship. Entertainment is a highlight on *Norwegian Bliss* and includes not only a Cuban dance show, but also a full-fledged Broadway production of *Jersey Boys* and a lounge featuring a Beatles tribute band.

Outside, you'll find the largest racetrack at sea where, for a fee, you can take a ride on the two-level competitive track. In the Laser Tag arena, which also charges a fee, you can participate in a stellar space-themed battle. There are also pools, hot tubs, waterslides, and an aqua park for children. Youth and teen clubs are large and offer a wide variety of age-appropriate activities and programs. For adults-only, the Vibe Beach Club offers serenity for a fee.

CABINS

Cabins: Cabin décor is chic and modern, but most balconies are disappointingly small. Storage space is adequate, but drawers are lacking. Bathrooms are moderately sized with small showers and large sinks. In mini-suites and above showers are expansive with multi-jet fixtures and vanities have double sinks. Shampoo and shower gel are provided in shower dispensers. All accommodations have a safe, hair dryer, minibar, flat-screen television, and good lighting.

Suites: Haven suites include access to an exclusive concierge lounge, restaurant, and shared open courtyard with pool, hot tub, sundeck, and small gym. Spa suites include access to the spa and thermal suite during the cruise.

Studios: Strictly for single passengers, the tiny studios have private bathrooms and access to the shared Studio Lounge.

Accessibility: Thirty-nine cabins are wheelchair accessible.

Top: *Norwegian Joy*
Bottom: Vibe Beach Club
on *Norwegian Bliss*

RESTAURANTS

Three main dining rooms serve open-seating breakfast, lunch, and dinner. Specialty restaurants include old favorites like Le Bistro and the new Jimmy Buffett's Margaritaville at Sea. Reservations are suggested and all include a charge, either set or à la carte. Casual selections are the Garden Café Lido buffet and The Local, serving classic pub fare around the clock. There is also a bakery, chocolate shop, gelato bar, and Starbucks—all with à la carte pricing. Available 24 hours a day, room service comes with a convenience charge of $7.95 per person, per order. Continental breakfast until 10 am is excluded and Suite Guests are not charged at any time.

SPAS

The huge spa offers beauty and medi-spa treatments; a full service salon; a barber shop; and large thermal suite with pools and hot tubs, a heated salt room, chilled snow grotto, sauna, steam room, and heated lounges for relaxation. The Fitness Center features a wide range of machines and free weights and fitness classes—some complimentary, others with a fee.

BARS AND ENTERTAINMENT

More than a dozen bars are located throughout the ship, including the Cavern Club, a nostalgic Liverpool-style bar where a Beatles tribute band entertains, a comedy club, and the Humidor cigar lounge. Happy Hour Prohibition—The Musical, set in a New Orleans–like speakeasy where madams share tales of bootleggers and serve Prohibition Era specialty cocktails, carries a cover charge. This show is not suitable for children under 16. The Broadway show *Jersey Boys* and ¡ *Havana*! which celebrates the music and culture of 1950's era Cuba, are both complimentary.

PROS AND CONS

Pros: you can make dining reservations on screens throughout the ship; the observation lounge has floor to ceiling windows for good visibility in Alaska ports; smoking is limited to small areas, but there is a lounge for cigar smokers.

Cons: there are charges for some of the entertainment, laser tag, and the racetrack; there is a charge for room service; charges can add up in the à la carte specialty restaurants.

Cabin Type	Size (sq. ft.)
Owner's Suite/Family Villa	1,458/538-622 sq. ft.
Penthouse	324-667 sq. ft.
Minisuite	249-439 sq. ft.
Ocean View with Balcony	207-367 sq. ft.
Ocean View	160-240 sq. ft.
Interior	135-201 sq. ft.
Studio	99 sq. ft.

FAST FACTS

- 16 passenger decks
- specialty restaurants, 3 dining rooms, buffet, ice cream parlor
- Wi-Fi, safe, refrigerator
- 3 pools, children's pool
- fitness classes, gym, hot tubs, sauna, spa, steam room
- 22 bars, casino, dance club, library, showroom, video game room
- children's programs
- dry cleaning, laundry service
- Internet terminal
- no-smoking cabins

Norwegian Bliss
Maltings Whiskey Bar

OCEANIA CRUISES

Oceania offers itineraries to smaller ports megaships can't reach and a near-luxury cruise experience for fares much lower than you would expect. The line first set sail in 2003, carving a unique niche in the cruise industry by offering a sophisticated vacation best suited

Oceania's *Regatta*

to inquisitive, well-traveled passengers. Its midsize ships carry fewer passengers than popular mainstream lines. Varied, destination-rich itineraries are an important characteristic of Oceania Cruises, and most sailings are in the 10- to 12-night range.

☎ 305/514–2300, 800/531–5658
⊕ www.oceaniacruises.com
☞ Cruise Style: Premium.

Intimate and cozy public spaces reflect the importance of socializing on Oceania ships. Indoor lounges feature numerous conversation areas, and even the pool deck is a social center. The Patio is a shaded slice of deck adjacent to the pool and hot tubs. Defined by billowing drapes and carpeting underfoot, it is furnished with plush sofas and chairs ideal for relaxation.

Thickly padded single and double loungers are arranged around the pool, but if more privacy appeals to you, private cabanas are available for rent. Each one has a double chaise longue with a view of the sea; overhead drapery can be drawn back for sunbathing, and the side panels can be left open or closed. Waiters are on standby to offer chilled towels or serve occupants with beverages or snacks. In addition, you can request a spa service in your cabana.

FOOD
Several top cruise-industry chefs were lured away from other cruise lines to ensure that the artistry of world-renowned master chef Jacques Pépin, who crafted five-star menus for Oceania, is properly carried out. The results are sure to please the most discriminating palate. Oceania simply serves some of the best food at sea, particularly impressive for a cruise line that charges

far less than luxury rates. The main restaurant offers trendy, French-Continental cuisine with an always-on-the-menu steak, seafood, or poultry choice and a vegetarian option.

Intimate specialty restaurants require reservations, but there's no additional charge for Toscana, the Italian restaurant, or Polo Grill, the steak house. On *Marina* and *Riviera,* passengers have those and more restaurants from which to choose—Jacques, the first restaurant to bear Jacques Pépin's name, serves French cuisine; Red Ginger features contemporary interpretations of Asian classics; Privée hosts private, seven-course menu degustation dinners for a single party of up to 10; and La Reserve serves exclusive wine and food pairings.

A casual dinner option is alfresco dining at the Terrace Café (the daytime Lido deck buffet). Although service is from the buffet, outdoor seating on the aft deck is transformed into a charming Mediterranean courtyard with candleholders and starched linens.

The Terrace Café also serves breakfast and lunch buffet-style, and has a small pizzeria window that operates during the day. At an outdoor poolside grill you can order up burgers, hot dogs, and sandwiches for lunch and then take a seat; waiters are at hand to serve you either at a nearby table or your lounge chair by the pool. Afternoon tea is a decadent spread of finger foods and includes a rolling dessert cart, which has to be seen to be believed.

ENTERTAINMENT
Culinary demonstrations by guest presenters and Oceania's own executive chefs are extremely popular. Lectures on varied topics, computer courses, hands-on arts and crafts classes, and wine or champagne seminars round out the popular enrichment series onboard. Before arrival in ports of call, lectures are presented on the historical background, culture, and traditions of the destinations.

Evening entertainment leans toward light cabaret, solo artists, music for dancing, and conversation with fellow passengers; however, you'll find lively karaoke sessions on the schedule as well. The sophisticated, adult atmosphere on days at sea is enhanced by a combo performing jazz or easy-listening melodies poolside. Enrichment programs feature guest lecturers who are experts in such topics as wine appreciation, culinary arts, history, and world events.

KNOWN FOR

■ **Cuisine:** Oceania Cruises' chefs are serious about food and serve noteworthy cuisine in all restaurants onboard.

■ **Great Destinations:** Oceania itineraries are destination-oriented and offer overnights in many top ports.

■ **Midsize Ships:** Oceania's deluxe ships are quite manageable in size: four ships have fewer than 850 passengers, the two largest fewer than 1,300 passengers.

■ **No Smoking:** Oceania ships are almost entirely smoke-free, with small, designated areas set aside for smokers.

■ **Surprisingly Affordable:** Cruises on Oceania approach true luxury in style, but not when it comes to fares—they are quite affordable.

3

OCEANIA CRUISES

Top: Penthouse suite
Bottom: Toscana Restaurant

Top: Cocktails before dinner
Middle: Veranda stateroom
Bottom: Martini bar

FITNESS AND RECREATION

The Canyon Ranch SpaClub spas and salons and well-equipped fitness centers are adequate for the number of passengers onboard. In addition to individual body-toning machines and complimentary exercise classes, there's a walking-jogging track circling the top of the ship. A personal trainer is available for individual instruction for an additional charge.

YOUR SHIPMATES

Oceania Cruises appeal to singles and couples from their late-thirties to well-traveled retirees who have the time for and prefer longer cruises. Most are American couples attracted to the casually sophisticated atmosphere, creative cuisine, and high level of service. Many are past passengers of the now-defunct Renaissance Cruises who are loyal to their favorite ships, which now offer a variety of in-depth destination-rich itineraries.

DRESS CODE

Leave the formal wear at home—attire on Oceania ships is country-club casual every evening, although some guests can't help dressing up to dine in the beautifully appointed restaurants. A jacket and tie are never required for dinner, but many men wear sport jackets, as they would to dine in an upscale restaurant ashore. Jeans, shorts, T-shirts, and tennis shoes are discouraged after 6 pm in public rooms.

JUNIOR CRUISERS

Oceania Cruises are adult-oriented and not a good choice for families, particularly those traveling with infants and toddlers. No dedicated children's facilities are available, and parents are completely responsible for their behavior and entertainment. Teenagers with sophisticated tastes (and who don't mind the absence of a video arcade) might enjoy the intriguing ports of call.

SERVICE

Highly personalized service by a mostly European staff is crisp and efficient without being intrusive. Butlers are

CHOOSE THIS LINE IF...

■ Socializing plays a more important role in your lifestyle than dancing the night away.

■ You love to read. These ships have extensive libraries that are ideal for curling up with a good book.

■ You have a bad back. You're sure to love the Tranquility Beds.

on hand to fulfill the requests of suite guests and will even assist with packing and unpacking when asked.

TIPPING

Gratuities of $16 per person per day are added to shipboard accounts for distribution to stewards and waitstaff; an additional $7 per person per day is added for occupants of suites with butler service. Passengers may adjust the amount based on the level of service experienced. An automatic 18% gratuity is added to all bar tabs for bartenders and drink servers and to all bills for salon and spa services.

PAST PASSENGERS

After you take two Oceania cruises, you'll receive several benefits along with a free subscription to the *OLife*magazine. Invitations to Shipboard Club parties hosted by the captain and senior officers, a club pin, savings on Oceania Cruises logo merchandise, and special pricing and mailings about upcoming promotions are some of the benefits. Members further qualify for elite-level status based on the number of sailings aboard Oceania Cruises, which include such benefits as shipboard credits, complimentary gratuities, spa treatments, and Internet. Once you take your 20th cruise, you receive the above and get a free cruise as well as complimentary spa treatments. After 60 cruises you also receive a complimentary beverage package, and complimentary laundry service.

3

OCEANIA CRUISES

HELPFUL HINTS

■ Many Oceania voyages include airfare in the fare pricing.

■ Pre- or post-cruise Hotel Collection Packages are available and include private group transfers.

■ There is never a dining charge on Oceania ships, but cocktail and wine prices are relatively high.

■ You may bring up to three bottles of wine per stateroom onboard upon embarkation or from ports of call, but there's a corkage fee of $25 per bottle if you bring wine to the dining room.

■ Oceania Cruises offers two shore excursion collections that must be reserved prior to sailing and can save a lot of money.

■ Oceania was the first cruise line to upgrade their bedding to the highest standard, so you can count on a good night's sleep on these ships.

DON'T CHOOSE THIS LINE IF...

■ You like the action in a huge casino. Oceania casinos are small, and seats at a poker table can be difficult to get.

■ You want to bring your children. Most passengers book with Oceania anticipating a kid-free atmosphere.

■ Glitzy production shows are your thing. Oceania's showrooms are decidedly low-key.

INSIGNIA, REGATTA, NAUTICA, SIRENA
Insignia, Regatta, Sirena

CREW MEMBERS	400
ENTERED SERVICE	1998, 1998, 1998
GROSS TONS	30,277
LENGTH	594 feet
NUMBER OF CABINS	342
PASSENGER CAPACITY	684 (824 max)
WIDTH	84 feet

700 ft.

500 ft.

300 ft.

Carefully furnished to impart the atmosphere of a private English country manor, these midsize ships are casual yet elegant, with sweeping central staircases and abundant flower arrangements. Brocade and toile fabrics window coverings, overstuffed sofas, and wing chairs create a warm and intimate feeling throughout.

Authentic-looking faux fireplaces are adjacent to cozy seating areas in the Grand Bar, near the martini bar's grand piano, and in the beautiful libraries—some of the best at sea, with an enormous selection. The casinos are quite small and can feel cramped, and smoking is prohibited. You may have to wait for a seat at a poker table, but there are enough slot machines to go around.

CABINS

Layout: Private balconies outfitted with chairs and tables add additional living space to nearly 75% of all outside cabins. All have a vanity-desk and a seating area with sofa, chair, and table, a generous closet, drawer/shelf storage, and bathroom shelves. Owner's and Vista suites have a separate living-dining room and powder room. Concierge-level accommodations and above include an iPad for use during the cruise. Several cabins accommodate third and fourth passengers, but few have connecting doors.

Suites: Owner's and Vista suites have an entertainment center, a small refrigerator, and a second TV in the bedroom; the main bathroom has a combination shower-whirlpool tub. Penthouse suites also have refrigerators and bathtubs. Butlers are on hand to coordinate reservations and serve evening canapés and dinner ordered from any of the ship's restaurants.

Amenities: Dark-wood cabinetry, soothing blue decor, mirrored accents, a safe, Prestige Tranquility Beds, 350-thread-count linens, goose-down pillows, and silk-cut duvets are typical stateroom features. Bathrooms have a hair dryer, shampoo, lotion, and bath gel, plus robes.

Accessibility: Three staterooms are designed for wheelchair accessibility.

RESTAURANTS

Oceania passengers enjoy the flexibility of open seating restaurants. The Grand Dining Room, open for breakfast, lunch, and dinner, serves Continental cuisine.

Top: Teatime in Horizons
Bottom: Breakfast in bed

Alternative, reservations-required dinner options are Toscana, which serves gourmet Italian dishes, and Polo Grill, the steak house. *Sirena* also features Red Ginger, the Asian restaurant, which debuted on *Marina* and *Riviera*. Terrace Café, the buffet restaurant, serves breakfast, lunch, and dinner and is transformed into Tapas on the Terrace after dark for a relaxed atmosphere and alfresco dining. All dining venues have nearby bars, and there's no additional cover charge for dining. A coffee bar serves complimentary specialty coffees and teas; soft drinks and bottled water are included in the fare. In addition, a poolside grill serves hamburgers and a variety of sandwiches and salads at lunchtime, and there is a pizzeria in the buffet area. Afternoon tea is an elaborate affair served in Horizons, the observation lounge. Room service is available 24 hours.

SPAS
The Canyon Ranch SpaClub offers a long menu of body wraps, massages, conditioning body scrubs, skin care and tanning treatments, and acupuncture. Thermal suites include complimentary single-sex aromatic steam rooms. A highlight of the tranquil open-air Spa Terrace is a therapy whirlpool, to which all Concierge-level and suite guests have unlimited complimentary access; all other guests must purchase passes.

BARS AND ENTERTAINMENT
Bars and lounges have an intimate quality, from the martini bar, where piano music is played, to the show lounge that offers small-scale cabaret-style entertainment ranging from headline acts and concerts to comedians and magicians. The observation lounge is a late-night hot spot with music for dancing and even karaoke led by the entertainment staff.

PROS AND CONS
Pros: a relaxed, social atmosphere pervades all areas onboard; the lobby staircase is a must-see—it's practically identical to the one in the movie *Titanic*; onboard, you'll find some of the most lavish afternoon teas at sea.

Cons: shipboard charges can add up fast, because drink prices and even Internet services are on the high side; there is only one self-serve laundry room; the absence of a sauna in the spa is an unfortunate oversight.

Cabin Type	Size (sq. ft.)
Owner's	962 sq. ft.
Vista Suite	786 sq. ft.
Penthouse Suite	322 sq. ft.
Concierge/ Ocean View with Balcony	216 sq. ft.
Deluxe Ocean View	165 sq. ft.
Standard Ocean View	150–165 sq. ft.
Inside	160 sq. ft.

FAST FACTS

- 9 passenger decks
- 2 specialty restaurants (3 on *Sirena*), dining room, buffet, pizzeria
- Wi-Fi, safe, refrigerator, DVD (some)
- pool
- fitness classes, gym, hot tubs, spa, steam room
- 4 bars, casino, dance club, library, showroom
- dry cleaning, laundry facilities, laundry service
- Internet terminal
- no-smoking cabins

Regatta at sea

PRINCESS CRUISES

Princess Cruises may be best known for introducing cruise travel to millions of viewers, when its flagship became the setting for *The Love Boat* television series in 1977. Since that heady time of small-screen stardom, the Princess fleet has grown both in the number and

Watch iceburgs float by from your balcony

size of ships. Although most are large in scale, Princess vessels manage to create the illusion of intimacy through the use of color and decor in understated yet lovely public rooms graced by multimillion-dollar art collections.

☎ *661/753–0000, 800/774–6237*
⊕ *www.princess.com*
☞ *Cruise Style: Premium.*

Princess has also become more flexible; Personal Choice Cruising offers alternatives for open seating dining (when you wish and with whom you please) and entertainment options as diverse as those found in resorts ashore.

Lovely chapels or the wide-open decks are romantic settings for weddings at sea with the captain officiating.

FOOD

Personal choices regarding where and what to eat abound, but because of the number of passengers, unless you opt for traditional assigned seating or make a reservation, you might have a short wait for a table in one of the open seating dining rooms. Menus are varied and extensive in the main dining rooms, and the results are good to excellent. Vegetarian and healthy lifestyle options are always on the menu. A separate menu is designed for children.

Alternative restaurants are a staple throughout the fleet but vary by ship class. Grand-class and newer ships have upscale steak houses and Sabatini's, an Italian restaurant; both require reservations and carry an extra cover charge. *Sun Princess* offers a similar steak-house option, although it's in a sectioned-off area of the buffet restaurant. On *Caribbean, Crown, Emerald,* and *Ruby Princess*, a casual evening alternative is the Crab Shack—adjacent to the Lido buffet restaurant, it serves shellfish such as Bayou-style boiled crawfish, clams, and mussels. With a few breaks in service, Lido buffets on all ships are almost always open, and a pizzeria and grill offer casual daytime snack choices. Open 24 hours a day, the International Café located in the Atrium Piazza is the place for an ever-changing array of small bite meals. The fleet's patisseries and ice cream bars charge for specialty coffee, some pastries, and premium ice cream. A complimentary daily British-style pub lunch served in the ships' Wheelhouse Bar is available fleet-wide, with the exception of the *Sun Princess* and *Island Princess*.

Ultimate Balcony Dining—either a champagne breakfast or full-course dinner—is a full-service meal served on your cabin's balcony. The Chef's Table allows guests (for a fee) to dine on a special menu with wine pairings. After a meeting with the executive chef in the galley (and some champagne and appetizers), guests sit at a special table in the dining room. The chef joins them for dessert.

ENTERTAINMENT

The roster of adult activities still includes standbys like bingo and art auctions, but you'll also find guest lecturers, cooking classes, wine-tasting seminars, pottery workshops, and computer and digital photography classes. Nighttime production shows tend toward Broadway-style revues presented in the main show lounge, and performers might include comedians, magicians, jugglers, and acrobats. Live bands play a wide range of musical styles for dancing and listening, and each ship has a dance club. The cruise director's staff leads lively evenings of fun with passenger participation. At the conclusion of the second formal night, champagne trickles down over a champagne waterfall. Ladies are invited to join the maître d' to assist in the pouring for a great photo op.

FITNESS AND RECREATION

Spa rituals include a variety of massages, body wraps, and facials; numerous hair and nail services are offered in the salons. Both the salons and spas are operated by Steiner Leisure. For a half-day fee, escape to The Sanctuary—the adults-only haven—which offers a relaxing outdoor spa-inspired setting with signature beverages, light meals, massages, attentive service, and relaxing personal entertainment.

KNOWN FOR

- **Accessibility:** Princess is a top choice for travelers with disabilities because the ships and even shore excursions offer more choices for them.

- **Movies Under the Stars:** An innovative feature copied by other cruise lines, Princess was the first line to offer movies and other programming on giant poolside LED screens.

- **Relaxation:** Ships in the Princess fleet feature another cruise industry first—The Sanctuary, where adults can get away from it all, has become a signature element imitated by many other lines.

- **Sophistication:** Princess Cruises' ships range from midsize to megaship, but all have a sophisticated ambience.

- **Weddings:** Noted as the "Love Boats," Princess ships were the first at sea to offer captain-officiated weddings, and unlike most cruise lines they still do.

Top: Place a bet in the casino

Top: Sunset at sea
Middle: Morning stretch
Bottom: Freshwater
Jacuzzi

Modern exercise equipment, a jogging track, and basic fitness classes are available at no charge. There's a fee for personal training, body composition analysis, and specialized classes such as yoga and Pilates. Grand-class ships have a resistance pool so you can get your laps in effortlessly.

YOUR SHIPMATES

Princess Cruises attract mostly American passengers, ranging from their mid-thirties to mid-fifties. Families enjoy cruising together on the Princess fleet, particularly during holiday seasons and in summer months, when many children are onboard. Longer cruises, especially those on *Pacific Princess*, appeal to well-traveled retirees and couples who have the time.

DRESS CODE

Two formal nights are standard on seven-night cruises; an additional formal night may be scheduled on longer sailings. Men are encouraged to wear tuxedos, but dark suits are appropriate. All other evenings are casual, although jeans are discouraged, and it's requested that no shorts be worn in public areas after 6 pm.

JUNIOR CRUISERS

For young passengers ages 3 to 17, each Princess vessel (except *Pacific Princess*) has a playroom, teen center, and programs of supervised activities designed for different age groups: ages 3 to 7, 8 to 12, and 13 to 17. Activities to engage youngsters include arts and crafts, pool games, and scavenger hunts. Events such as dance parties, athletic contests, karaoke, and pizza parties occupy teenagers. Children also participate in learning programs focused on the environment and wildlife in areas where the ships sail.

Youth centers operate as usual during port days, including lunch with counselors. For an additional charge, group babysitting is available nightly from 10 pm until 1 am. Infants under 6 months are not permitted; private in-cabin babysitting is not available on any Princess

CHOOSE THIS LINE IF...

■ You're a traveler with a disability. Princess ships are some of the most accessible at sea.

■ You like to gamble but hate a smoke-filled casino. Princess casinos are no-smoking areas.

■ You want a balcony. Princess ships feature them in abundance at affordable rates.

vessel. Children under age 3 are welcome in the playrooms if supervised by a parent.

SERVICE

Professional service by an international staff is efficient and friendly. It's not uncommon to be greeted in passageways by smiling stewards who know your name.

TIPPING

A gratuity of $13.50 per person per day ($15.50 for passengers in suites and minisuites) is added to shipboard accounts for distribution to stewards and waitstaff. An automatic 15% is added to all bar tabs.

PAST PASSENGERS

Membership in the Captain's Circle is automatic following your first Princess cruise. All members receive a free subscription to *Captain's Circle*, a quarterly magazine, as well as discounts on selected cruises.

Perks are determined by the number of cruises or cruise days completed: Gold (one cruise), Ruby (31–50 cruise days), Platinum (51–150 cruise days), and Elite (151 and above cruise days). Benefits really begin to accrue once you've completed five cruises. Platinum members receive expedited check-in, a debarkation lounge to wait in on the ship, and, best of all, limited free Internet access during the cruise (150 minutes for 7 days). Elite benefits are even more lavish, with complimentary services such as a mini bar consisting of a selection of liquors, soft drinks, beer, still and sparkling water; deluxe canapés on formal nights; afternoon tea served in your stateroom; upgraded bathroom amenities; and complimentary laundry service.

HELPFUL HINTS

■ Princess Cruises pioneered the concept of affordable balcony accommodations and continues to lead the industry in that regard.

■ If you're unsure, select Traditional dining when you reserve your cruise; it is impossible to change from Anytime Dining to Traditional onboard, but it's easy to go the other way.

■ Princess Cruises is the only contemporary cruise line that offers deluxe Ultimate Balcony Dining—either an intimate breakfast or romantic dinner served by your own dedicated waiters on your stateroom balcony.

■ A Princess cruise can be enhanced by adding a Cruisetour, a five- to eight-day in-depth land tour, to your voyage to create a land-and-sea vacation.

3

PRINCESS CRUISES

DON'T CHOOSE THIS LINE IF...

■ You have a poor sense of direction. Most ships are very large.

■ You think Princess is still as depicted in *The Love Boat*. That was just a TV show, and it was more than three decades ago.

■ You're too impatient to stand in line or wait. Debarkation from the large ships can be lengthy.

CORAL-CLASS
Coral Princess, Island Princess

CREW MEMBERS	900
ENTERED SERVICE	2003
GROSS TONS	92,000
LENGTH	964
NUMBER OF CABINS	987
PASSENGER CAPACITY	1,970
WIDTH	106 feet

700 ft.
500 ft.
300 ft.

All the Personal Choice features attributed to the larger Grand-class ships were incorporated into the design of the slightly smaller Coral Class ships. The four-story atrium is similar to that on *Sun Princess*, but public rooms are mainly spread fore and aft on two lower decks.

CABINS

Layout: Stepped out in wedding-cake fashion, more than 83% of ocean-view staterooms include Princess Cruises' trademark private balconies. Even the least expensive inside categories have plentiful storage and a small seating area with a chair and table. Suites have two TVs, a seating area, a wet bar, a large walk-in closet, and a separate bathtub and shower. Minisuites have a separate seating area, two TVs, a walk-in closet, and a combination bathtub/shower.

Suites: Occupants of 16 suites receive complimentary Internet access, dry cleaning, and shoe polishing, afternoon tea and evening canapés delivered to their suites, and priority embarkation, disembarkation, and tendering privileges. An extended room service menu is also available for them, as are priority reservations for dining and shore excursions.

Amenities: Decorated in pastels and light-wood tones, typical staterooms have a safe, hair dryer, refrigerator, and bathrobes for use during the cruise. Bathrooms have shampoo, lotion, and bath gel.

Accessibility: Twenty staterooms are designed for wheelchair accessibility and range in size from 217 to 374 square feet, depending on category.

RESTAURANTS

Passengers may choose between traditional dinner seating times in one assigned dining room or open seating in the other formal dining room; breakfast and lunch are open seating. Alternative dinner options include reservations-only Sabatini's Italian Trattoria and Bayou Café & Steakhouse (both with an extra charge). With a few breaks in service, Lido buffets are almost always open. A pub lunch is served in the Wheelhouse Bar, and a pizzeria and grill offer casual daytime snack choices. The International Cafe serves light snacks, panini, and pastries, most of which are complimentary, although there is a charge for specialty coffees. The ice cream bar charges for premium ice cream. Ultimate Balcony Dining

Top: Fast-paced shows
Bottom: Plenty of locations on the ship to enjoy spectacular views

and Chef's Table options are available, as is afternoon tea, and 24-hour room service.

SPAS
The spa, which is operated by Steiner Leisure, offers a menu of massages, body wraps, and facials, including treatments specifically designed for men, teens, and couples. Acupuncture is also available. Thermal suites have relaxing aromatic wet and dry saunas and heated loungers and are complimentary for those in suites, but there is a fee for everyone else. Adults can escape to The Sanctuary, a relaxing outdoor spa-inspired setting for which there is also a fee. Complimentary to all are saunas adjacent to men's and women's changing rooms.

BARS AND ENTERTAINMENT
Nighttime production shows tend toward musical revues presented in the main show lounge; other performers might include comedians, magicians, jugglers, and acrobats. Live bands play a wide range of musical styles for dancing and listening in the lounges, and each ship has a dance club. The cruise director's staff leads lively evenings of fun with passenger participation. Movies Under the Stars with popcorn and other movie fare are a popular option.

PROS AND CONS
Pros: the pizzeria serves some of the best pizza at sea; cabins that sleep third and fourth passengers are numerous; the Fine Art Gallery is a dedicated area, so displays don't clutter other public spaces.

Cons: the library and card room often become noisy passageways; there are only 16 suites on each ship; engine pods on the funnel give the ships a futuristic space-age appearance but are mainly decorative.

Cabin Type	Size (sq. ft.)
Suite	470 sq. ft.
Minisuite	285–302 sq. ft.
Ocean View Balcony	217–232 sq. ft.
Deluxe	212 sq. ft.
Inside	156–166 sq. ft.
Ocean View Standard	162 sq. ft.

FAST FACTS

- 11 passenger decks
- 2 specialty restaurants, 2 dining rooms, buffet, ice cream parlor, pizzeria
- Wi-Fi, safe, refrigerator, DVD (some)
- 3 pools (1 indoor), children's pool
- fitness classes, gym, hot tubs, sauna, spa
- 7 bars, casino, 2 dance clubs, library, 2 showrooms, video game room
- children's programs
- dry cleaning, laundry facilities, laundry service
- Internet terminal
- no kids under 6 months, no-smoking cabins

Lavish buffets in Horizon Court

3 PRINCESS CRUISES

GRAND-CLASS
Grand Princess, Golden Princess, Star Princess

CREW MEMBERS	1,100, 1,100, 1,200
ENTERED SERVICE	1998, 2001, 2002
GROSS TONS	109,000
LENGTH	951 feet
NUMBER OF CABINS	1,300
PASSENGER CAPACITY	2,600
WIDTH	118 feet

700 ft.

500 ft.

300 ft.

When *Grand Princess* was introduced as the world's largest cruise ship in 1998, futuristic Skywalker's Disco hovered approximately 150 feet above the waterline, but in a dramatic—and fuel-saving—transformation, it was removed from *Grand Princess* in 2011 and replaced with a more conventional nightclub in the heart of the ship. Subsequent ships did not have the same design problem, so Skywalker's remains.

Like their predecessors, the interiors of Grand-class ships have splashy glamour in the sweeping staircases and marble-floor atriums. Surprisingly intimate for such large ships, human scale in public lounges is achieved by judicious placement of furniture as unobtrusive room dividers. The 300-square-foot Times Square–style LED screens that hover over the pools show up to seven movies or events daily.

CABINS
Layout: On these ships, 80% of the outside staterooms have balconies. The typical stateroom has a seating area with a chair and table; even the cheapest categories have ample storage. Minisuites have a separate seating area, a walk-in closet, a combination shower-tub, and a balcony, as well as two TVs. More deluxe suites have even more room, some with sofa beds. Two Family suites have interconnecting staterooms with a balcony that can sleep up to eight people (D105/D101 and D106/D102). Staterooms in a variety of categories will accommodate three and four people, and some adjacent cabins can be interconnected through interior doors or by unlocking doors in the balcony dividers.

Amenities: Decorated in attractive pastel hues, all cabins have a refrigerator, hair dryer, safe, and bathrobes to use during the cruise. Bathrooms have shampoo, lotion, and bath gel.

Accessibility: Twenty-eight staterooms are wheelchair accessible.

RESTAURANTS
Passengers choose between two assigned dinner seatings or open seating; breakfast and lunch are open seating. Alternative dinner options include the reservations-only Crown Grill and Sabatini's Italian restaurants (both with cover). Lido buffets are open around the clock. Crab Shack—adjacent to the Lido buffet—serves

Top: *Star Princess* at sea
Bottom: *Golden Princess* grand plaza atrium

shellfish for an extra charge. A pub lunch is served in the Wheelhouse Bar, and a pizzeria and grill offer casual daytime snack choices. The International Café serves light snacks, panini, and pastries, most of which are complimentary, although there is a charge for specialty coffees. The ice cream bar charges for premium ice cream. A wine bar serves extra-charge evening snacks and artisan cheeses. Ultimate Balcony Dining and Chef's Table options are available, as is afternoon tea and 24-hour room service.

SPAS

Spas operated by Steiner Leisure offer a menu of massages, body wraps, and facials, as well as treatments specifically designed for men, teens, and couples. Acupuncture is also available. Only *Star Princess* has a thermal suite (complimentary for those in suites but open to others for a fee), but saunas and steam rooms adjacent to men's and women's changing rooms are complimentary on all three ships. Adults can escape to The Sanctuary, a relaxing outdoor spa-inspired setting for which there is a fee.

BARS AND ENTERTAINMENT

Nighttime production shows presented in the main show lounge lean toward musical revues; guest performers might include comedians, magicians, jugglers, and acrobats. Live bands play a wide range of musical styles for dancing and listening in the lounges, and each ship has a disco. The cruise director's staff leads lively evenings of fun with passenger participation. Movies Under the Stars, where popcorn is free, is a popular evening option.

PROS AND CONS

Pros: Skywalker's Disco on *Golden Princess* and *Star Princess* is virtually deserted during the day, when it's the ideal quiet spot to watch the sea; self-service passenger laundry rooms have ironing stations; the nautical Wheelhouse Bar is a Princess tradition for cocktails and dancing.

Cons: sports bars get jam-packed—and stuffy—during big games; accommodations aft and above the Vista lounge are noisy when bands crank up the volume; minisuites don't include the perks offered to full suites.

Cabin Type	Size (sq. ft.)
Grand Suite	730/ 1,314* sq. ft.
Other Suites	468–591 sq. ft.
Family Suite	607 sq. ft.
Minisuite	323 sq. ft.
Ocean-View Balcony	232–274 sq. ft.
Standard	168 sq. ft.
Inside	160 sq. ft.

All dimensions include the square footage for balconies.

Grand Princess dimensions followed by *Golden Princess* and *Star Princess*

FAST FACTS

- 14 passenger decks
- 2 specialty restaurants, 3 dining rooms, buffet, ice cream parlor, pizzeria
- Wi-Fi, safe, refrigerator
- 4 pools (1 indoor), children's pool
- fitness classes, gym, hot tubs, sauna, spa, steam room
- 9 bars, casino, 2 dance clubs, library, 2 showrooms, video game room
- children's programs
- dry cleaning, laundry facilities, laundry service
- Internet terminal
- no kids under 6 months, no-smoking rooms

Grand-class balcony stateroom

PRINCESS CRUISES 3

GRAND-PLUS CLASS
Caribbean Princess, Crown Princess, Emerald Princess, Ruby Princess

CREW MEMBERS	
1,200, 1,200, 1,200, 1,225	
ENTERED SERVICE	
2004, 2006, 2007, 2008	
700 ft. **GROSS TONS**	
113,000	
LENGTH	
951 feet	
500 ft. **NUMBER OF CABINS**	
1,557, 1,538, 1,532, 1540	
PASSENGER CAPACITY	
3,080	
300 ft. **WIDTH**	
118 feet	

With dramatic atriums and Skywalker's Nightclub (the spoiler hovering 150 feet above the stern), *Caribbean Princess* is a supersize version of the older Grand-class vessels with an extra deck of passenger accommodations. Not quite identical to *Caribbean Princess*, the younger ships in the class, *Crown, Emerald,* and *Ruby Princess* have introduced more dining options. Several signature public spaces have been redesigned or relocated on these ships as well—the atrium on *Crown, Emerald,* and *Ruby Princess* resembles an open piazza and sidewalk café; Sabatini's Italian Trattoria is found on a top deck with views on three sides and alfresco dining; and Skywalker's Disco is forward near the funnel (where it's topped with a sports court). Inside spaces on all three vessels are quietly neutral, with touches of glamour in the sweeping staircases and marble-floor atriums. Surprising intimacy is achieved by the number of public rooms and restaurants that swallow up passengers.

CABINS
Layout: On these ships 80% of the outside staterooms have balconies. The typical stateroom has a seating area with a chair and table; all have ample storage. Minisuites have a separate seating area, a walk-in closet, a combination shower-tub, and a balcony, as well as two TVs. Larger deluxe suites have separate sitting rooms and walk-in closets, some with sofa beds. Two Family suites have interconnecting staterooms with a balcony and sleep up to eight (D105/D101 and D106/D102). Some staterooms can accommodate three and four, and some adjacent cabins can be connected through interior doors or balcony dividers.

Amenities: Decorated in attractive pastel hues, all cabins have a refrigerator, a hair dryer, a safe, and bathrobes to use during the cruise. Bathrooms have shampoo, lotion, and bath gel.

Accessibility: Twenty-five staterooms are wheelchair accessible on *Caribbean Princess* and *Crown Princess*; *Emerald Princess* and *Ruby Princess* have 31.

RESTAURANTS
Passengers choose between two assigned dinner seatings or open seating; breakfast and lunch are always open seating. Dinner options include reservations-only Sabatini's and Crown Grill (both with cover). Casual

Top: Movies Under the Stars
Bottom: Broadway-style revue

options with a cover charge are The Crab Shack—adjacent to the Lido buffet, which serves shellfish, and The Salty Dog Gastropub, where pub fare includes gourmet burgers. The International Café serves light snacks, panini, and pastries, most of which are complimentary, although there is a charge for specialty coffees. Lido buffets on all ships are almost always open. A pub lunch is served in the Wheelhouse Bar, and a pizzeria and grill offer casual daytime snack choices. The wine bars and ice cream bars charge for artisan cheeses and premium ice cream. Ultimate Balcony Dining and Chef's Table options are available, as are afternoon tea and 24-hour room service.

SPAS

Spas operated by Steiner Leisure offer the standard treatments, including a variety of massages, body wraps, and facials, as well as some designed specifically for men, teens, and couples. Medi-Spa treatments are also available. The spas' thermal suites have relaxing aromatic wet and dry saunas and heated loungers that are complimentary for those in suites, but a fee is charged for everyone else. Complimentary to all are saunas and steam rooms adjacent to men's and women's changing rooms.

BARS AND ENTERTAINMENT

Nighttime production shows tend toward musical revues presented in the main show lounge, and performers might include comedians, magicians, jugglers, and acrobats. Live bands play a wide range of musical styles for dancing and listening in the lounges and each ship has a dance club. The cruise director's staff leads lively evenings of fun with passenger participation. Movies Under the Stars with popcorn and other movie fare are a popular option.

PROS AND CONS

Pros: Movies Under the Stars on the huge poolside screen have proven to be a big hit; the Wheelhouse Bar serves complimentary pub lunch at noon; the adults-only Sanctuary is a private deck with posh loungers for a fee.

Cons: priority dining reservations are extended only to Elite Captain's Circle members; the terrace overlooking the aft pool is a quiet spot after dark, but the nearest bar often closes early; opt for Anytime Dining and you may encounter a wait for a table.

Cabin Type	Size (sq. ft.)
Grand Suite	1,279 sq. ft.
Other Suites	461–689 sq. ft.
Family Suite	607 sq. ft.
Minisuite	324 sq. ft.
Ocean View with Balcony	233–285 sq. ft.
Ocean View	158–182 sq. ft.
Inside	163 sq. ft.

FAST FACTS

- 15 passenger decks
- 2 specialty restaurants, 3 dining rooms, buffet, ice cream parlor, pizzeria
- Wi-Fi, safe, refrigerator, DVD (some)
- 4 pools (1 indoor), children's pool
- fitness classes, gym, hot tubs, sauna, spa, steam room
- 9 bars, casino, 2 dance clubs, library, 2 showrooms, video game room
- children's programs
- dry cleaning, laundry facilities, laundry service
- Internet terminal
- no kids under 6 months, no-smoking cabins

Sailing at sunset

REGENT SEVEN SEAS CRUISES

This luxurious fleet of vessels owned by Norwegian Cruise Line Holdings offers a nearly all-inclusive cruise experience in sumptuous, contemporary surroundings. The line has generous staterooms with abundant amenities, a variety of dining options, and superior

The end of a perfect day

lecture and enrichment programs. Guests are greeted with champagne on boarding and find an all-inclusive beverage policy that offers not only soft drinks and bottled water, but also cocktails and select wines at all bars and restaurants throughout the ships.

☎ *877/505–5370*
⊕ *www.rssc.com*
☞ *Cruise Style: Luxury.*

Round-trip air, ground transfers, gratuities, and shore excursions in every port are included in the cruise fare. Onboard, casinos are more akin to Monaco than Las Vegas. All ships display tasteful and varied art collections, including pieces that are for sale.

FOOD
Menus include the usual beef Wellington and Maine lobster, but in the hands of Regent Seven Seas chefs the results are some of the most outstanding meals at sea. Specialty dining varies within the fleet, with the sophisticated Chartreuse, featuring the most authentic modern French cuisine to be found outside of Paris, on all ships except *Seven Seas Navigator*. Prime 7, on all ships, is a contemporary adaptation of the classic American steak house offering fresh, distinctive decor and an innovative menu of the finest prime-aged steak and chops, along with fresh seafood and poultry specialties. In addition, Mediterranean-influenced bistro dinners that need no reservations are served in Sette Mari at La Veranda, the venue that is the daytime casual Lido buffet restaurant. Coffee Connection serves light breakfast and lunch as well as snacks during the day. The Pool Grill is a come-as-you-are option that serves grilled burgers, seafood, salad, milkshakes, and ice cream.

Wine Connoisseurs Dinners are offered occasionally on longer cruises. Each course on the degustation menu is complemented by a wine pairing. The cost varies according to the special vintage wines that are included.

Room-service menus are fairly extensive, and you can also order directly from the restaurant menus during regular serving hours.

Although special dietary requirements should be relayed to the cruise line before sailing, general considerations such as vegetarian, low-salt, or low-cholesterol food requests can be satisfied onboard the ships simply by speaking with the dining room staff. Wines chosen to complement dinner menus are freely poured each evening.

ENTERTAINMENT

Most sailings host guest lecturers, including historians, anthropologists, naturalists, and diplomats, and there are often discussions and workshops. Spotlight cruises center around popular pastimes and themes, such as food and wine, photography, history, archaeology, literature, performing arts, design and cultures, active exploration and wellness, antiques, jewelry and shopping, the environment, and marine life. All passengers have access to these unique experiences onboard and on shore.

Activities and entertainment are tailored for each of the line's distinctive ships with the tastes of sophisticated passengers in mind. Don't expect napkin-folding demonstrations or nonstop action. Production revues, cabaret acts, concert-style piano performances, solo performers, and comedians may be featured in show lounges, with combos playing for listening and dancing in lounges and bars throughout the ships.

FITNESS AND RECREATION

Although gyms and exercise areas are well equipped, these are not large ships, so the facilities tend to be limited in size. Each ship has a jogging track, and the larger ones feature a variety of sports courts. The spas and salons aboard Regent Seven Seas ships are operated by Canyon Ranch SpaClub, which offers an array of customizable treatments and services.

YOUR SHIPMATES

Regent Seven Seas Cruises are inviting to active, affluent, well-traveled couples ranging from their late-thirties to retirees who enjoy the ship's chic ambience and destination-rich itineraries. Longer cruises attract veteran passengers in the over-sixty age group.

3

Top: Sunrise jog
Bottom: *Seven Seas Navigator*

Top: Fitness center
Middle: Pool decks are
never crowded
Bottom: Pampering in the
Carita of Paris spa

DRESS CODE

Elegant casual is the dress code for most nights; formal and semiformal attire is optional on sailings of 16 nights or longer, but it's no longer required. It's requested that dress codes be observed in public areas after 6 pm.

JUNIOR CRUISERS

Regent Seven Seas' vessels are adult-oriented and do not have dedicated children's facilities. However, a Club Mariner youth program for children ages 5 to 8, 9 to 12, and 13 to 17 is offered on select sailings, both during summer months and during school holiday periods. Supervised by counselors, the organized, educational activities focus on nature and the heritage of the ship's destinations. Activities, including games, craft projects, movies, and food fun, are organized to ensure that every child has a memorable experience. Teens are encouraged to help counselors select the activities they prefer. Only infants that are one year of age before the first day of the cruise may sail.

SERVICE

The efforts of a polished, unobtrusive staff go almost unnoticed, yet special requests are handled with ease. Butlers provide an additional layer of personal service to guests in the top-category suites.

TIPPING

Gratuities are included in the fare, and none are expected. To show their appreciation, passengers may elect to make a contribution to a crew welfare fund that benefits the ship's staff.

PAST PASSENGERS

Membership in the Seven Seas Society is automatic on completion of a Regent Seven Seas cruise. Members receive discounted cruise fare savings on select sailings, exclusive shipboard and shore-side special events on select sailings, a Seven Seas Society recognition cocktail party on every sailing, and *Inspirations* newsletter highlighting special events, sailings, and destination- and travel-related information. The tiered program offers

CHOOSE THIS LINE IF...

■ You want to learn the secrets of cooking like a Cordon Bleu chef (for a charge, of course).

■ You don't want the hassle of signing bar tabs or extra expense of shore excursions.

■ A really high-end spa experience is on your agenda.

rewards based on the number of nights you have sailed with RSSC. The more you sail, the more you accrue. Bronze benefits that include a cocktail reception and savings offers are awarded to members with 7 to 20 nights. From 21 through 74 nights, Silver members also receive limited free pressing, and an hour of free phone time. From 75 through 199 nights, Gold members are given priority disembarkation at some ports, free Wi-Fi, an additional two hours of complimentary phone time, more complimentary pressing, an exclusive Gold, Platinum & Titanium activity aboard or ashore on every sailing, and priority reservations at restaurants and spas. From 200 through 399 nights, Platinum members can add complimentary air deviation services (one time per sailing), nine hours of complimentary phone use, and unlimited free pressing and laundry services. Titanium members who have sailed 400 or more nights also get free dry cleaning and free transfers.

HELPFUL HINTS

■ Other luxury lines don't always include round-trip air, ground transfers, and unlimited shore excursions in every port of call.

■ Regent Seven Seas ships offer all-suite accommodations.

■ Regent Choice Shore Excursions carry a supplement, but they delve much deeper into a region's culture and history.

■ Multinight pre- and post-cruise land programs are available to extend your cruise vacation.

■ Regent Seven Seas ships are luxurious but not stuffy, and there's a "block party" on every cruise where passengers are invited to meet their neighbors in adjacent suites.

DON'T CHOOSE THIS LINE IF...

■ Connecting cabins are a must. Very few are available, and only the priciest cabins connect.

■ You can't imagine a cruise without the hoopla of games in the pool; these ships are much more discreet.

■ You don't want to dress up for dinner. Most passengers still dress more formally than on other lines.

SEVEN SEAS MARINER/VOYAGER
Seven Seas Mariner, Seven Seas Voyager

CREW MEMBERS	445, 447
ENTERED SERVICE	2001, 2003
GROSS TONS	50,000, 46,000
LENGTH	709 feet, 670 feet
NUMBER OF CABINS	350
PASSENGER CAPACITY	700
WIDTH	93 feet, 95 feet

700 ft.
500 ft.
300 ft.

The world's first all-balcony, all-suite ships continue the Regent Seven Seas tradition of offering posh accommodations on vessels with generous space for every passenger.

Lounges are predominantly decorated in soothing neutrals and cool marine blues with splashes of bold color, soft leather, and glass-and-marble accents. Even areas that can accommodate all (or nearly all) passengers at once, including the formal dining room and show lounge, appear intimate. Good design elements don't hint at their size, and indoor spaces seem smaller than they actually are. With so much room, public areas are seldom crowded, and you won't have to hunt for a deck chair by the swimming pool. The two-tiered Constellation Theater has a full-size proscenium stage, where cabaret revues, headline entertainers, and Broadway-inspired shows are presented.

CABINS

Layout: Rich-textured fabrics and warm wood finishes add a touch of coziness to the larger-than-usual suite accommodations. Every suite has a vanity-desk, walk-in closet, and seating area with sofa, chairs, and table. Marble bathrooms have a separate tub and shower. Most balconies are about 50 square feet.

Top-Category Suites: The top three suite categories feature Bose music systems, an iPad, and an iPod docking station. Butler service is available for passengers in Master, Grand, Navigator, and Penthouse suites. The top-category Master suites have a separate sitting–dining room, two bedrooms (each has its own TV), a powder room, and two full bathrooms (the master bath has dual vanities, a bidet, separate shower, and whirlpool tub), but some do not have the powder room or whirlpool tub.

Amenities: All suites have an entertainment center with CD/DVD player, stocked refrigerator, stocked bar, safe, hair dryer, and fine linens and duvets on the bed. Passengers in Concierge suites and higher receive 15 minutes of free ship-to-shore phone time and unlimited Internet access of up to four logins for four devices, per suite. Bathrooms have robes and toiletries, including shampoo, lotion, and bath gel.

Top: *Seven Seas Mariner* observation lounge
Bottom: The Library on *Seven Seas Mariner*

Accessibility: Four suites are designed for wheelchair accessibility and are equipped with showers only.

RESTAURANTS

Three restaurants offer open-seating dining. In addition to Compass Rose, the main dining room, which serves breakfast, lunch, and dinner, evening choices include the French restaurant Chartreuse (reservations required); classic steak house Prime 7 (reservations required); and La Veranda, the daytime buffet for breakfast and lunch that's converted to Mediterranean bistro for dinner. Wines are chosen to complement each night's menu, and there is no charge for any specialty dining. At least once during each cruise, dinner is served alfresco on the pool deck. In addition to the buffet, Coffee Connection serves light breakfast and lunch as well as snacks during the day; an additional choice for casual lunch and snacks is the poolside grill. Afternoon tea is served daily, and room service is available 24 hours. Dinner can be ordered from the main dining room menu during restaurant hours and served en suite, course by course.

SPAS

Operated by Canyon Ranch SpaClub, the spas on these ships offer an array of massages, facials, and body wraps utilizing organic and natural materials that can be individually customized. Guests can also enjoy complimentary aromatic steam rooms infused with pure plant essences or Finnish-style saunas.

BARS/ENTERTAINMENT

Dining and socializing are major evening pursuits, and there's music for dancing before and after dinner, as well as deck parties in fine weather and even a late-night disco. Dance hosts are on hand to lead unaccompanied ladies on the dance floor. The main show lounge features small-scale production shows; guest entertainers range from classical to modern vocalists and musicians.

PROS AND CONS

Pros: after an effortless check-in and champagne greeting, you are escorted to your suite; self-service laundries with ironing stations are complimentary; every stateroom is a suite, and every suite has a balcony.

Cons: seasonal kids' programs take place in unused public rooms; specialty dining is popular and should be booked online before the cruise; few organized activities are scheduled, so be prepared to make your own fun.

Cabin Type	Size (sq. ft.)
Master Suite	1,204 sq. ft. (Mariner), 1,152–1,216 sq. ft. (Voyager)
Grand Suite	903 sq. ft. (Mariner), 753 sq. ft. (Voyager)
Seven Seas Suite	441–561 sq. ft.
Other Suites	320–650 sq. ft.
Deluxe Suite	252 sq. ft. (Mariner), 306 sq. ft. (Voyager)

FAST FACTS

- 9 passenger decks
- 2 specialty restaurants, dining room, buffet, ice cream parlor, pizzeria
- Wi-Fi, safe, refrigerator, DVD
- pool
- fitness classes, gym, hot tubs, sauna, spa, steam room
- 5 bars, casino, dance club, library, showroom
- children's programs
- dry-cleaning, laundry facilities, laundry service
- Internet terminal
- no-smoking cabins

Sailing among the icebergs

ROYAL CARIBBEAN INTERNATIONAL

Big, bigger, biggest! Royal Caribbean has the largest modern mega cruise liners in the world, as well as some of the most innovative technology on its newest ships, from robot bartenders to the fastest Wi-Fi at sea. Its fleet of 25 and counting are all-around favorites of

Adventure of the Seas solarium

passengers—arguably the most multigenerational (and Millennial) crowd at sea—who enjoy traditional cruising ambience with a touch of daring and whimsy. Each ship in the fleet has action-packed activities such as surfing pools, rock-climbing walls, and on the newest ships, skydiving simulators, and 10-story slides.

☎ 305/539–6000, 800/327–6700
⊕ www.royalcaribbean.com
☞ Cruise Style: Mainstream.

Expansive multideck atriums and promenades, as well as the generous use of brass and floor-to-ceiling glass windows, give each vessel a sense of spaciousness and style. The action is nonstop in casinos and dance clubs after dark, while daytime hours are filled with poolside games and traditional cruise activities. Port talks tend to lean heavily on shopping recommendations and the sale of shore excursions.

FOOD

Dining is an international experience, with nightly changing themes and cuisines from around the world. Passenger preference for casual attire and a resort-like atmosphere has prompted the cruise line to add laid-back alternatives to the formal dining rooms: the Windjammer Café and, on certain ships, Johnny Rockets Diner. Royal Caribbean offers you the choice of early or late dinner seating and has introduced an open seating program fleet-wide.

Room service is available 24 hours, but for orders between midnight and 5 am there's a $3.95 service charge, not to mention a limited menu.

Royal Caribbean has introduced a more upscale and intimate dinner experience in the form of an Italian specialty restaurant and/or a steak house on all ships and more specialty dining options on the newest ships, such as the Asian-inspired Izumi and imaginative cuisine of Wonderland.

ENTERTAINMENT

A variety of lounges and high-energy stage shows draws passengers of all ages out to mingle and dance the night away. Production extravaganzas showcase singers and dancers in lavish costumes. Comedians, acrobats, magicians, jugglers, and solo entertainers fill show lounges on nights when the ships' companies aren't performing. Broadway shows are featured on the newest ships. Professional ice shows are a highlight of cruises on Voyager-, Freedom-, and Oasis-class ships—the only ships at sea with ice-skating rinks.

FITNESS AND RECREATION

Royal Caribbean has pioneered such new and previously unheard-of features as rock-climbing walls, ice-skating rinks, and even the first self-leveling pool tables on a cruise ship. Interactive water parks, boxing rings, surfing simulators, and cantilevered whirlpools suspended 112 feet above the ocean made their debuts on the Freedom-class ships.

Facilities vary by ship class, but all Royal Caribbean ships have state-of-the-art exercise equipment, jogging tracks, and rock-climbing walls; passengers can work out independently or in classes guaranteed to sweat off extra calories. Some exercise classes are included in the fare, but there's a fee for specialized spin, yoga, and Pilates classes, as well as the services of a personal trainer. Spas and salons are top-notch, with full menus of day spa–style treatments and services for pampering and relaxation for adults and teens.

YOUR SHIPMATES

Royal Caribbean cruises have a broad appeal for active couples and singles, mostly in their thirties to fifties. Families are partial to the newer vessels that have larger staterooms, huge facilities for children and teens, and seemingly endless choices of activities and dining options.

DRESS CODE

Two formal nights are standard on seven-night cruises; one formal night is the norm on shorter sailings. Men may wear tuxedos, but dark suits or sport coats and ties are more prevalent. All other evenings are casual, although jeans are discouraged in restaurants. It's requested that no shorts be worn in public areas after

KNOWN FOR

■ **A Step Above:** Offering the same value as other mainstream lines, Royal Caribbean's ships are more sophisticated than its competitors'.

■ **Big Ships:** The Royal Caribbean fleet boasts the world's largest cruise ships.

■ **Extra Charges:** You will have to break out your wallet quite often once onboard, as the cruise fare is far from inclusive.

■ **Recreation:** Gym rats and sports and fitness buffs find multiple facilities available to satisfy their active lifestyles while at sea.

■ **Something for Everyone:** With activities that appeal to a broad demographic, Royal Caribbean is a top choice for multigenerational cruise vacations.

Top: Adventure Beach for kids Bottom: Voyager-class interior stateroom

3

Top: Miniature golf
Middle: *Adventure of the Seas* Bottom: *Serenade of the Seas* rock-climbing wall

6 pm, although there are passengers who can't wait to change into them after dinner.

JUNIOR CRUISERS

Supervised age-appropriate activities are designed for children ages 3 through 17; babysitting services are available as well. Children are assigned to the Adventure Ocean youth program by age. They must be at least three years old and toilet-trained to participate (children who are in diapers and pull-ups or who are not toilet-trained are not allowed in swimming pools or whirlpools; however, they may use the Baby Splash Zone designated for them on the *Freedom, Liberty, Independence, Oasis,* and *Allure of the Seas*). Youngsters who wish to join a different age group must participate in one daytime and one night activity session with their proper age group first; the manager will then make the decision based on their maturity level.

Interactive 45-minute Aqua Babies and Aqua Tots play sessions for children ages 6 months to 36 months are hosted by youth staff members; these programs were designed by early childhood development experts for parents and their babies and toddlers, and teach life skills through playtime activities. Nurseries have been added for babies 6 to 36 months old on select ships, with drop-off options during the day and evening—and if parents supply diapers, attendants will change them. There is an hourly fee, and a limited number of babies and toddlers can be accommodated at a time.

A teen center with a disco is an adult-free gathering spot that will satisfy even the pickiest teenagers.

SERVICE

Service on Royal Caribbean ships is friendly but inconsistent. Assigned meal seatings assure that most passengers get to know the waiters and their assistants, who in turn get to know the passengers' likes and dislikes; however, that can lead to a level of familiarity that is uncomfortable for some people. Most ships have

CHOOSE THIS LINE IF...

■ You want to see the sea from atop a rock wall—it's one of the few activities on these ships that's free.

■ You're active and adventurous. Even if your traveling companion isn't, there's an energetic staff onboard to cheer you on.

■ You want your space. There's plenty of room to roam; quiet nooks and crannies are there if you look.

a concierge lounge for the use of suite occupants and top-level past passengers.

TIPPING

Tips that are not prepaid when the cruise is booked are automatically added to shipboard accounts in the amount of $14.50 per person, per day ($17.50 for suites), to be shared by dining and housekeeping staff. A 15% gratuity is automatically added to all bar tabs and spa and salon services.

PAST PASSENGERS

After one cruise, you can enroll in the Crown & Anchor Society. Tiered membership levels are achieved according to a point system. One Cruise Point is earned for every night you sail and double the points are earned when you book a suite. All members receive the *Crown & Anchor* magazine and have access to the member section on the Royal Caribbean website. All members receive an Ultimate Value Booklet and an invitation to a welcome-back party. Platinum members also have the use of a private departure lounge and receive priority check-in (where available), the onboard use of robes during the cruise, an invitation to an exclusive onboard event, and complimentary custom air arrangements. As points are added to your status, the benefits increase to Emerald, Diamond, Diamond Plus, and Pinnacle Club. For instance, Diamond and above receive such perks as access to a private lounge, select behind-the-scenes tours, and priority seating for certain events.

DON'T CHOOSE THIS LINE IF...

■ Patience is not one of your virtues. Lines are not uncommon.

■ You want to do your own laundry. There are no self-service facilities on any Royal Caribbean ships.

■ You don't want to hear announcements. There are a lot on Royal Caribbean ships.

RADIANCE-CLASS
Radiance of the Seas, Brilliance of the Seas, Serenade of the Seas, Jewel of the Seas

CREW MEMBERS	857
ENTERED SERVICE	2001, 2002, 2003, 2004
GROSS TONS	90,090
LENGTH	962 feet
NUMBER OF CABINS	1,056
PASSENGER CAPACITY	2,112 (2,501 max)
WIDTH	106 feet

700 ft.

500 ft.

300 ft.

Considered by many people to be the most beautiful vessels in the Royal Caribbean fleet, Radiance-class ships are large but sleek and swift, with sun-filled interiors and panoramic elevators that span 10 decks along the ships' exteriors.

CABINS
Layout: With a high percentage of outside cabins, standard staterooms are bright and cheery as well as roomy. Nearly three-quarters of the outside cabins have private balconies. Every cabin has adequate closet and drawer/shelf storage, as well as bathroom shelves.

Suites: All full suites and Family suites have private balconies and include concierge service. Top-category suites have wet bars, separate living-dining areas, multiple bathrooms, entertainment centers with flat-screen TVs, DVD players, and stereos. Some bathrooms have twin sinks, steam showers, and whirlpool tubs. Junior suites have a seating area, vanity area, and bathroom with a tub.

Amenities: Light-wood cabinetry, a small refrigerator-minibar, Wi-Fi connection, a vanity-desk, a TV, a safe, a hair dryer, and a seating area with sofa, chair, and table are typical Radiance-class features in all categories. Bathroom extras include shampoo and bath gel.

Accessibility: Fifteen staterooms are designed for wheelchair accessibility on *Radiance* and *Brilliance*; 19 on *Serenade* and *Jewel*.

RESTAURANTS
The double-deck-high formal dining room serves open seating breakfast and lunch; dinner is served in two assigned seatings, but open seating is an option. For a more upscale dinner, each ship has an Italian restaurant and a steak house. All but *Jewel* have an Asian restaurant; *Radiance* has Samba Grill, a Brazilian-style steak house. There is a supplement charged for specialty dining, and reservations are required. The casual Lido buffet serves nearly around the clock for breakfast, lunch, dinner, and snacks. Seaview Café is open for quick lunches and dinners on *Jewel of the Seas*. The Solarium features Park Café for casual deli-style fare, and *Radiance* also serves custom hot dogs at Boardwalk Doghouse. The coffee bar features specialty coffees and pastries, for which there is a charge. Room service is available 24 hours; however there is a delivery charge after midnight.

Top: Pool deck
Bottom: Shared moments on your personal balcony

SPAS

The full-service spa operated by Steiner Leisure offers an extensive treatment menu including facials, tooth whitening, body wraps and scrubs. Spa rituals also include treatments designed especially for men and teens. There are thermal suites for a fee as well as complimentary saunas, and steam rooms are located in men's and women's changing rooms.

BARS AND ENTERTAINMENT

Nightlife options range from Broadway-style productions in the main show lounge to movies in the cinema or on the outdoor screen overlooking the pool. Bars and lounges include a piano bar and wine bar, and most have music for dancing or listening. There's also a pub or sports bar and a lounge for billiards. Look high above for aerial performances in the central atriums on these ships.

PROS AND CONS

Pros: aft on deck 6, four distinct lounges and a billiard room form a clubby adult entertainment center; spacious family ocean-view cabins sleep up to six people; ships offer a wide range of family-friendly activities and games.

Cons: upgraded features of the fleet are not consistent throughout this ship class, so check before booking; dining options that charge have replaced some that were previously complimentary; libraries are tiny and poorly stocked for ships this size.

Cabin Type	Size (sq. ft.)
Royal Suite	1,001 sq. ft.
Royal Family Suite	533–586 sq. ft.
Owner's Suite	512 sq. ft.
Grand Suite	358–384 sq. ft.
Family Ocean View	319 sq. ft.
Junior Suites	293 sq. ft.
Superior Ocean View	204 sq. ft.
Deluxe Ocean View	179 sq. ft.
Large Ocean View	170 sq. ft.
Interior	165 sq. ft.

FAST FACTS

■ 12 passenger decks

■ 2 specialty restaurants on *Jewel*, 4 on *Serenade* and *Brilliance*, 5 on *Radiance*; dining room, buffet, pizzeria

■ Wi-Fi, safe, refrigerator, DVD (some)

■ 2 pools (1 indoor), children's pool

■ fitness classes, gym, hot tubs, sauna, spa, steam room

■ 11 bars, casino, dance club, library, showroom, video game room

■ children's programs

■ dry cleaning, laundry service

■ Internet terminal

■ no-smoking cabins

VOYAGER-CLASS
Voyager of the Seas, Explorer of the Seas, Adventure of the Seas, Navigator of the Seas, Mariner of the Seas

CREW MEMBERS	1,185
ENTERED SERVICE	1999, 2000, 2001, 2002, 2003
GROSS TONS	142,000
LENGTH	1,020 Feet
NUMBER OF CABINS	1,557
PASSENGER CAPACITY	3,114 (3,835 max)
WIDTH	158 feet

700 ft.
500 ft.
300 ft.

A truly impressive building program introduced one of these gigantic Voyager-class ships per year over a five-year period. With their rock-climbing walls, ice-skating rinks, in-line skating tracks, miniature golf, and multiple dining venues, they are destinations in their own right. Sports enthusiasts will be thrilled with nonstop daytime action.

The unusual horizontal, multiple-deck promenade-atriums on Voyager-class vessels can stage some of the pageantry for which Royal Caribbean is noted. Fringed with boutiques, bars, and even coffee shops, the mall-like expanses set the stage for evening parades and events, as well as spots to simply kick back for some people watching.

Other public rooms are equally dramatic. Though it's considered to be three separate dining rooms, the triple-deck height of the single space is stunning. These ships not only carry a lot of people, but carry them well. Space is abundant, and crowding is seldom an issue.

CABINS
Layout: As on other Royal Caribbean ships, cabins are bright and cheerful. Although more than 60% are outside—and a hefty 75% of those have private veran-das—there are still plenty of bargain inside cabins, some with a bowed window for a view overlooking the action-packed promenade. Cabins in every category have adequate closet and drawer/shelf storage and bathroom shelves. Junior suites have a seating area, vanity area, and bathroom with bathtub. Family ocean-view cabins with a window sleep up to six people and can accommodate a roll-away bed and/or crib, have two twin beds (convertible to a queen), and additional bunk beds in a separate area, a separate seating area with a sofa bed, a vanity area, and a private bathroom with shower.

Amenities: Wood cabinetry, a small refrigerator-minibar, broadband Internet connection, a vanity-desk, a TV, a safe, a hair dryer, and a seating area with sofa, chair, and table are typical Voyager-class features in all categories. Bathrooms have shampoo and bath gel.

Accessibility: Twenty-six staterooms are designed for wheelchair accessibility.

Top: *Voyager of the Sea* main theater
Bottom: Playing roulette in the casino

RESTAURANTS

Triple-deck-high formal dining rooms serve open seating breakfast and lunch; dinner is served in two evening assigned seatings or open seating My Timing Dining. For a more upscale dinner, each ship has an Italian specialty restaurant; *Mariner* and *Navigator* also have a steak house. Both specialty restaurants charge a supplement and require reservations. The casual Lido buffet offers service nearly around the clock for meals and snacks, including dinner; *Mariner*, *Explorer*, and *Navigator* also serve Asian fare in their Jade section. Johnny Rockets is a popular option for casual meals, though it also has a separate charge. In the promenade are a pizzeria, coffee bar, and Ben & Jerry's ice cream, which charges for frozen treats. All but *Mariner* have Park Café, which serves casual fare. Room service is available 24 hours; however, there is a delivery charge after midnight.

SPAS

The full-service spa operated by Steiner Leisure offers an extensive treatment menu including facials, tooth whitening, body wraps and scrubs, massages, acupuncture, and FDA-approved Medi-Spa treatments performed by trained physicians. Spa rituals also include treatments designed especially for men and teens. While there are no thermal suites, complimentary saunas and steam rooms are located in men's and women's changing rooms.

BARS/ENTERTAINMENT

Nightlife runs the gamut from Broadway-style production shows to bars and lounges that include a piano bar, pub, wine bar, and disco, and on *Mariner* and *Navigator*, a Latin-themed bar. Music abounds for dancing or listening, or you can choose to end the evening with a movie on the outdoor screen overlooking the pool.

PROS AND CONS

Pros: Royal Promenade may elicit the biggest "Wow!" onboard when a parade is center stage; professional ice-skating performances are staged twice during each cruise; equipment to participate in sports activities is provided at no additional charge.

Cons: with the exception of the gym and some fitness classes, nearly everything else onboard carries a price tag; although there is no charge to attend, you must get tickets for the ice-skating shows; smokers may be frustrated to find that smoking is prohibited in cabins, on balconies, and in most indoor areas.

Cabin Type	Size (sq. ft.)
Royal Suite	1,188–1,325 sq. ft.
Other Suites*	277–618 sq. ft.
Superior/Deluxe/Family Ocean View**	173–328 sq. ft.
Large Ocean View	211 sq. ft.
Standard Ocean View	161–180 sq. ft.
Interior	153–167 sq. ft.

*Owner's (506–618 sq. ft.), Grand (381–390 sq. ft.), Royal family (512–610 sq. ft.), Junior (277–299 sq. ft.).

**Superior (202–206 sq. ft.), Deluxe (173–184 sq. ft.), Family (265–328 sq. ft.).

FAST FACTS

- 14 passenger decks
- 1 specialty restaurant (2 on *Mariner* and *Navigator*), dining room, buffet, ice cream parlor, pizzeria
- Internet, Wi-Fi, safe, refrigerator, DVD (some)
- 3 pools, children's pool (only *Voyager*, *Explorer*, and *Adventure*)
- fitness classes, gym, hot tubs, sauna, spa, steam room
- 12 bars, casino, 2 dance clubs, library, 3 showrooms, video game room
- children's programs
- dry-cleaning, laundry service
- Internet terminal
- no-smoking cabins

QUANTAM-CLASS
Ovation of the Seas

CREW MEMBERS	1,300
ENTERED SERVICE	2016
GROSS TONS	168,666
LENGTH	1,145 feet
NUMBER OF CABINS	2,090
PASSENGER CAPACITY	4,180
WIDTH	134 ft.

700 ft.

500 ft.

300 ft.

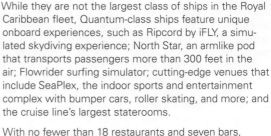

While they are not the largest class of ships in the Royal Caribbean fleet, Quantum-class ships feature unique onboard experiences, such as Ripcord by iFLY, a simulated skydiving experience; North Star, an armlike pod that transports passengers more than 300 feet in the air; Flowrider surfing simulator; cutting-edge venues that include SeaPlex, the indoor sports and entertainment complex with bumper cars, roller skating, and more; and the cruise line's largest staterooms.

With no fewer than 18 restaurants and seven bars, including Royal Caribbean's Bionic Bar with robotic bartenders, these ships hit the mark to satisfy a wide variety of tastes. There is plenty to like about the open spaces on the ship, including pools, hot tubs, rock-climbing walls, and a jogging track high above the ship with unobstructed views of the sea.

CABINS
Layout: A dizzying number of accommodations options can be narrowed down to inside cabins, ocean view cabins (with or without a balcony), junior suites, suites, and loft-style suites. Many cabins are adjoining and some are designated as family accommodations. For solo cruisers, there are studio cabins in a variety of locations from inside to those with a balcony. Standard accommodations feature small sitting areas, desk/vanity, TV, hair dryer, refrigerator, and safe. Storage is adequate, but can be tight for more than two people. Inside cabins all feature a "virtual balcony" with a live image of the view outside the ship projected to an inside wall.

Suites: Suite and junior suite passengers receive special amenities, such as bathrobes, coffee and tea service, and a suite concierge for special requests. Ideal for families, the multibedroom loft suites span two decks and can accommodate four to six guests. Spa Junior Suite bathrooms have rain showerheads and separate tubs and have a split-bath arrangement with toilet and sink separate from the shower and bath area.

Accessibility: Thirty-four staterooms are wheelchair accessible.

RESTAURANTS
The four main dining rooms serve open seating breakfast and lunch; dinner is served in either assigned or open seating. Several specialty

Top: *Ovation of the Seas*
Bottom: *Music Hall,
Ovation
of the Seas*

restaurants—Wonderland imaginative cuisine, Jamie's Italian, Michael's Genuine Pub, Chops Grille, Izumi Japanese, and the Chef's Table charge either à la carte or a fixed fee and most require reservations. For casual and complimentary fare, the Windjammer Marketplace buffet restaurant is open nearly around the clock for breakfast, lunch, dinner, and snacks; Solarium Bistro serves light spa cuisine for breakfast and lunch; The Cafe@Two70 serves casual bites all day; Sorrento's pizza serves slices of pie; the Café Promenade offers freshly brewed coffee, pastries or small sandwiches. Room service is available 24 hours a day; however, there is a delivery charge after midnight.

SPAS

The full-service spa offers a treatment menu including facials, teeth whitening, body wraps, massages, and FDA-approved Medi-Spa treatments. There is a tiny thermal suite with six heated tiled chairs, a rain shower, a sauna, and a steam room.

BARS/ENTERTAINMENT

Nightlife runs the gamut from a Broadway show to the acrobatic song-and dance cabaret revues in Two70. In the Music Hall you can dance or listen to tribute bands, enjoy drinks, or participate in karaoke. Although only a few bars don't double as entertainment spaces or restaurants, the somewhat gimmicky Bionic Bar is where bartending "robots" mix up drinks ordered via tablet.

PROS AND CONS

Pros: accommodations, including connecting cabins well suited to families, are spacious retreats; cabins have plenty of outlets and USB ports for charging devices; Internet service is lightning fast.

Cons: there are extra charges for nearly everything; some activities require reservations and lines form everywhere on a ship this large; there are no free steam rooms or saunas in the fitness center.

Cabin Type	Size (sq. ft.)
Loft Suites	696–1,640 sq. ft.
Suites	351–543 sq. ft.
Family Suites	301–543 sq. ft.
Junior Suites	267–276 sq. ft.
Balcony Ocean View	177–198 sq. ft.
Ocean View	214–301 sq. ft.
Interior	166 sq. ft.

FAST FACTS

- 16 passenger decks
- 5 specialty restaurants, dining room, buffet, ice cream parlor, pizzeria
- Wi-Fi, safe, refrigerator, DVD (some)
- 3 pools, children's pool
- fitness classes, gym, hot tubs, sauna, spa, steam room
- 9 bars, casino, 2 dance clubs, library, 3 showrooms, video game room
- children's programs
- dry cleaning, laundry service
- Internet terminal
- no-smoking cabins

3

SEABOURN CRUISE LINE

A leader in small-ship, luxury cruising, Seabourn has an elegant fleet of ships that appeal to sophisticated, independent-minded passengers whose lifestyles demand the best. In addition to personalized service, Seabourn delivers all the expected extras—complimentary wines and spirits, a stocked minibar in all suites, and elegant amenities. Expect the unexpected as well—from exclusive travel-document portfolios and luggage tags to the pleasure of a complimentary mini-massage while lounging at the pool.

Seabourn in Alaska

☎ *800/929–9391*
⊕ *www.seabourn.com*
☞ *Cruise Style:*
Luxury.

Peace and tranquility reign on these ships, so the daily roster of events is somewhat thin. Wine tastings, lectures, and other quiet pursuits might be scheduled, but most passengers are satisfied to simply do what pleases them. One don't-miss activity is the daily team trivia contest. Prizes are unimportant: it's the bragging rights that most guests seek.

Although the trio of original Seabourn ships were sold, the line now has five larger, even more luxurious ships in service.

FOOD

As expected from a member of Chaîne des Rôtisseurs, Seabourn offers exceptional cuisine prepared *à la minute* and served in open seating dining rooms. Upscale menu offerings include foie gras, quail, fresh seafood, and jasmine crème brûlée. Dishes low in cholesterol, salt, and fat, as well as vegetarian selections, are prepared with the same artful presentation and attention to detail. Wines are chosen to complement each day's luncheon and dinner menus, and caviar is always available. A background of classical music sets the tone for afternoon tea.

The Grill features steakhouse favorites and table-side preparations of Caesar salad and ice cream sundaes. The Colonnade, a more casual, indoor/outdoor alternative centered on an open kitchen, features lavish buffets or table service for breakfasts and lunch, and serves regionally themed, bistro-style dinners with table service nightly. Relaxed poolside dining at The Patio offers lunch buffets, salads, soups, grilled specialties, and pizza. Each evening The Patio features an array of fresh, inventive dishes for alfresco dining on deck. Alternative dining restaurants require reservations for dinner, but happily there is no additional charge.

Room service is always available. Dinner can even be served course by course in your suite during restaurant hours.

ENTERTAINMENT

Dining and evening socializing are generally more stimulating to Seabourn passengers than splashy song-and-dance revues. Still, proportionately scaled production shows and cabarets are presented in the main show room and smaller lounges. The library stocks not only books but also DVDs for those who prefer to watch movies in the privacy of their suites—popcorn will naturally be delivered with a call to room service.

The inspiring enrichment program features guest appearances by luminaries in the arts, literature, politics, and world affairs; during certain culinary-focused sailings you can learn the secrets of the world's most innovative chefs. Due to the size of Seabourn ships, passengers have the opportunity to mingle with presenters and interact one-on-one.

FITNESS AND RECREATION

A full array of exercise equipment, free weights, and basic fitness classes is available in the state-of-the-art gym, while some specialized fitness sessions are offered for a fee.

Many passengers are drawn to the pampering spa treatments, including a variety of massages, body wraps, and facials. Hair and nail services are offered in the salon. Both spa and salon are operated by Steiner Leisure.

YOUR SHIPMATES

Seabourn's yachtlike vessels appeal to well-traveled, affluent couples of all ages who enjoy destination-intense itineraries, a subdued atmosphere, and exclusive service. Passengers tend to be 50-plus and retired couples who are accustomed to evening formality.

3

Top: *Seabourn Encore* Veranda Suite
Bottom: *Seabourn Encore* Pool Deck

Top: Pool on *Seabourn Odyssey*
Middle: The Colonnade, *Seabourn Sojourn*
Bottom: Seabourn Square, *Seabourn Sojourn*

DRESS CODE

At least one formal night is standard on seven-night cruises and three to four nights, depending on the itinerary, on two- to three-week cruises. Men are required to wear tuxedos or dark suits after 6 pm, and the majority prefers black tie. All other evenings are elegant casual, and slacks with a jacket over a sweater or shirt for men and a sundress or skirt or pants with a sweater or blouse for women are suggested.

JUNIOR CRUISERS

Seabourn Cruise Line is adult-oriented and does not accommodate children under six months (or under one year for transocean sailings and voyages of 15 days or longer). A limited number of suites are available for triple occupancy. No dedicated children's facilities are present on these ships, so parents are responsible for the behavior and entertainment of their children.

SERVICE

Personal service and attention by the professional staff are the orders of the day. Your preferences are noted and fulfilled without the necessity of reminders. It's a mystery how nearly every staff member knows your name within hours, if not minutes, after you board.

TIPPING

Tipping is neither required nor expected.

PAST PASSENGERS

Once you have completed your first Seabourn cruise, you are automatically enrolled in the Seabourn Club for past guests. Within Seabourn Club, there are six membership levels, determined by the number of Seabourn Club Points the member has earned: Club Member, Silver Member, Gold Member, Platinum Member, Diamond Member, and Diamond Elite Member. Each level has a unique set of benefits, which include discounts on selected cruises (not combinable with Early Booking Savings); the Seabourn Club newsletters and periodic mailings featuring destinations, special programs, and exclusive savings; and an exclusive online email contact

CHOOSE THIS LINE IF...

■ You consider fine dining the highlight of your vacation.

■ You own your own tuxedo. These ships are dressy, and most men wear them on formal evenings.

■ You feel it's annoying to sign drink tabs; everything is included on these ships.

point to the club desk through the membership page on the Seabourn website.

On the ships, club members receive a 5% discount on future bookings, special recognition for frequent cruising, and a club party hosted by the captain. As members reach Silver, Gold, Platinum, Diamond, and Diamond Elite levels, the benefits increase. Milestone Awards offer a complimentary cruise of up to seven days when 140 days sailed have been completed, or a complimentary cruise of up to 14 days when 250 days sailed is reached.

HELPFUL HINTS

■ Seabourn's shore excursions often include privileged access to historic and cultural sites when they are not open to the general public.

■ Most warm-weather cruises include a beach picnic (albeit one with champagne and caviar); on itineraries where a beach isn't available, a similar party is held on the ships' water-sports marina.

■ A Vintage Seabourn pre-purchase wine option offers access to a varied selection of premium wines from the ships' well-stocked cellars at advantageous prices.

■ Every passenger gets a complimentary canvas logo tote bag.

■ Ground transfers are included in air and sea packages purchased through Seabourn, but passengers traveling independently are responsible for their own transfer to the ship.

DON'T CHOOSE THIS LINE IF...

■ Dressing down is on your agenda.

■ You absolutely must smoke on your private balcony. It's not allowed.

■ You need to be stimulated by constant activity.

SEABOURN ODYSSEY, SEABOURN SOJOURN, SEABOURN QUEST

Seabourn Odyssey, Seabourn Sojourn, Seabourn Quest

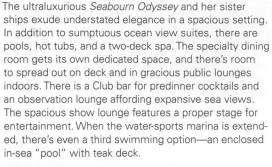

CREW MEMBERS	330
ENTERED SERVICE	2009, 2010, 2011
GROSS TONS	32,000
LENGTH	650 feet
NUMBER OF CABINS	225
PASSENGER CAPACITY	450
WIDTH	84 feet

700 ft.

500 ft.

300 ft.

The ultraluxurious *Seabourn Odyssey* and her sister ships exude understated elegance in a spacious setting. In addition to sumptuous ocean view suites, there are pools, hot tubs, and a two-deck spa. The specialty dining room gets its own dedicated space, and there's room to spread out on deck and in gracious public lounges indoors. There is a Club bar for predinner cocktails and an observation lounge affording expansive sea views. The spacious show lounge features a proper stage for entertainment. When the water-sports marina is extended, there's even a third swimming option—an enclosed in-sea "pool" with teak deck.

CABINS

Cabins: All suites, 90% with balconies, are located midship to forward; none are aft. Eight categories of roomier accommodations are true suites, with separate bedrooms in all but the least expensive. Even the most modest suites have walk-in closets, a seating area with coffee table that converts to a dining table for meals, a dressing table–desk, and a granite-topped bathroom with double-sink vanities and a separate shower and tub (some with whirlpool tubs).

Amenities: Amenities include flat-screen TV with DVD player, safe, hair dryer, fully stocked minibar, fresh fruit and flowers, world atlas, personalized stationery, shampoo, conditioner, designer soap and lotion, Egyptian-cotton towels and robes, slippers, umbrellas, and beds dressed with silky, high-thread-count linens. Top-category suites have a butler's pantry and guest powder room. Wintergarden and Signature suites can be configured with two bedrooms.

Accessibility: Seven suites are designed for wheelchair accessibility.

RESTAURANTS

The formal Restaurant serves breakfast, lunch, and dinner in open seating. In The Grill (reservations required), steakhouse favorites are prepared individually by the chef. For casual indoor-outdoor dining, The Colonnade serves breakfast, lunch, and dinner from an open kitchen, with à la minute preparation. Breakfast, lunch, and dinner are also offered poolside at the Patio Grill. Espresso and cappuccino are available at the coffee bar. Meals and snacks can be ordered from an extensive

Top: *Seabourn Sojourn*, The Restaurant
Bottom: *Seabourn Sojourn*, Veranda Suite

room-service menu around the clock. During restaurant hours, dinner can be served course by course en suite.

SPAS

Treatments in the spa operated by Steiner Leisure include massages, facials, and body wraps that incorporate natural ingredients. Along with a treatment, you receive use of the thermal suite, with a large hydrotherapy pool (on *Seabourn Odyssey*) or the Kneipp Walk, a walking pool with hot water on one side and cold water on the other, utilized to stimulate circulation (on *Sojourn* and *Quest*). Heated loungers surround the pools, and a variety of steam and thermal rooms are included. Day passes (for a fee) are available for just the thermal suite, or you can opt for the free sauna in changing rooms.

BARS/ENTERTAINMENT

Proportionately scaled production shows, performances by guest artists, and cabarets are presented in the Grand Salon and smaller Club lounge, where dancing is held most nights. A pianist entertains in the Observation Bar. Movies and a deck party with dancing are scheduled on the wind-protected pool deck on most cruises as long as the weather permits.

PROS AND CONS

Pros: kayaks, waterskiing, and other complimentary water toys are available at the fold-down marina when the ships are at anchor; the fully equipped gym has a Kinesis Wall, an innovative method of exercise utilizing a pulley-and-cable system; there is never a cover charge for specialty dining.

Cons: choose your suite location carefully—not all balconies are equal, even within the same category; although the spa is opulent, it's still operated by Steiner, which operates spas on most cruise ships; past passengers take a proprietary interest in the ships and may seem cliquish to newcomers.

Cabin Type	Size (sq. ft.)
Wintergarden Suite	914 sq. ft.
Signature Suite	859 sq. ft.
Owner's Suite	526–593 sq. ft.
Penthouse	436 sq. ft.
Veranda	300 sq. ft.
Ocean View	295 sq. ft.

FAST FACTS

- 8 passenger decks
- specialty restaurant, dining room, buffet
- Wi-Fi, safe, refrigerator, DVD
- 2 pools
- fitness classes, gym, hot tubs, sauna, spa
- 5 bars, casino, dance club, library, show room
- dry cleaning, laundry facilities, laundry service
- Internet terminal

SILVERSEA CRUISES

In 2018 Royal Caribbean International purchased a large stake in Silversea Cruises, adding a new luxury option to their portfolio. Intimate ships with spacious suites, exclusive amenities, and unparalleled hospitality are the hallmarks of the line. Every suite is assigned a

The most captivating view on board

butler, so you can expect even the most unusual requests to be fulfilled. In addition, your all-inclusive air-and-sea fares can be customized to include not just round-trip airfare but all transfers, porterage, and deluxe pre-cruise accommodations as well.

☎ 954/522–2299,
877/276–6816
⊕ www.silversea.com
☞ Cruise Style:
Luxury.

Personalization is a Silversea maxim. Their ships offer more activities than other comparably sized luxury vessels. Take part in those that interest you, or opt instead for a good book and any number of quiet spots to read or snooze in the shade.

Silversea's third generation of ships introduced even more luxurious features when the 36,000-ton *Silver Spirit* launched late in 2010 and the 40,700-ton *Silver Muse* entered service in 2017. Silversea's fleet of exploration ships are the top choice for luxurious soft adventure expedition cruising, including *Silver Galapagos* that sails exclusively in the Galápagos Islands.

FOOD
Dishes from the galleys of Silversea's master chefs are complemented by those of La Collection du Monde, created by Silversea's culinary partner, the world-class chefs of Relais & Châteaux. Menus include hot and cold appetizers, at least four entrée selections, a vegetarian alternative, and Cruiselite cuisine (low in cholesterol, sodium, and fat). Special off-menu orders are prepared whenever possible, provided that the ingredients are available onboard. In the event that they aren't, you may find after a day in port that a trip to the market was made in order to fulfill your request.

At La Terrazza (by day, a casual buffet) the menu showcases the finest in Italian cooking, from classic favorites to Tuscan fare. The restaurant carries no surcharge. Seating is limited, so reservations are a must to ensure a table—it's one reservation you'll be glad you took the time to book. Or dine beneath the stars at The Grill, where you can prepare your own fish, vegetables, and meat at your table on volcanic rocks heated to 400 degrees.

ENTERTAINMENT

Guest lecturers are featured on nearly every cruise; language, dance, and culinary lessons and excellent wine-appreciation sessions are always on the schedule of events. Silversea also schedules culinary arts cruises and a series of wine-focused voyages that feature award-winning authors, international wine experts, winemakers, and acclaimed chefs from the world's top restaurants. During afternoon tea the ranks of highly competitive trivia teams increase every successive day.

After dark, Dolce Vita is a predinner gathering spot and the late-night place for dancing to a live band. A multitiered show lounge is the setting for talented singers and musicians, classical concerts, magic shows, big-screen movies, and folkloric entertainers from ashore. A small casino offers slot machines and gaming tables.

FITNESS AND RECREATION

The rather small gyms are equipped with cardiovascular and weight-training equipment, and fitness classes on *Silver Whisper* and *Silver Shadow* are held in the mirror-lined, but somewhat confining, exercise room. *Silver Spirit* and *Silver Muse* introduced more expansive spas and more spacious fitness centers.

South Pacific–inspired Zagara Spa offers numerous treatments including exotic-sounding massages, facials, and body wraps. Hair and nail services are available in the busy salon. A plus is that appointments for spa and beauty salon treatments can be made online from 60 days until 48 hours prior to sailing.

Golfers can sign up with the pro onboard for individual lessons utilizing a high-tech swing analyzer and attend complimentary golf clinics or participate in a putting contest.

YOUR SHIPMATES

Silversea Cruises appeal to sophisticated, affluent couples who enjoy the country club–like atmosphere, exquisite cuisine, and polished service onboard, not

3

Top: Stylish entertainment
Bottom: La Terrazza alfresco dining

Top: Table tennis
Middle: Caring personal
service Bottom: Verandah
Suite

to mention the exotic ports and unique experiences ashore.

DRESS CODE

One formal night is standard on cruises of up to nine nights and two to three nights, depending on the itinerary, on longer sailings. Men are required to wear tuxedos or dark suits after 6 pm. All other evenings are either informal, when a jacket is called for (a tie is optional, but most men wear them), or casual, when slacks with a jacket over an open-collar shirt for men and sporty dresses or skirts or pants with a sweater or blouse for women are suggested.

JUNIOR CRUISERS

Silversea Cruises is adult-oriented, does not accommodate children less than six months of age, and the cruise line limits the number of children under the age of three onboard. The availability of suites for a third passenger is capacity controlled. A youth program staffed by counselors is available on holiday and select sailings. No dedicated children's facilities are available, so parents are responsible for the behavior and entertainment of their children.

SERVICE

Personalized service is exacting and hospitable yet discreet. The staff strives for perfection and often achieves it. The attitude is decidedly European and begins with a welcome-aboard flute of champagne, then continues throughout as personal preferences are remembered and satisfied. The word *no* doesn't seem to be in the staff vocabulary in any language. Guests in all suites are pampered by butlers.

TIPPING

Tipping is neither required nor expected.

PAST PASSENGERS

Membership in the Venetian Society is automatic on completion of one Silversea cruise, and members begin accruing benefits: Venetian Society cruise days and eligibility for discounts on select voyages, onboard

CHOOSE THIS LINE IF...

■ Your taste leans toward learning and exploration.

■ You enjoy socializing as well as the option of live entertainment, just not too much of it.

■ You like to plan ahead. You can reserve shore tours, salon services, and spa treatments online.

recognition and private parties, milestone rewards, exclusive gifts, the *Venetian Society Newsletter*, ship visitation privileges, and complimentary early embarkation or late debarkation at certain milestones. After reaching the 500-day milestone, the Venetian Society member will receive a complimentary seven-day voyage for each additional 150 days sailed.

HELPFUL HINTS

■ Every Silversea voyage includes an exclusive Silversea Experience—a complimentary shoreside event, such as private access to museums after hours.

■ Silversea offers a customized collection of pre- and post-cruise land programs linking some of Relais & Châteaux's worldwide properties together with Silversea's global itineraries.

■ For a fee, Silversea will pick up your bags at home and deliver them to the ship, or vice versa.

■ If adults travel with minors under the age of 18 who are not their children, a signed parental consent guardianship form is required.

■ Requests must be made in writing no later than 14 days prior to departure if you want to arrange a Bon Voyage Party or have visitors board the ship at your embarkation port.

DON'T CHOOSE THIS LINE IF...

■ You want to dress informally at all times on your cruise. Passengers on these cruises tend to dress up.

■ You need highly structured activities and have to be reminded of them.

■ You prefer the glitter and stimulation of Las Vegas to the understated glamour of Monte Carlo.

SILVER SHADOW/WHISPER
Silver Shadow, Silver Whisper

CREW MEMBERS	
	295
ENTERED SERVICE	
	2000, 2001
700 ft. **GROSS TONS**	
	28,258
LENGTH	
	610 feet
500 ft. **NUMBER OF CABINS**	
	191
PASSENGER CAPACITY	
	382
300 ft. **WIDTH**	
	82 feet

The logical layout of these sister ships, with suites in the forward two-thirds of the ship and public rooms aft, makes orientation simple. The clean, modern decor that defines public areas and lounges might seem almost stark, but it places the main emphasis on large expanses of glass for sunshine and sea views as well as passenger comfort.

Silversea ships boast unbeatable libraries stocked with best sellers, travel books, classics, and movies for en suite viewing. Extremely wide passageways in public areas are lined with glass-front display cabinets full of interesting and unusual artifacts from the places the ships visit. The Connoisseur's Corner is a clubby cigar-smoking room with overstuffed leather seating and a ventilation system that makes it possible for even non-smokers to appreciate.

CABINS

Layout: Every suite has an ocean view, and more than 80% have a private teak-floor balcony. Standard suites have a seating area that can be curtained off from the bed. Marble bathrooms have double sinks and a separate glass-enclosed shower as well as a tub. All suites have generous walk-in closets.

Top Suites: In addition to much more space, top-category suites have all the standard amenities plus dining areas and separate bedrooms. Silver suites and above have whirlpool tubs. The top three categories have espresso makers and separate powder rooms. All are served by butlers.

Amenities: Standard suites have a TV, personalized stationery, cocktail cabinet, safe, and stocked refrigerator. A hair dryer is provided at a vanity table, and you can request a magnifying mirror. Beds are dressed with high-quality linens and your choice of synthetic or down pillows. Bathrooms have huge towels and terry robes for use during the cruise as well as designer shampoo, soaps, and lotion.

Accessibility: Two suites are designed for wheelchair accessibility.

RESTAURANTS

The Restaurant offers open seating breakfast, lunch, and dinner. Le Champagne (reservation, cover charge) offers a gourmet meal and wine pairings; La Terrazza serves

Top: The casino
Bottom: *Silver Shadow* at sea

Italian cuisine at dinner. For casual meals, La Terrazza has indoor and outdoor seating for buffet-style breakfast and lunch. The outdoor Grill offers a laid-back lunch option with poolside table service. The do-it-yourself Black Rock Grill allows you to cook meats and seafood to your liking on preheated volcanic stones table-side. Elaborate afternoon tea is served daily. An evening poolside barbecue is a weekly dinner event as a galley brunch. Room service is available anytime and arrives with crystal, china, and a linen tablecloth; if desired, service can be course by course.

SPAS

South Pacific–inspired Zagara Spa, a division of Steiner Leisure, offers treatments including exotic-sounding massages, facials, and body wraps, tooth whitening, acupuncture, and Medi-Spa Cosmetic treatments. There is no thermal suite, but complimentary saunas and steam rooms are in the men's and ladies' locker rooms.

BARS AND ENTERTAINMENT

The show lounge is the setting for singers and musicians, classical concerts, magic shows, big-screen movies, and folkloric entertainers from ashore. The Bar is the most popular predinner gathering spot and a late-night place for dancing to a live band. A pianist or other entertainers perform in the Panorama Lounge for listening and dancing. Concerts or movies are presented on deck, weather permitting.

PROS AND CONS

Pros: champagne flows freely throughout your cruise; sailing on a Silversea ship is like spending time as a guest at a home in the Hamptons where everything is at your fingertips; Silversea is so all-inclusive that you'll seldom use your room card for anything but opening your suite door.

Cons: lines can form to use a washing machine in the smallish (yet totally free) laundry rooms; in an odd contrast to the contents of display cases and lovely flower arrangements, artwork on the walls is fairly ho hum; the spa's complimentary saunas and steam rooms are quite small.

Cabin Type	Size (sq. ft.)
Grand Suite	1,286–1,435 sq. ft.
Royal Suite	1,312–1,352 sq. ft.
Owner's Suite	1,208 sq. ft.
Silver Suite	701 sq. ft.
Medallion Suite	521 sq. ft.
Veranda Suite	345 sq. ft.
Terrace Suite	287 sq. ft.
Vista Suite	287 sq. ft.

FAST FACTS

- 7 passenger decks
- 2 specialty restaurants, dining room, buffet
- Wi-Fi, safe, refrigerator
- pool
- fitness classes, gym, hot tubs, sauna, spa, steam room
- 3 bars, casino, dance club, library, showroom
- dry cleaning, laundry facilities, laundry service
- Internet terminal
- no-smoking cabins

The Poolside Grill serves lunch and light snacks.

SILVER DISCOVERER
Silver Discoverer

CREW MEMBERS	96
ENTERED SERVICE	2014
GROSS TONS	5,218
LENGTH	338 feet
NUMBER OF CABINS	62
PASSENGER CAPACITY	120
WIDTH	51 feet

700 ft.

500 ft.

300 ft.

Silversea's smallest ship, *Silver Discoverer*, is an expedition vessel that is dispatched to explore the more inaccessible locations in such destinations as the Galápagos, Alaska, and the South Pacific. The yachtlike vessel has a shallow draft and carries a dozen inflatable Zodiac landing craft. While cabins have the same style as those on a full-size Silversea ship, they are generally smaller, and fewer have balconies. Given the ship's size, there are fewer dining options.

CABINS

Cabins: Champagne on ice awaits in all suites upon arrival, and your refrigerator and bar are stocked with your preferences and replenished as requested. To complete the luxury appointments are a selection of European-designer bath amenities from which to choose, down duvets, fine bed and bath linens, premium mattresses, a selection from a pillow menu, personalized stationery, a flat-screen TV with on-demand movies and satellite news programming, a combination radio/alarm clock with a docking station, hair dryer, and plush slippers and robe. Beds are twins that can be combined to form a queen with storage drawers beneath them. In addition to daily service and nightly turndown, butlers are on hand to assist guests in all five accommodations categories.

Layout: All suites are decorated in soothing neutral tones but are on the small side when compared with the other luxury ships in the Silversea fleet. Only Medallion and Veranda suites have balconies, and they measure 27 and 35 square feet respectively. All accommodations have a sitting area with a writing desk, but only the Medallion suite is an actual two-room suite with a bedroom separate from the living room and an additional TV. The sitting area in four of the Veranda suites has a sofa bed to accommodate a third guest, who must be age 14 or under. All marble bathrooms feature a walk-in shower. Explorer suites have two portholes, while View and Vista suites feature picture windows.

Accessibility: There are no accommodations designed for wheelchair accessibility.

RESTAURANTS

The Restaurant, which is the main dining room, is only in service for dinner; all meals are open seating, which allows you to dine when you please and with whom you

Top: Discoverer Lounge
Bottom: Seeing the scenery

wish. Menus feature international classical and modern cuisine along with dishes prepared from locally sourced ingredients and accompanied by wine to complement the meal. Vegetarian, low-calorie, and low-carb options are available upon request. Breakfast and lunch buffets, afternoon tea, and snacks are served in the Discoverer Lounge, where a self-service coffee, tea, and juice bar is always available. Located poolside, The Grill serves light breakfast and lunch selections and is transformed in the evening into the Hot Rock dining spot, where you can grill your own fresh seafood and steaks on heated volcanic plates. Room service is available from 6 am until 11 pm.

SPAS

The small spa has one treatment room and offers a limited range of massages.

BARS AND ENTERTAINMENT

As on other expedition vessels, formal entertainment on *Silver Discoverer* is limited to a pianist who plays in the Explorer Lounge before and after dinner. With its expansive views, the lounge also serves as the venue for daily briefings and recaps by the Expedition Team, lectures, and social gatherings.

PROS AND CONS

Pros: a rarity on expedition vessels, *Silver Discoverer* has a small swimming pool; every voyage features complimentary excursions led by the Expedition Team; expedition binoculars and an umbrella are provided for use while onboard.

Cons: children under age six are not allowed on Zodiacs (and an adult must remain onboard the ship with the child); special meal requests may not be available on *Silver Discoverer* as they are on other Silversea ships; there are no steam rooms, saunas, or hot tubs.

Cabin Type	Size (sq. ft.)
Medallion Suite	381 sq. ft.
Vista Suite	269 sq. ft.
Veranda Suite	245 sq. ft.
Explorer Suite	186 sq. ft.
View Suite	181 sq. ft.

FAST FACTS

- 5 passenger decks
- dining room
- Wi-Fi, safe, refrigerator
- pool
- gym, spa
- 2 bars
- laundry service
- no kids under 1, no-smoking cabins

Vista Suite

UNCRUISE ADVENTURES

With more than 20 years of experience plying Alaska waters, UnCruise Adventures offers nature-focused small ship cruises for travelers who like to go off the beaten path and stay unplugged on vacation. The captain and crew navigate inlets and waterways on

Wilderness Discoverer at sea

the lookout for tailor-made experiences for their guests. If whales are breaching nearby or a bear is spotted fishing for salmon on the shore, the captain will swing the vessel around for a better look. There are fewer better ways to see Alaska's wonders up close than with UnCruise's expedition-style active exploration.

☎ *206/284–0300, 888/862–8881*
⊕ *www.uncruise.com*
☞ *Cruise Style: Small-ship.*

UnCruise Adventures offers several small-ship cruising styles from which to choose—Active Adventures, Luxury Adventures, and Heritage Adventures—each designed to provide a unique experience. Active Adventures are expedition-style cruises offering more active adventures and delivering them aboard expedition vessels at an economical price point. Luxury Adventures are offered aboard more upscale, yachtlike ships that are loaded with extra amenities; soft-adventure activities are emphasized, and fares range from moderate to high. Heritage Adventures focus on history, both on the ship and ashore. Living History programs are offered aboard a replica Victorian-style steamship for a moderate to high price. All the line's ships are also available for charter by private groups.

All cruises, regardless of the style, include guided tours ashore, but more included excursions are offered on Luxury Adventures. Heritage Adventures offer more port calls with shore visits to museums and historical sites. Kayaks and paddleboards are available at no charge on Active and Luxury Adventures, but there is a nominal daily use charge for snorkeling gear and wet suits on Active Adventures. Limited quantities of hiking poles, binoculars, mud boots, and rain gear are available onboard for use during your cruise.

FOOD

Chefs serve a choice of nicely presented dinner entrées, featuring fresh local ingredients and plenty of seafood. Both Luxury and Heritage cruises are nearly all-inclusive, so premium wines and liquors are available at every meal, and guests are welcome to help themselves to the well-provisioned bar as well as snack options set up between meals. Meals on Active cruises are simpler and often served buffet-style, and on these cruises there is a separate charge for alcoholic beverages. Espresso, coffee, and tea are available 24 hours a day on all ships.

ENTERTAINMENT

Expert naturalists give informative presentations onboard and are available throughout the trip as a resource for assistance and information. Libraries are stocked with books and DVDs. The Victorian-style steamship SS *Legacy* has a dance floor for evenings onboard for its Heritage cruises.

FITNESS AND RECREATION

Exercise equipment, hot tubs, a sauna, and yoga sessions are featured onboard. Kayaking and nature hikes are offered for a more adventurous workout.

YOUR SHIPMATES

Typical passengers tend to be inquisitive couples from mid-thirties to retirees. Children are welcome, but there are no facilities specifically designed for them.

DRESS CODE

Dress is always comfortably casual, so guests can feel free to pack any clothing they like. Although there are a limited number of rain slickers, rain pants, and mud boots onboard for passenger use, guests may also bring their own to ensure the best fit. Evening attire tends to be more upscale casual on Luxury and Heritage Adventures.

JUNIOR CRUISERS

With the exception of the smaller yachts, children are welcome on any sailing. There are kid-friendly DVDs and books onboard for their enjoyment and enrichment, and children ages eight and older can join Exploration Guides on hiking and kayaking adventures to see wildlife.

KNOWN FOR

■ **Flexible Itineraries:** Itineraries are flexible to take advantage of wildlife sightings.

■ **Wilderness Access:** Maneuverability of the small vessels offers unique access to wilderness areas for viewing wildlife and exploration by skiff.

■ **Intimate Tours:** Small groups that do not overwhelm the areas visited allow more up-close discoveries ashore on excursions led by trained leaders and guides.

■ **Personal Encounters:** Insightful cultural encounters ashore are a highlight of off-the-beaten path explorations.

■ **Eco-Friendly:** The line follows a "Leave No Trace" policy to protect the environment.

■ By supporting and promoting local culture, the line makes a positive impact on communities.

Kayaking

3

Top: Comfortable deck on
Wilderness Adventurer
Middle: Scenic views from
Wilderness Discoverer
Bottom: Enjoying the
outdoors

SERVICE

Crew members tend to passenger needs discreetly, yet in a personal way—they know your name and preferences and your needs will be satisfied in an attentive manner.

TIPPING

Tips are discretionary, but a generous 10% of the fare is suggested. A lump sum is pooled and shared among the crew after the cruise.

SHIPS OF THE LINE

UnCruise Adventures currently sails seven vessels for soft adventure cruising to regions throughout Alaska, and eight vessels for the Columbia and Snake rivers, coastal Washington state and British Columbia, the Hawaiian Islands, and Mexico's Sea of Cortés. Vessels are comfortable and feature modern amenities, although these vary by ship.

Wilderness Adventurer, Wilderness Discoverer, Wilderness Explorer. The Active Adventure ships, with capacities of 60, 76, and 74 respectively, provide maximum comfort and upgraded amenities that are often unexpected on expedition ships this size. Casual and inviting public areas decorated in contemporary colors impart the feeling of a 1940s-era National Park Service Lodge crossed with a neighborhood pub that features a bar top made from salvaged wood. On deck you'll find plenty of space to view the passing scenery, either at the rail, from a deck chair, or in a strategically placed hot tub. The top decks have covered areas where exercise equipment and saunas—with a view—are located. The ships also feature kayak-launching platforms for convenience and safety. They are not, however, very accessible to passengers with disabilities.

Safari Endeavour, Safari Explorer, Safari Quest. The line's Luxury Adventure ships have capacities of 86, 36, and 22 respectively. *Safari Endeavour* is exquisitely appointed with features such as an intimate wine bar and spa area including two hot tubs, sauna, fitness equipment,

CHOOSE THIS LINE IF...

■ You consider yourself more an adventurer than a tourist.

■ Your idea of a fun evening includes board games and quiet conversation.

■ You want to get up close to glaciers, waterfalls, whales, and other wildlife.

yoga classes, and massage suite (with a complimentary massage.) *Safari Explorer's* three public decks offer comfort amid casually elegant appointments. The library and cozy salons for dining and socializing are nicely balanced, with a large open viewing deck highlighted by a hot tub and nearby sauna. *Safari Quest* has warm wood trim throughout and plenty of outer deck space for spotting wildlife and taking in the scenery. A top deck lounge is a pleasant hideaway from which to enjoy the views. Hydrophones for listening to below-surface sounds are found on all three ships. There is no Internet access onboard, and cell-phone service is available only when the ships are near shore and within range of a cell tower. Smoking is limited to designated outside deck areas. No cabins are wheelchair-accessible.

SS Legacy. Refurbished before entering service in 2013 as the Heritage Adventures vessel, the 86-passenger SS *Legacy* emulates the old-world ambience and charm of an early turn-of-the-20th-century coastal steamer. Appointed with period decor, the vessel features carved wooden appointments. The Grand Salon, complete with a full bar and dance floor, and the Pesky Barnacle Saloon each have an adjacent outdoor viewing area. Two hot tubs, a sauna, fitness equipment, yoga classes, and a massage suite are features accessible to all guests. The ship's four decks provide ample outside viewing spaces and public areas for gathering with fellow passengers. Elevator access is available to three of the public decks. Smoking is limited to designated areas on outside decks away from doors and windows. There are no wheelchair-accessible cabins.

DON'T CHOOSE THIS LINE IF...

■ You can't entertain yourself; except for dancing on Heritage cruises, there is no organized entertainment at night.

■ You have to ask the price—except for Active cruises, these are primarily expensive trips.

■ You would rather play a slot machine than attend an evening lecture.

VIKING OCEAN CRUISES

Known for their fleet of river boats that ply the waterways of Europe and Asia, Viking River Cruises' parent company expanded into ocean cruising with Viking Ocean Cruises. After the christening of their first ocean passenger ship in 2015, an aggressive ship-

Viking Sea, Main Pool Chaises

building program followed with at least one new identical ship entering the fleet each year, making Viking Ocean Cruises the industry's largest small ship cruise line. The upscale ships are noted for their beautiful, Scandinavian-inspired interior design.

☎ 855/338–4546
⊕ www.vikingocean-cruises.com
☞ Cruise Style: Small-ship.

Viking Ocean Cruises' small ships are designed to allow direct access to most ports for easy and efficient embarkation and disembarkation. Itineraries range from eight to fifteen days and are planned to maximize the time passengers have to spend in ports, either participating in the tours included in the fare, excursions with an add-on fee, or exploring independently. Prior to cruises, Viking provides materials online, such as reading recommendations, cultural profiles, and videos to help passengers plan their journey.

Aboard the Nordic-inspired ships, which are some of the most beautifully designed, contemporary spaces at sea, all accommodations feature private verandas. A variety of restaurant options, including alfresco dining, are available. An exhibit that explores the history and legacy of the Viking explorers and specially curated book collections can be found in the library.

FOOD
Menus that change daily, including regional specialties prepared with fresh ingredients and American dishes are found in The Restaurant, the ships' main dining room.

Alternative restaurants, for which there is no additional charge, include The Chef's Table, serving international cuisine with wine pairings and Manfredi's Italian Restaurant, featuring Mediterranean dishes. Mamsen's, located in the Explorers' Lounge, is inspired by traditional Scandinavian delis and is named for the founder's family matriarch. It offers Norwegian specialties for breakfast, lunch, and afternoon or evening snacks. Tea and scones, finger sandwiches, and pastries are served daily at the Wintergarden on deck beneath a trellised wood canopy.

For casual meals, the World Café is the ship's buffet restaurant. Alfresco dining is a highlight of the Aquavit Terrace, the World Café, and The Restaurant. The Pool Grill serves hamburgers and other casual fare, including salads, for lunch and afternoon snacks poolside. Room service is available around the clock. Occupants of the Owner's Suite can order service from any of the ship's restaurants during open hours.

ENTERTAINMENT

Bringing classical music alive, the ship's resident pianist, guitarist, violinist, and flautist perform calming classical compositions throughout the ship. Each Viking itinerary includes one or more cultural performances specific to the region. To complement onshore experiences, the onboard lecture program is designed to offer insight into a destination's art, architecture, music, geopolitics, and natural world. They are hosted by a wide range of experts, from authors and archaeologists to former diplomats and news correspondents. Ship historians provide an enhanced level of enrichment, delivering lectures specific to your journey. Also included are roundtable discussions, where you can engage in a smaller, more intimate group setting, and daily "office hours" for one-on-one time for individual attention. Gain an overview of your next day's port of call through informative multimedia presentations covering the history and culture of your destination, as well as highlights of must-see landmarks.

In the onboard cooking school, The Kitchen Table, the ship's chefs bring local flavors from market to table. On port days, passengers can accompany the chef to a local market to select ingredients, and then learn to prepare regional dishes in a three-course meal.

FITNESS AND RECREATION

While the fitness center is housed in a relatively small space, it features cardio machines and open areas for yoga or Pilates. A personal trainer is on hand. In addition to the usual spa treatments you'll find on cruise ships,

KNOWN FOR

■ **Inclusiveness:** Viking Ocean Cruises offers a variety of included amenities in the fare.

■ **Intimacy:** The line's small ships can call on smaller ports larger ships cannot reach.

■ **Mature Clientele:** Passengers on Viking cruises tend to be older and more well traveled than on most cruise lines.

■ **All Balconies:** All accommodations on Viking ships have a balcony.

The Explorer's Lounge Library sitting area on the *Viking Star*

including Swedish massage, facials, and body wraps, you'll find one of the most unique spa experiences at sea: a chilling Snow Grotto. In true Scandinavian tradition, you can alternate the experience with a hot sauna.

There's a running track on Deck Eight for joggers, while walkers can stroll along the Deck Two 360° promenade, where four laps equal one mile. Two swimming pools are located on Deck Seven. The main pool has a sliding roof that can be closed when weather is inclement; at the aft is an infinity pool that offers a sense of swimming in the ocean. A hot tub is adjacent to each pool.

YOUR SHIPMATES
Viking is inviting to mature couples who have enjoyed the company's river cruises and tend to place more importance on the destination than the vessel that gets them there. They also appreciate the inclusiveness of the line, which offers a complimentary shore excursion in each port, unlimited free Wi-Fi, no charge for alternative restaurants, complimentary beer, wine, and soft drinks at lunch and dinner, and specialty coffees, teas, and bottled water available at all times.

DRESS CODE
Daytime dress is casual and comfortable including shorts (if the day is warm), slacks or jeans and comfortable shoes for walking tours. When the sun goes down, attire is "elegant casual" for all dining venues. Attire for ladies includes a dress, skirt, or slacks with a sweater or blouse; for men, trousers and a collared shirt. A tie and jacket are optional; jeans are not permitted, except in the World Café where the dress remains casual.

JUNIOR CRUISERS
Viking ships are adult-oriented and do not have dedicated children's facilities. Teenagers with mature tastes might enjoy the intriguing ports of call and, being teenagers, they would certainly appreciate unlimited Internet access.

Top: Mamsen's dining area on the *Viking Sea*
Middle: Wintergarden
Bottom: *Viking Sea*, Infinity Pool

CHOOSE THIS LINE IF...

■ You want an upscale atmosphere at a reasonable fare.

■ Reading is important to you. These ships have extensive libraries and nooks for curling up with a good book.

■ Socializing is more important to you than dancing the night away.

SERVICE

Unobtrusive professional service is offered by the international staff both onboard and ashore during complimentary port tours.

TIPPING

A discretionary charge of $15 per guest, per day is added to shipboard accounts to be shared among the onboard staff. Changes to the gratuity amount can be made at any time. A 15% gratuity is added to bar tabs. Local excursion guides or drivers may be tipped in cash at the end of each tour.

PAST PASSENGERS

Once you travel with Viking, you are automatically enrolled in the Viking Explorer Society, a community of travelers whose members enjoy benefits with Viking. They are among the first to be informed about new Viking itineraries and new ships, so they always have first choice of destinations and departure dates. They also receive news about special limited-time offers.

To encourage passengers to cruise with them again, Viking Ocean Cruises offers credit on upcoming travel with the line. Whether you select the rivers or oceans for your next journey, you will receive travel credits according to the amount of time that has elapsed since your last Viking voyage. If you reserve within one year, you receive $200 per passenger in travel credit; if you reserve within two years, you receive $100 per passenger. You will also be invited to an exclusive Viking Explorer Society members-only cocktail party during your next journey, where you can mingle with fellow repeat passengers, get to know the ship's staff, and enjoy a complimentary cocktail.

HELPFUL HINTS

■ In addition to the complimentary shore tours, there are premium excursions for an additional charge.

■ Reservations for specialty restaurants should be made as soon as possible because they fill up fast.

■ There is a fee for the interactive culinary experience at The Kitchen Table, where you shop ashore for ingredients and learn to prepare regional cuisine with the chef.

■ Complimentary laundry rooms with ironing boards are located on most accommodations decks, and even detergent is free.

■ Guests requiring special diets (low salt, diabetic, gluten-free, and low cholesterol) should alert Viking 90 days prior to departure and follow up with the maître d' when onboard.

DON'T CHOOSE THIS LINE IF...

■ Gambling in a casino is a must-have experience. These ships don't feature casinos.

■ Your children must accompany you. They will likely be bored.

■ You must be entertained all the time. Viking ships tend to be low-key.

VIKING ORION
Viking Orion

CREW MEMBERS	545
ENTERED SERVICE	2018
GROSS TONS	47,800
LENGTH	745
NUMBER OF CABINS	465
PASSENGER CAPACITY	930
WIDTH	94.5 feet

700 ft.

500 ft.

300 ft.

Graceful and refined, Viking ships borrow many of the attributes from the parent company's river cruise line. With blond woods, clean lines, and an airy feel, the decor is decidedly Scandinavian.

The heart of the ship and the center for much of the entertainment is the Living Room, a three-deck atrium with a variety of seating areas and a bar that also serves coffee drinks. Comfortable and spacious, it has shops, guest services, and the spa and fitness center clustered nearby. A classical trio, a pianist, and a guitarist often perform here.

Other public rooms, such as the Living Room, feature walls of floor-to-ceiling windows for optimal views of the sea and the destination while in port, but only the panoramic Explorers' Lounge offers stunning 180° views. There's also a Norwegian-inspired deli, Mamsen's, and a library filled with travel books.

CABINS
Cabins: Decorated in soothing shades of blue and cream, all accommodations include a veranda, a seating area, desk, king-size bed, flat-screen interactive television with on-demand movies, safe, hair dryer, spacious closet and drawer storage, and refrigerators stocked with soft drinks, water, and snacks. Robes and slippers are provided for use onboard and spacious bathrooms are stocked with Freyja toiletries and have a large shower and heated floor. Deluxe Veranda cabins also have binoculars and a coffeemaker.

Suites: Penthouse and Suite occupants are greeted with a bottle of champagne and their refrigerators are stocked with alcoholic beverages as well as soft drinks and water. In addition to more space, they are given priority for spa bookings, specialty restaurant reservations, and shore excursion reservations. Amenities include binoculars, a coffeemaker, and complimentary shoe shining and pressing services. Junior Suites and above add complimentary laundry and dry cleaning. The Owner's Suite, the largest accommodation onboard, includes a living room, dining room, bedroom, two guest bathrooms and a large master bathroom with a separate shower and bathtub, double-sink vanity, heated floor, and anti-fog mirror. For relaxation, there is a dry sauna with an ocean view.

Explorers' Lounge

Accessibility: Two cabins are wheelchair accessible.

RESTAURANTS

The open seating main dining room, simply named The Restaurant, serves a variety of international dishes and American classics. Specialty restaurants include Manfredi's, a classic Italian restaurant with a Tuscan bent, and The Chef's Table, which rotates through a series of set four-course menus with wine pairings included.

The World Cafe is a buffet with an outdoor seating area called Aquavit Terrace at the rear of the ship. Sections of the buffet include prepared-to-order pasta and wok stations, a deli section, seafood and sushi bar, dessert bar, and pizza.

The Pool Grill offers burgers and hot sandwiches, plus a small salad bar. Mamsen's, located in the Explorers Lounge, serves a selection of Norwegian sandwiches, soup, and pastries. Afternoon tea, with scones, finger sandwiches, and pastries is served in the Wintergarden.

SPAS

Viking's Nordic roots are hard to miss in the spa. The complimentary thermal suite features Norway's hot/cold bath treatments with a snow grotto, cold plunge pools, a warm saltwater pool, and dry saunas. The spa offers the usual array of massages, facials, and other treatments. There are also a salon and barbershop.

BARS/ENTERTAINMENT

Most of the entertainment takes place in the Star Theater, which has a main stage and two cinemas. Onstage you might find an ABBA tribute show in the evening after a day of port talks. Movies are shown on a big screen overlooking the pool on some nights. The Torshavn bar has live music and dancing at night.

PROS AND CONS

Pros: the excellent library has a wide selection of books; reasonably priced beverage packages are available; the atmosphere is casual yet sophisticated.

Cons: unless you prebook specialty restaurant tables, you could find them unavailable after boarding; slow-paced evening entertainment isn't satisfying if you prefer Vegas-style shows; the fitness center is tiny.

Cabin Type	Size (sq. ft.)
Owner's Suite	1,448 sq. ft.
Explorer Suite	757 sq. ft.
Penthouse Jr Suite	405 sq. ft.
Penthouse Veranda	338 sq. ft.
Veranda/Deluxe Veranda	270 sq. ft.

FAST FACTS

- 6 passenger decks
- 2 specialty restaurants, dining room, buffet
- Wi-Fi, safe, refrigerator
- 2 pools, 2 hot tubs, sauna, spa, gym, fitness classes
- 6 bars, library
- laundry service
- Internet terminal
- no-smoking cabins

3

WINDSTAR CRUISES

For years, Windstar Cruises' fleet traditionally consisted of three majestic motor-sail yachts with billowing sails, but in 2015 the line doubled in size with a trio of 212-passenger luxury yachts. All of the upscale yachts often visit ports of call inaccessible to huge, tra-

Windstar Cruises

ditional cruise ships and offer a unique perspective of any cruising region. Windstar's sailing ships seldom depend on wind alone to sail, but if conditions are perfect, as they sometimes are, the complete silence of pure sailing is heavenly.

☎ 206/292–9606
☎ 800/258–7245
⊕ www.windstarcruises.com
☞ Cruise Style: Luxury.

Whether on the sailing ships or megayachts, it doesn't take long to read the daily schedule of activities on a typical Windstar cruise. Simply put, there are few scheduled activities. Diversions are for the most part social, laid-back, and impromptu. You can choose to take part in the short list of daily activities; borrow a book, game, or DVD from the library; or do nothing at all. There's never pressure to join in or participate if you simply prefer relaxing.

Multimillion-dollar upgrades last took place in 2012, when each sailing ship was enhanced from bow to stern with chic decor that mimics the colors of the sky and sandy beaches. The Yacht Club is designed to be the social hub of the ship, with computer stations, a coffee bar, and an expansive feel. The yachts Windstar acquired in 2015 from Seabourn were substantially renovated before they entered the fleet. The all-suite accommodations, restaurants, pool deck, and public spaces were upgraded in the move.

FOOD

Dining on Windstar ships is as casually elegant as the dress code. There's seldom a wait for a table in open seating AmphorA dining rooms, where tables for two are plentiful. Whether meals are taken in the open and airy buffet restaurants, with floor-to-ceiling windows and adjacent tables outside, or in the formal dining room, dishes are as creative as the surroundings. Expect traditional entrées but also items that incorporate regional ingredients, such as plantains, for added interest. Save room for petits fours with coffee and a taste of the fine cheeses from the after-dinner cheese cart.

In a nod to healthy dining, low-calorie and low-fat spa cuisine alternatives for breakfast, lunch, and dinner are prepared to American Heart Association guidelines. Additional choices are offered from the vegetarian menu.

A midcruise deck barbecue featuring grilled seafood and other favorites is fine dining in an elegantly casual alfresco setting. Desserts are uniformly delightful, and you'll want to try the bread pudding, a Windstar tradition available at the luncheon buffet. With daily tea and hot and cold hors d'oeuvres served several times during the afternoon and evening, no one goes hungry. Room service is always available, and you can place your order for dinner from the restaurant's menu during scheduled dining hours.

ENTERTAINMENT

Evening entertainment is informal, with a small dance combo playing in the main lounges. Compact casinos offer games of chance and slot machines, but don't look for bingo or other organized games. A weekly show by the crew is delightful; attired in the traditional costumes of their homelands, they present music and dance highlighting their cultures. You may find occasional movies in the main lounges, which are outfitted with state-of-the-art video and sound equipment. Most passengers prefer socializing, either in the main lounge or an outdoor bar where Cigars Under the Stars attracts not only cigar aficionados but stargazers as well.

Welcome-aboard and farewell parties are hosted by the captain, and most passengers attend those as well as the nightly informational sessions regarding ports of call and activities that are presented by the staff during predinner cocktails.

FITNESS AND RECREATION

Most of the line's massage and exercise facilities are quite small, as would be expected on ships that carry 212 and fewer passengers; however, *Wind Surf's* Wind-Spa and fitness areas are unexpectedly huge. An array of exercise equipment, free weights, and basic fitness classes are available in the gym and Nautilus room.

3

Star Pride

Top: Chefs on *Star Pride*
Middle: Windstar dining
Bottom: *Star Legend*

There is an extra charge for Pilates and yoga classes. A wide variety of massages, body wraps, and facial treatments are offered in the spa, while hair and nail services are available for women and men in the salon. Both spa and salon are operated by Steiner Leisure.

Stern-mounted water-sports marinas are popular with active passengers who want to kayak, windsurf, and water-ski. Watery activities are free, including the use of snorkel gear that can be checked out for the entire cruise. The only charge is for diving; PADI-certified instructors offer a two-hour course for noncertified divers who want to try scuba and are also available to lead experienced certified divers on underwater expeditions. The dive teams take care of everything, even prepping and washing down the gear. If you prefer exploring on solid ground, sports coordinators are often at hand to lead an early-morning guided walk in port.

YOUR SHIPMATES

Windstar Cruises appeal to upscale professional couples in their late thirties to sixties who enjoy the unpretentious, yet casually sophisticated atmosphere, creative cuisine, and refined service.

Windstar's sailing ships were not designed for accessibility, and are not a good choice for the physically challenged. Although every attempt is made to accommodate passengers with disabilities, *Wind Surf* has only two elevators, and the smaller ships have none. There are no staterooms or bathrooms with wheelchair accessibility, and gangways can be difficult to navigate, depending on the tide and angle of ascent. The megayachts are better, with suites that have been modified for accessibility. Bathrooms have a shower only, and there is a step into the bathroom with a portable ramp. Service animals are permitted to sail if arrangements are made at the time of booking.

DRESS CODE

All evenings are country-club casual, and slacks with a jacket over a sweater or shirt for men, and sundresses,

BOX TITLE

■ You want a high-end experience yet prefer to dress casually every night of your vacation.

■ You love water sports, particularly scuba diving, kayaking, and windsurfing.

■ You're a romantic: tables for two are plentiful in the dining rooms.

skirts, or pants with a sweater or blouse for women are suggested. Coats and ties for men are not necessary, but some male passengers prefer to wear a jacket with open-collar shirt to dinner.

JUNIOR CRUISERS

Windstar Cruises' unregimented atmosphere is adult-oriented, and children are not encouraged. No dedicated children's facilities are available, so parents are responsible for the behavior and entertainment of their children.

SERVICE

Personal service and attention by the professional staff is the order of the day. Your preferences are noted and fulfilled without the necessity of reminders. Expect to be addressed by name within a short time of embarking.

TIPPING

A service charge of $13.50 per guest per day (including children) is added to each shipboard account. A 15% service charge is added to all bar bills. All these proceeds are paid directly to the crew.

PAST PASSENGERS

Windstar guests who cruise once with the line are automatically enrolled in the complimentary Foremast Club. Member benefits include savings on many sailings in addition to the Advance Savings Advantage Program discounts, Internet specials, and a free subscription to the *Foremast Club* magazine.

BOX TITLE

■ You must have a spacious private balcony. There are few.

■ You're bored unless surrounded by constant stimulation. Activities are purposely low-key.

■ You have mobility problems. These ships are simply not very good for passengers in wheelchairs.

STAR LEGEND
Star Legend

CREW MEMBERS	153
ENTERED SERVICE	2015
700 ft. **GROSS TONS**	9,975
LENGTH	440 feet
500 ft. **NUMBER OF CABINS**	106
PASSENGER CAPACITY	212
300 ft. **WIDTH**	63 feet

One of three yachts Windstar acquired in 2015, *Star Legend* went through major upgrades when it joined the fleet. The all-suite accommodations, restaurants, and public spaces were upgraded in the move. The pool deck received extensive attention with the addition of a small swim-against-the-current pool and adjacent hot tub.

Like its fleetmates, *Star Legend* offers an "almost luxury" experience. Unlike other luxury lines, the cruise fare isn't all-inclusive; however, all nonalcoholic beverages (soda, water, specialty coffee and tea drinks) are included, but there is a charge for alcoholic beverages. Shore excursions incur a fee with the exception of Windstar's special complimentary private event, which might be a beach barbecue or a visit to a cultural center for a concert or wine tasting. All dining options, including the intimate Candles, are complimentary.

CABINS

Cabins: All accommodations are termed suites, although in lower categories only a curtain separates the bed from the sitting area. You have to book one of the top categories to have a bedroom separate from the living and dining area. All feature Egyptian cotton linens, a robe and slippers for use during the cruise, a flat-screen TV with DVD player, a fully stocked minibar, a personal safe, hair dryers, walk-in closets, and ample drawer space. Bathrooms have a granite vanity with a magnifying mirror, a full-size tub, and a shower, plus L'Occitane bath amenities.

Suites: Some Ocean View Suites have a French-style "balcony," which is actually just a sliding door that opens—there is no sitting area. For a true balcony you have to move up to the larger Classic Suite, which also features two walk-in closets. The luxurious Owner's Suites offer living room and dining areas separate from the bedroom, plus a balcony, two flat-screen TVs and DVD players, and a full master bath and separate powder room.

Accessibility: Four suites are modified-accessible. Bathrooms are shower only with a small lip into the shower, a step into the bathroom with a portable ramp, and standard interior and exterior doorways.

Star Legend

RESTAURANTS

AmphorA, the main dining room, only serves dinner with open seating. Breakfast and lunch are served in Veranda, the buffet that features indoor seating and open-air dining both at the back of the ship and directly in front of the restaurant in a covered area. Veranda converts in the evening into Candles, a romantic steak and seafood restaurant, where you can dine alfresco. Reservations are required, and passengers are allowed to dine here only once per cruise, unless tables are available for a repeat meal. The Yacht Club offers coffee and Continental breakfast of pastries, fruit, and yogurt parfaits in the morning and sandwiches and sweets in the afternoon.

SPAS

The small WindSpa, operated by Steiner Leisure, features Elemis products and treatments ranging from aroma and hot-stone therapy to Swedish massages. There are two treatment rooms. The equally small salon offers hair care, shaves, manicures and pedicures, tooth whitening, and waxing. The fitness center adjacent to the WindSpa is outfitted with exercise equipment such as stationary bikes, free weights, and treadmills. Yoga and Pilates classes are complimentary.

BARS/ENTERTAINMENT

Few activities are held at night with the exception of live music and dancing in the Lounge, Star Bar, and Compass Rose. The ship's Voyage Leader gives a short briefing on the evening before every port call to share information on the port, docking position, shuttles, and shore excursions. Windstar brings lecturers onboard for some itineraries. Movies are shown in The Screening Room, which has movie theater-style armchairs. There is also a tiny casino.

PROS AND CONS

Pros: the Sun Deck is wide enough to allow for jogging; a Premium Beverage Package includes unlimited cocktails and beer; an open bridge policy allows you to visit the ship's control center at almost any time.

Cons: Internet packages are on the pricey side; the swim-against-the-current splash pool is tiny; children over seven are allowed, but will probably be bored.

Cabin Type	Size (sq. ft.)
Owner's Suite	575 sq. ft.
Classic Suite	400–530 sq. ft.
Balcony and Ocean View	277 sq. ft.

FAST FACTS

- 6 passenger decks
- specialty restaurant, dining room, buffet
- Wi-Fi, safe, refrigerator, DVD
- pool, fitness classes, gym, hot tub, sauna, spa
- 4 bars, casino, dance club, library
- laundry service
- Internet terminal
- no-smoking cabins

Tracy Arm, *Star Legend*

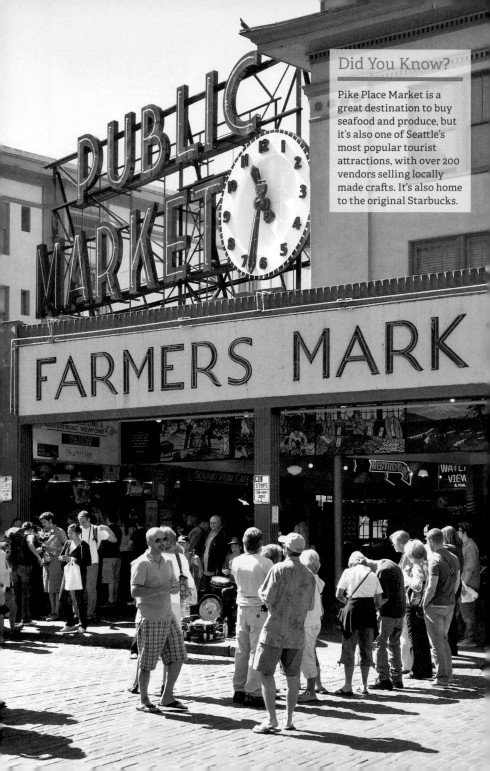

Pike Place Market is a great destination to buy seafood and produce, but it's also one of Seattle's most popular tourist attractions, with over 200 vendors selling locally made crafts. It's also home to the original Starbucks.

Chapter 4

PORTS OF EMBARKATION

Updated by Teeka
Ballas, Joey Besl,
Chris McBeath,
and AnnaMaria
Stephens

4

Many northbound cruises begin in Vancouver, British Columbia, and Seattle. Small-ship cruise lines usually begin and end their itineraries in Alaska, offering sailings from such ports as Juneau, Petersburg, and Sitka, Alaska.

Anchorage is the primary starting point for cruise passengers heading south, but most ships don't actually dock there. Instead, travelers fly into and may overnight in Anchorage before being transported by bus or train to the ports of Seward or Whittier for southbound departures.

Cruise travelers frequently opt for combination packages that include a one-way north- or southbound Inside Passage cruise plus a tour by bus or train through interior Alaska (and sometimes the Yukon). Denali National Park, too far inland to be included on round-trip Inside Passage cruises, is a particular focus of these "CruiseTour" trips (⇨ *see Chapter 6, "Inland Cruise Tour Destinations," for more information*).

Before or after the cruise, travelers with a more independent streak may want to rent a car and strike out on their own to places not often visited by cruise ships, such as Homer or Valdez (⇨ *see Chapter 5, "Ports of Call," for more information on these cities*).

Port Essentials

Car Rentals

If you plan on lingering before or after your cruise, rental cars are available in most Alaska ports of embarkation, as well as in Seattle and Vancouver. In Anchorage and other major destinations, expect to pay at least $55 to $75 a day or $300 (and up) a week for an economy or compact car with automatic transmission and unlimited mileage. Some locally owned companies offer lower rates for older cars. Also, be sure to ask in advance about discounts if you have a AAA or Costco card, or are over age 50.

MAJOR AGENCIES Alamo ☎ *844/354–6962* ⊕ *www.alamo.com.* **Avis** ☎ *800/230–4898* ⊕ *www.avis.com.* **Budget** ☎ *800/218–7992* ⊕ *www.budget.com.* **Hertz** ☎ *800/654–3131* ⊕ *www.hertz.com.* **National Car Rental** ☎ *844/382–6875* ⊕ *www.nationalcar.com.*

Dining

Given the seaside location of the embarkation towns, it's no surprise that fresh fish and other seafood are especially popular. Fresh halibut and salmon are available throughout the summer, along with specialties such as shrimp, oysters, and crab.

Seafood meals can be simply prepared fast food, like beer-battered fish-and-chips, or more-elaborate dinners of halibut baked in a macadamia-nut crust with fresh mango chutney. If seafood isn't your first choice, rest assured that all the staples—including restaurants serving steaks, burgers, pizza, or Mexican or Chinese food—can also be found.

What it Costs

$	$$	$$$	$$$$
RESTAURANTS			
under $15	$15–$20	$21–$25	over $25
HOTELS			
under $125	$125–$175	$176–$225	over $225

Lodging

Whether you're driving or flying into your port of embarkation, it's often more convenient to arrive the day before or to stay for a day (or longer) after your cruise. Cruise travelers often stay in one of the larger downtown hotels booked by the cruise lines to be closer to the ports, but you might like to make your own arrangements for a pre- or post-cruise sojourn. Therefore, we offer lodging suggestions for each port.

The hotels we list are convenient to the cruise port and the cream of the crop in each price category. Properties are assigned price categories based on the range between their least and most expensive standard double room in high season (excluding holidays).

Assume that hotels do not include meals unless specified in the review.

Anchorage

By far Alaska's largest and most sophisticated city, Anchorage is situated in a truly spectacular location. The permanently snow-covered peaks and volcanoes of the Alaska Range lie to the west of the city while part of the craggy Chugach Range is within the eastern edge of the municipality; the Talkeetna and Kenai ranges are visible to the north and south. Two arms of Cook Inlet embrace the town's western and southern borders, and on clear days Denali looms on the northern horizon.

Anchorage is Alaska's medical, financial, and banking center, and home to the executive offices of most of the Native corporations. The city has a population of roughly 290,000, approximately 40% of the people in the state. The relative affluence of this white-collar city—with a sprinkling of olive drab from nearby military bases—fosters fine restaurants and pricey shops, and first-rate entertainment.

Boom and bust periods followed major events: an influx of military bases during World War II; a massive buildup of Arctic missile-warning stations during the Cold War; reconstruction after the devastating Good Friday earthquake of 1964; and in the late 1960s the biggest jackpot of all—the discovery of oil at Prudhoe Bay and the construction of the Trans-Alaska Pipeline. Not surprisingly, Anchorage positioned itself as the perfect home for the pipeline administrators and support industries, and it continues to attract a large share of the state's oil-tax dollars.

THE CRUISE PORT

Anchorage is the starting (or ending) point for many Alaskan cruises, but few ships call here directly. However, if your cruise originates in or ends in Alaska, it's very likely you'll be flying into or out of the Anchorage airport, and some passengers choose to spend time before or after a cruise in Anchorage.

Cruises board or disembark either in Seward (125 miles south on Resurrection Bay) or in Whittier (59 miles southwest of Anchorage), on the western shore of Prince William Sound.

Access between Anchorage and these ports is by bus or train. Transfers are offered by the cruise lines, either as an add-on to your fare or, in the case of some luxury cruise lines or small-ship cruise lines, included in the price of your cruise. Cruise-line representatives meet airport arrivals to make the process as effortless as possible. You spend virtually no shore time in either Seward or Whittier before you embark or after disembarkation—buses and the train also offer dock-to-airport service in both places; however, it is possible to spend time in Seward or Whittier and make your own transportation arrangements. The few ships that do dock at Anchorage proper dock just north of downtown. There's an information booth on the pier. It's only a 15- or 20-minute walk from the town to the dock, but this is through an industrial area with heavy traffic, so it's best to take a taxi.

The Glenn Highway enters Anchorage from the north and becomes 5th Avenue near Merrill Field; this route leads directly into downtown. Gambell Street leads out of town to the south, becoming New Seward Highway at about 20th Avenue. South of town, it becomes the Seward Highway.

GETTING HERE AND AROUND
AIR TRAVEL TO ANCHORAGE
Ted Stevens Anchorage International Airport is 6 miles from downtown. Taxis queue up outside baggage claim. A ride downtown runs about $20, not including tip.

AIRPORT INFORMATION Ted Stevens Anchorage International Airport (ANC) ☎ 907/266–2525 ⊕ www.dot.alaska.gov/anc.

RENTAL CARS
Anchorage is the ideal place to rent a car for exploring sites farther afield before or after your cruise. National Car Rental has a downtown office. All the major companies (and several local operators) have airport desks and free shuttle service to the airport to pick up cars.

TAXIS
If you need a taxi, call one of the cab companies for a pickup; it's not common to hail one. Prices are $2.75 for a pickup, plus an additional $2.50 for each mile. Allow 20 minutes for arrival of the cab during morning and evening rush hours. Alaska Yellow Cab has taxis with wheelchair lifts.

CONTACT Alaska Yellow Cab ☎ 907/222–2222.

HOURS
During the summer cruise season, most attractions are open daily. Stores are generally open from 10 to 7 or 8, but government offices and banks may have earlier closing times.

VISITOR INFORMATION
CONTACTS Log Cabin and Visit Anchorage Information Center ⊠ 546 W. 4th Ave., Downtown ☎ 907/276–4118, 800/478–1255 to order visitor guides ⊕ www.anchorage.net.

 Sights

Alaska Aviation Museum
MUSEUM | FAMILY | The state's unique aviation history is presented here with more than 25 vintage aircraft, a flight simulator, a theater, and an observation deck along the world's busiest seaplane base. Highlights include a Stearman C2B, the first plane to land on Denali back in the early 1930s, and a recently restored 1931 Fairchild Pilgrim aircraft. You may see volunteers busily restoring an aircraft, and docents eager to talk about their bush pilot experiences. A free shuttle to and from Anchorage Airport is available,

as is luggage storage. ✉ *4721 Aircraft Dr., West Anchorage* ☎ *907/248–5325* ⊕ *www.alaskaairmuseum.org* ✉ *$15.*

Alaska Botanical Garden

GARDEN | FAMILY | The garden showcases perennials hardy enough to make it in Southcentral Alaska in several large display gardens, a pergola-enclosed herb garden, and a rock garden amid 110 acres of mixed boreal forest. There's a 1-mile nature trail loop to Campbell Creek, with views of the Chugach Range and a wildflower trail between the display gardens. Interpretive signs guide visitors and identify plants along the trail. Docent tours are available upon request. ✉ *4601 Campbell Airstrip Rd., off Tudor Rd. (park at Benny Benson School), East Anchorage* ☎ *907/770–3692* ⊕ *www.alaskabg. org* ✉ *$12.*

Alaska Heritage Museum at Wells Fargo

MUSEUM | More than 900 Alaska Native artifacts are the main draw in the quiet unassuming lobby of a large Midtown bank—it's reputed to be one of the largest private collections of Native artworks in the country. Also here you'll find paintings by Alaskan artists, a library of rare books, and a 46-troy-ounce gold nugget. The gallery is free to stroll through; call ahead to arrange a guided tour. ✉ *Wells Fargo Bank, 301 W. Northern Lights Blvd., at C St., Midtown* ☎ *907/265–2834* ⊕ *www.wellsfargohistory.com/museums* ✉ *Free* ⊘ *Closed weekends.*

★ Alaska Native Heritage Center

NATIVE SITE | FAMILY | On a 26-acre site facing the Chugach Mountains, this facility provides an introduction to Alaska's Native peoples. The spacious Gathering Place has interpretive displays, artifacts, photographs, demonstrations, Native dances, storytelling, and films, along with a gift shop selling crafts and artwork. Step outside for a stroll around the adjacent lake, where seven village exhibits represent 11 Native cultural groups through traditional structures and exhibitions. As you enter the homes in these villages, you can visit with the hosts, hear their stories, and try some of the tools, games, and utensils used in the past. ✉ *8800 Heritage Center Dr., (Glenn Hwy. at Muldoon Rd.), East Anchorage* ☎ *907/330–8000, 800/315–6608* ⊕ *www.alaskanative.net* ✉ *$25* ⊘ *Closed mid-Sept.–mid-May.*

Alaska Public Lands Information Center

INFO CENTER | FAMILY | Stop here for information on all of Alaska's public lands, including national and state parks, national forests, and wildlife refuges. You can plan a hiking, sea kayaking, bear viewing, or fishing trip; purchase state and national park passes; find out about public-use cabins; learn about Alaska's plants and animals; or head to the theater for films highlighting different parts of the state. The bookstore also sells maps and nature books. Guided walks to historic Downtown sights depart daily throughout the summer at 11 am and 3:15 pm. The center is housed in a federal facility, meaning a security screening is required to enter. ✉ *605 W. 4th Ave., at F St., Suite 105, Downtown* ☎ *907/644–3661, 866/869–6887* ⊕ *www.alaskacenters. gov/anchorage.cfm.*

★ Anchorage Museum

MUSEUM | FAMILY | This striking, contemporary building with first-rate exhibits is an essential stop for visitors who want to celebrate the history of the North. The star of the museum is the Smithsonian Arctic Studies Center, which features more than 600 objects from Alaska Native cultures and short films that teach visitors about modern-day Native life. Wander the Art of the North galleries filled with works that showcase Alaska landscape, history, and beauty. The Alaska Exhibition shares Alaska's diversity and history with a knock-out eye for design. Cap the visit in the 9,000-square-foot, kid-focused Discovery Center, which includes a planetarium. Curated exhibitions rotate regularly and frequently spotlight Arctic issues, Northern design,

Downtown

W. 2nd Ave.
W. 3rd Ave.
W. 4th Ave.
W. 5th Ave.
W. 6th Ave.
W. 7th Ave.
W. 8th Ave.

L St.
K St.
J St.
H St.
G St.
F St.
E St.
D St.
C St.
B St.
A St.

0   1/8 mile
0   1/8 kilometer

Tony Knowles
Coastal Trail

Knik Arm

N St.
L St.
K St.
J St.

Delaney Park

P St.
N St.
L St.
14

KEY
1 Sights
1 Restaurants
1 Hotels

Cook Inlet

Tony Knowles
Coastal Trail

W. Marston Dr.

Fish Creek

Westchester
Lagoon

Hillcrest Dr.

Turnagain Pkwy.

Forest Park Dr.

Arlington Dr.

Spenard Rd.

TO
EARTHQUAKE PARK

Northern Lights Blvd. W.
W. 29th St.
W. 30th Ave.
W. 31st Ave.
W. 32nd Ave.

Turnagain St.
Barbara St.

Lois Dr.

Benson Blvd.

Minnesota Dr.

W. 34th Ave.
W. 35th Ave.

Aero Ave.

Wisconsin Dr.

McRae Dr.

Spenard Rd.

SPENARD
W. 40th Ave.

Lois Dr.

Lake
Hood

44th Ave.

Northwood Dr.

1
**Anchorage
International Airport**

Lake
Spenard

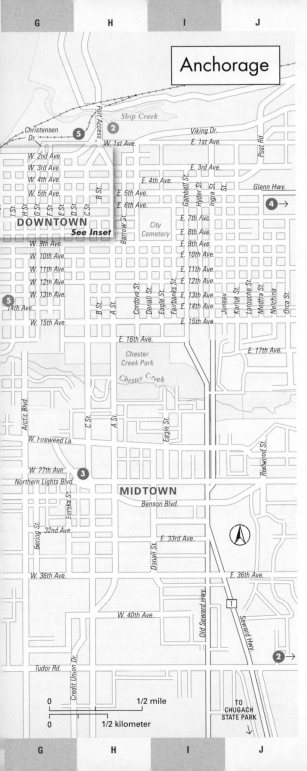

Sights ▼

1 Alaska Aviation Museum **A9**
2 Alaska Botanical Garden **J8**
3 Alaska Heritage Museum
  at Wells Fargo **H6**
4 Alaska Native Heritage Center.... **J3**
5 Alaska Public Lands
  Information Center **H2**
6 Anchorage Museum **E3**
7 Tony Knowles Coastal Trail **A1**

Restaurants ▼

1 Crow's Nest Restaurant. **B2**
2 Crush Wine Bistro and Cellar **B1**
3 Glacier BrewHouse **B2**
4 Marx Bros. Cafe **C1**
5 New Sagaya's City Market **G4**
6 Snow City Cafe..................... **A2**
7 Wild Scoops........................ **C2**

Hotels ▼

1 Anchorage Marriott
  Downtown.......................... **B3**
2 Comfort Inn Downtown
  Ship Creek.......................... **H2**
3 Historic Anchorage Hotel.......... **C2**
4 Hotel Captain Cook **B2**
5 Oscar Gill House **F3**

4

Ports of Embarkation ANCHORAGE

and the unique perspective of life at these latitudes. The bright and modern Muse restaurant serves delicious lunches and dinners, and the gift shop is one of Anchorage's best places to buy Alaska Native art and other souvenirs. ✉ *625 C St., Downtown* ☎ *907/929–9200* ⊕ *www. anchoragemuseum.org* 🎟 *$18* ⊗ *Closed Mon. in winter.*

★ Tony Knowles Coastal Trail

TRAIL | Strollers, runners, bikers, dog walkers, and in-line skaters cram this recreation trail on sunny summer evenings, particularly around Westchester Lagoon. In winter, cross-country skiers take to it by storm. The trail begins off 2nd Avenue, west of Christensen Drive, and curls along Cook Inlet for approximately 11 miles to Kincaid Park, beyond the airport. In summer you might spot beluga whales offshore in Cook Inlet. Access points are on the waterfront at the ends of 2nd and 5th avenues and at Westchester Lagoon near the end of 15th Avenue. When you get to the high points in the trail, look north; Denali is visible on clear days. ✉ *Anchorage.*

🍴 Restaurants

Smoking is banned in all Anchorage restaurants. Most local restaurants are open daily in summer, with reduced hours in winter. Only a few places require reservations, but it's always best to call ahead, especially for dinner.

★ Crow's Nest Restaurant

$$$$ | **EUROPEAN** | An absolute must for epicures and adventurous eaters, Crow's Nest uses inspired combinations to highlight, but never overpower, the freshest ingredients Alaska has to offer. Located on the top floor of the Hotel Captain Cook, this is also the best restaurant view in Anchorage, spanning the Chugach Mountains to the east, the Alaska Range to the north and west, and the city 20 stories below. **Known for:** unforgettable views and atmosphere;

excellent steaks and seafood; 10,000-bottle wine cellar. ⑤ *Average main: $44* ✉ *Hotel Captain Cook, 939 W. 5th Ave., 20th fl., Downtown* ☎ *907/343–2217* ⊕ *www.captaincook.com* ⊗ *Closed Sun. No lunch.*

★ Crush Wine Bistro and Cellar

$$ | **ECLECTIC** | The combination of shared small plates and an international wine list makes this Anchorage's most conversation-friendly dining venue. The menu—ranging from crab tartine to pork empanadas—is both inventive and budget-friendly. **Known for:** daily brunch; charcuterie plates; expansive next-door bottle shop. ⑤ *Average main: $17* ✉ *328 G St., Downtown* ☎ *907/865–9198* ⊕ *www.crushak.com* ⊗ *No dinner Sun.*

Glacier BrewHouse

$$$ | **AMERICAN** | The scent of hops permeates the cavernous, wood-beam BrewHouse, where at least a dozen beers are brewed on the premises. Locals mingle with visitors in this noisy, always-busy heart-of-town restaurant, and dinner selections range from chili-lime shrimp to fettuccine jambalaya and fresh seafood (in season). **Known for:** brick-oven pizzas; can't-miss dessert menu; great home-brewed beer. ⑤ *Average main: $25* ✉ *737 W. 5th Ave., Downtown* ☎ *907/274–2739* ⊕ *www.glacierbrewhouse.com.*

★ Marx Bros. Cafe

$$$$ | **AMERICAN** | Inside a small frame house built in 1916, this nationally recognized 14-table restaurant opened in 1979 and is still going strong thanks to a daily-changing menu that highlights classic Alaskan ingredients. The wine list encompasses more than 700 international choices. **Known for:** exceptionally deep wine cellar; table-made Caesar salads; homemade butter pecan ice cream. ⑤ *Average main: $47* ✉ *627 W. 3rd Ave., Downtown* ☎ *907/278–2133* ⊕ *www. marxcafe.com* ⊗ *Closed Sun. and Mon. No lunch.*

New Sagaya's City Market

$ | ECLECTIC | Stop at either the Downtown or Midtown New Sagaya's grocery stores for quick lunches, healthy to-go food (perfect for hiking or camping), and Kaladi Brothers coffee. The in-house bakery and deli, L'Aroma, makes specialty breads, sandwiches, California-style pizzas, and a wide range of snack-worthy pastries. **Known for:** fresh seafood counter; Asian ingredients galore; outdoor seating. $ *Average main: $9* ✉ *900 W. 13th Ave., Downtown* ☎ *907/274–6173* ⊕ *www. newsagaya.com.*

★ Snow City Cafe

$ | ECLECTIC | On summer days, Snow City attracts some serious crowds— and for good reason. This modern but unassuming café, convenient to many of the Downtown hotels, serves one of Anchorage's best (and reasonably priced) breakfasts all day long. **Known for:** inventive eggs Benedict; build-your-own omelets with snow crab and salmon; long waits unless you go early or make a reservation. $ *Average main: $13* ✉ *1034 W. 4th Ave., Downtown* ☎ *907/272–2489* ⊕ *www.snowcitycafe.com* ☽ *No dinner.*

Wild Scoops

$ | ECLECTIC |FAMILY | Step inside this Downtown microcreamery for Alaska-inspired ice cream flavors like almond birch brittle and rhubarb crumble. The homemade, small-batch ice cream options rotate constantly, emphasizing local ingredients like honey, blueberries, sea salt, and even beer. **Known for:** the favorite ice cream of Alaskan locals; innovative ingredients; fresh and unique flavors. $ *Average main: $5* ✉ *429 E St., Downtown* ☎ *907/744–7295* ⊕ *www. wildscoops.com.*

🛏 Hotels

Lodging for most cruise-ship travelers is typically included in package tours set up through a travel agency, an online site, or directly from the cruise line. If you prefer to pick your own hotel or bed-and-breakfast, make your reservations well ahead of time, since many central hotels fill up months in advance for the peak summer season. Rooms are generally available, though you may be staying in Midtown, 2 miles from Downtown.

Anchorage Marriott Downtown

$$$$ | HOTEL | One of Anchorage's biggest lodgings, the brightly decorated Marriott appeals to business travelers, tourists, and corporate clients. **Pros:** great views; modern, up-to-date facilities; near Downtown's best restaurants. **Cons:** extra charge for Wi-Fi; pricey valet parking; cruise-ship crowds at times in summer. $ *Rooms from: $359* ✉ *820 W. 7th Ave., Downtown* ☎ *907/279–8000, 800/228–9290* ⊕ *www.marriott.com/ancdt* ⬎ *392 rooms* ⦿ *No meals.*

Comfort Inn Downtown Ship Creek

$$$ | HOTEL |FAMILY | The namesake Ship Creek gurgles past this popular family hotel, which is a short walk northeast of the Alaska Railroad Historic Depot and practically on top of the Creek's parallel paved walking trail. **Pros:** free parking; pet-friendly rooms; loaner poles for guests with fishing licenses. **Cons:** walk into Downtown is an uphill climb; train noise; close to an industrial part of town. $ *Rooms from: $249* ✉ *111 Ship Creek Ave., Downtown* ☎ *907/277–6887, 800/424–6423* ⊕ *www.choicehotels.com* ⬎ *100 rooms* ⦿ *Breakfast.*

Historic Anchorage Hotel

$$$ | HOTEL | Part of the Anchorage landscape since 1916, experienced travelers call this little building the most charming hotel in town. **Pros:** excellent staff; on the National Register of Historic Places; complimentary breakfast in the hotel's former saloon. **Cons:** some rooms are small; no airport shuttle; street noise affects some rooms. $ *Rooms from: $219* ✉ *330 E St., Downtown* ☎ *907/272–4553, 800/544–0988* ⊕ *www.historicanchoragehotel.com* ⬎ *26 rooms* ⦿ *Breakfast.*

★ Hotel Captain Cook

$$$$ | HOTEL | Recalling Captain Cook's voyages to Alaska and the South Pacific, dark teak paneling lines the hotel's interior, and a nautical theme continues into the guest rooms. **Pros:** very well-trained and accommodating staff; excellent lobby bar and rooftop restaurant; destination hotel for visiting dignitaries, including President Obama in 2015. **Cons:** 24-hour parking passes cost $30; lots of lobby traffic; no airport shuttle. ⑤ *Rooms from: $300* ✉ *939 W. 5th Ave., Downtown* ☎ *907/276–6000, 800/843–1950* ⊕ *www. captaincook.com* ⇆ *642 rooms* ⦿ *No meals.*

Oscar Gill House

$$ | B&B/INN | Originally built by Gill in the settlement of Knik (north of Anchorage) in 1913, this historic home has been transformed into a comfortable B&B in a quiet neighborhood along Delaney Park Strip, with Downtown attractions a short walk away. **Pros:** great breakfast; cozy home with some old Anchorage history; very hospitable owners. **Cons:** shared bath in two of the rooms; no king-size beds; no elevator to second floor. ⑤ *Rooms from: $135* ✉ *1344 W. 10th Ave., Downtown* ☎ *907/279–1344* ⊕ *www.oscargill.com* ⇆ *3 rooms, 1 with bath* ⦿ *Breakfast.*

Nightlife

Anchorage does not shut down when it gets dark—well, that is when it actually does get dark (it's still light at 3 am in the summer!). Bars here—and throughout Alaska—open early (in the morning) and close as late as 3 am on weekends. The listings in the Alaska Dispatch News entertainment section, published on Friday, and in the free weekly Anchorage Press (⊕ *www.anchoragepress.com*) cover concerts, theater performances, movies, and a roundup of nightspots featuring live music.

49th State Brewing Company

BREWPUBS/BEER GARDENS | The rustic interior here is all stone, wood, and antlers, but the real attraction is the sun-soaked back deck and rooftop, where, on clear days, you can see Denali hovering over the northern horizon. The menu of pizzas and hearty bar bites emphasizes all things Alaska, including giant burgers appropriately named for noteworthy peaks. Beers are brewed on-site using local ingredients like Sitka spruce tips and Talkeetna birch syrup. The restaurant also hosts a range of events in its on-site theater, including improv comedy and trivia nights. ✉ *717 W. 3rd Ave., Downtown* ☎ *907/277–7727* ⊕ *www.49statebrewing.com.*

★ Chilkoot Charlie's

BARS/PUBS | A rambling timber building with sawdust floors, loud music, weekend DJs, and rowdy customers, Chilkoot Charlie's is where young Alaskans go to get crazy. The legendary bar has many unusual nooks and crannies, including a room filled with Russian artifacts and a reconstructed version of Alaska's infamous Birdhouse Bar. ✉ *2435 Spenard Rd., Spenard* ☎ *907/272–1010* ⊕ *www. koots.com.*

Club Paris

BARS/PUBS | Lots of old-timers favor the dark bar of Club Paris. This is your spot if you like a stiff, no-nonsense drink. ✉ *417 W. 5th Ave., Downtown* ☎ *907/277–6332* ⊕ *www.clubparisrestaurant.com.*

★ Humpy's Great Alaskan Alehouse

MUSIC CLUBS | One of Anchorage's best bars, Humpy's Great Alaskan Alehouse serves up rock, blues, and folk several nights a week, including an open mike on Sunday, along with dozens of microbrews (more than 40 beers are on tap) and surprisingly tasty pub grub. Trivia buffs should head to Humpy's on Tuesday night for the weekly pub quiz. You can grab one of Humpy's delicious halibut burgers on your way out of town—the company has a satellite restaurant in Terminal B of the

Anchorage airport. ✉ *610 W. 6th Ave., Downtown* ☎ *907/276–2337* ⊕ *www. humpys.com.*

Simon & Seafort's Saloon & Grill
BARS/PUBS | A trendy place for the dressy crowd, the bar at Simon & Seafort's Saloon & Grill has stunning views of Cook Inlet, a special single-malt-Scotch menu, and tempting cocktails. The lavender martini is a highlight. Take advantage of the two happy hours each day, including a late-night stretch starting at 9 pm. ✉ *420 L St., Downtown* ☎ *907/274–3502* ⊕ *www.simonandseaforts.com.*

🛍 Shopping

Stock up for your travels around Alaska in Anchorage, where there's no sales tax. The weekend markets are packed with Alaskan-made products of all types, and you're likely to meet local artisans.

BOOKS
Title Wave Books
BOOKS/STATIONERY | Easily the largest independent bookstore in Alaska, Title Wave Books fills a 24,000-square-foot space in the Northern Lights Center. The shelves are filled with nearly half a million used books, CDs, and DVDs across more than 1,600 categories, including a large section of Alaska-focused books. The staff is very knowledgeable, and the store hosts regular game nights and children's story times. Anyone can bring in used books and trade them for store credit. ✉ *1360 W. Northern Lights Blvd., Spenard* ☎ *907/278–9283, 888/598–9283* ⊕ *www.wavebooks.com.*

MARKETS
★ Anchorage Market and Festival
OUTDOOR/FLEA/GREEN MARKETS | On weekends from mid-May to mid-September, the Anchorage Market and Festival opens for business in the parking lot at 3rd Avenue and E Street. Dozens of vendors offer Alaskan-made crafts, ethnic imports, and deliciously fattening food. Stock up on birch candy and salmon jerky

to snack on while traveling or as perfect made-in-Alaska gifts for friends back home. ✉ *3rd Ave. between E and C Sts., Downtown* ☎ *907/272–5634* ⊕ *www. anchoragemarkets.com.*

NATIVE CRAFTS
Oomingmak
CLOTHING | The Alaska Native–owned cooperative Oomingmak sells items made of qiviut, the ubersoft and warm undercoat of musk ox, from inside one of the few small houses remaining in Downtown. Scarves, shawls, hats, and tunics are knitted in traditional patterns by women in villages across Alaska. ✉ *604 H St., Downtown* ☎ *907/272–9225, 888/360–9665* ⊕ *www.qiviut.com.*

Seattle

Seattle has much to offer: a gorgeous setting, lively arts and entertainment, innovative restaurants, friendly residents, green spaces galore, and Pike Place Market, which provides a wonderfully earthy focal point for downtown Seattle, with views of the ferries crossing Elliott Bay. Visitors to the city will almost certainly wish they had set aside more time to take in Seattle's charms.

Seattle, like Rome, is said to be built on seven hills. As a visitor, you're likely to spend much of your time on only two of them (Capitol Hill and Queen Anne Hill), but the city's hills are indeed the most definitive element of the city's natural and spiritual landscape. Years of largely thoughtful building practices have kept tall buildings from obscuring the lines of sight, maintaining vistas in most directions and around almost every turn. The hills are lofty, privileged perches from which residents are constantly reminded of the beauty of the forests, mountains, and waters surrounding the city—that is, when it stops raining long enough for you to enjoy those amazing views.

Seattle is also one of the fastest-growing urban centers in the United States, buoyed by a booming tech industry in particular. At times it feels as though the entire city is under construction—or stuck in traffic. Be sure to factor in a bit of wiggle room when you're out exploring, and keep in mind that everything books up quickly during the peak summer tourist season.

In the heart of downtown Seattle's bustling retail core, the Seattle Convention and Visitors Bureau offers ticket sales, reservation and concierge services, dining suggestions, and a handy visitor information packet and coupon book that can be emailed to you.

THE CRUISE PORT

Ships from Norwegian Cruise Line and Oceania Cruises dock at the Bell Street Pier Cruise Terminal at Pier 66. Pier 66 is within walking distance of downtown attractions, and a city bus wrapped in the Waterfront Streetcar logo (the real 1927 Waterfront Streetcars are out of commission until they can be upgraded) provides trolley service along the shoreline to the cruise terminal.

Holland America Line, Princess Cruises, Celebrity Cruises, Carnival Cruise Line, and Royal Caribbean dock at the newer Smith Cove Cruise Terminal at Pier 91, at the north end of the downtown waterfront. It is best accessed by cruise-line motor-coach transfer, taxi, or shuttle service.

Many cruise passengers drive themselves to the port via I–90 west. The Port of Seattle website has clear maps and directions to each pier.

CONTACTS Bell Street Cruise Terminal at Pier 66 ⊠ *2225 Alaskan Way* ☎ *206/787–3900* ⊕ *www.cruiseterminalsofamerica. com.* **Smith Cove Cruise Terminal at Pier 91** ⊠ *2001 W. Garfield St.* ☎ *206/787–3900* ⊕ *www.cruiseterminalsofamerica.com.*

GETTING HERE AND AROUND
AIRPORT TRANSFERS

The major gateway is Seattle–Tacoma International Airport (Sea-Tac). Sea-Tac is about 15 miles south of downtown on Interstate 5 (I–5). It takes 25–40 minutes to ride between the airport and downtown, depending on traffic. Metered cabs make the trip for around $40–$45. Shuttle Express Downtown Airporter has the only 24-hour door-to-door service, from $19.99 per person each way between the airport to downtown. You can make arrangements at the Downtown Airporter counter upon arrival at Sea-Tac or online. If you're traveling directly to Pier 91 from the airport ($36 per person, one-way), contact Shuttle Express. A more affordable option is the Link light rail system, which whisks passengers from Sea-Tac to downtown's Westlake Station; trains depart every 7–15 minutes for the 35-minute ride ($3).

Transfers to the piers between Sea-Tac Airport and designated hotels are offered by the cruise lines, either as an add-on to your fare or, in the case of some luxury cruise lines or small-ship cruise lines, included in the price of your cruise. Cruise-line representatives meet airport arrivals and are present at hotel transfer points to make the process virtually seamless.

AIRPORT INFORMATION Seattle–Tacoma International Airport ☎ *206/787–5388, 800/544–1965* ⊕ *www.portseattle.org.*

AIRPORT TRANSFER Shuttle Express ☎ *425/981–7000* ⊕ *www.shuttleexpress. com.*

PUBLIC TRANSPORTATION

The bus system, Metro Bus, will get you anywhere you need to go, although some routes farther afield require a time commitment and several transfers. Within the downtown core, however, the bus is efficient. King County Metro's Trip Planner is a useful resource. Bus fare is a flat $2.75 regardless of the time of travel.

Built for the 1962 World's Fair, the monorail is the shortest transportation system in the city. It runs from Westlake Center (at 5th and Pine) to Seattle Center. But it is a great option for visitors who plan to spend a day at the Space Needle and the Seattle Center's museums. A single ride is $2.50.

The Seattle Streetcar, the second-shortest system in the city, was built to connect downtown to the up-and-coming neighborhood of South Lake Union (which is directly east of Seattle Center). It runs from Westlake and Olive to the southern shore of Lake Union. In 2016, Seattle Streetcar debuted its First Hill line, which connects downtown's Pioneer Square and Capitol Hill. A single ride is $2.25.

CONTACTS Metro Transit ☎ *206/553–3000 for customer service, schedules, and information, 206/263–3582 for bus-pass and ticket sales* ⊕ *metro.kingcounty.gov.* **Seattle Center Monorail** ☎ *206/905–2620* ⊕ *www.seattlemonorail.com.* **Seattle Streetcar** ☎ *866/205–5001, 206/553–3000* ⊕ *www.seattlestreetcar.org.* **Sound Transit** ☎ *888/889–6368, 206/398–5000* ⊕ *www. soundtransit.org.*

TAXIS

Seattle's taxi fleet is small, but you can sometimes hail a cab on the street, especially downtown. Most of the time you must call for one. Except on Friday and Saturday nights, you rarely have to wait more than a few minutes for pickup. Cab rides can be pricey but useful, especially late at night when buses run infrequently. Yellow Cab is your best bet. Many locals rely on so-called ride-sharing services like Uber or Lyft rather than taxis, which can be tough to hail even near popular tourist haunts. To use either, you'll need to download and install an app, follow the simple prompts (be sure to read the fine print), and enter your credit-card information. Ride-sharing services are especially useful if you want to explore off-the-beaten path. Both tend to be cheaper than cabs.

CONTACTS Lyft ⊕ *www.lyft.com.* **Uber** ⊕ *www.uber.com.* **Yellow Cab** ☎ *206/622– 6500* ⊕ *www.seattleyellowcab.com.*

TRAIN TRAVEL

Amtrak provides train service north to Vancouver; south to Portland, Oakland, and Los Angeles; and east to Spokane, Chicago, and other cities. Amtrak's King Street Station is just south of downtown at 3rd Avenue South and South King Street.

CONTACTS Amtrak ☎ *800/872–7245* ⊕ *www.amtrak.com.*

HOURS

Most attractions are open from 10 to 6 (some with extended hours during the summer), but some museums may close on Monday. Businesses are usually open from 10 to 6 (or later). ■TIP→ **Many of the city's busiest attractions offer advance booking; for an additional fee, some will even allow you to choose a time slot, so you don't waste time in long lines.**

PARKING

Note that parking at both piers fills up fast, and both parking lots discussed here offer handicapped parking spaces. If you're driving to Pier 66, you can reserve a parking space at Bell Street Pier Garage (directly across from the pier) at a discount online with Republic Parking. Fares are $22 per day (discounted if prepaid online). Note that there are no facilities for oversize vehicles such as RVs.

If you're sailing from Pier 91 (Smith Cove Terminal), you can also reserve a spot ahead of time with Republic Parking. Fares are $27 per day (discounted if prepaid online). RV and overheight vehicles for those sailing from Pier 66 can also park here ($40 per day for RVs and overheight; $60 if over 40 feet). For those parking here but departing from Pier 66, a taxi voucher is provided. While

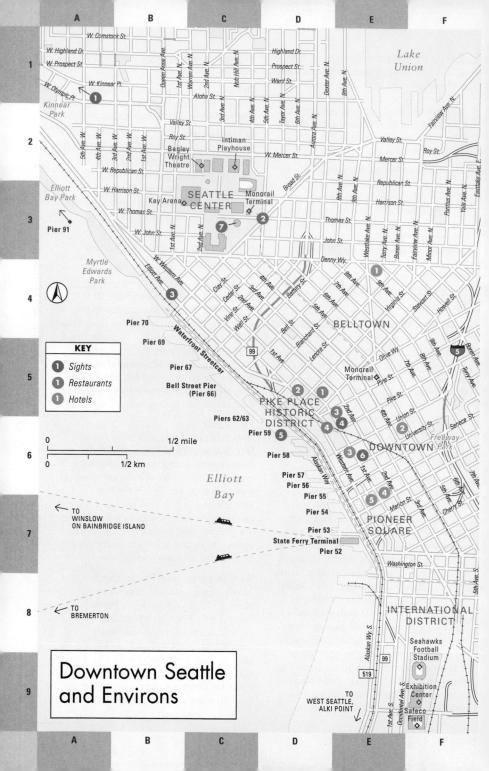

4

Ports of Embarkation SEATTLE

not required, prepaid reservations are recommended to guarantee a spot.

CONTACTS Republic Parking ☎ *206/783–4144 Ext 1113 cruise parking* ⊕ *www.rpnw.com.* **Port of Seattle** ⊕ *www.portseattle.org.*

VISITOR INFORMATION
CONTACTS Seattle Visitors Center ✉ *Suite 800, 701 Pike Street* ☎ *866/732–2695 visitor information* ⊕ *www.visitseattle.org.*

Sights

The Elliott Bay waterfront is one of Seattle's most fascinating features, and Pike Place Market, the Seattle Aquarium, and the Seattle Art Museum (SAM) are all within close walking distance. Just south of downtown is the historic Pioneer Square area, and a short distance north of Pike Place Market lies the Olympic Sculpture Park, a magnificent waterfront urban playground filled with gigantic works of art. North of the sculpture park is Seattle Center, a civic gathering place that's home to the Space Needle, the Museum of Pop Culture (MoPOP), the Children's Museum, and the Pacific Science Center.

★ Olympic Sculpture Park
PUBLIC ART | An outdoor branch of the Seattle Art Museum is a favorite destination for picnics, strolls, and quiet contemplation. Nestled at the edge of Belltown with views of Elliott Bay, the gently sloping green space features native plants and walking paths that wind past bigger-than-life public artwork. On sunny days, the park frames an astounding panorama of the Olympic Mountains, but even the grayest afternoon casts a favorable light on the site's sculptures. The grounds are home to works by such artists as Richard Serra, Louise Bourgeois, and Alexander Calder, whose bright-red steel "Eagle" sculpture is a local favorite (and a nod to the bald eagles that sometimes soar above). "Echo," a 46-foot-tall elongated

girl's face by Spanish artist Jaume Plensa, is a beautiful and bold presence on the waterfront. The park's PACCAR Pavilion has a gift shop, café, and information about the artworks. ✉ *2901 Western Ave., between Broad and Bay Sts., Belltown* ☎ *206/654–3100* ⊕ *www.seattleartmuseum.org* ⊠ *Free.*

★ Pike Place Market
MARKET | FAMILY | One of the nation's largest and oldest public markets dates from 1907, when the city issued permits allowing farmers to sell produce from parked wagons. At one time the market was a madhouse of vendors hawking their produce and haggling with customers over prices; now you might find fishmongers engaging in frenzied banter and hilarious antics, but chances are you won't get them to waver on prices. There are many restaurants, bakeries, coffee shops (including the flagship Starbucks), lunch counters, and ethnic eateries. Go to Pike Place hungry and you won't be disappointed. The flower market is also a must-see—gigantic fresh arrangements can be found for around $10. It's well worth wading through dense crowds to enjoy the market's many corridors, where you'll find specialty-food items, quirky gift shops, tea, honey, jams, comic books, beads, eclectic crafts, and cookware. In spring 2017, Pike Place Market debuted a significant expansion, fulfilling a decades-long vision for Seattle's Market Historic District. The market's new digs feature artisanal-food purveyors, an on-site brewery, four public art installations, and a 30,000-square-foot open public space with a plaza and a viewing deck overlooking Elliott Bay. ✉ *Pike Pl. at Pike St., west of 1st Ave., Downtown* ☎ *206/682–7453* ⊕ *www.pikeplacemarket.org.*

★ Seattle Aquarium
ZOO | FAMILY | Located right at the water's edge, the Seattle Aquarium is one of the nation's premier aquariums. Among

Seattle is a city of many hills—and many spectacular views.

its most engaging residents are the sea otters—kids, especially, seem able to spend hours watching the delightful antics of these creatures and their river cousins. In the Puget Sound Great Hall, "Window on Washington Waters," a slice of Neah Bay life, is presented in a 20-foot-tall tank holding 120,000 gallons of water. The aquarium's darkened rooms and large, lighted tanks brilliantly display Pacific Northwest marine life. The "Life on the Edge" tide pools re-create Washington's rocky coast and sandy beaches—kids can touch the starfish, sea urchins, and sponges. Huge glass windows provide underwater views of the harbor seal exhibit; go up top to watch them play in their pools. If you're visiting in fall or winter, dress warmly— the Marine Mammal area is outside on the waterfront and catches all of those chilly Puget Sound breezes. The café serves Ivar's chowder and kid-friendly food like burgers and chicken fingers; the balcony has views of Elliott Bay. ⊠ *1483 Alaskan Way, Pier 59, Downtown* ☎ *206/386–4300* ⊕ *www.seattleaquarium.org* ✉ *$29.95.*

★ **Seattle Art Museum**

MUSEUM | Sculptor Jonathan Borofsky's several-stories-high "Hammering Man" greets visitors to SAM, as locals call this pride of the city's art scene. SAM's permanent collection surveys American, Asian, Native American, African, Oceanic, and pre-Columbian art. Collections of African dance masks and Native American carvings are particularly strong. SAM's free floors have the best attractions for kids, including an installation of cars hanging upside down from the ceiling and the WaMu OpenStudio. ⊠ *1300 1st Ave., Downtown* ☎ *206/654–3100* ⊕ *www.seattleartmuseum.org* ✉ *$24.95; fee for special exhibitions; free 1st Thurs. of month* ⊗ *Closed Tuesday.*

★ **Discovery Park**

NATIONAL/STATE PARK | **FAMILY** | You won't find more spectacular views of Puget Sound, the Cascades, and the Olympics. Located on Magnolia Bluff, northwest of Downtown, Seattle's largest park covers

534 acres and has an amazing variety of terrain: shaded, secluded forest trails lead to meadows, saltwater beaches, sand dunes, a lighthouse, and 2 miles of protected beaches. The North Beach Trail, which takes you along the shore to the lighthouse, is a must-see. Head to the South Bluff Trail to get a view of Mt. Rainier. The park has several entrances—if you want to stop at the visitor center to pick up a trail map before exploring, use the main entrance at Government Way. The North Parking Lot is much closer to the North Beach Trail and to Ballard and Fremont, if you're coming from that direction. First-come, first-served beach parking passes for the disabled, elderly, and families with small children are available at the Learning Center. Note that the park is easily reached from Ballard and Fremont. It's easier to combine a park day with an exploration of those neighborhoods than with a busy Downtown itinerary. ✉ *3801 W. Government Way, Magnolia* ✥ *From Downtown, take Elliot Ave. W (which turns into 15th Ave. W), and get off at Emerson St. exit and turn left onto W. Emerson. Make a right onto Gilman Ave. W (which eventually becomes W. Government Way). As you enter park, road becomes Washington Ave.; turn left on Utah Ave.* ☎ *206/386–4236* ⊕ *www.seattle.gov/parks/find/parks/discovery-park* ✉ *Free.*

★ Museum of Pop Culture (MoPOP)

MUSEUM | FAMILY | Formerly EMP, Seattle's most controversial architectural statement is the 140,000-square-foot complex designed by architect Frank Gehry, who drew inspiration from electric guitars to achieve the building's curvy metallic design. It's a fitting backdrop for rock memorabilia from the likes of Bob Dylan and the grunge-scene heavies. Two permanent exhibits provide a primer on the evolution of Seattle's music scene, focusing on Nirvana and Jimi Hendrix, respectively. In the Science Fiction Museum and Hall of Fame—now a permanent exhibit—you'll find iconic artifacts from sci-fi literature, film, television, and art, including an Imperial Dalek from *Doctor Who,* the command chair from the classic television series *Star Trek,* and Neo's coat from *The Matrix Reloaded.* ✉ *325 5th Ave. N, between Broad and Thomas Sts., Central District* ☎ *206/770–2700* ⊕ *www.mopop.org* ✉ *$36 (less if purchased online).*

Space Needle

BUILDING | FAMILY | More than 50 years old, Seattle's most iconic building is as quirky and beloved as ever. The distinctive, towering, 605-foot-high structure is visible throughout much of Seattle—but the view from the inside out is even better. A less-than-one-minute ride up to the observation deck yields 360-degree vistas of Downtown Seattle, the Olympic Mountains, Elliott Bay, Queen Anne Hill, Lake Union, and the Cascade Range. Built for the 1962 World's Fair, the Needle has educational kiosks, interactive trivia game stations for kids, and the glass-enclosed SpaceBase store and Pavilion spiraling around the base of the tower. The top-floor SkyCity restaurant is "revolutionary" (literally—watch the skyline evolve as you dine) and the elevator trip and observation deck are complimentary with your reservation. For an extra $5, you can test your mettle on The Loupe, the world's first and only rotating glass floor that turns 500-feet above street level. If the forecast says you may have a sunny day during your visit, schedule the Needle for that day! If you can't decide whether you want the daytime or nighttime view, for an extra 10 bucks you can buy a ticket that allows you to visit twice in one day. (Also look for package deals with Chihuly Garden and Glass.) ✉ *400 Broad St., Central District* ☎ *206/905–2100* ⊕ *www.spaceneedle.com* ✉ *From $32.50.*

Restaurants

Downtown is a good area for lunch; come evening, its action centers on hotel restaurants and a handful of watering holes. Belltown, on the other hand, comes alive nightly with chic restaurants and bars, plus music and other entertainment. Pioneer Square is a bit more rough around the edges at night and features bars and restaurants that cater to baseball fans.

Lola

$$$ | MEDITERRANEAN | Tom Douglas dishes out his signature Northwest style, spiked with Greek and Mediterranean touches—another huge success for the local celebrity chef. Try a sensational tagine of Northwest seafood; a variety of meat kebabs; and scrumptious spreads including hummus, tzatziki, and *harissa* (a red-pepper concoction). **Known for:** Greek food; breakfast; doughnuts. $ *Average main: $24* ⊠ *2000 4th Ave., Belltown* ☎ *206/441-1430* ⊕ *www.lolaseattle.com.*

Le Pichet

$$$ | FRENCH | Located a few minutes' walking from Pike Place Market, this small french bistro is about as authentic as it gets. It offers an all day charcuterie snacking selection, a Casse-Croute menu for smaller appetites, as well as lunch and dinner menus featuring traditional French faves like chicken roasted to order with Basque-style sweet pepper–pancetta ragout and pork loin escalope. **Known for:** superb service; intimate yet lively atmosphere; value. $ *Average main: $23* ⊠ *1933 1st Ave.* ☎ *206/256-1499* ⊕ *lepichetseattle.com.*

★ Matt's in the Market

$$$$ | PACIFIC NORTHWEST | One of the most beloved of Pike Place Market's restaurants, Matt's is all about intimate dining, fresh ingredients, and superb service. You can perch at the bar for pints and the signature deviled eggs or be seated at a table—complete with vases filled with flowers from the market—for

Seattle CityPass

If you're in Seattle for several days before or after your cruise, look into the CityPASS, which gives admission to five different attractions for just $89 ($69 for kids 12 and under)—nearly half off what admission for all five would be without a discount. The pass covers admission to the Space Needle, the Seattle Aquarium, a Seattle harbor tour, and the Woodland Park Zoo or the Museum of Pop Culture (MoPop), and the Pacific Science Center OR the Chihuly Garden & Glass. See ⊕ *www.citypass.com/seattle* for more information.

a seasonal menu that synthesizes the best picks from the restaurant's produce vendors and an excellent wine list. **Known for:** view; seafood; celebrity chef Dan Bugge. $ *Average main: $39* ⊠ *94 Pike St., Downtown* ☎ *206/467-7909* ⊕ *www.mattsinthemarket.com* ⊙ *Closed Sun.*

Place Pigalle

$$$ | MODERN AMERICAN | Large windows look out on Elliott Bay in this cozy spot tucked behind a meat vendor in Pike Place Market's main arcade. In nice weather, open windows let in the fresh salt breeze. $ *Average main: $33* ⊠ *81 Pike St., Downtown* ☎ *206/624-1756* ⊕ *www.placepigalle-seattle.com.*

🛏 Hotels

Alexis Hotel

$$$$ | HOTEL | Two historic buildings (on the National Register of Historic Places, in fact) near the waterfront use exposed brick, walls of windows, and nouveau-baroque touches to appeal to aesthetes and modern romantics, and ornate leather chairs and wood-burning fireplaces

4

Ports of Embarkation SEATTLE

recall a different era. **Pros:** close to waterfront; unique, beautiful rooms; suites aren't prohibitively expensive. **Cons:** small lobby; not entirely soundproofed against old building and city noise; some rooms can be a bit dark. ⑤ *Rooms from: $285* ✉ *1007 1st Ave., Downtown* ☎ *206/624–4844, 888/850–1155* ⊕ *www.alexishotel.com* ➦ *88 rooms* ⦿ *No meals.*

★ The Fairmont Olympic Hotel

$$$$ | **HOTEL** | **FAMILY** | With marble floors, soaring ceilings, massive chandeliers, and sweeping staircases, the lobby of this very centrally located hotel personifies old-world elegance, while guest rooms have a modern twist. **Pros:** great location; excellent service; fabulous on-site dining and amenities. **Cons:** not much in the way of views; water pressure on higher floors can be low; some rooms on the small side. ⑤ *Rooms from: $479* ✉ *411 University St., Downtown* ☎ *206/621–1700, 888/363–5022* ⊕ *www.fairmont.com/seattle* ➦ *450 rooms* ⦿ *No meals.*

★ Four Seasons Hotel Seattle

$$$$ | **HOTEL** | **FAMILY** | Just south of the Pike Place Market and steps from the Seattle Art Museum, this Downtown gem is polished and elegant, with Eastern accents and plush furnishings in comfortable living spaces in which Pacific Northwest materials, such as stone and fine hardwoods, take center stage. **Pros:** fantastic location with amazing water views; large rooms with luxurious bathrooms with deep soaking tubs; lovely spa. **Cons:** Four Seasons regulars might not click with this modern take on the brand; street-side rooms not entirely soundproofed; some room views are partially obscured by industrial sites. ⑤ *Rooms from: $699* ✉ *99 Union St., Downtown* ☎ *206/749–7000, 800/332–3442* ⊕ *www.fourseasons.com/seattle* ➦ *134 rooms* ⦿ *No meals.*

Loews Hotel 1000

$$$$ | **HOTEL** | **FAMILY** | Since Loews took over this hotel in 2016, it has been reimagined into a very chic, modern, and inviting locale with luxurious tech-savvy rooms. **Pros:** terrific location near Pike Place Market; golf simulator and spa; speakeasy-style lobby bar. **Cons:** bar attracts a lot of tourists; a handful of no-view rooms look out to a cement wall. ⑤ *Rooms from: $425* ✉ *1000 1st Ave., Downtown* ☎ *206/957–1000, 844/244–4973* ⊕ *www.hotel1000seattle.com* ➦ *120 rooms* ⦿ *No meals.*

★ Pan Pacific Hotel Seattle

$$$$ | **HOTEL** | Located in one of Seattle's most vibrant and transforming neighborhoods, this hotel has undeniable draws, from the attractive and comfortable modern rooms to a happening lobby bar-restaurant serving Northwest cuisine and tapas, to the impressive views of the Space Needle and Lake Union. **Pros:** no touristy vibe like Downtown hotels; feels more luxurious than it costs; award-winning sustainability efforts. **Cons:** long walk to Downtown (though streetcar access and the hotel's free car service help with that); bathroom design isn't the most private. ⑤ *Rooms from: $350* ✉ *2125 Terry Ave., South Lake Union* ☎ *206/264–8111* ⊕ *www.panpacific.com/seattle* ➦ *131 rooms* ⦿ *No meals.*

Nightlife

The grunge-rock legacy of Nirvana, Soundgarden, and Pearl Jam still reverberates in local music venues, which showcase up-and-coming pop, punk, heavy metal, and alternative bands, along with healthy doses of other genres.

Two free papers, the *Stranger* and *Seattle Weekly* (see ⊕ *www.thestranger.com* or ⊕ *www.seattleweekly.com*), provide detailed music, art, and nightlife listings. Friday editions of the *Seattle Times* have pullout sections detailing weekend events.

Bars and clubs stay open until 2 am. Cabs are easy to find, and some buses run until the early morning hours (see

metro.kingcounty.gov). After the witching hour, cabs are the best option for those not willing to hoof it.

BARS AND CLUBS

Black Bottle

BARS/PUBS | This sleek and sexy gastro-tavern makes the northern reaches of Belltown look good. The interior is simple but stylish, with black chairs and tables and shiny wood floors. It gets crowded on nights and weekends with a laid-back but often dressed-up clientele. A small selection of beers on tap and a solid wine list (with Washington, Oregon, California, and beyond well represented) will help you wash down the sustainably sourced and creatively presented snacks and shareable dishes, including house-smoked wild boar ribs, pork belly with kimchi, and oysters on the half shell. Vegan and nut-, dairy- and gluten-free options are plentiful. ✉ *2600 1st Ave., Belltown* ☎ *206/441–1500* ⊕ *www.blackbottleseattle.com.*

★ The Crocodile

MUSIC CLUBS | The heart and soul of Seattle's music scene since 1991 has hosted the likes of the Beastie Boys, Pearl Jam, and Mudhoney, along with countless other bands. There's a reason *Rolling Stone* once called the 525-person Crocodile one of the best small clubs in America. Nightly shows are complemented by cheap beer on tap and pizza at the Back Bar. All hail the Croc! ✉ *2200 2nd Ave., Belltown* ☎ *206/441–7416* ⊕ *www.thecrocodile.com.*

★ Zig Zag Café

BARS/PUBS | A mixed crowd of mostly locals hunts out this unique spot at Pike Place Market's Street Hill Climb (walk past the Gum Wall—yes, it really is as disgusting as it sounds—to find a nearly hidden stairwell leading down to the piers). In addition to pouring a perfect martini, Zig Zag features a revolving cast of memorable cocktails. A Mediterranean-inspired food menu offers plenty of tasty bites to accompany the excellent cocktails. A small patio is the place to be on a summery happy-hour evening. Zig Zag is friendly—retro without being obnoxiously ironic—and very Seattle, with the occasional live music show to boot. ✉ *1501 Western Ave., Downtown* ☎ *206/625–1146* ⊕ *zigzagseattle.com.*

💼 Shopping

Seattle's retail core might feel business-crisp by day, but it's casual and arts-centered by night, and the shopping scene reflects both these moods. Within a few square blocks—between 1st Avenue to the west and Boren Avenue to the east, and from University Street to Olive Way—you can find department-store flagships, several glossy vertical malls, dozens of upper-echelon boutiques, and retail chains. One block closer to Elliott Bay, on Western Avenue, high-end home-furnishings showrooms make up an informal "Furniture Row." The Waterfront, with its small, kitschy stores and open-air restaurants, is a great place to dawdle. ■ TIP➔ **Seattle's best shopping is found in the small neighborhood made up of 4th, 5th, and 6th avenues between Pine and Spring streets, and 1st Avenue between Virginia and Madison streets.**

Kobo

ART GALLERIES | The Japanese word *kobo* translates to "artist's workspace," and true to its ethos, this unusual gallery-shop is a showcase of Japanese and Northwest art, jewelry, and artsy housewares in practically all genres: textiles, ceramics, acrylics, wood, and more. Hanako Nakazato is a 14th-generation potter, Michael Zitka is a local modern-day folk artist and wood carver, and the very popular Rob Vetter is known for Seattle landscapes. Many pieces are highly unusual; treasures abound. ✉ *608 South Jackson St., Capitol Hill* ☎ *206/381–3000* ⊕ *www.koboseattle.com* ⊘ *Closed Mon.*

★ **Peter Miller Architectural & Design Books and Supplies**

BOOKS/STATIONERY | Aesthetes and architects haunt this shop, which is stocked with all things design. Rare, international architecture, art, and design books (including titles for children) mingle with high-end products from Alessi and Iittala; sleek notebooks, bags, portfolios, and drawing tools round out the collection. This is a great shop for quirky, unforgettable gifts, like a pentagram typography calendar, an Arne Jacobsen wall clock, or an aerodynamic umbrella. ⊠ *304 Alaskan Way South, Post Alley, Belltown ✛ entrance off alley* ☎ *206/441–4114* ⊕ *www. petermiller.com.*

★ **REI**

CLOTHING | The enormous flagship for Recreational Equipment, Inc. (REI) has an incredible selection of outdoor gear—polar-fleece jackets, wool socks, down vests, hiking boots, raingear, and much more—as well as its own 65-foot climbing wall. The staff is extremely knowledgeable; there always seems to be enough help on hand, even when the store is busy. You can test things out on the mountain-bike test trail or in the simulated rain booth. REI also rents gear such as tents, sleeping bags, skis, snowshoes, and backpacks. Bonus: the outdoor behemoth offers an hour of free parking. ⊠ *222 Yale Ave. N, South Lake Union* ☎ *206/223–1944* ⊕ *www.rei.com.*

Seward

It is hard to believe that a place as beautiful as Seward exists. Surrounded on all sides by Kenai Fjords National Park, Chugach National Forest, and Resurrection Bay, Seward offers all the quaint realities of a small railroad town with the bonus of jaw-dropping scenery. This little town of about 2,750 citizens was founded in 1903, when survey crews arrived at the ice-free port and began planning a railroad to the Interior. Since its inception,

Seward Best Bets

■ **Get your sea legs.** Seward's main claims to fame are Resurrection Bay and Kenai Fjords National Park.

■ **Landlubber?** Visit the park at Exit Glacier north of town, hike any of the numerous trails, or shop at one of the stores near the small-boat harbor or downtown.

■ **Rainy day?** The SeaLife Center is not to be missed. It's a combination aquarium, rescue facility for marine animals, and research center. If the seas are too rough or the rain is too bothersome, there's interesting stuff here for all ages.

4

Ports of Embarkation SEWARD

Seward has relied heavily on tourism and commercial fishing. It is also the launching point for excursions into Kenai Fjords National Park, where it is quite common to see marine life and calving glaciers.

Seward is an important embarkation and disembarkation port for cruise-ship travelers. Many large cruise ships terminate (or start) their seven-day Alaskan voyages in Seward. Although many cruise ships stop here, travelers are often shunted off to Anchorage on waiting buses or train cars, with no time to explore this lovely town.

THE CRUISE PORT

Most cruises that begin in Alaska actually start or end in Seward, but transportation from (or to) Anchorage is either included in your cruise fare or available as an add-on. Check with your cruise line for tours to the SeaLife Center that can be added on to an airport transfer. Cruise ships dock approximately a half mile from downtown.

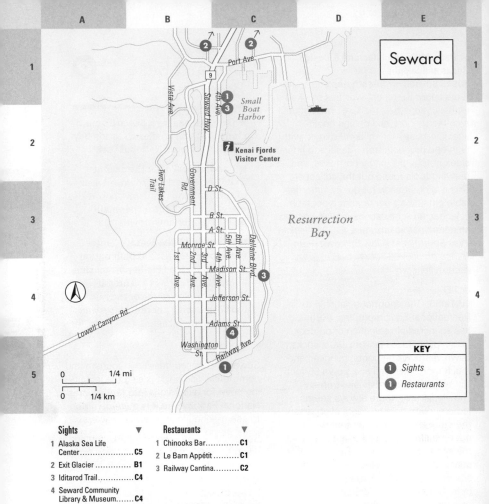

Seward

Resurrection Bay

Small Boat Harbor

Port Ave.

Kenai Fjords Visitor Center

KEY

①	Sights
①	Restaurants

0   1/4 mi

0   1/4 km

TOURS

Kenai Fjords Tours

TOUR—SPORTS | FAMILY | From May to September, this outfit offers five different Resurrection Bay wildlife tours. Cruise options include visits to Fox Island, interpretive programs by National Park Service rangers, up-close viewing of calving glaciers, and opportunities to see orcas, puffins, otters, harbor seals, porpoises, and sea lions. Lunch or dinner of prime rib and salmon on Fox Island is included in some tours. ⊠ *Seward* ☎ *888/478–3346* ⊕ *www.kenaifjords.com* ⌑ *From $80.*

Major Marine Tours

TOUR—SPORTS | This family-run operation has been offering aquatic tours of the fjords for more than 25 years. Onboard, a National Park Service ranger narrates the half- and full-day cruises of Resurrection Bay and Kenai Fjords National Park. For an additional price ($24), meals of salmon, prime rib, or vegetarian chili are available on the five- and six-hour cruises; all other trips include a deli-style lunch. Whether whale watching or glacier gazing, you're sure to have extraordinary wildlife sightings and awe-inspiring views. Major Marine can arrange transportation between Anchorage and Seward. ⊠ *Seward* ☎ *907/274–7300, 800/764–7300* ⊕ *www.majormarine.com* ⌑ *From $84.*

VISITOR INFORMATION

The **Seward Chamber of Commerce** has a visitor information center at the cruise-ship dock that is staffed when ships are in port. The **Kenai Fjords National Park visitor center** is within walking distance: turn left as you leave the pier, then left again onto 4th Avenue; the center is two blocks ahead.

CONTACTS Seward Chamber of Commerce

⊠ *2001 Seward Hwy.* ☎ *907/224–8051* ⊕ *www.seward.com.*

Maritime Explorations

The protected waters of the bay provide the perfect environment for sailing, fishing, sea kayaking, and marine wildlife–watching. There are numerous tours to choose from—just check out the boardwalk area adjacent to the docks. Half-day tours include Resurrection Bay, and all-day tours also allow you to view parts of spectacular Kenai Fjords National Park. The more adventurous trips venture out of the bay and into the Gulf of Alaska when the notoriously fickle weather permits visits to the more distant glaciers and attractions.

◉ Sights

★ Alaska SeaLife Center

ZOO | FAMILY | A research center as well as visitor center, Alaska SeaLife rehabilitates injured marine wildlife and provides educational experiences for the general public. The facility includes massive cold-water tanks and outdoor viewing decks as well as interactive displays of cold-water fish, seabirds, and marine mammals, including harbor seals and a 2,000-pound sea lion. The center was partially funded with reparations money from the *Exxon Valdez* oil spill. Films, hands-on activities, a gift shop, and behind-the-scenes tours where you can interract with different animals ($74.95) complete the offerings. ⊠ *301 Railway Ave.* ☎ *907/224–6300, 800/224–2525* ⊕ *www.alaskasealife.org* ⌑ *$25.*

Exit Glacier

NATURE SITE | A mass of ice that caps the Kenai Mountains, the Harding Icefield covers more than 1,100 square miles, and oozes more than 40 glaciers from its edges and down the mountainsides;

Exit Glacier is the most accessible part of the ice field. Just outside Seward, if you hike a mile up the paved trail that starts at the parking lot, you'll find yourself at the terminal moraine of Exit Glacier. Look for the marked turnoff at Mile 3.7 as you enter town, or you can take the hourly shuttle from downtown ($15 round-trip). There's a small walk-in campground here, a ranger station, and access to the glacier. The hike to the ice field from the parking lot is a 9-mile round-trip that gains 3,000 feet in elevation, so it's not for the timid or out of shape. But if you're feeling up to the task, the hike and views are breathtaking. Local wildlife includes mountain goats and bears both black and brown, so keep a sharp eye out for them. Due to recent ice fall at the toe of the glacier, the entire toe is currently off-limits. ✉ *Herman Leirer Rd.* ⊕ *www.nps.gov/kefj/planyourvisit/exit-glacier-area.htm.*

Iditarod Trail

TRAIL | The first mile of the historic original trail—at first called the Seward-to-Nome Mail Trail—runs along the beach and makes for a nice, easy stroll. ✉ *Seward.*

Seward Community Library & Museum

LIBRARY | Seward's museum, community center, and library is a one-stop attraction, with the museum just downstairs from the library. The museum displays art by prominent Alaskan artists as well as relics that weave together the stories of the gold rush, Russian settlements, and the upheaval created by the 1964 earthquake. A movie illustrating the disaster and one about the Iditarod Trail are played back-to-back daily ($4 suggested donation). ✉ *239 6th Ave.* ☎ *907/224–3902* ⊕ *www.cityofseward.us/libmus* 🎞 *Movie $5.*

🍴 Restaurants

Chinooks Bar

$$$ | **SEAFOOD** | Just about everything at this restaurant in the small-boat harbor is made on-site, from the salad dressings to the infused liquors in the inventive libations. The award-winning chef prepares only sustainable Alaskan seafood, and information is provided about where it comes from and when it's in season. **Known for:** fantastic cocktail menu; inventive fresh seafood dishes; upstairs seating with views of the harbor and mountains. ⑤ *Average main: $25* ✉ *1404 4th Ave.* ☎ *907/224–2207* ⊕ *www.chinooksak.com* ⊘ *Closed Jan. and Feb.*

★ Le Barn Appétit

$$ | **FRENCH FUSION** | This little restaurant and inn serves some of the finest crepes in Alaska with options that range from savory like creamed beef and spinach to sweet like strawberries, Nutella, and whipped cream. The delightful proprietor is known to throw together fantastic French dinners for parties that call ahead, and if you're lucky, you'll also taste his quiche lorraine or chicken cordon bleu. **Known for:** best French crepes in Alaska; great hospitality; good for groups. ⑤ *Average main: $18* ✉ *11786 Old Exit Glacier Rd.* ☎ *907/224–8706* ⊕ *www.lebarnappetit.com* ⊘ *No dinner (except by special advance reservation).*

Railway Cantina

$$ | **MEXICAN** | This harbor-area hole-in-the-wall is locally renowned for its flavorful burritos, quesadillas, and great halibut and rockfish tacos. Various hot sauces, some contributed by customers who brought them from their travels, and beer complement the fare. **Known for:** fantastic blackened halibut burrito; grab-and-go hot food; excellent hot sauce collection. ⑤ *Average main: $14* ✉ *1401 4th Ave.* ☎ *907/224–8226* ⊕ *www.railwaycantina.com* ▭ *No credit cards.*

Shopping

Ranting Raven

GIFTS/SOUVENIRS | **FAMILY** | The shelves at this gallery and art shop are packed with local artwork, Alaska Native crafts and jewelry, and ravens—lots of them,

Fishing is an important industry and popular recreational activity in Seward.

including a couple of murals that adorn the side exterior. ⊠ *238 4th Ave.* ☏ *907/224–2228.*

Resurrect Art Coffeehouse

FOOD/CANDY | A darling coffeehouse and gallery-gift shop, Resurrect is located inside a 1932 church—the ambience and the views from the old choir loft are reason enough to stop by. This a good place to find Alaskan gifts, many of them by local artists and craftspeople, that aren't mass-produced. ⊠ *320 3rd Ave.* ☏ *907/224–7161* ⊕ *www.resurrectart. com.*

 Activities

FISHING

The Fish House

FISHING | This booking agency has a fleet of more than 40 Resurrection Bay and Kenai Peninsula fishing charters specializing in silver salmon and halibut fishing. You can book a half- or full-day charter (full-day only for halibut). The Fish House is also a supplier of tackle,

gear, and clothing. ⊠ *1303 4th Ave.* ☏ *907/224–3674, 800/257–7760* ⊕ *www. thefishhouse.net* ☝ *From $199.*

HIKING

For a comprehensive listing of all the trails, cabins, and campgrounds in the Seward Ranger District of Chugach National Forest, check the website of the U.S. Forest Service.

Caines Head Trail

HIKING/WALKING | This 4½-mile trail that starts at Lowell Point allows easy, flat hiking south along the coast, but with a hitch. Much of the hike is over tidal mudflats, so care must be taken to time it correctly: with tides here running in the 10- to 20-foot range, bad planning isn't just a case of getting your feet wet. It's officially advised that the trail be hiked only when there's a "plus 4-foot tide or greater" in summer. Two cabins can be rented (call ahead to book) at Derby Cove and Callisto Canyon. ⊠ *Seward* ☏ *877/444–6777.*

Mt. Marathon Race
FESTIVALS | FAMILY | An event held every July 4 since 1915, this race attracts runners and spectators from near and far while the entire town celebrates. The whole affair takes less than an hour, but the route is arduous: straight up the mountain (3,022 feet) and back down to the center of town. Racers are chosen on a lottery basis; enter before April for a chance, and be sure to book a hotel room well in advance. ✉ Seward 🕾 907/224–8051 ⊕ www.mmr.seward.com.

Vancouver, British Columbia

Cosmopolitan Vancouver has a spectacular setting. Tall fir trees stand practically downtown, the Coast Mountains tower close by, the ocean laps at the doorstep, and people from every corner of Earth create a youthful and vibrant atmosphere.

Vancouver is a young city, even by North American standards. It was not yet a town in 1871, when British Columbia became part of the Canadian confederation. The city's history, such as it is, remains visible to the naked eye: eras are stacked east to west along the waterfront like some century-old archaeological dig—from cobblestone, late-Victorian Gastown to shiny postmodern glass cathedrals of commerce grazing the sunset.

Long a port city in a resource-based province, Vancouver is relatively new to tourism and, for that matter, to its now-famous laid-back West Coast lifestyle. Most locals mark Expo '86, when the city cleaned up old industrial sites and generated new tourism infrastructure, as the turning point. Little did they know that was a mere dress rehearsal for what was to come: the 2010 Winter Games not only brought Vancouver to the forefront of the world's attention, but

was the major impetus to expand the convention center, upgrade many sports and community venues, build a rapid-transit connection between the airport and downtown, and develop the last of Vancouver's former industrial areas along the shores of False Creek. This is where the former Athlete's Village was located and which is now finding new life as the fashionable hub of a sustainable, upscale, and mixed-housing neighborhood. There is much to see and do in Vancouver, but when time is limited (as it usually is for cruise-ship passengers), the most popular options are a stroll through Gastown and Chinatown; a visit to Granville Island; or a driving, horse-drawn-carriage, or biking tour of Stanley Park. A hop-on/hop-off tour is always a terrific option. If you have more time, head to the Museum of Anthropology, on the University of British Columbia campus; it's worth a trip.

AIRPORT TRANSFERS

Vancouver International Airport is 16 km (10 miles) south of downtown in the suburb of Richmond. It takes 30 to 45 minutes to get downtown from the airport.

Taxi stands are in front of the terminal building; the fare from the airport to downtown is about C$35. Local cab companies include Black Top Cabs and Yellow Cab, both of which serve the whole Vancouver area. Limousine service from AeroCar costs about C$65–C$70 one-way. There is no shared shuttle service between the airport and downtown Vancouver.

The Canada Line, part of Vancouver's rapid transit system, runs passengers directly from Vancouver International Airport to the Canada Place cruise-ship terminal (and stops en route) in just 25 minutes. The station is inside the airport, on Level 4 between the domestic and international terminals. The trains, which are fully wheelchair accessible and allow plenty of room for luggage, begin running before 5 am and leave every 4 to 6 minutes during peak hours, and every 10 minutes from 11 pm until end of service (between 12:30 and 1:15 am). Fares are C$5 plus the cost of a fare for the time of day you're traveling (C$2.95 in Vancouver; up to C$4.70 to Vancouver suburbs). Passes such as DayPasses or FareSavers are exempt from the extra C$5 charge. Visit TransLink's website for more fare details.

AIRPORT INFORMATION Vancouver International Airport (YVR) ☎ *604/207–7077* ⊕ *www.yvr.ca.*

AIRPORT TRANSFERS AeroCar
☎ *604/298–1000, 888/821–0021* ⊕ *www. aerocar.ca.* **Airport Link Shuttle** ☎ *604/594– 3333* ⊕ *www.airportlinkshuttle.com.* **Black Top & Checker Cabs** ☎ *604/731–1111, 800/494–1111* ⊕ *www.btccabs.ca.* **TransLink** ☎ *604/953–3333* ⊕ *www. translink.ca.* **Yellow Cab** ☎ *604/681–1111* ⊕ *www.yellowcabonline.com.*

THE CRUISE PORT

Embarkation or disembarkation in Vancouver makes a scenic start or finish to an Alaska cruise. Sailing through Burrard Inlet, ships pass the forested shores of Stanley Park and sail beneath the graceful sweep of the Lions Gate Bridge. Ships calling at Vancouver dock at the Canada Place cruise-ship terminal on the downtown waterfront, a few minutes' walk from the city center. Its rooftop of dramatic white sails makes it instantly recognizable.

Transfers between the airport and the piers are offered by the cruise lines, either as a fare add-on or, in the case of some luxury cruise lines or small-ship cruise lines, included in the price of your cruise. Cruise-line representatives meet airport arrivals or are present at hotel transfer points to make the process stress-free.

From the south, Interstate 5 from Seattle becomes Highway 99 at the U.S.–Canada border. Vancouver is a three-hour drive (226 km [140 miles]) from Seattle.

It's best to avoid border crossings during peak times such as holidays and weekends. Highway 1, the Trans-Canada Highway, enters Vancouver from the east. To avoid traffic, arrive after rush hour (8:30 am).

Vancouver's evening rush-hour traffic starts early—about 3 pm on weekdays. The worst bottlenecks outside the city center are the North Shore bridges, the George Massey Tunnel on Highway 99 south of Vancouver, and Highway 1 through Coquitlam and Surrey. The BC Ministry of Transportation (☎ *800/550– 4997* ⊕ *www.drivebc.ca*) has updates.

CONTACTS Canada Place Cruise Terminal ✉ *999 Canada Place Way* ☎ *604/665– 9000* ⊕ *www.portvancouver.com.*

HOURS

Most stores are open from 10 am to 6 pm, with extended hours on Thursday and Friday until 9 pm. Sunday hours are likely to be from noon to 6 pm. Although many banks are open on Saturday, services may be limited to over-the-counter transactions. ATMs are plentiful.

PARKING

Vinci Park offers secure underground parking in a two-level garage at Canada Place. Rates are C$26 per day for cruise passengers if reserved in advance. The entrance is at the foot of Howe Street.

CONTACTS Vinci Park ✉ *999 Canada Place Way* ☎ *604/684–2251, 866/856– 8080* ⊕ *www.canadaplace.westpark. com.*

TOURS

Vancouver Trolley Company
TOUR—SIGHT | The Vancouver Trolley Company's fully narrated, hop-on/hop-off tour of Vancouver operates year-round with more than 30 stops (including a few in Stanley Park) on its 2½-hour circuit. From late June through September, it also offers a Stanley Park Shuttle that goes to 15 major park sights. It runs every 20 minutes; see website for map and pickup locations.

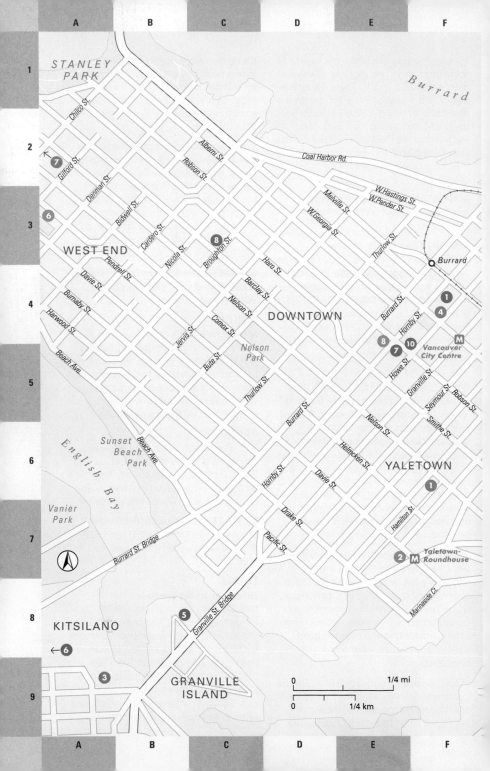

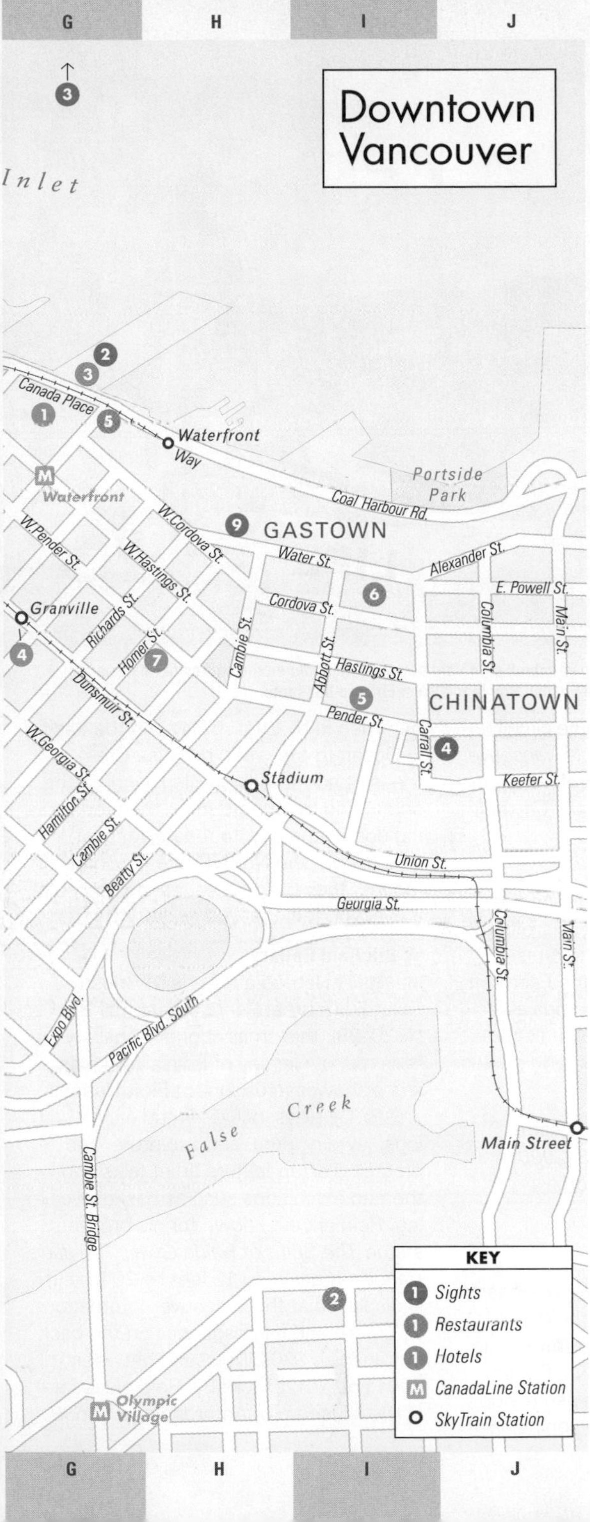

Downtown Vancouver

4

Sights ▼

1 Bill Reid Gallery **F4**
2 Canada Place **G2**
3 Capilano Suspension Bridge **G1**
4 Dr. Sun Yat-Sen
  Chinese Garden................... **J5**
5 Granville Island Public Market... **B8**
6 Museum of Anthropology......... **A8**
7 Robson Street...................... **E5**
8 Roedde House Museum **C3**
9 Steam Clock **H4**
10 Vancouver Art Gallery............. **F5**

Restaurants ▼

1 Blue Water Cafe & Raw Bar **F6**
2 Craft Beer Market **I9**
3 Go Fish **A9**
4 Hawksworth......................... **F4**
5 Miku Restaurants................. **G3**
6 Salt Tasting Room................. **I4**
7 The Teahouse in Stanley Park.... **A2**

Hotels ▼

1 Fairmont Waterfront............... **G3**
2 OPUS Vancouver Hotel **E7**
3 Pan Pacific Vancouver............ **G2**
4 St. Regis Hotel **G4**
5 Skwachays Lodge................. **I6**
6 Sylvia Hotel........................ **A3**
7 Victorian Hotel **H4**
8 Wedgewood Hotel & Spa.......... **E4**

KEY

- **1** Sights
- **1** Restaurants
- **1** Hotels
- **M** CanadaLine Station
- **O** SkyTrain Station

Inlet

Canada Place

Waterfront Way

Waterfront

Portside Park

Coal Harbour Rd.

GASTOWN

W. Pender St.
W. Cordova St.
W. Hastings St.
Water St.
Alexander St.
E. Powell St.

Granville

Richards St.
Homer St.
Cordova St.
Cambie St.
Abbott St.
Hastings St.
Carrall St.
Columbia St.
Main St.

Dunsmuir St.

CHINATOWN

Pender St.

Keefer St.

W. Georgia St.
Hamilton St.
Cambie St.
Beatty St.

Stadium

Union St.

Georgia St.

Expo Blvd.

Pacific Blvd. South

Columbia St.
Main St.

Cambie St. Bridge

False Creek

Main Street

Olympic
Village

Beaches might not be the first thing you think of in Vancouver, but in summer, the shores of Kits Beach, Second Beach in Stanley Park, and English Bay in the West End are hot spots.

The City-only tour is a 90-minute circuit. Tickets are valid for 24 hours. ⊠ *Vancouver* ☎ *604/801–5515* ⊕ *www.westcoastsightseeing.com* ⊠ *C$54 dual circuit; City only C$39; Stanley Park only $49.*

VISITOR INFORMATION

For maps and information, stop at the Vancouver Visitors Centre. It's across the street from Canada Place (the cruiseship terminal), next door to the Fairmont Waterfront Hotel. Tourism Victoria also offers information on Vancouver accommodation listings, attractions, and guides on its website.

CONTACTS Vancouver Visitors Centre ⊠ *200 Burrard St.* ☎ *604/683–2000* ⊕ *www.tourismvancouver.com.*

Sights

Vancouver is easy to navigate. The heart of the city—which includes the downtown area, the Canada Place cruise-ship terminal, Gastown, Chinatown, Stanley Park, and the West End high-rise residential neighborhood—sits on a peninsula

hemmed in by English Bay and the Pacific Ocean to the west; by False Creek, the inlet home to Granville Island, to the south; and by Burrard Inlet, the working port of the city, to the north, past which loom the North Shore Mountains. Indeed, they become your compass point if ever you feel that you're getting lost.

★ Bill Reid Gallery

MUSEUM | Named after one of British Columbia's preeminent artists, Bill Reid (1920–98), this small aboriginal gallery is as much a legacy of Reid's works as it is a showcase of current First Nations artists. Displays include wood carvings, jewelry, print, and sculpture, and programs often feature artist talks and themed exhibitions such as basket weaving. Reid is best known for his bronze statue *The Spirit of Haida Gwaii, The Jade Canoe*—measuring 12 feet by 20 feet; it is displayed at the Vancouver International Airport, and its image was on the back of Canadian $20 bills issued between 2004 and 2012. More Bill Reid pieces are at the Museum of Anthropology. ⊠ *639*

Hornby St., Downtown ☎ *604/682–3455*
🌐 *www.billreidgallery.ca* 🏷 *C$13*
🕐 *Closed Mon. and Tues., Oct.–May.*

Canada Place

CONVENTION CENTER | Extending four city blocks (about a mile and a half) north into Burrard Inlet, this complex mimics the style and size of a luxury ocean liner, complete with exterior esplanades and a landmark roofline that resembles five sails (it was made with NASA-invented material: a Teflon-coated fiberglass once used in astronaut space suits). Home to Vancouver's cruise-ship terminal, Canada Place can accommodate up to four liners at once. All together, the giant building is definitely worth a look and the very cool **Flyover Canada** *(604/620–8455, www.flyovercanada.com, C$33, daily 10–9; online discount offered)* attraction, a simulated flight that takes you on a soaring and swooping virtual voyage across the country, is an excellent reason to go inside. If this dramatic journey above Niagara Falls, the Rocky Mountains, and the vast Arctic sparks your curiosity about other parts of Canada, follow the **Canadian Trail** on the west side of the building, which has displays about the country's provinces and territories. Use your smartphone or tablet to access multimedia content along the way: there's free Wi-Fi. Canada Place is also home to the posh **Pan Pacific Hotel** and the east wing of the **Vancouver Convention Centre**. On its western side stands the new convention center—its plaza stages the 2010 Olympic cauldron and the Digital Orca sculpture by Canadian artist Douglas Coupland. A waterfront promenade from Canada Place winds all the way to (and around) Stanley Park, with spectacular vantage points from which to view Burrard Inlet and the North Shore Mountains; plaques posted at intervals have historical information about the city and its waterfront. At the recently renovated **Port of Vancouver Discovery Centre** at Canada Place *(604/665–9000, free, daily 8–6)*, at the north end of the Canada Place complex, you can take in

Night Market

If you're in the area in summer on a Friday, Saturday, or Sunday, check out Chinatown's small and bustling Night Market for food and tchotchkes: the 200 block of East Pender and Keefer is closed to traffic from 6:30 to 11 pm (until midnight on Saturday). Or hop aboard the SkyTrain for a 20-minute ride to Bridgeport, and one of the two much larger night markets in Richmond.

a history wall with artifacts, imagery, and interactive displays. ✉ *999 Canada Pl. Way, Downtown* ☎ *604/665–9000* 🌐 *www.canadaplace.ca.*

★ Capilano Suspension Bridge

BRIDGE/TUNNEL | **FAMILY** | Swaying 230 feet above the Capilano River, the bridge is Vancouver's oldest continuously running attraction—and the quintessential rainforest experience. Cross the very sturdy bridge to explore canopy walkways through and above the forest floor as well as easy trails with informative signs referencing the region's ecology and habitat. If you can hold your nerve, there's even a cliff-edge walk that most kids love. Although it's located halfway up Grouse Mountain, the bridge is easily accessible: a free shuttle runs every half-hour from Canada Place, making the 20-minute trip there very doable. ✉ *3735 Capilano Rd.* ☎ *604/985–7474* 🌐 *www. capbridge.com* 🏷 *C$46.95.*

Dr. Sun Yat-Sen Chinese Garden

GARDEN | The first authentic Ming Dynasty–style garden outside China, this small garden was built in 1986 by 52 Chinese artisans from Suzhou. No power tools, screws, or nails were used in the construction. It incorporates design elements and traditional materials from several of Suzhou's centuries-old private gardens. Guided tours (45 minutes long), included in the ticket price, are conducted on the hour between mid-June and the end of August (call ahead or check the website for off-season tour times); these are valuable for understanding the philosophy and symbolism that are central to the garden's design. Covered walkways make this a good rainy-day choice. A concert series, including classical, Asian, world, jazz, and sacred music, plays on Thursday evenings in July and August. The free public park next door is a pleasant place to sit, but lacks the context that you get with a tour of the Sun Yat-Sen garden. ⊠ *578 Carrall St., Chinatown* ☎ *604/662–3207* ⊕ *www.vancouverchinesegarden.com* ⊠ *C$14; C$12 in winter* ☉ *Closed Mon., Oct.–Apr.* Ⓜ *Stadium-Chinatown.*

★ Granville Island Public Market

MARKET | FAMILY | The dozens of stalls in this 50,000-square-foot building sell locally grown fruits and vegetables direct from the farm and farther afield; other stalls stock crafts, chocolates, artisanal cheeses and pastas, fish, meat, flowers, and exotic foods. On Thursday in summer, farmers sell fruit and vegetables from trucks outside. At the north end of the market, you can pick up a snack, lunch, or coffee from one of the many prepared-food vendors. The Market Courtyard, on the waterside, has great views of the city and is also a good place to catch street entertainers—be prepared to get roped into the action, if only to check the padlocks of an escape artist's gear. Weekends can get madly busy. ⊠ *1689 Johnston St., Granville Island* ☎ *604/666–6655* ⊕ *www.granvilleisland.com.*

★ Museum of Anthropology

MUSEUM | Part of the University of British Columbia, the MOA has one of the world's leading collections of Northwest Coast First Nations art. The Great Hall has dramatic cedar poles, bentwood boxes, and canoes adorned with traditional Northwest Coast–painted designs. On clear days, the gallery's 50-foot-tall windows reveal a striking backdrop of mountains and sea. Another highlight is the work of the late Bill Reid, one of Canada's most respected Haida artists. In *The Raven and the First Men* (1980), carved in yellow cedar, he tells a Haida story of creation. Reid's gold-and-silver jewelry work is also on display, as are exquisite carvings of gold, silver, and argillite (a black shale found on Haida Gwaii, also known as the Queen Charlotte Islands) by other First Nations artists. The museum's visible storage section displays, in drawers and cases, contain thousands of examples of tools, textiles, masks, and other artifacts from around the world. The Koerner Ceramics Gallery contains 600 pieces from 15th- to 19th-century Europe. Behind the museum are two Haida houses, set on the cliff over the water. Free guided tours—given several times daily (call or check the website for times)—are immensely informative. The MOA also has an excellent book and fine-art shop, as well as a café. To reach the museum by transit, take any UBC-bound bus from Granville Street downtown to the university bus loop, a 15-minute walk, or connect to a shuttle that scoots around the campus and will drop you off opposite the MOA at the Rose Garden. Pay parking is available in the Rose Garden parking lot, across Marine Drive from the museum. A UBC Museums and Gardens Pass will save you money if you're planning to visit several attractions at UBC. ⊠ *University of British Columbia, 6393 N.W. Marine Dr., Point Grey* ☎ *604/822–5087* ⊕ *www.moa.ubc.ca* ⊠ *C$18; Thurs. 5–9 C$10* ☉ *Closed Mon. mid-Oct.–mid-May.*

Robson Street

NEIGHBORHOOD | Running from the Terry Fox Plaza outside BC Place Stadium down to the West End, Robson is Vancouver's busiest shopping street, where fashionistas hang out at see-and-be-seen sidewalk cafés, high-end boutiques, and chain stores. Most of the designer action takes place between Jervis and Burrard streets, and that's also where you can find buskers and other entertainers in the evenings. ⊠ *Downtown* ⊕ *www. robsonstreet.ca.*

Roedde House Museum On a pretty residential street, the Roedde (pronounced *roh*-dee) House Museum is an 1893 home in the Queen Anne Revival style, set among Victoriana gardens. Tours of the restored, antiques-furnished interior take about an hour. On Sunday, tours are followed by tea and cookies. Museum hours can vary, so it's a good idea to phone before visiting. The gardens (free) can be visited anytime. The museum also hosts a concert series (classical music on the second Sunday of the month at 3 pm, jazz on the second Thursday at 7 pm). ⊠ *1415 Barclay St., between Broughton and Nicola Sts., West End* ☎ *604/684–7040* ⊕ *www.roeddehouse. org* ☎ *C$5; Sun. C$8 including tea and cookies* ⊘ *Closed Mon. and Sat.*

Vancouver Art Gallery
MUSEUM | Canadian painter Emily Carr's haunting evocations of the British Columbian hinterland are among the attractions at western Canada's largest art gallery. Carr (1871–1945), a grocer's daughter from Victoria, BC, fell in love with the wilderness around her and shocked middle-class Victorian society by running off to paint it. Her work accentuates the mysticism and danger of BC's wilderness, and records the diminishing presence of native cultures during that era (there's something of a renaissance now). The gallery, which also hosts touring historical and contemporary exhibitions, is housed in a 1911 courthouse that Canadian architect Arthur Erickson redesigned in the early 1980s as part of the Robson Square redevelopment. Stone lions guard the steps to the Georgia Street side (the plaza is often the site of festivals and other events); the main entrance is accessed from Robson Square or Hornby Street. ⊠ *750 Hornby St., Downtown* ☎ *604/662–4719* ⊕ *www. vanartgallery.bc.ca* ☎ *C$24; higher for some exhibits; by donation Tues. 5–9.*

Steam Clock
CLOCK | An underground steam system, which also heats many local buildings, supplies the world's first steam clock— possibly Vancouver's most photographed attraction. On the quarter hour, a steam whistle rings out the Westminster chimes, and on the hour a huge cloud of steam spews from the apparatus. The ingenious design, based on an 1875 mechanism, was built in 1977 by Ray Saunders of Landmark Clocks to commemorate the community effort that saved Gastown from demolition. Fun fact: yes, the clock does use steam power, but three electric motors help it run, too. ⊠ *Water St. at Cambie St., Gastown.*

🍴 Restaurants

A diverse gastronomic experience awaits you in cosmopolitan Vancouver. A wave of Asian immigration and tourism has brought a proliferation of upscale Asian eateries. Cutting-edge restaurants currently perfecting and defining Pacific Northwest fare—including homegrown regional favorites such as salmon and oysters, accompanied by British Columbia wines—have become some of the city's leading attractions.

You're also spoiled for choice when it comes to casual and budget dining. Good choices include Asian cafés or any of the pubs listed in the Nightlife section; many have both an adults-only pub and a separate restaurant section where kids are welcome. A bylaw bans smoking indoors in all Vancouver restaurants, bars, pubs, and patios.

Vancouver dining is fairly informal. Casual but neat dress is appropriate everywhere. A 15% tip is expected. A 5% sales tax (GST) is added to the bill.

★ Blue Water Cafe & Raw Bar

$$$$ | SEAFOOD | Executive chef Frank Pabst focuses his menu on both popular and lesser-known local seafood (including frequently overlooked varieties like mackerel or herring) at his widely heralded, fashionable fish restaurant. You can dine in the warmly lighted interior or outside on the former loading dock that's now a lovely terrace. **Known for:** seafood-centric menu; top-notch sushi; great local wine list. $ *Average main: C$36* ⊠ *1095 Hamilton St., Yaletown* ☎ *604/688–8078* ⊕ *www.bluewatercafe.net* ☾ *No lunch.*

Craft Beer Market

$$ | PACIFIC NORTHWEST | Unique brews and fresh local food is the name of the game here, where there are more than 100 beers (local and international) on tap. The happening cavernous tavern is a celebration of the ever-evolving craft beer industry. **Known for:** craft beer. $ *Average main: C$17* ⊠ *85 West 1st Ave., Olympic Village* ☎ *604/709–2337* ⊕ *www.craftbeermarket.ca.*

★ Go Fish

$ | SEAFOOD | If the weather's fine, head for this seafood stand on the seawall overlooking the docks beside Granville Island. The menu is short—highlights include fish-and-chips, grilled salmon or tuna sandwiches, and fish tacos—but the quality is first-rate. **Known for:** seaside location; fish and chips; long queues. $ *Average main: C$10* ⊠ *Fisherman's Wharf, 1505 W. 1st Ave., Kitsilano* ☎ *604/730–5040* ☾ *Closed Mon. No dinner.*

Hawksworth

$$$$ | CONTEMPORARY | Professional foodies consistently rank this hotel restaurant among the top fine-dining tables in the city. The lively vibe is eclectic with a glamorous, art deco influence—original artwork prevails, and the food from breakfast through to dinner is just as imaginative. **Known for:** lobster with Iberico ham risotto; impressive wine list; seven-course tasting menu. $ *Average main:* *C$46* ⊠ *Rosewood Hotel Georgia, 801 W. Georgia St., Downtown* ☎ *604/673–7000* ⊕ *www.hawksworthrestaurant.com.*

Miku Restaurant

$$$$ | SUSHI |FAMILY | Considered one of the top sushi destinations in the world, Miku is an absolute must-visit. Located right beside the cruise ship terminal, the restaurant delivers cutting-edge flavors and creativity. **Known for:** Aburi (flame-seared sushi); sharing plates; great dessert. $ *Average main: C$32* ⊠ *70-200 Granville St., at Granville Square* ☎ *604/568–3900* ⊕ *www. mikurestaurant.com.*

Salt Tasting Room

$$ | ECLECTIC | If your idea of a perfect light meal revolves around fine cured meats, artisanal cheeses, and a glass of wine from a wide-ranging list, find your way to this sleek space in a decidedly unsleek Gastown location. The restaurant has no kitchen and simply assembles the selection of top-quality provisions—perhaps smoked beef tenderloin or British Columbian–made Camembert, with accompanying condiments—into artfully composed delights. **Known for:** local charcuterie; extensive wine list; three-course set menu. $ *Average main: C$16* ⊠ *45 Blood Alley, off Abbott St., Gastown* ☎ *604/633–1912* ⊕ *www.salttastingroom. com* ☾ *No lunch.*

🛏 Hotels

Accommodations in Vancouver range from luxurious waterfront hotels to neighborhood B&Bs and basic European-style pensions. Many of the best choices are in the downtown core, either in the central business district or in the West End near Stanley Park. From mid-October through May, rates throughout the city can drop as much as 50%. Vancouver hotels do not allow smoking in either rooms or public areas.

For expanded hotel reviews, visit Fodors. com.

Take a walk and explore the outdoor totem poles at Vancouver's Museum of Anthropology.

★ Fairmont Waterfront

$$$$ | HOTEL | Stunning views of the harbor, mountains, and Stanley Park from the floor-to-ceiling windows of the guest rooms are one of the highlights of this luxuriously modern 23-story hotel across the street from Vancouver's cruise-ship terminal. **Pros:** harbor views; proximity to the waterfront; inviting pool terrace. **Cons:** long elevator queues; busy lobby lounge. ⑤ *Rooms from: C$630* ✉ *900 Canada Pl. Way, Downtown* ☎ *866/540–4509* ⊕ *www.fairmont.com/waterfront-vancouver* ⊷ *513 rooms* ⵔ *No meals.*

★ OPUS Vancouver Hotel

$$$$ | HOTEL | Groundbreakingly trendy when it opened in 2002, the OPUS continues to reinvent itself and live up to the motto of being a "place to be, not just a place to stay." The design team created a set of online fictitious characters, then decorated the rooms to suit each "persona." Guests are matched with room styles using the Lifestyle Concierge. **Pros:** great Yaletown location, right by rapid transit; funky and hip vibe; the lobby

bar is a fashionable meeting spot. **Cons:** trendy nightspots nearby can be noisy at night; expensive and limited parking. ⑤ *Rooms from: C$475* ✉ *322 Davie St., Yaletown* ☎ *604/642–6787, 866/642–6787* ⊕ *www.vancouver.opushotel.com* ⵔ *96 rooms* ⵔ *No meals.*

★ Pan Pacific Vancouver

$$$$ | HOTEL | Located in the waterfront Canada Place complex, the sophisticated Pan Pacific has easy access to the city's convention center and the cruise-ship terminal. **Pros:** lovely harbor views; staff has a "go the extra mile" attitude. **Cons:** atrium is open to the convention center, so it's often full of executives talking shop; parking is expensive. ⑤ *Rooms from: C$599* ✉ *999 Canada Pl., Downtown* ☎ *604/662–8111, 800/663–1515 in Canada, 800/937–1515 in U.S.* ⊕ *www.panpacific.com/en/hotels-resorts/canada/vancouver.html* ⵔ *504 rooms* ⵔ *No meals.*

Skwachays Lodge

$$$$ | HOTEL | As Canada's first aboriginal arts hotel—with First Nations owners

and operators—Skwachays offers a one-of-a-kind experience. **Pros:** lively First Nations cultural narrative embodied in the design and style; unique experience in Vancouver hotels. **Cons:** on the edge of downtown, so a bit out of the heart of the action; need to take a taxi at night. $ *Rooms from: C$245* ⊠ *31 W. Pender St., Gastown* ☎ *604/687–3589, 888/998–0797* ⊕ *www.skwachays.com* ↪ *18 rooms* ⊚ *No meals.*

St. Regis Hotel

$$$$ | **HOTEL** | It's the oldest continuously operating hotel in the city, but edgy, modern decor livens up the 1913 boutique property and Canadian artwork and select heritage furnishings gives it a unique sense of place. **Pros:** hot location; complimentary global long-distance calling; à la carte breakfast for two. **Cons:** no views; slow elevator can mean the stairs are faster (plus there is original artwork in the stairwell). $ *Rooms from: C$329* ⊠ *602 Dunsmuir St., Downtown* ☎ *604/681–1135, 800/770–7929* ⊕ *www.stregishotel.com* ↪ *65 rooms* ⊚ *Breakfast.*

Sylvia Hotel

$$$$ | **HOTEL** |**FAMILY** | This Virginia-creeper-covered 1912 heritage building is continually popular because of its affordable rates and near-perfect location: a stone's throw from the beach on scenic English Bay, two blocks from Stanley Park, and a 20-minute walk from Robson Street. **Pros:** beachfront location; close to restaurants; a good place to mingle with the locals. **Cons:** older building; parking can be difficult; walk to Downtown is slightly uphill. $ *Rooms from: C$275* ⊠ *1154 Gilford St., West End* ☎ *604/681–9321, 877/681–9321* ⊕ *www.sylviahotel.com* ↪ *120 rooms* ⊚ *No meals.*

★ Victorian Hotel

$$$$ | **B&B/INN** | This handsome boutique hotel, on the edge of Downtown and historic Gastown, is one of Vancouver's best values—note that some rooms have shared bathrooms. **Pros:** nice small-hotel feel; complimentary continental breakfast; historic atmosphere. **Cons:** take a cab after midnight in this area; some shared bathrooms (but they are very nice); no in-room safes (items can be left with the front desk). $ *Rooms from: C$235* ⊠ *514 Homer St., Downtown* ☎ *604/681–6369, 877/681–6369* ⊕ *www.victorianhotel.ca* ↪ *47 rooms, 28 with private baths* ⊚ *Breakfast.*

★ Wedgewood Hotel & Spa

$$$$ | **HOTEL** | A member of the exclusive Relais & Châteaux Group, the luxurious, family-owned Wedgewood is all about pampering. **Pros:** personalized service; great location close to shops; Bacchus Lounge is a destination in its own right. **Cons:** small size means it books up quickly. $ *Rooms from: C$435* ⊠ *845 Hornby St., Downtown* ☎ *604/689–7777, 800/663–0666* ⊕ *www.wedgewoodhotel.com* ↪ *83 rooms* ⊚ *No meals.*

▼ Nightlife

For information on events, pick up a free copy of the *Georgia Straight,* available at cafés and bookstores around town, or look in the entertainment section of the *Vancouver Sun* (Thursday's paper has listings).

Tickets for many venues can be booked via Ticketmaster either by phone or online. Tickets Tonight sells half-price day-of-the-event tickets and full-price advance tickets to the theater, concerts, festivals, and other performing arts events around the city. It's at the Vancouver Tourist Info Centre.

★ The Diamond

TAPAS BARS | At the top of a narrow staircase above Maple Tree Square, the Diamond occupies the second floor of one of the city's oldest buildings. A cool hangout and cocktail lounge, the venue serves a mix of historic tipples and inventive house concoctions. There's a daily, and very welcoming, after-work happy hour. ⊠ *6 Powell St., at Carrall St., Gastown* ⊕ *www.di6mond.com.*

★ **Pourhouse Vancouver**

BARS/PUBS | The brick-and-beam 1910 architecture, antiques, and a 38-foot bar are in keeping with the menu of classic cocktails. Most are inspired by the 1862 bartending bible *How to Mix Drinks* by Jerry Thomas, the first bartending manual ever to put oral traditions to print, with recipes such as a Tom Collins. Book ahead for one of the family-style dinners that serve four to six people: everything is set in the center of the kitchen table, and it's a help-yourself affair, just like at home. There's also live music Sunday through Thursday nights. ✉ *162 Water St., Gastown* ☎ *604/568–7022* ⊕ *www. pourhousevancouver.com.*

Prohibitions

GATHERING PLACES | While the name gives a nod to the building itself, which opened in 1927 during Prohibition, its interior exudes a very modern take on the speakeasy era. Think very low lighting, lavish velvet drapery, black leather pillars, and a sleek sophistication that invites tête-à-têtes. Live jazz, solo artists, and a late-night DJ appeal to those who like to dress up for an evening of entertainment and imaginative, true-to-the-era cocktails. The entrance is a rather "prohibitive"-looking wooden door on Howe Street. ✉ *Georgia Rosewood Hotel, 801 W. Georgia St.* ☎ *604/673–7089* ⊕ *www. prohibitionrhg.com.*

Ticketmaster

NIGHTLIFE OVERVIEW | ☎ *855/985–5000, 866/448–7849 Automated Express purchase* ⊕ *www.ticketmaster.ca.*

Tickets Tonight

NIGHTLIFE OVERVIEW | ✉ *200 Burrard St., Downtown* ☎ *604/684–2787* ⊕ *www. ticketstonight.ca.*

 # Shopping

Unlike many cities where suburban malls have taken over, Vancouver is full of individual boutiques and specialty shops. Ethnic markets, art galleries, gourmet-food shops, and high-fashion outlets abound, and both Asian and First Nations influences in crafts, home furnishings, and foods are quite prevalent.

Stretching from Burrard to Bute, **Robson Street** is the city's main fashion-shopping and people-watching artery. The Gap and Banana Republic have their flagship stores here, as do Canadian fashion outlets Club Monaco, Lululemon Athletica, and Roots. Souvenir shops and cafés fill the gaps. One block north of Robson, **Alberni Street** is geared to the higher-income visitor, and is where you'll find duty-free shopping. At the stores in and around Alberni and around Burrard, you'll find names such as Tiffany & Co., Louis Vuitton, Gucci, Coach, Hermès, Burberry and De Beers. Treasure hunters like the 300 block of **West Cordova Street** in **Gastown**, where offbeat shops sell curios, vintage clothing, and locally designed clothes. Bustling **Chinatown**—centered on Pender and Main streets—is full of Chinese bakeries, restaurants, herbalists, tea merchants, and import shops. Frequently described as Vancouver's SoHo, **Yaletown** on the north bank of False Creek is home to boutiques and restaurants—many in converted warehouses—that cater to a trendy, moneyed crowd. On the south side of False Creek, **Granville Island** has a lively food market and a wealth of galleries, crafts shops, and artisans' studios.

NATIVE CRAFTS

★ **Hill's Native Art**

ART GALLERIES | This highly respected store has Vancouver's largest selection of First Nations art. The place is crammed with souvenirs, keepsakes, and high-quality pieces, including carvings, masks, and drums. If you think that's impressive, head for one-of-a-kind collector pieces and limited editions. Its recent move from Gastown to East Broadway makes it a 10-minute cab ride from downtown, but the larger and brighter space makes for easy browsing. ✉ *120 E. Broadway,*

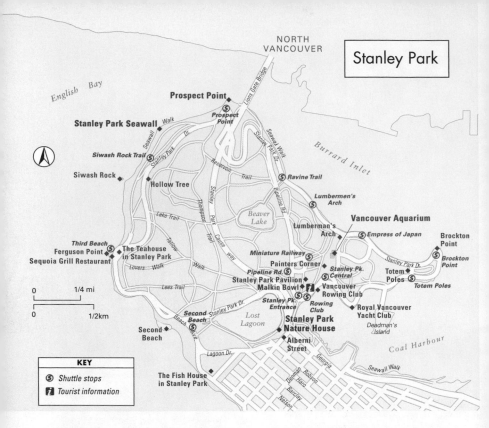

Mt. Pleasant ☎ *604/685–4249, 866/685–5422* ⊕ *www.hills.ca.*

Stanley Park

A 1,000-acre wilderness park, only blocks from the downtown section of a major city, is a rare treasure. Vancouverites use it, protect it, and love it with such zeal that when it was proposed that the 120-year-old Hollow Tree be axed because of safety concerns, citizens rallied, raised funds, and literally engineered its salvation.

Stanley Park is, perhaps, the single most prized possession of Vancouverites, who make use of it fervently to cycle, walk, jog, Rollerblade, play cricket and tennis, and enjoy outdoor art shows and theater performances alongside attractions such as the renowned aquarium.

When a storm swept across the park's shores in December 2006, it destroyed close to 10,000 trees as well as parts of the perimeter seawall. Locals contributed thousands of dollars to the cleanup and replanting effort in addition to the monies set aside by local authorities. The storm's silver lining was that it cleared some deadwood areas, making room for the reintroduction of many of the park's original species of trees.

GETTING HERE AND AROUND

To get to the park by public transit, take Stanley Park Bus 19 from the corner of Pender and Howe, downtown. It's possible to see the park by car, entering at the foot of Georgia Street and driving counterclockwise around the one-way Stanley Park Drive.

Coming nose-to-nose with a beluga whale—these underwater views are star attractions at the Vancouver Aquarium.

 Sights

Prospect Point

VIEWPOINT | At 211 feet, Prospect Point is the highest point in the park and provides striking views of the Lions Gate Bridge (watch for cruise ships passing below), the North Shore, and Burrard Inlet. There's also a year-round souvenir shop, a snack bar with terrific ice cream, and a restaurant. From the seawall, you can see where cormorants build their seaweed nests along the cliff ledges. ⊠ *Stanley Park.*

Stanley Park Nature House

COLLEGE | Vancouver's only ecology center is a treasure trove of information and showcases Stanley Park's true natural beauty with a host of programs and guided walks. The Nature House is on the south shore of Lost Lagoon, at the foot of Alberni Street. ⊠ *Stanley Park, Alberni St., north end, under viewing platform, Stanley Park* ☎ *604/257–8544* ⊕ *www. stanleyparkecology.ca* ⊠ *Programs and guided walks vary in price* ⊙ *Closed*

Mon. in July and Aug.; closed weekdays rest of year.

★ Stanley Park Seawall

TRAIL | Vancouver's seawall path includes a 9 km (5½-mile) paved shoreline section within Stanley Park. It's one of several car-free zones in the park and it's popular with walkers and cyclists. If you have the time (about a half day) and the energy, strolling the entire seawall is an exhilarating experience. It extends an additional mile east past the marinas, cafés, and waterfront condominiums of Coal Harbour to Canada Place in downtown, so you could start your walk or ride from there. From the south side of the park, the seawall continues for another 28 km (17 miles) along Vancouver's waterfront to the University of British Columbia, allowing for a pleasant, if ambitious, day's bike ride. Along the seawall, cyclists must wear helmets and stay on their side of the path. Within Stanley Park, cyclists must ride in a counterclockwise direction. The seawall can get crowded on summer weekends, but inside the park is a 28-km (17-mile) network of peaceful walking and cycling paths through old- and second-growth forest. The wheel-chair-accessible Beaver Lake Interpretive Trail is a good choice if you're interested in park ecology. Take a map—they're available at the park-information booth and many of the concession stands—and don't go into the woods alone or after dusk. ⊠ *Stanley Park.*

★ Vancouver Aquarium

ZOO | FAMILY | Massive floor-to-ceiling windows let you get face-to-face with sea otters, sea lions, dolphins, and harbor seals at this award-winning research and educational facility. In the Amazon Gallery you walk through a rain-forest jungle populated with piranhas, caimans, and tropical birds; in summer, hundreds of free-flying butterflies add to the mix. The Tropic Zone is home to exotic freshwater and saltwater life, including clown fish, moray eels, and black-tip reef sharks. Other displays, many with hands-on features for kids, show the underwater life of coastal British Columbia and the Canadian Arctic. Sea lion and dolphin shows, as well as dive shows (where divers swim with aquatic life, including sharks) are held daily. Be sure to check out the stingray touch pool, as well as the "4-D" film experience (it's a multisensory show that puts mist, smell, and wind into the 3-D equation). For an extra fee, you can help the trainers feed and train otters, belugas, and sea lions. There's also a café and a gift shop. Be prepared for lines on weekends and school holidays. In summer, the quietest time to visit is before 11 am or after 4 pm; in other seasons, the crowds are smaller before noon or after 2 pm. ⊠ *845 Avison Way, Stanley Park* ☎ *604/659–3474 information line* ⊕ *www.vanaqua.org* ⊠ *C$38.*

 Restaurants

The Teahouse in Stanley Park

$$$$ | **CANADIAN** | The former officers' mess at Ferguson Point in Stanley Park is a prime location for water views by day, and for watching sunsets at dusk. The Pacific Northwest menu is not especially innovative, but its broad appeal will please those looking for local fish, rack of lamb, steaks, and a host of other options, including gluten-free pasta. **Known for:** tasting boards; lovely patio; Pacific Northwest cuisine. $ *Average main: C$30* ⊠ *7501 Stanley Park Dr., Stanley Park* ✢ *At Ferguson Point* ☎ *604/669–3281* ⊕ *www.vancouverdine.com/teahouse.*

Whittier

The entryway to Whittier is unlike any other: a 2½-mile drive atop railroad tracks through the Anton Anderson Memorial Tunnel, cut through the Chugach Mountain Range. Once on the other side of the tunnel, you enter the mysterious world of Whittier, the remnants of a military town developed in World War II. The only way to get to Whittier was by boat or train until the tunnel opened to traffic in 2000.

This quaint hamlet, nestled at the base of snow-covered peaks at the head of Passage Canal on the Kenai Peninsula, has an intriguing history. In the 1940s the U.S. Army constructed a port in Whittier and built the Hodge and Buckner buildings to house soldiers. These enormous monoliths are eerily reminiscent of Soviet-era communal apartment buildings. The Hodge Building (now called Begich Towers) houses almost all of Whittier's 215 year-round residents. The town averages 30 feet of snow in the winter, and in summer gets a considerable amount of rainfall. Whittier's draw is primarily fishing, but there are a number of activities to be had on Prince William Sound, including kayaking and glacier

Continued on page 243

AMAZING WHALES
OF ALASKA

(top) A breaching humpback (left) An orca whale

It's unforgettable: a massive, barnacle-encrusted humpback breaches skyward from the placid waters of an Alaskan inlet, shattering the silence with a thundering display of grace, power, and beauty. Welcome to Alaska's coastline.

Alaska's cold, nutrient-rich waters offer a bounty of marine life that's matched by few regions on earth. Eight species of whales frequent the state's near-shore waters, some migrating thousands of miles each year to partake of Alaska's marine buffet. The state's most famous cetaceans (the scientific classification of marine mammals that includes whales, dolphins, and porpoises) are the humpback whale, the gray whale, and the orca (a.k.a. the killer whale).

BEST REGIONS TO VIEW WHALES

Whales can be viewed throughout the world; after all, they are migratory animals. But thanks to its pristine environment, diversity of cetacean species, and jaw-dropping beauty, Alaska is perhaps the planet's best whale-watching locale.

From April through October, humpbacks visit many of Alaska's coastal regions, including the Bering Sea, the Aleutian Islands, and Prince William Sound. The **Inside Passage,** though, is the best place to see them: it's home to a migratory population of up to 600 humpbacks. Good bets for whale-viewing include taking a trip on the **Alaska Marine Highway,** spending time in **Glacier Bay National Park,** or taking a day cruise out of any of Southeast's main towns. While most humpbacks return to Hawaiian waters in

A gray whale greets whale-watchers

the winter, some spend the whole year in Southeast Alaska.

Gray whales favor the coastal waters of the Pacific, which terminate in the Bering Sea. Their healthy population—some studies estimate that 30,000 gray whales populate the west coast of North America—make them relatively

---

THE HUMPBACK: Musical, Breaching Giant

Humpbacks' flukes allow them to breach so effectively that they can propel two-thirds of their massive bodies out of the water.

Known for their spectacular breaching and unique whale songs, humpbacks are captivating. Most spend their winters in the balmy waters off the Hawaiian Islands, where females, or sows, give birth. Come springtime, humpbacks set off on a 3,000-mile swim to their Alaskan feeding grounds.

Southeast Alaska is home to one of the world's only groups of bubble-net feeding humpbacks. Bubble-netting is a cooperative hunting technique in which one humpback circles below a school of baitfish while exhaling a "net" of bubbles, causing the fish to gather. Other humpbacks then feed at will from the deliciously dense group of fish.

The Song of the Humpback

All whale species communicate sonically, but the humpback is the most musical. During mating season, males emit haunting, songlike calls that can last for up to 30 minutes at a time. Most scientists attribute the songs to flirtatious, territorial, or competitive behaviors.

QUICK FACTS:

Scientific name: *Megaptera novaeangliae*

Length: Up to 50 ft.

Weight: Up to 90,000 pounds (45 tons)

Coloring: Dark blue to black, with barnacles and knobby, lighter-colored flippers

Life span: 30 to 40 years

Reproduction: One calf every 2 to 3 years; calves are generally 12 feet long at birth, weighing up to 2,000 pounds (1 ton)

easy to spot in the spring and early summer months, especially around **Sitka** and **Kodiak Island** and south of the **Kenai Peninsula,** where numerous whale-watching cruises depart from Seward into **Resurrection Bay**.

Orcas populate nearly all of Alaska's coastal regions. They're most commonly viewed in the **Inside Passage** and **Prince William Sound,** where they reside year-round. A jaunt on the Alaska Marine Highway is one option, but so is a kayaking or day-cruising trip out of **Whittier** to Prince William Sound.

When embarking on a whale-watching excursion, don't forget rain gear, a camera, and binoculars!

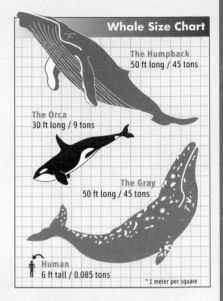

Whale Size Chart

The Humpback
50 ft long / 45 tons

The Orca
30 ft long / 9 tons

The Gray
50 ft long / 45 tons

Human
6 ft tall / 0.085 tons

* 1 meter per square

THE GRAY WHALE: Migrating Leviathan

Though the average lifespan of a gray whale is 50 years, one individual was reported to reach 77 years of age—a real old-timer.

While frequenting Alaska during the long days of summer, gray whales tend to stay close to the coastline. They endure the longest migration of any mammal on earth—some travel 14,000 miles each way between Alaska's Bering Sea and their mating grounds in sunny Baja California.

Gray whales are bottom-feeders that stir up sediment on the sea floor, then use their baleen—a comblike collection of long, stiff hairs inside their mouths—to filter out sediment and trap small crustaceans and tube worms.

Their predilection for near-shore regions, coupled with their easygoing demeanor—some "friendly" gray whales have even been known to approach small tour boats—cements their spot on the short list of Alaska's favorite cetacean celebrities. (Gray whales aren't always in such amicable spirits: whalers dubbed mother gray whales "devilfish" for the fierce manner in which they protected their young.)

QUICK FACTS:

Scientific name: *Eschrichtius robustus*

Length: Up to 50 ft.

Weight: Up to 90,000 pounds (45 tons)

Coloring: Gray and white, usually splotched with lighter growths and barnacles

Life span: 50 years

Reproduction: One calf every 2 years; calves are generally 15 feet long at birth, weighing up to 1,500 pounds (3/4 ton)

AN AGE-OLD CONNECTION

Nearly every major Native group in Alaska has relied on whales for some portion of its diet. The Inupiaq and Yup'ik counted on whales for blubber, oil, meat, and intestines to survive. Aleuts used whale bones to build their semisubterranean homes. Even the Tlingit, for whom food was perennially abundant, considered a beached whale a bounty.

Subsistence whaling lives on in Alaska: although gray-whale hunting was banned in 1996, the Eskimo Whaling Commission permits the state's Native populations to harvest 50 bowhead whales every year.

Other Alaskan whale species:
Bowhead, northern right, minke, fin, and beluga whales also inhabit Alaskan waters.

BARNACLES These ragged squatters of the sea live on several species of whales, including humpbacks and gray whales. They're conspicuously absent from smaller marine mammals, such as orcas, dolphins, and porpoises. The reason? Speed. Scientists theorize that barnacles are only able to colonize the slowest-swimming cetacean species, leaving the faster swimmers free from their unwanted drag.

THE ORCA: Conspicuous, Curious Cetacean

Why the name killer whale? Perhaps for this animal's skilled and fearsome hunting techniques, which are sometimes used on other, often larger, cetaceans.

Perhaps the most recognizable of all the region's marine mammals, orcas (also called killer whales) are playful, inquisitive, and intelligent whales that reside in Alaskan waters year-round. Orcas travel in multigenerational family groups known as pods, which practice cooperative hunting techniques.

Orcas are smaller than grays and humpbacks, and their 17-month gestation period is the longest of any cetacean. They are identified by their white-and-black markings, as well as by the knifelike shape of their dorsal fins, which, in the case of mature males, can reach 6 feet in height.

Pods generally adhere to one of three common classifications: residents, which occupy inshore waters and feed primarily on fish; transients, which occupy larger ranges and hunt sea lions, squid, sharks, fish, and whales; and offshores, about which little is known.

QUICK FACTS:

Scientific name:
Orcinus orca

Length: Up to 30 ft.

Weight: Up to 18,000 pounds (9 tons)

Coloring: Smooth, shiny black skin with white eye patches and chin and white belly markings

Life span: 30 to 50 years

Reproduction: One calf every 3 to 5 years; calves are generally 6 feet long at birth, weighing up to 400 pounds (0.2 ton)

tours with some of the best glacier viewing in Southcentral Alaska. Whittier is very small, and there is not much to look at in town, but the location is unbeatable. Surrounding peaks cradle alpine glaciers, and when the summer weather melts the huge winter snow load you can catch glimpses of the brilliant blue ice underneath. Sheer cliffs drop into Passage Canal and provide nesting places for flocks of black-legged kittiwakes, while sea otters and harbor seals cavort in the small-boat harbor and salmon return to spawn in nearby streams. A short boat ride out into the sound reveals tidewater glaciers, and an alert wildlife watcher can catch sight of mountain goats clinging to the mountainsides and black bears patrolling the beaches and hillsides in their constant search for food.

THE CRUISE PORT
Ships dock in Whittier, and there is a small cruise terminal. Within easy walking distance of the dock are other seasonal shops and casual restaurants. There are also a couple of lodging options, but most people will prefer Anchorage, which has many more choices. Whittier is reached by rail or road, though both trains and road traffic pass through the same tunnel.

HOURS
Seasonal shops and restaurants open when a ship is in port.

 Restaurants

China Sea
$$ | CHINESE | This MSG-free Chinese restaurant features local seafood and amazingly fresh vegetables. The grilled halibut is fantastic, and for nonfish lovers, the Mongolian beef and kung pao chicken are excellent choices. **Known for:** one of the best Chinese restaurants in Southcentral Alaska; fresh fish and vegetables (a rarity in these parts); location right near the ferry terminal. $ *Average main:* $15 ⊠ *6 Harbor Rd.* ☎ *907/472–3663* ✆ *Closed mid-Sept.–late May.*

Lazy Otter Café & Gifts
$ | CAFÉ | Amid the summer shops and docks, this little café offers warm drinks and soups, sandwiches, and fresh-baked pastries, along with an Alaskan favorite, soft-serve ice cream. The busy shop has only a couple of indoor seats, but there's outdoor seating overlooking the harbor, which is quite pleasant on sunny days. **Known for:** excellent seafood chowder and salmon spread; outdoor seating with views of harbor; only good coffee in town. $ *Average main:* $9 ⊠ *Lot 2, Whittier Harbor* ☎ *907/472–6887.*

Varly's Ice Cream & Pizza Parlor
$ | PIZZA | On a hot summer day and even on not-so-hot days, locals yearn for some Varly's ice cream or if the weather's cold and rainy, for some decent pizza. The owners (who also manage Varly's Swiftwater Seafood Café) take great pride in what they do, and it shows: the homemade pizza here is certainly something to write home about. **Known for:** homemade pizza dough and breads; outdoor seating; authentic frontier feel. $ *Average main: $9* ⊠ *Lot 1A Triangle Lease Area, Whittier Harbor* ☎ *907/472–2547* ⊕ *www.swiftwaterseafoodcafe.com* ✆ *Closed Oct.–Apr.*

Varly's Swiftwater Seafood Café
$$ | SEAFOOD | The epicurean heart of Whittier for more than two decades, Varly's offers delightful surprises like its famed calamari burger—squid tenderized and fried in a secret batter. Other menu items include burgers, homemade chowders, rockfish, halibut, and salmon. **Known for:** best fried fish in the state; fresh seafood straight out of the water; true fishermen's wharf atmosphere. $ *Average main: $20* ⊠ *Harbor Loop* ☎ *907/472–2550* ⊕ *www.swiftwaterseafoodcafe.com* ✆ *Closed mid-Sept.–May.*

Hotels

Inn at Whittier
$$$ | HOTEL | With its lighthouse-tower design and its weathered-looking gray slats, this hotel set among shanties and

harbor boats blends in well with its surroundings. **Pros:** comfortable beds; great views; nice restaurant and bar. **Cons:** no kitchen amenities; some downstairs rooms have only parking lot views; some rooms don't have working televisions. ⑤ *Rooms from: $180* ✉ *5a Harbor Rd.* ☎ *907/472-3200* ⊕ *www.innatwhittier. com* ⊗ *Closed Oct.–Mar.* ⇌ *25 rooms* ⧖ *Breakfast.*

June's Whittier Condo Suites

$$ | **HOTEL** | A former military housing tower that is now home to most of the town's residents, June's also offers bed-and-breakfast condos, half with million-dollar bay views and half with gorgeous mountain and glacier views. **Pros:** full amenities including Wi-Fi; lovely views; quirky decor. **Cons:** unattractive exterior; rooms with the best views cost more; some rooms could use updating. ⑤ *Rooms from: $165* ✉ *Begich Towers, 100 Kenai St.* ☎ *907/472-6001 office, 907/841-5102 cell* ⊕ *www.juneswhittiercondosuites.com* ⇌ *10 rooms* ⧖ *No meals.*

🏃 Activities

BOATING AND WILDLIFE VIEWING
Alaska Sea Kayakers

BOATING | This outfit supplies sea kayaks and gear for exploring Prince William Sound and conducts guided day trips, multiday tours, instruction, and boat-assisted and boat live-aboard kayaking trips. The company practices a leave-no-trace camping ethos, and is very conscientious about avoiding bear problems. All guides are experienced Alaska paddlers, and group sizes are kept small. ✉ *Whittier* ☎ *907/472-2534, 877/472-2534* ⊕ *www. alaskaseakayakers.com* ✉ *Day trips from $89.*

Lazy Otter Charters

BOATING | With three boats and two landing craft, Lazy Otter runs sightseeing trips, operates a water taxi to Forest Service cabins, drops off sea kayakers at scenic points, and has ride-along

and share-a-ride programs, a way to see Prince William Sound on a smaller budget. Customized sightseeing trips last from four to nine hours. Day trips include lunch from the Lazy Otter Café. ✉ *Whittier* ☎ *800/587-6887, 907/694-6887* ⊕ *www.lazyotter.com* ✉ *Custom sightseeing trips from $255 per person (minimum of four).*

Major Marine Tours

BOATING | Major Marine Tours runs a five-hour cruise from Whittier that visits two tidewater glaciers. The waters of Prince William Sound are well protected and relatively calm, making this a good option if you tend to get seasick. Seabirds, waterfowl, and bald eagles are always present, and the chance to get close to the enormous walls of glacier ice is not to be missed. A number of different cruises are available from mid-March to mid-September, ranging from $119 to $150 per person. ✉ *Whittier* ☎ *907/274-7300* ⊕ *www.majormarine.com.*

★ 26 Glacier Cruise

BOATING | Phillips Cruises & Tours has been running the 26 Glacier Cruise through Prince William Sound for many years. The high-speed catamaran covers 135 miles of territory in 4½ hours, leaving Whittier and visiting Port Wells, Barry Arm, and College and Harriman fjords. The boat is a very stable platform, and even visitors prone to seasickness take this cruise with no ill effects. The heated cabin has large windows, upholstered booths, and wide aisles, and a snack bar and a saloon are onboard. Potential wildlife sightings include humpback whales, orcas, sea otters, harbor seals, sea lions, bears, mountain goats, and eagles. You can drive to Whittier and catch the boat at the dock, or you can arrange with the company to travel from Anchorage by rail or bus. The tour rate includes a hot lunch of cod or chicken. ✉ *Cliffside Marina, 100 W. Camp Rd.* ☎ *907/276-8023* ⊕ *www. phillipscruises.com* ✉ *$159.*

Chapter 5

PORTS OF CALL

Updated by
Teeka Ballas,
Amy Fletcher, and
Chris McBeath

There's never a dull day on an Alaskan cruise, and whether your ship is scheduled to make a port call, cruise by glaciers, or glide through majestic fjords, you'll have constant opportunities to explore the culture, wildlife, history, and amazing scenery that make Alaska so unique.

Most port cities are small and easily explored on foot, but if you prefer to be shown the sights, your ship will offer organized shore excursions at each stop along the way.

Popular activities include city tours, flightseeing, charter fishing, whale watching, river rafting, and visits to Native communities. You can also, for the sake of shorter trips or more active excursions, readily organize your own tour through a local vendor.

Going Ashore

The ports visited on an Alaska cruise and the amount of time spent in each vary depending on the cruise line and itinerary, but most ships stop in Ketchikan, Juneau, and Skagway—the three big draws in Southeast Alaska. Some ports, such as Homer and Wrangell, are visited by only a couple of the small-ship cruise lines, whereas other adventure ships head out to explore the wild places in the Bering Sea.

Each town has its highlights. For example, Ketchikan has a wealth of Native artifacts, Skagway has lots of gold-rush history, Sitka has a rich Russian and Native heritage, and Juneau has glacier trips. There are also ample shopping opportunities in most ports, but beware of tacky tourist traps. Nearly all Southeast towns, but especially Haines, Sitka, and Ketchikan, have great art galleries.

To help you plan your trip, we've compiled a list of the most worthwhile excursions available in each port of call. Also look out for "Best Bets" boxes; these highlight a port's top experiences so you don't shell out for a flightseeing trip in one place, for example, when the experience would be better elsewhere.

Arriving in Port

When your ship arrives in a port, it will tie up alongside a dock or anchor out in a harbor. If the ship is docked, passengers walk down the gangway to go ashore. Docking makes it easy to move between the shore and the ship.

TENDERING

If your ship anchors in the harbor, you will have to take a small boat—called a launch or tender—to get ashore. Tendering is a nuisance; however, participants in shore excursions are given priority. Passengers wishing to disembark independently may be required to gather in a public room, get sequenced tendering passes, and wait until their numbers are called. The ride to shore may take as long as 20 minutes. If you don't like waiting, plan to go ashore an hour or so after the ship drops its anchor. On a very large ship, the wait for a tender can be quite long and frustrating.

Because tenders can be difficult to board, passengers with mobility problems may not be able to visit certain ports. The larger ships are more likely to use tenders. It is usually possible to learn before booking a cruise whether the ship will dock or anchor at its ports of call.

Before anyone is allowed to walk down the gangway or board a tender, the ship must be cleared for landing. Immigration and customs officials board the vessel to examine the ship's manifest or possibly passports and sort through red tape. It may be more than an hour before you're allowed ashore. You will be issued a boarding pass, which you'll need to get back onboard.

Returning to the Ship

Cruise lines are strict about sailing times, which are posted at the gangway and elsewhere and announced in the daily schedule of activities. Be sure to be back onboard (not on the dock waiting to get a tender back to the ship) at least an hour before the announced sailing time or you may be stranded. If you are on a shore excursion that was sold by the cruise line, however, the captain will wait for your group before casting off. That is one reason many passengers prefer ship-packaged tours.

If you're not on one of the ship's tours and the ship sails without you, immediately contact the cruise line's port representative, whose phone number is often listed on the daily schedule of activities. You may be able to hitch a ride on a pilot boat, although that is unlikely.

Passengers who miss the boat must pay their own way to the next port.

Alaska Essentials
Currency

Alaska cruises may call in ports in either the United States or Canada (Canadian ports are much more likely on itineraries that focus on the Inside Passage). In such cases, you may need to change some currency into Canadian dollars, though U.S. dollars are accepted in some places.

Keeping in Touch

Internet cafés are less common than they used to be, but you'll sometimes find Internet access in the cruise-ship terminal itself, or perhaps in an attached or nearby shopping center. Such access is often Wi-Fi. If you want to call home, most cruise-ship terminal facilities have phones that accept credit cards or phone cards (local phone cards are almost always the cheapest option). But mobile phones work in almost all those ports, though you will likely have to pay a roaming charge if you make a call in Canada, depending on your cell phone calling plan.

Where to Eat

Not surprisingly, seafood dominates most menus. In summer, salmon, halibut, crab, cod, and prawns are usually fresh. Restaurants are informal and casual clothes are the norm; you'll never be sent away for wearing jeans in an Alaskan restaurant. However, prices are typically higher than in the continental United States.

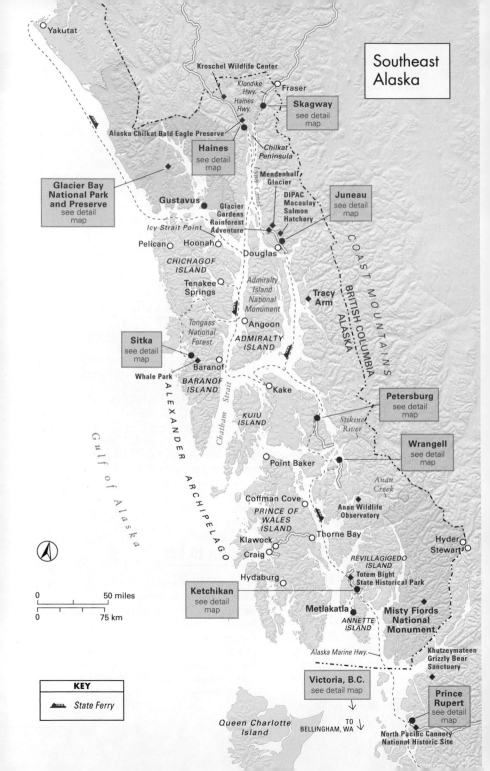

Southeast Alaska

Yakutat

Kroschel Wildlife Center

Klondike Hwy.
Fraser

Haines Hwy.

Skagway
see detail map

Alaska Chilkat Bald Eagle Preserve

Haines
see detail map

Chilkat Peninsula

Mendenhall Glacier

DIPAC Macaulay Salmon Hatchery

Juneau
see detail map

Glacier Bay National Park and Preserve
see detail map

Gustavus

Glacier Gardens Rainforest Adventure

Icy Strait Point

Pelican   Hoonah

Douglas

CHICHAGOF ISLAND

Admiralty Island National Monument

Tenakee Springs

Tracy Arm

Tongass National Forest

Angoon

ADMIRALTY ISLAND

Sitka
see detail map

Baranof

Whale Park

BARANOF ISLAND

Kake

KUIU ISLAND

Petersburg
see detail map

Stikine River

Wrangell
see detail map

Point Baker

Anan Creek

Coffman Cove

PRINCE OF WALES ISLAND

Anan Wildlife Observatory

Thorne Bay

Klawock

Craig

REVILLAGIGEDO ISLAND

Hyder
Stewart

Hydaburg

Totem Bight State Historical Park

Ketchikan
see detail map

Metlakatla

ANNETTE ISLAND

Misty Fiords National Monument

Khutzeymateen Grizzly Bear Sanctuary

Alaska Marine Hwy.

Victoria, B.C.
see detail map

TO
BELLINGHAM, WA

Prince Rupert
see detail map

Queen Charlotte Island

North Pacific Cannery National Historic Site

Gulf of Alaska

ALEXANDER ARCHIPELAGO

Chatham Strait

COAST MOUNTAINS

BRITISH COLUMBIA
ALASKA

0   50 miles
0   75 km

KEY

State Ferry

What it Costs			
$	$$	$$$	$$$$
AT DINNER			
under $15	$15–$20	$21–$25	over $25

Outdoor Activities

There are hikes and walks in or near every Alaska port town. Well-maintained trails are easily accessible from even the largest cities; lush forests and wilderness areas, port and glacier views, and mountaintop panoramas are often within a few hours' walk of downtown areas. More adventurous travelers will enjoy paddling sea kayaks in the protected waters of Southeast and Southcentral Alaska; companies in most ports rent kayaks and give lessons and tours. Fishing enthusiasts from all over the world come to Alaska for a chance to land a trophy salmon or halibut. Cycling, glacier hikes, flightseeing, or bear-viewing shore excursions in some ports also offer cruise passengers an opportunity to engage with Alaska's endless landscape.

Shopping

Alaskan Native handicrafts range from Tlingit totem poles—a few inches high to more than 30 feet tall—to Athabascan beaded slippers and fur garments. Traditional pieces of art (or imitations thereof) are found in gift shops up and down the coast: Inupiat spirit masks, Yupik dolls and dance fans, Tlingit button blankets and silver jewelry, and Aleut grass baskets and carved wooden items. Salmon, halibut, crab, and other frozen fish are very popular souvenirs (shipped home to meet you, of course) and make great gifts. Although Ketchikan is probably your best bet, with several outlets, most towns have at least one local company that packs and ships fresh, smoked, or frozen seafood.

To ensure authenticity, buy items tagged with the state-approved "authentic Native handcraft from Alaska" or "Silverhand" label, or look for the polar-bear symbol indicating products made in Alaska. Although these symbols are designed to ensure authentic Alaskan and Native-made products, not all items lacking them are inauthentic. Better prices tend to be found in the more remote villages, in museum shops, or in crafts fairs such as Anchorage's downtown Saturday Market. *For more on buying Native crafts, see Made in Alaska in this chapter.*

Shore Excursions

Shore excursions arranged by the cruise line are a convenient way to see the sights, but you'll pay extra for this convenience. Before your cruise, you'll receive a booklet or be directed to a Web page describing the shore excursions your cruise line offers. Most cruise lines let you book excursions in advance online, where you'll find descriptions and pricing; all sell them onboard during the cruise. If you cancel your excursion, you may incur penalties, the amount varying with the number of days remaining until the tour. Because these trips are specialized, many have limited capacity and are sold on a first-come, first-served basis.

Glacier Bay National Park and Preserve

Your cruise experience in Glacier Bay will depend partly on the size of your ship. Large cruise ships tend to stay midchannel, while small yachtlike ships spend more time closer to shore. Smaller ships give you a better view of the calving ice and wildlife, but on a big ship you can get

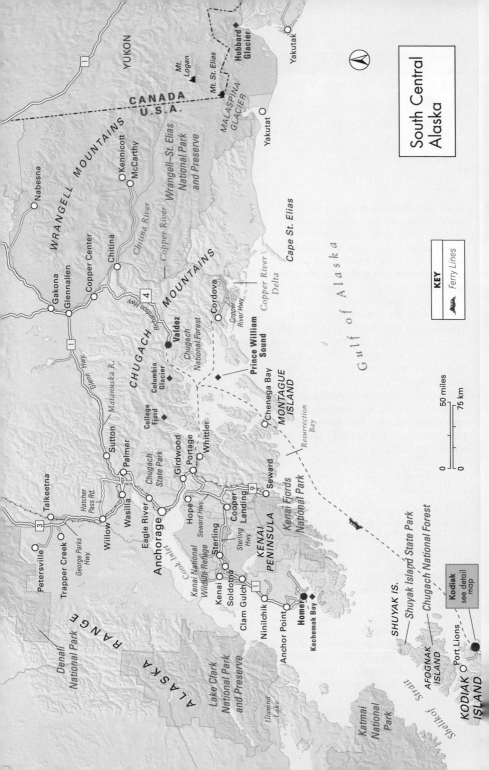

South Central Alaska

KEY

Ferry Lines

Don your jacket and head to the outside deck for spectacular views of Glacier Bay.

a loftier perspective. Both come within a quarter mile of the glaciers themselves.

GLACIER RUNDOWN

The most frequently viewed glaciers are in the west arm of Glacier Bay. Ships linger in front of five glaciers, giving you ample time to admire their stunning and ever-changing faces. First, most ships stop briefly at Reid Glacier, which flows down from the Brady Icefield, before continuing on to Lamplugh Glacier—one of the bluest in the park—at the mouth of Johns Hopkins Inlet. Next, at the end of the inlet, is the massive Johns Hopkins Glacier, where you're likely to see a continuous shower of calving ice. (Sometimes there are so many icebergs in the inlet that ships must avoid the area. And access isn't allowed early in the season because it's where sea lions give birth to their babies.) Farther north, near the end of the western arm, is Margerie Glacier, which is also quite active. Adjacent is Grand Pacific Glacier, the largest glacier in the park.

Competition for entry permits into Glacier Bay is fierce. To protect the humpback whale, which feeds here in summer, the Park Service limits the number of ships that can call. Check your cruise brochure to make sure Glacier Bay is included in your sailing. Most ships that do visit spend at least one full day exploring the park. There are no shore excursions or landings in the bay—the steep-sided and heavily forested fjords aren't conducive to pedestrian exploration—but a Park Service naturalist boards every cruise ship to offer a running commentary throughout the day.

★ **Glacier Bay National Park and Preserve**
NATIONAL/STATE PARK | Tidewater glaciers in Glacier Bay National Park calve icebergs into the sea with loud blasts. Humpback whales breach, spout, and slap their tails against the water. Coastal brown bears feed on sedge, salmon, and berries. Bald eagles soar overhead, and mountains in the Fairweather Range come in and out of view. This magical place rewards those who get out on

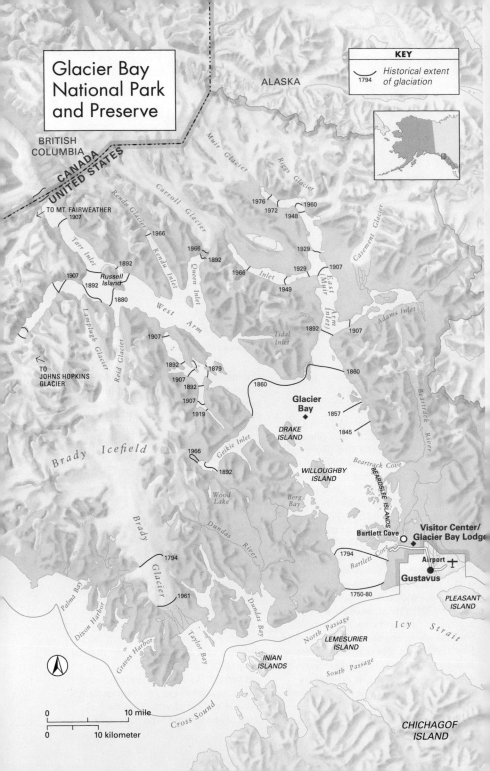

Glacier Bay National Park and Preserve

BRITISH COLUMBIA

CANADA
UNITED STATES

ALASKA

KEY

1794 Historical extent of glaciation

TO MT. FAIRWEATHER
1907

Muir Glacier

Riggs Glacier

Rendu Glacier

Carroll Glacier

Casement Glacier

1976
1972
1948
1960

1966

1929

Tarr Inlet
1892

1966
1892

Inlet
1929
1907

Russell Island
1907
1892
1880

Rendu Inlet

Queen Inlet

1966

1949

East Arm Muir Inlet

Casement Glacier

Lamplugh Glacier

West Arm

1907
1892

1892
1907

Adams Inlet

TO JOHNS HOPKINS GLACIER

Reid Glacier

1907
1892
1879

1860

Tidal Inlet

Beartrack River

1907
1919

1860

Glacier Bay

DRAKE ISLAND

1857
1845

Brady Icefield

1966
1892

Geikie Inlet

WILLOUGHBY ISLAND

Beartrack Cove

BEARDSLEE ISLANDS

Wood Lake

Berg Bay

Bartlett Cove

Visitor Center/ Glacier Bay Lodge

Brady Glacier

Dundas River

1794

Bartlett Cove

Airport

Gustavus

Palma Bay

Dixon Harbor

1961

Dundas Bay

1750-80

PLEASANT ISLAND

Graves Harbor

Taylor Bay

North Passage

LEMESURIER ISLAND

Icy Strait

INIAN ISLANDS

South Passage

0   10 mile

0   10 kilometer

Cross Sound

CHICHAGOF ISLAND

the water—whether it be in a cruise, a day boat, or a kayak. Glacier Bay is a marvelous laboratory for naturalists of all persuasions. Glaciologists, of course, can have a field day. Animal lovers can hope to see the rare glacial "blue" bears of the area, a variation of the black bear, which is here along with the brown bear; mountain goats in late spring and early summer; and seals on floating icebergs. Humpback whales are also abundant in these waters; the best time to see them is June through early August. Birders can look for the more than 200 species that have already been spotted in the park, and you are assured bald eagle sightings. The bay is a still-forming body of water fed by the runoff of the icefields, glaciers, and mountains that surround it. Today many glaciers in the park, including the namesake glacier of naturalist John Muir, who was one of the region's earliest proponents, continue to retreat: the Muir Glacier's terminus is now scores of miles farther up the bay from the small cabin he built there. However, some of the glaciers are still healthy, such as the Johns Hopkins Glacier and the Marjorie Glacier, which receive enough snow to maintain their size or even grow. **Bartlett Cove**, an area that's been ice-free for more than 200 years, has a lush spruce-and-hemlock rain forest as well as the 2,500-square-foot **Huna Tribal House** (Xunaa Shuká Hít), a space for tribal members and for visitors to learn about Tlingit history and culture. ⌧ *Gustavus* ☎ *907/697–2230, 907/697–2627 boating information* ⊕ *www.nps.gov/glba.*

Gustavus

50 miles west of Juneau, 75 miles south of Skagway.

For airborne visitors, Gustavus is the gateway to Glacier Bay National Park and Preserve. The long, paved jet airport, built as a refueling strip during the Second World War, is all the more impressive

because of the limited facilities at the field. Gustavus itself is less of a town than a scattering of homes, farmsteads, a craft studio, fishing and guiding charter companies, an art gallery, and other tiny enterprises run by hospitable individuals. Visitors enjoy the unstructured outdoor activities in the area, including beach and trail hiking in the Nature Conservancy's Forelands Preserve.

COMING ASHORE
Large cruise ships do not dock anywhere in Glacier Bay, and only a few small cruise lines stop in nearby Gustavus, 9 miles down the road. Small ships that dock here use the same dock as the ferries of the Alaska Marine Highway.

🏃 Activities

Glacier Bay is best experienced from the water, whether from the deck of a cruise ship, on a tour boat, or from the level of a sea kayak. National Park Service naturalists often come aboard to explain the great glaciers and to help spot bears, mountain goats, whales, porpoises, and birds. Those ships lucky enough to land in Gustavus will have other opportunities to see Glacier Bay.

BOAT TOURS
Glacier Bay Day Boat Tour
BOATING | Daily summertime boat tours, operated by Glacier Bay Lodge and Tours, leave from the dock at Bartlett Cove, near Glacier Bay Lodge, at 7:30 am and return at 3:30 pm. These eight-hour trips into Glacier Bay have a Park Service naturalist aboard a high-speed 155-passenger catamaran. A light lunch is included. Campers and sea kayakers heading up the bay ride the same boat. ⌧ *179 Bartlett Cove* ☎ *888/229–8687* ⊕ *www.visitglacierbay.com* ⌧ *$225.*

FLIGHTSEEING
★ Alaska Seaplanes
TOUR—SPORTS | Besides daily scheduled air service to 14 Southeast communities, Alaska Seaplanes also offers flightseeing

tours and charters to other Southeast destinations. ✉ *1873 Shell Simmons Dr., Juneau* ☎ *907/789–3331* ⊕ *www.flyalaskaseaplanes.com.*

HIKING

Glacier Bay's steep and heavily forested slopes aren't the most conducive to hiking, but there are several short hikes that begin at the Glacier Bay Lodge. Among the most popular is the **Forest Loop Trail,** a pleasant 1-mile jaunt that begins in a forest of spruce and hemlock and finishes on the beach. Also beginning at the lodge is the **Bartlett River Trail**—a 5-mile round-trip hike that borders an intertidal lagoon, culminating at the Bartlett River estuary. The **Bartlett Lake Trail,** part of a 6-mile walk that meanders through rain forest, ends at the quiet lakeshore. The entire Gustavus beachfront was set aside by the Nature Conservancy, enabling visitors to hike the shoreline for miles without getting lost. The beachfront is part of the **Alaska Coastal Wildlife Viewing Trail** (⊕ *wildlife.alaska.gov*). The spring and fall bird migrations are exceptional on Gustavus estuaries, including Dude Creek Critical Habitat Area, which provides a stopover before crossing the ice fields for sandhill cranes. Maps and wildlife-viewing information are available from the **Alaska Division of Wildlife Conservation** (⊕ *wildlife.alaska.gov*).

SEA KAYAKING

The most adventurous way to explore Glacier Bay is by paddling your own kayak through the bay's icy waters and inlets. But unless you're an expert, you're better off signing on with the guided tours.

Alaska Discovery

KAYAKING | You can book a six-day or an eight-day guided expedition through Alaska Discovery. Operated by Mountain Travel Sobek, the company provides safe, seaworthy kayaks and tents, gear, and food. Its guides are tough, knowledgeable Alaskans, and they've spent enough time in Glacier Bay's wild country to know what's safe and what's not. Private

Gustavus Best Bets

■ **Glacier Bay Boat Tours.** Whether you are on a simple boat tour or a whale-watching trip, the best way to see Glacier Bay up close and personal is aboard a smaller boat.

■ **Flightseeing.** Alaska Seaplanes, based at the Gustavus airport, offers flights over the glaciers.

■ **Hiking.** The Gustavus Forelands Preserve, set aside by the Nature Conservancy, stretches along the beach and into the surrounding wetlands, providing plentiful opportunities for hiking and wildlife viewing.

and custom-designed tours for small groups can also be organized through this company. ✉ *Gustavus* ☎ *888/831–7526* ⊕ *www.mtsobek.com/trips/br/region-north-america* ☞ *From $4,195.*

Alaska Mountain Guides

KAYAKING | Take day kayaking trips for whale watching at Point Adolphus, a premier humpback gathering spot, as well as multiday sea-kayaking expeditions next to tidewater glaciers in Glacier Bay National Park, with Alaska Mountain Guides. ✉ *Gustavus* ☎ *907/313–4422, 800/766–3396* ⊕ *www.alaskamountain-guides.com* ☞ *From $460.*

Glacier Bay Sea Kayaks

KAYAKING | Kayak rentals for Glacier Bay exploring and camping can be arranged through Glacier Bay Sea Kayaks. You will be given instructions on handling the craft plus camping and routing suggestions for unescorted trips. Guided day trips with knowledgeable guides are available in Bartlett Cove. The company is an official NPS concession for guided day kayak trips. ✉ *Bartlett Cove*

☎ *907/697–2257* ⊕ *www.glacierbay-seakayaks.com* ✉ *Trips from $95.*

Spirit Walker Expeditions

KAYAKING | Take one- to seven-day sea-kayaking trips from Gustavus to various parts of Icy Strait with Spirit Walker Expeditions. Trips to Glacier Bay and other remote areas of Southeast Alaska, including Fords Terror and West Chichagof, are also offered on a limited basis. ⊠ *Gustavus* ☎ *800/529–2537* ⊕ *www.seakayakalaska.com.*

WHALE WATCHING

The *Taz* Whale Watching Tours

WHALE-WATCHING | Step aboard the M/V *TAZ* and check out Icy Strait and Point Adolphus, near the entrance to Glacier Bay, for awesome views of humpback whales and many other marine mammals. All tours out of Gustavus include binoculars, snacks, and hot beverages. Half-day tours and custom charters accommodating up to 28 passengers are offered, as well as "Weddings with the Whales," where you can get married while surrounded by humpbacks. ⊠ *Gustavus* ☎ *907/321–2302, 888/698–2726* ⊕ *www.taz.gustavus.com* ✉ *From $123.*

Haines

Haines encompasses an area that has been occupied by Tlingit peoples for centuries on the collar of the Chilkat Peninsula, a narrow strip of land that divides the Chilkat and Chilkoot inlets. Missionary S. Hall Young and famed naturalist John Muir were intent on establishing a Presbyterian mission in the area, and, with the blessing of local chiefs, they chose the site that later became Haines. It's hard to imagine a more beautiful setting—a heavily wooded peninsula with magnificent views of Portage Cove and the snowy Coast Range.

The downtown area is small, and the town exudes a down-home friendliness. Perhaps this is because Haines sees

fewer cruise ships, or maybe it's the grand landscape and ease of access to the mountains and sea. Whatever the cause, visitors should be prepared for a relative lack of souvenir and T-shirt shops compared with other ports. Local weather is drier than in much of Southeast Alaska.

COMING ASHORE

Cruise ships and catamaran ferries dock in front of Ft. Seward, and downtown Haines is just a short walk away (about a half mile). Complimentary shuttle service is provided to downtown and the Ft. Seward area.

TOURS

Jilkaat Kwaan Heritage Center

NATIVE SITE | Built near Klukwan, a Native village 23 miles up the road from Haines, this site offers visitors the chance to learn more about Tlingit culture, language, and traditions. Visit the site's Long House, built using traditional methods; find out about traditional Native crafts, including wood carving, beading, and the distinctive Chilkat blanket; see the process for smoking salmon; and much more. ⊠ *32 Chilkat Ave., Klukwan* ☎ *907/767–5485* ⊕ *jilkaatkwaanheritagecenter.org* ✉ *$15* ⊗ *Closed mid-Sept.–mid-May; Sun.*

VISITOR INFORMATION

CONTACTS Haines Convention and Visitors Bureau ⊠ *122 2nd Ave. S* ☎ *907/766–6418, 800/458–3579* ⊕ *www.haines.ak.us.*

Sights

Alaska Chilkat Bald Eagle Preserve

NATURE PRESERVE | In winter, the section of the preserve between Mile 19 and Mile 21 of the Haines Highway harbors the largest concentration of bald eagles in the world. In November and December, more eagles gather outside Haines than live in the continental United States. Thousands come to feast on the late run of salmon in the clear, ice-free waters

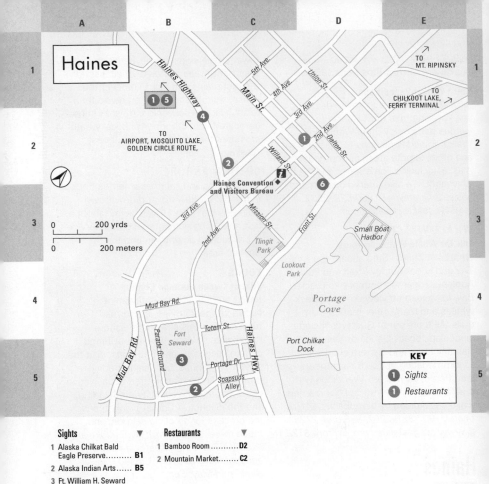

Haines

A **B** **C** **D** **E**

TO
MT. RIPINSKY

TO
CHILKOOT LAKE,
FERRY TERMINAL

5th Ave.

4th Ave.

Union St.

Main St.

3rd Ave.

2nd Ave.

Dalton St.

TO
AIRPORT, MOSQUITO LAKE,
GOLDEN CIRCLE ROUTE,

Willard St.

Haines Convention
and Visitors Bureau

Haines Highway

3rd Ave.

2nd Ave.

Mission St.

Front St.

Small Boat
Harbor

Tlingit
Park

Lookout
Park

Portage
Cove

200 yrds

200 meters

Mud Bay Rd.

Parade Ground

Fort
Seward

Totem St.

Haines Hwy.

Port Chilkat
Dock

Portage Dr.

Soapsuds
Alley

KEY

1 *Sights*

1 *Restaurants*

Sights ▼

1 Alaska Chilkat Bald
   Eagle Preserve.......... **B1**

2 Alaska Indian Arts...... **B5**

3 Ft. William H. Seward
   National Historic
   Landmark................ **B5**

4 Haines Highway **B2**

5 Kroschel Wildlife
   Center.................... **B1**

6 Sheldon Museum and
   Cultural Center.......... **D3**

Restaurants ▼

1 Bamboo Room **D2**

2 Mountain Market........ **C2**

of the Chilkat River, which is heated by underground warm springs. ⊠ *Haines Hwy* ☎ *907/766-2292* ⊕ *www.dnr.alaska.gov/parks/units/eagleprv.htm.*

Alaska Indian Arts

NATIVE SITE | FAMILY | Dedicated to the preservation and continuation of Alaska Native art, this nonprofit organization occupies what was Ft. Seward's hospital. You can watch artisans doing everything from carving totem poles to creating delicate silver jewelry. ⊠ *Ft. Seward, south side of parade ground* ☎ *907/766-2160* ⊕ *www.alaskaindianarts.com* ⊠ *Free.*

Ft. William H. Seward National Historic Landmark

INFO CENTER | Stately clapboard homes stand against a mountain backdrop on the sloping parade grounds of Alaska's first U.S. Army post. As you enter you'll soon see the gallant, white-columned former commanding officer's quarters, now part of the **Hotel Halsingland.** Circle the parade ground if you like, passing the other homes along Officers Row. On the parade ground's south side at **Alaska Indian Arts,** you can watch artists at work. The Haines Convention and Visitors Bureau has a walking-tour brochure of the fort. ⊠ *Ft. Seward Dr.* ⊕ *www.nps.gov/places/fort-william-h-seward.htm.*

★ Haines Highway

SCENIC DRIVE | The breathtaking Haines Highway, a National Scenic Byway, starts at Mile 0 in Haines and continues 152 miles to Haines Junction. You don't have to drive the entire length to experience its beauty, as worthwhile stops are all along the route. At about Mile 6 a delightful picnic spot is near the Chilkat River. At Mile 9.5 the view of Cathedral Peaks, part of the Chilkat Range, is magnificent. At Mile 9 begins the **Alaska Chilkat Bald Eagle Preserve.** In winter the stretch between Mile 19 and Mile 21 harbors the largest concentration of bald eagles in the world. At Mile 33 is a roadside restaurant called, aptly, **33-Mile Roadhouse** (*www.33mileroadhouse.com*), where

Haines Best Bets

■ **Float the Chilkat River.** Running through one of Alaska's most stunning mountain ranges, the mellow Chilkat caters more to sightseers than to thrill-seekers.

■ **Pound the pavement.** Haines has a delightfully funky vibe welcoming to visitors; Mountain Market, Sheldon Bookstore, and the public library are favorite local hangouts.

■ **Hit the road.** The Haines Highway is one of the nation's most beautiful roads. Whether you enlist a local tour operator or rent a car, a drive up this highway is an unforgettable experience.

you fill your tank and coffee mug, grab a burger and, most important, a piece of pie—do not leave without trying the pie. The United States–Canada border lies at Mile 42; stop at Canadian customs and set your clock ahead one hour. ⊠ *Haines Hwy.* ☎ *907/766-2234* HCVB ⊕ *www.haines.ak.us/highway.*

Kroschel Wildlife Center

NATURE PRESERVE | A must for animal lovers, this privately run operation 28 miles north of Haines provides an up close look at Alaskan wildlife, including bears, caribou, moose, wolverines, porcupines, foxes, and wolves. More sanctuary than zoo, the center hosts small group tours, usually booked through cruise lines or other tourist outlets, but with notice may be able to arrange a visit for independent travelers. ⊠ *Mile 1.8 Mosquito Lake Rd.* ☎ *907/767-5464* ⊕ *www.kroschelfilms.com* ⊠ *Rates vary depending on tour; expect to pay about $50.*

Sheldon Museum and Cultural Center

MUSEUM | In the 1880s, Steve Sheldon began assembling Native artifacts, items from historic Ft. Seward, and gold-rush memorabilia, such as Jack Dalton's sawed-off shotgun, and started an exhibit of his finds in 1925. Today his collection is the core of this museum's impressive array of artifacts, including Chilkat blankets, a model of a Tlingit tribal house, and the original lens from the Eldred Rock lighthouse just south of Haines on the Lynn Canal. Repatriated Bear Clan items such as an 18th-century carved ceremonial Murrelet hat are also on display. ⊠ *11 Main St.* ☎ *907/766–2366* ⊕ *www.sheldonmuseum.org* ⊠ *$10* ⊗ *Closed Sun.*

Restaurants

Bamboo Room

$ | AMERICAN | Pop culture meets greasy spoon in this unassuming coffee shop with red-vinyl booths that has been in the same family for more than 50 years. The menu doesn't cater to light appetites—it includes sandwiches, burgers, fried chicken, chili, and halibut fish-and-chips—but the place really is at its best for an all-American breakfast (available until 2 pm). **Known for:** diner-style breakfast; burgers; retro, relaxed atmosphere. ⑤ *Average main: $10* ⊠ *11 2nd Ave., near Main St.* ☎ *907/766–2800* ⊕ *www.bamboopioneer.net.*

Mountain Market

$ | AMERICAN | Meet the locals over espresso, brewed from fresh-roasted beans, and a fresh-baked pastry at this busy corner natural-foods store, deli, café, wine-and-spirits shop, de facto meeting hall, and hitching post. Mountain Market is great for lunchtime sandwiches, wraps, soups, and salads. **Known for:** coffee (roasted on the premises); pizza; one-stop shop. ⑤ *Average main: $8* ⊠ *151 3rd Ave.* ☎ *907/766–3340* ⊕ *www.mountain-market.com.*

Shopping

A surprising number of artists live in the Haines area and sell their works in local galleries.

Wild Iris Gallery

ART GALLERIES | Haines's most charming gallery displays attractive jewelry, prints, and fashion wear created by owner Fred Shields and his daughter Melina. Other local artists are also represented. The gallery is just up from the cruise-ship dock, and its summer gardens alone are worth the visit. ⊠ *Portage St.* ☎ *907/766–2300.*

Activities

BOATING AND FISHING
★ Alaska Fjordlines

TOUR—SPORTS | The company operates a high-speed catamaran from Skagway and Haines to Juneau and back throughout the summer, stopping along the way to watch sea lions, humpbacks, and other marine mammals. One-way service is also available. ⊠ *Haines* ☎ *907/766–3395, 800/320–0146* ⊕ *www.alaskafjordlines.com* ⊠ *$169 round-trip, $130 one-way.*

Chilkat River Adventures

TOUR—SPORTS | The flat-bottom jet-boat tours offered by Chilkat River Adventures are a great way to experience the bald eagle preserve in majestic Chilkat River Valley. ⊠ *Haines* ☎ *907/766–2050, 800/478–9827* ⊕ *www.jetboatalaska.com* ⊠ *From $139.*

HIKING
Battery Point Trail

HIKING/WALKING | A fairly level path that hugs the shoreline for 1.2 miles, Battery Point provides fine views across Lynn Canal. The trail begins a mile east of town, and a campsite can be found at Kelgaya Point near the end. For other hikes, pick up a copy of "Haines Is for Hikers" at the Haines Convention and Visitors Bureau. ⊠ *Beach Rd., east end* ⊕ *www.seatrails.org/com_haines/trl-battery.htm.*

NATURE TOURS
Alaska Nature Tours
TOUR—SPORTS | This company conducts bird-watching and natural-history tours through the Alaska Chilkat Bald Eagle Preserve, operates brown bear–watching excursions in July and August, and leads hiking treks in summer. ⊠ *109 2nd Ave.* ☎ *907/766–2876* ⊕ *www.alaskanature-tours.net* ✉ *From $80.*

Homer

It's a shame that of the hundreds of thousands of cruise passengers who visit Alaska each year, only a very few get to see Homer. Its scenic setting on Kachemak Bay, surrounded by mountains, spruce forest, and glaciers, makes Homer unique even in Alaska.

Founded in the late 1800s as a gold-prospecting camp, this community was later used as coal-mining headquarters. Chunks of coal are still common along local beaches; they wash into the bay from nearby slopes where the coal seams are exposed. Today the town of Homer is an eclectic community with most of the tacky tourist paraphernalia relegated to the Spit (though the Spit has plenty else to recommend it, not the least of which is the 360-degree view of the surrounding mountains); the rest of the town is full of local merchants and artisans. The community is an interesting mix of fishermen, actors, artists, and writers. Much of the commercial fishing centers on halibut, and the popular Homer Jackpot Halibut Derby is often won by fish weighing more than 300 pounds. The local architecture includes everything from dwellings that are little more than assemblages of driftwood to steel commercial buildings and magnificent homes on the hillside overlooking the surrounding bay, mountains, forests, and glaciers.

Homer Best Bets

■ **Charter a fishing boat.** Nothing beats wrestling a monster halibut out of the icy depths.

■ **People-watch on the Spit.** Homer is home to a thriving arts community, and makes for an interesting cultural mix.

■ **Cruise to a waterfront gallery.** Crossing the bay to Halibut Cove for gallery hopping is another favorite experience.

COMING ASHORE
Ships and Alaska Marine Highway ferries dock at the end of the Homer Spit, where you can find charters, restaurants, and shops. The routine for cruise lines calling in Homer is to provide a shuttle from the Spit to downtown. Since Homer isn't a common port and the town itself offers so much to explore, shore-excursion offerings aren't as predictable here as in other ports of call. Your ship may offer boat charters to Gull Island (a nearby island chock-full of cacophonous seagulls and other seabirds) or Seldovia (a small, scenic town with quality art galleries across Kachemak Bay). Halibut fishing is also huge here, and if you take one fishing-charter excursion during your trip this would be the place to do it.

VISITOR INFORMATION
Visit Homer
⊠ *201 Sterling Hwy.* ☎ *907/235–8766* ⊕ *www.homeralaska.org.*

Sights

Halibut Cove
TOWN | A small artists' community directly across from the tip of Homer Spit, Halibut Cove is a fine place to spend time meandering along the boardwalk and

visiting galleries. The cove is lovely, especially during salmon runs, when fish leap and splash in the clear water. The *Danny J* ferries people across from Homer Spit, with a stop at the rookery at Gull Island and two or three hours to walk around Halibut Cove. The ferry makes two trips daily: the first ($58) leaves Homer at noon and returns at 5 pm, and the second ($35) leaves at 5 pm and returns at 10 pm. Central Charters and the Saltry Restaurant handle all bookings. Several lodges are on this side of the bay, on pristine coves away from summer crowds. Mako's Taxi provides service to most of the lodging destinations in the area. ✉ *Homer* ☎ *907/399–2683* ⊕ *www.halibut-cove-alaska.com/ferry.htm* ☉ *Closed Oct.–Apr.*

★ Homer Spit

BODY OF WATER | FAMILY | Protruding into Kachemak Bay, Homer Spit provides a sandy focal point for visitors and locals. A 4½-mile paved road runs the length of the Spit, making it the world's longest road into the ocean. A commercial-fishing-boat harbor at the end of the path has restaurants, hotels, charter-fishing businesses, sea-kayaking outfitters, art galleries, and on-the-beach camping spots. Fly a kite, walk the beaches, drop a line in the Fishing Hole, or just wander through the shops looking for something interesting; this is one of Alaska's favorite summertime destinations. ✉ *Homer.*

★ Islands and Ocean Visitors Center

MUSEUM | FAMILY | This center provides a wonderful introduction to the Alaska Maritime National Wildlife Refuge. The refuge covers some 3½ million acres spread across some 2,500 Alaskan islands, from Prince of Wales Island in the south to Barrow in the north. The 37,000-square-foot eco-friendly facility with towering windows facing Kachemak Bay is a must-see for anyone interested in wild places. A film takes visitors along on a voyage of the Fish and Wildlife Service's research ship, the MV *Tiglax.* Interactive exhibits

detail the birds and marine mammals of the refuge (the largest seabird refuge in America), and one room even re-creates the noisy sounds and pungent smells of a bird rookery. In summer, guided bird-watching treks and beach walks are offered, and you can take a stroll on your own on the walkways in the Beluga Slough, where Alaskan poet Wendy Erd's commissioned work lines the way. ✉ *95 Sterling Hwy.* ☎ *907/235–6961* ⊕ *www. islandsandocean.org* ⊠ *Free.*

Kachemak Bay

BODY OF WATER | The bay abounds with wildlife, including a large population of puffins and eagles. Tour operators take visitors past bird rookeries or across the bay to gravel beaches for clam digging. Most fishing charters include an opportunity to view whales, seals, porpoises, and birds close-up. At the end of the day, walk along the docks on one of the largest coastal parks in America. ✉ *Homer.*

Mako's Water Taxi

✉ *Homer Spit Rd.* ☎ *907/235–9055* ⊕ *www.makoswatertaxi.com.*

Pratt Museum

MUSEUM | FAMILY | The Pratt is an art gallery and a cultural and natural-history museum rolled into one. In addition to monthly exhibits showcasing some of Alaska's finest artists, the museum has an exhibit on the 1989 *Exxon Valdez* oil spill; botanical gardens; nature trails; a gift shop; and pioneer, Russian, and Alaska Native displays. You can spy on wildlife with robotic video cameras set up on a seabird rookery and at the McNeil River Bear Sanctuary. A refurbished homestead cabin and outdoor summer exhibits are along the trail out back. ✉ *Bartlett St., off Pioneer Ave.* ☎ *907/235–8635* ⊕ *www. prattmuseum.org* ⊠ *$10* ☉ *Closed Jan.*

🍴 Restaurants

Fritz Creek General Store

$ | ECLECTIC | Be sure to check out this old-fashioned country store, gas station,

Continued on page 266

NATIVE ARTS AND CRAFTS

Intricate Aleut baskets, Athabascan birch-bark wonders, Inupiaq ivory carvings, and towering Tlingit totems are just some of the eye-opening crafts you'll encounter as you explore the 49th state. Alaska's native peoples—who live across 570,000 square miles of tundra, boreal forest, arctic plains, and coastal rain forest—are undeniably hardy, and their unique artistic traditions are just as resilient and enduring.

TIPS ON CHOOSING AN AUTHENTIC ITEM

1 The Federal Trade Commission has enacted strict regulations to combat the sale of falsely marketed goods; it's illegal for anything made by non-native Alaskans to be labeled as "Indian," "Native American," or "Alaska Native."

2 Some authentic goods are marked by a silver hand symbol or are labeled as an "Authentic Native Handicraft from Alaska."

3 The "Made in Alaska" label, often accompanied by an image of a polar bear with cub, denotes that the handicraft was made in the state.

4 Be sure to ask for written proof of authenticity with your purchase, as well as the artist's name. You can also request the artist's permit number, which may be available.

5 The Alaska State Council on the Arts, in Anchorage, is a great resource if you have additional questions or want to confirm a permit number. Call 907/269–6610 or 888/278–7424 in Alaska.

6 Materials must be legal. For example, only some feathers, such as ptarmigan and pheasant feathers, comply with the Migratory Bird Act. Only Native artisans are permitted to carve new walrus ivory. The seller should be able to answer your questions about material and technique.

THE NATIVE PEOPLE OF ALASKA

There are many opportunities to see the making of traditional crafts in native environments, including the Southeast Alaska Indian Cultural Center in Sitka and Anchorage's Alaska Native Heritage Center.

After chatting with the artisans, pop into the gift shops to peruse the handmade items. Also check out prominent galleries and museum shops.

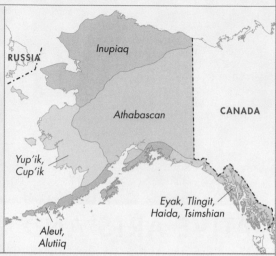

NORTHWEST COAST INDIANS: TLINGIT, HAIDA & TSIMSHIAN

Scattered throughout Southeast Alaska's rain forests, these highly social tribes traditionally benefited from the region's mild climate and abundant salmon, which afforded them a rare luxury: leisure time. They put this time to good use by cultivating highly detailed crafts, including ceremonial masks, elaborate woven robes, and, most famously, totem poles.

TOWERING TOTEM POLES

Throughout the Inside Passage's braided channels and forested islands, Native peoples use the wood of the abundant cedar trees to carve totem poles, which illustrate history, pay reverence, commemorate a potlatch, or cast shame on a misbehaving person.

Every totem pole tells a story with a series of animal and human figures arranged vertically. Traditionally the totem poles of this area feature ravens, eagles, killer whales, wolves, bears, frogs, the mythic thunderbird, and the likenesses of ancestors.

A Tlingit totem reaches for the skies in Ketchikan

K'alyaan Totem Pole

Carved in 1999, the K'alyaan totem pole is a tribute to the Tlingits who lost their lives in the 1804 Battle of Sitka between invading Russians and Tlingit warriors. Tommy Joseph, a venerated Tlingit artist from Sitka, and an apprentice spent three months carving the pole from a 35-ft western red cedar. It now stands at the very site of the skirmish, in Sitka National Historical Park.

Woodworm: The woodworm—a Tlingit clan symbol—is a wood-boring beetle that leaves a distinctive mark on timber.

Beaver: Sporting a fearsome pair of front teeth, this beaver symbol cradles a child in its arms, signifying the strength of Tlingit family bonds.

Frog: This animal represents the Kik.sádi Clan, which was very instrumental in organizing the Tlingit's revolt against the Russian trespassers. Here, the frog holds a raven helmet—a tribute to the Kik.sádi warrior who wore a similar headpiece into battle.

Raven: Atop the pole sits the striking raven, the emblem of one of the two moieties (large multi-clan groups) of Tlingit culture.

Sockeye Salmon (above) and Dog/Chum Salmon (below): These two symbols signify the contributions of the Sockeye and Dog Salmon Clans to the 1804 battle. They also illustrate the symbolic connection to the tribe's traditional food sources.

TOOLS AND MATERIALS
As do most modern carvers, Joseph used a steel adz to carve the cedar. Prior to European contact—and the accompanying introduction of metal tools—Tlingit artists carved with jade adzes. Totem poles are traditionally decorated with paint made from salmon-liver oil, charcoal, and iron and copper oxides.

ALEUT & ALUTIIQ

The Aleut inhabit the Alaska Peninsula and the windswept Aleutian Islands. Historically they lived and died by the sea, surviving on a diet of seals, sea lions, whales, and walruses, which they hunted in the tumultuous waters of the Gulf of Alaska and the Bering Sea. Hunters pursued their prey in *Sugpiaq*, kayaklike boats made of seal skin stretched over a driftwood frame.

WATERPROOF KAMLEIKAS

The Aleut prize seal intestine for its remarkable waterproof properties; they use it to create sturdy cloaks, shelter walls, and boat hulls. To make their famous cloaks, called *kamleikas*, intestine is washed, soaked in salt water, and arduously scraped clean. It is then stretched and dried before being stitched into hooded, waterproof pullovers.

FINE BASKETRY

Owing to the region's profusion of wild rye grass, Aleutian women are some of the planet's most skilled weavers, capable of creating baskets with more than 2,500 fibers per square inch. They also create hats, socks, mittens, and multipurpose mats. A long, sharpened thumbnail is their only tool.

ATHABASCANS

Inhabiting Alaska's rugged interior for 8,000 to 20,000 years, Athabascans followed a seasonally nomadic hunter-gatherer lifestyle, subsisting off of caribou, moose, bear, and snowshoe hare. They populate areas from the Brooks Range to Cook Inlet, a vast expanse that encompasses five significant rivers: the Tanana, the Kuskokwim the Copper, the Susitna, and the Yukon.

BIRCH BARK: WATERPROOF WONDER

Aside from annual salmon runs, the Athabascans had no access to marine mammals—or to the intestines that made for such effective boat hulls and garments. They turned to the region's birch, the bark of which was used to create canoes. Also common were birch-bark baskets and baby carriers.

FUNCTIONAL & ORNAMENTED PIECES

Much like that of the neighboring Eskimos, Athabascan craftwork traditionally served functional purposes. But tools, weapons, and clothing were often highly decorated with colorful embroidery and shells. Athabascans are especially well known for ornamenting their caribou-skin clothing with porcupine quills and animal hair—both of which were later replaced by imported western beads.

INUPIAQ, YUP'IK & CUP'IK

Residing in Alaska's remote northern and northwestern regions, these groups are often collectively known as Eskimos or Inupiaq. They winter in coastal villages, relying on migrating marine mammals for sustenance, and spend summers at inland fish camps. Ongoing artistic traditions include ceremonial mask carving, ivory carving (not to be confused with scrimshaw), sewn skin garments, basket weaving, and soapstone carvings.

Thanks to the sheer volume of ivory art in Alaska's marketplace, you're bound to find a piece of ivory that fits your fancy—regardless of whether you prefer traditional ivory carvings, scrimshaw, or a piece that blends both artistic traditions.

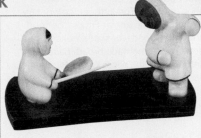

IVORY CARVING

While in Alaska, you'll likely see carved ivory pieces, scrimshaw, and some fake ivory carvings (generally plastic). Ivory carving has been an Eskimo art form for thousands of years. After harvesting ivory from migrating walrus herds in the Bering Sea, artisans age tusks for up to one year before shaping it with adzes and bow drills.

KEEP IN MIND

The Marine Mammal Protection Act states that only native peoples are allowed to harvest fresh walrus ivory, which is legal to buy after it's been carved by a native person. How can you tell if a piece is real and made by a native artisan? Real ivory is likely to be pricey; be suspect of anything too cheaply priced. It should also be hard (plastic will be softer) and cool to the touch. Keep an eye out for mastery of carving technique, and be sure to ask questions when you've found a piece you're interested in buying.

WHAT IS SCRIMSHAW?

The invention of scrimshaw is attributed to 18th-century American whalers who etched the surfaces of whale bone and scrap ivory. The etchings were filled with ink, bringing the designs into stark relief.

More recently the line between traditional Eskimo ivory carving and scrimshaw has become somewhat blurred, with many native artisans incorporating both techniques.

TIPS

Ivory carving is a highly specialized native craft that is closely regulated. As it is a by-product of subsistence hunting, all meat and skin from a walrus hunt is used.

Ivory from extinct mammoths and mastodons (usually found buried underground or washed up on beaches) is also legal to buy in Alaska; many native groups keep large stores of it, as well as antique walrus tusk, for craft purposes. Many of the older pieces have a caramelized color.

liquor store, post office, video-rental shop, and deli. The latter is the primary reason for stopping at Fritz's: the food is amazingly good—brisket smoked right out back, homemade bread, pastries, and pizza by the slice. **Known for:** best sandwiches in town; great place to mingle with locals; off-the-beaten path vibe. ⑤ *Average main: $10* ⊠ *Mile 8.2, 55770 E. End Rd.* ☎ *907/235–6753.*

★ La Baleine

$ | AMERICAN | One of the few places on the Spit open at 5 am, this is a perfect stop before a day of fishing, but lunch is an equally fulfilling experience. La Baleine serves fantastic breakfast sandwiches on fresh ciabatta rolls—complimentary cup of locally roasted coffee included. **Known for:** best breakfast sandwiches in town; fantastic homemade ramen bowls; locally sourced ingredients. ⑤ *Average main: $12* ⊠ *4450 Homer Spit Rd.* ☎ *907/299–6672* ⊕ *www.labaleinecafe. com* ☾ *Closed Mon. No dinner.*

Two Sisters Bakery

$ | CAFÉ | This very popular café is a short walk from Bishops Beach, Beluga Slough, and the Islands and Ocean Visitors Center. In addition to fresh breads and pastries, Two Sisters specializes in deliciously healthy lunches, such as vegetarian focaccia sandwiches, homemade soups, quiche, and salads. **Known for:** fantastic fresh bread; best place to drink coffee and read the morning paper; wraparound porch perfect for summer. ⑤ *Average main: $10* ⊠ *233 E. Bunnell Ave.* ☎ *907/235–2280* ⊕ *www.twosistersbakery.net* ☾ *Closed Sun. No dinner.*

🛍 Shopping

A variety of art by the town's residents can be found in the galleries on and around Pioneer Avenue.

Bunnell Street Arts Center

ART GALLERIES | The gallery, which occupies the first floor of a historic trading post, showcases and sells innovative Alaskan-made contemporary art. It also hosts workshops, lectures, musical performances, and other community events. ⊠ *106 W. Bunnell Ave., at Main St.* ☎ *907/235–2662* ⊕ *www.bunnellarts. org.*

Coal Point Seafood Company

FOOD/CANDY | Homer is famous for its halibut, salmon, and Kachemak Bay oysters. For fresh fish, head to Coal Point Seafood Company, which can also package and ship fish that you catch. ⊠ *4306 Homer Spit Rd.* ☎ *907/235–3877, 800/325–3877* ⊕ *www.welovefish.com.*

Nomar

CLOTHING | The company manufactures equipment and clothing for commercial fishermen. Its Homer shop sells Polarfleece garments and other rugged outerwear, plus duffels, rain gear, and children's clothing. ⊠ *104 E. Pioneer Ave.* ☎ *907/235–8363, 800/478–8364* ⊕ *www. nomaralaska.com.*

Ptarmigan Arts

ART GALLERIES | A cooperative gallery, Ptarmigan shows photographs, paintings, pottery, jewelry, woodworking, and other pieces by local fine and craft artists. ⊠ *471 E. Pioneer Ave.* ☎ *907/235–5345* ⊕ *www.ptarmiganarts.com.*

Activities

BEAR WATCHING

Emerald Air Service

WILDLIFE-WATCHING | Homer is a favorite departure point for viewing Alaska's famous brown bears in Katmai National Park. Emerald Air is one of several companies offering daylong and custom photography trips. ⊠ *Homer* ☎ *907/235–4160, 877/235–9600* ⊕ *www.emeraldairservice.com* 🎫 *From $650.*

Hallo Bay Wilderness

WILDLIFE-WATCHING | This outfit delivers guided close-range viewing without the crowds. The day trips are eventful, but the overnight stays at Hallo Bay's eco-friendly coastal lodging provide the ultimate in world-class bear and wildlife viewing. ⊠ *Homer* ☎ *907/235–2237, 888/535–2237* ⊕ *www.hallobay.com* ☒ *Day trip $625, overnight trips from $1,299.*

FISHING

Homer is a major commercial fishing port (especially for halibut) and a popular destination for sport anglers in search of giant halibut or feisty king and silver salmon. Quite a few companies offer charter fishing in summer, from about $250 to $350 per person per day, including bait and tackle. The pricing is usually based on how many different types of fish you're going after.

Fishing Hole

BOATING | Near the end of the Spit, Homer's famous Fishing Hole, aka the Nick Dudiak Fishing Lagoon, is a small bight stocked with king and silver salmon smolt (baby fish) by the Alaska Department of Fish and Game. The salmon then head out to sea, returning several years later to the Fishing Hole, where they are easy targets for wall-to-wall bankside anglers throughout summer. The Fishing Hole isn't anything like casting for salmon along a remote stream, but your chances are good and you don't need to drop $800 for a flight into the wilderness. Fishing licenses and rental poles are available from fishing-supply stores on the Spit. ⊠ *Homer.*

CHARTERS
Central Charters & Tours

TOUR—SPORTS | Central can arrange fishing trips in outer Kachemak Bay and Lower Cook Inlet—areas known for excellent halibut fishing. Boat sizes vary considerably; some have a six-person limit, whereas others can take up to 16 passengers. The company also conducts nonfishing boat tours and bear-viewing trips. ⊠ *4241 Homer Spit Rd.* ☎ *907/235–7847* ⊕ *www.centralcharter.com* ☒ *Boat tours from $59, fishing trips from $295, bear viewing from $675.*

Homer Jackpot Halibut Derby

FISHING | Anyone heading out on a halibut charter is advised to buy a $10 ticket for the derby, which ends with the season in September. First prize for the largest halibut is $10,000, plus 50¢ per ticket sold. In addition, more than 100 fish are tagged; anglers who catch them win cash or other prizes worth up to $50,000. Food for thought: in 2013, the angler who caught the fish bearing the $50K tag hadn't bought a derby ticket. ⊠ *Homer* ☎ *907/235–7740* ⊕ *www.homerhalibutderby.com.*

Homer Ocean Charters

TOUR—SPORTS | Locally owned and operated, Homer Ocean Charters has been in business since 1979, setting up fishing, sea-kayaking, and sightseeing trips. It also offers water-taxi services and bare-bones cabin rentals on Otter Cove. ⊠ *4287 Homer Spit Rd.* ☎ *800/426–6212* ⊕ *www.homerocean.com* ☒ *From $250.*

Inlet Charters

TOUR—SPORTS | Try Inlet Charters for fishing charters (halibut and salmon), fish processing, water-taxi services, lodging, sea kayaking, and wildlife cruises. ⊠ *Homer* ☎ *800/770–6126* ⊕ *www.halibutcharters.com* ☒ *From $250.*

SEA KAYAKING
True North Kayak Adventures

KAYAKING | Several local companies offer guided sea-kayaking trips to protected coves within Kachemak Bay State Park and nearby islands. True North has a range of such adventures, including a three-day trip and a boat and kayak day trip to Yukon Island (both trips include round-trip water taxi to the island base camp, guide, all kayak equipment, and meals). ⊠ *Homer* ☎ *907/235–0708* ⊕ *www.truenorthkayak.com* ☒ *Day trips from $115; overnight from $375.*

Hubbard Glacier

The 24-million-acre international wilderness that embraces Hubbard can only be described with superlatives. For example, the massive St. Elias and Fairweather ranges form the largest nonpolar glaciated mountain system in the world. British Columbia's only winter range for Dall sheep is here, and the region supports a population of both grizzlies and rare, silver-blue "glacier" bears.

This glacier is famous for "surging"—moving forward quickly. Most glaciers slide an inch or two a day. However, in 1986, the Hubbard Glacier made headlines around the world by advancing to the mouth of Russell Fjord, damming it, and creating a huge lake that lasted five months. By September it was advancing 30 meters a day. This was an event without precedent in recent geologic history, and it was mapped by the Landsat 5 satellite from 6 miles above Earth. Seals, sea lions, and porpoises were trapped behind the dam, and efforts were mounted to relocate them. "Russell Lake" eventually reached a level almost 90 feet higher than the level of Disenchantment Bay. When the dam broke on October 8, it produced an enormous rush of freshwater—something like a tidal wave in reverse.

The glacier surged again in summer 2002, creating another dam in the space of a month—by coincidence, just about the time glaciologists convened in Yakutat for an international symposium on fast glacier flow. Nervous Yakutat residents continue to lobby the government to build a channel to make sure the glacier cannot form "Russell Lake" again. They fear this would change river courses, endanger important fisheries, and inundate the Yakutat Airport, the chief transportation link with the rest of Alaska.

◉ Sights

The Hubbard Glacier is an icy tongue with its root on Mt. Logan in Yukon Territory. The vast Hubbard ice field originates near 15,300-foot Mt. Hubbard and flows 76 miles to lick the sea at Yakutat and Disenchantment bays. With its 400-foot snout, Hubbard Glacier is also a prime pausing point for cruise ships. Hubbard calves great numbers of icebergs, making it difficult to get close. There are no roads to the glacier. Unless you are a seasoned mountaineer with ice experience, Hubbard Glacier is no shore excursion.

Juneau

Juneau, Alaska's capital and third-largest city, is on the North American mainland but can't be reached by road. Bounded by steep mountains and water, the city's geographic isolation and compact size make it much more akin to an island community such as Sitka than to other Alaskan urban centers, such as Fairbanks or Anchorage.

Juneau is full of contrasts. Its dramatic hillside location and historic downtown buildings provide a frontier feeling, but the city's cosmopolitan nature comes through in fine museums, noteworthy restaurants, and a literate and outdoorsy populace. The finest of the museums, the Alaska State Museum, was completely rebuilt in 2016 following several years of planning and exhibit research. Another new facility, the Walter Soboleff Building, offers visitors a chance to learn about the indigenous cultures of Southeast Alaska—Tlingit, Haida, and Tsimshian. Other highlights include the Mt. Roberts Tramway, plenty of densely forested wilderness areas, quiet bays for sea kayaking, and even a famous drive-up glacier, Mendenhall Glacier. For goings-on, pick up the Juneau Empire (⊕ www.juneauempire.com), which keeps tabs on state politics, business, sports, and local news.

COMING ASHORE

Most cruise ships dock on the south edge of town between the **Marine Park** and the **A.J. Dock**. Several ships can tie up at once; others occasionally anchor in the harbor. Juneau's downtown shops are a pleasant walk from the docks. A shuttle bus ($5 all day) runs from the A.J. Dock to town whenever ships are in port.

VISITOR INFORMATION

Pick up maps, bus schedules, charter-fishing information, and tour brochures at the small kiosks on the pier at Marine Park and in the cruise-ship terminal on South Franklin Street. Both are staffed when ships are in port.

Sights

Alaska State Capitol

GOVERNMENT BUILDING | Completed in 1931, this unassuming building houses the governor's office and hosts state legislature meetings in winter, placing it at the epicenter of Alaska's animated political discourse. Historical photos line the upstairs walls. Feel free to stroll right in. You can pick up a self-guided tour brochure as you enter. ⊠ *Seward and 4th Sts.* 🕿 *907/465–4648* ⊕ *www.akleg.gov* 🖭 *Free.*

★ Alaska State Library, Archives, and Museum

MUSEUM | FAMILY | The Andrew P. Kashevaroff State Library, Archives, and Museum, which opened in 2016 on the site of the old state museum, is among the most impressive cultural attractions in Alaska. In the permanent gallery, visitors weave through interconnected spaces that present Alaska's unique stories through carefully selected objects and culturally diverse narratives. Kids will love the pirate ship (built for them to climb on) and the eagle tree in the lobby, viewable from multiple levels. The new state-of-the-art building also houses Alaska's most important books, photographs, and documents, offering increased

Juneau Best Bets

■ **Walk South Franklin Street.** Juneau's historic downtown still retains much of its hardscrabble mining feel. While away hours in the saloons and shops of this charming district.

■ **Ride the Mt. Roberts Tram.** On Juneau's favorite attraction, enjoy panoramic views of the area's stunning scenery from 1,800 feet above town.

■ **Marvel at the Mendenhall Glacier.** With an otherworldly blue hue, Alaska's most accessible—and most popular—glacier is a must-see.

opportunities for researchers as well as more casual visitors. ⊠ *395 Whittier St.* 🕿 *907/465–2901* ⊕ *museums.alaska.gov* 🖭 *$12 summer, $7 winter* ⊘ *Closed Sun. and Mon. Oct.–Apr.*

DIPAC Macaulay Salmon Hatchery

FISH HATCHERY | FAMILY | Salmon are integral to life in Southeast Alaska, and Alaskans are proud of their healthy fisheries. A visit to the hatchery is a great introduction to the complex considerations involved in maintaining the continued vitality of this crucial resource. Watch through an underwater window as salmon fight their way up a fish ladder from mid-June to mid-October. Inside the busy hatchery, which produces almost 125 million young salmon annually, you will learn about the environmental considerations of commercial fishermen and the lives of salmon. A retail shop sells gifts and salmon products. The salmon hatchery is part of a larger nonprofit, Douglas Island Pink & Chum, Inc., and is usually referred to locally by its acronym, DIPAC. ⊠ *2697 Channel Dr.* ✛ *3 miles northwest of downtown Juneau* 🕿 *907/463–5114,*

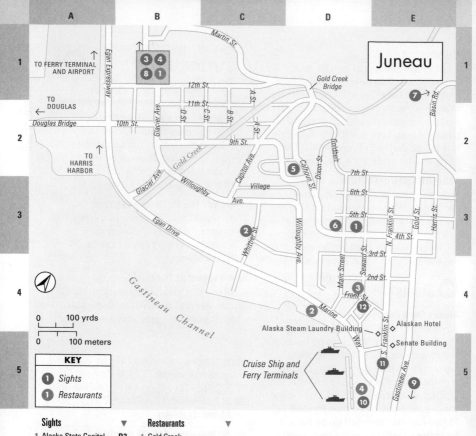

Juneau

TO FERRY TERMINAL AND AIRPORT

TO DOUGLAS

Douglas Bridge

TO HARRIS HARBOR

Gold Creek Bridge

Egan Expressway
Egan Drive
Glacier Ave.
Gold Creek
Willoughby Ave.
12th St.
11th St.
10th St.
9th St.
Martin St.
D St.
C St.
B St.
A St.
Capitol Ave.
Whittier St.
Village
Willoughby Ave.
7th St.
6th St.
5th St.
4th St.
3rd St.
2nd St.
Goldbelt
Calhoun St.
Dixon St.
Main Street
Seward St.
Front St.
Marine Way
S. Franklin St.
N. Franklin St.
Gold St.
Harris St.
Gastineau Ave.
Basin Rd.

Gastineau Channel

Alaska Steam Laundry Building
Alaskan Hotel
Senate Building

Cruise Ship and Ferry Terminals

0   100 yrds
0   100 meters

KEY

- **1** Sights
- **1** Restaurants

Best Ports for Kids

Juneau: For a day of family togetherness, the Gold Creek Salmon Bake hits the spot. After an all-you-can-eat buffet lunch of barbecued fresh Alaska salmon (there are chicken and ribs for picky eaters), baked beans, corn bread, and blueberry cake, the kids can roast marshmallows over the open fire and explore the abandoned Wagner Mine. If you're lucky, you'll spot salmon spawning in the clear water beneath the Salmon Creek waterfall.

Ketchikan: One of the cheesiest, yet most kid-pleasing tastes of old-time woodsman skills is the Great Alaskan Lumberjack Show. All summer long this hour-long contest demonstrates such authentic "sports" as sawing, ax throwing, chopping, and a log-rolling duel. There's even a speed climb up a 50-foot tree. At 50 Main Street, all the fun's within walking distance of the cruise-ship pier.

Skagway: Spend the day in real Alaskan wilderness. Get a map at the Convention and Visitors Bureau and take the entire family on the inexpensive city bus to 23rd Avenue, where a 10-minute walk on a dirt road leads to the Gold Rush Cemetery. Let the kids discover where the town's villain Soapy Smith and its hero Frank Reid are buried, and then continue along the trail a quarter mile to Reid Falls.

877/463–2486 ⊕ www.dipac.net ⊠ $4, including short tour ⊙ Closed Oct.–Apr.

Glacier Gardens Rainforest Adventure

FOREST | One of the upsides to living in a rain forest is the lush proliferation of plants and trees. At Glacier Gardens, they've turned local flora into an art form. Spread over 50 acres of rain forest, the family-owned Glacier Gardens has ponds, waterfalls, hiking paths, a large atrium, and gardens. The roots of fallen trees, turned upside down and buried in the ground, act as bowls to hold planters that overflow with begonias, fuchsias, and petunias. Guided tours in covered golf carts lead you along the 4 miles of paved paths, and a 580-foot-high overlook provides dramatic views of the Mendenhall wetlands wildlife refuge, Chilkat Mountains, and downtown Juneau. A café and gift shop are here, and the conservatory is a popular wedding spot. Admission includes a guided tour. The Juneau city bus, which departs from multiple locations downtown, stops in front of Glacier Gardens. ⊠ 7600 Glacier Hwy. ⊹ 6½

miles northwest of downtown Juneau ☎ 907/790–3377 ⊕ www.glaciergardens.com ⊠ $27 ⊙ Closed Oct.–Apr.

Governor's Mansion

HOUSE | This stately colonial-style home completed in 1912 overlooks downtown Juneau. With 14,400 square feet, 6 bedrooms, and 10 bathrooms, it's no miner's cabin. Out front is a totem pole that tells three tales: the history of man, the cause of ocean tides, and the origin of Alaska's ubiquitous mosquitoes. Unfortunately, tours of the residence are not permitted. ⊠ 716 Calhoun Ave.

Juneau-Douglas City Museum

MUSEUM | FAMILY | Exhibits at this city-run museum interpret pioneer, mining, and Tlingit history. A diorama of a fire assay lab shows how the Bureau of Mines measured the gold content of rock samples, and there's a reconstructed Tlingit fish trap. Pioneer artifacts include a century-old store and kitchen. Digital story kiosks shed light on Alaska's quest for statehood, how government works here, civil rights in Alaska, and the cultures of

Juneau. In the hands-on room, youngsters can try on clothes similar to ones worn by the miners and look at gold-rush stereoscopes. Engaging historic walking tours of downtown ($25) take place from May through September. ⊠ *114 4th St.* ☎ *907/586–3572* ⊕ *www.juneau.org/ library/museum/index.php* ⊠ *$6 May– Sept., free Oct.–Apr.; $25 walking tour (includes museum admission)* ⊙ *Closed Sun. and Mon. Oct.–Apr.*

Last Chance Mining Museum

A 1½-mile hike or taxi ride behind town, this small museum is housed in the former compressor building of Juneau's historic AJ Gold Mine. The collection includes old mining tools, railcars, minerals, and a 3-D map of the ore body. If you have time, and didn't arrive on foot, meander down back toward town. Unlike most of Juneau, Basin Road is flat and relatively quiet. The surrounding country is steep and wooded, with trails leading in all directions, including one to the summit of Mt. Juneau. At the base of the Perseverance Trail, not far from the museum, you can see the boarded-up opening to an old mining tunnel; even from a safe distance you can feel a chilly breeze wafting through the cracks. ⊠ *1001 Basin Rd.* ☎ *907/586–5338* ⊠ *$4.*

★ Mendenhall Glacier

NATURE SITE | FAMILY | Glaciers are abundant in Southeast Alaska, but only a very few are as accessible as the Mendenhall Glacier. Alaska's most-visited drive-up glacier spans 12 miles and is fed by the massive Juneau Icefield. Like many other Alaska glaciers, it is retreating, losing more than 100 feet a year as huge chunks of ice calve into the small lake separating the glacier from the **Mendenhall Visitor Center**. The center has interactive and traditional exhibits, a theater and bookstore, and panoramic views. Nature trails lead along Mendenhall Lake, to Nugget Falls, and into the mountains overlooking Mendenhall Glacier; the trails are marked by posts and paint stripes delineating the historic location of the glacier, providing a sharp reminder of the Mendenhall's hasty retreat. An elevated viewing platform allows visitors to look for spawning sockeye and coho salmon—and the bears that eat them—at Steep Creek, a half mile south of the visitor center along the Moraine Ecology Trail. Several companies lead bus tours to the glacier. A glacier express bus leaves from the cruise-ship terminal and heads right out to Mendenhall Glacier; ask at the visitor information center there. You can also get within a mile and a half of the glacier on the city bus, which is $2 one-way. For a different perspective, you can travel by helicopter to the surface of the glacier, or hire a guide to take you to one of the amazing, electric blue ice caves. Note that because the caves are inherently unstable, the Forest Service doesn't recommend self-guided tours. ⊠ *End of Glacier Spur Rd. off Mendenhall Loop Rd.* ⊕ *13 miles north of downtown Juneau* ☎ *907/789–0097* ⊕ *www. fs.usda.gov/detail/tongass/about-forest/ offices* ⊠ *Visitor center $5 May–Sept., free Oct.–Apr.* ⊙ *Closed Mon.–Thurs. Oct.–Apr.*

★ Mt. Roberts Tramway

VIEWPOINT | FAMILY | One of Southeast's most popular tourist attractions whisks you from the cruise terminal 1,800 feet up the side of Mt. Roberts. After the six-minute ride, you can take in a film on the history and legends of the Tlingits, visit the nature center, go for an alpine walk on hiking trails (including the 5-mile round-trip hike to Mt. Roberts's 3,819-foot summit), purchase Native arts and peruse the on-site gallery, or enjoy a meal while savoring mountain views. You can also get an up-close view of an "education" eagle in her mew. A local company leads guided wilderness hikes from the summit, and the bar serves locally brewed beers. Plan to spend one to two hours at the top. For a workout, hike up the mountain from town or hike up to Father Brown's Cross from the top; each takes about an hour. ✉ *490 S. Franklin St.* ☎ *907/463–3412, 888/461–8726* ⊕ *www.mountrobertstramway.com* 🍴 *$34* ⊙ *Closed Oct.–Apr.*

Red Dog Saloon

RESTAURANT—SIGHT | The frontierish quarters of the Red Dog have housed an infamous Juneau watering hole since 1890. Nearly every conceivable surface in this two-story bar is cluttered with graffiti, business cards, and memorabilia, including a pistol that reputedly belonged to Wyatt Earp, who failed to reclaim the piece after checking it in at the U.S. Marshall's office on June 27, 1900. The saloon's food menu includes halibut, reindeer sausage, potato skins, burgers, and locally brewed beers. A little atmospheric sawdust covers the floor, and musicians pump out ragtime piano tunes when cruise ships are docked. ✉ *278 S. Franklin St.* ☎ *907/463–3658* ⊕ *www.reddogsaloon.com.*

South Franklin Street

NEIGHBORHOOD | The buildings on South Franklin Street and neighboring Front Street, among the oldest and most inviting structures in the city, house curio and crafts shops, snack shops, and a salmon shop. Many reflect the architecture of the 1920s and '30s. When the small Alaskan Hotel opened in 1913, Juneau was home to 30 saloons; the Alaskan gives today's visitors the most authentic glimpse of the town's whiskey-rich history. The barroom's massive, mirrored oak back bar is accented by Tiffany lights and panels. Topped by a wood-shingled turret, the 1901 Alaska Steam Laundry Building now houses a toy store and other shops. The Senate Building, another of South Franklin's landmarks, is across the street. ✉ *S. Franklin St.*

★ Walter Soboleff Building

MUSEUM | This center devoted to Alaska Native art, culture, and language is operated by Sealaska Heritage Institute and named for a local Tlingit elder who died at age 102 in 2011. It includes a gallery, a traditional clan house, a living-history center, research areas, and a shop selling work by Northwest Coast artists. The building's three major public art pieces—exterior red metal panels, a carved cedar house facade, and a modern glass screen in the clan house itself—were created by three of the top Northwest Coast artists in the world (Robert Davidson, David Boxley, and Preston Singletary), and represent the three indigenous tribes of Southeast Alaska—Haida, Tsimshian, and Tlingit, respectively. The art pieces also highlight the center's dual role in honoring tradition while remaining forward-facing and contemporary. Among the goals of this downtown historical district facility are promoting Juneau's role as a hub of Northwest Coast art and fostering cross-cultural understanding between Native and non-Native populations. ✉ *105 Seward St.* ☎ *907/463–4844* ⊕ *www.sealaskaheritage.org* 🍴 *$5* ⊙ *Store closed Sun. and Mon. Oct.–Apr.*

🍴 Restaurants

Gold Creek Salmon Bake

$$$$ | SEAFOOD | Trees, mountains, and the rushing water of Salmon Creek surround the comfortable, canopy-covered benches and tables at this authentic, all-you-can-eat salmon bake operated through Alaska Travel Adventures. After dinner you can pan for gold in the stream, wander up a hill to explore the remains of a gold mine, or roast marshmallows over a fire. **Known for:** fresh-caught salmon cooked over fire; forest experience; picnic-style eating. ⑤ *Average main: $55* ✉ *1061 Salmon Lane Rd.* ☎ *907/789–0052, 800/323–5757* ⊕ *www.bestofalaskatravel.com/alaska_day_tours/pages/j_gold_creek_salmon.htm* ⊙ *Closed Oct.–Apr.*

The Hangar on the Wharf

$$ | ECLECTIC | Crowded with locals and travelers, the Hangar occupies the building where Alaska Airlines started business, and though flight-theme

The spectacular and accessible Mendenhall Glacier is actually within the city limits of Juneau and one of the most visited sights in the area.

puns (e.g., "Pre-flight Snacks" and the "Plane Caesar") dominate the menu, the comfortably worn wood and the vintage airplane photos create a casual experience that trumps the kitsch. Every seat has views of the Gastineau Channel and Douglas Island, and on warm days you can sit outdoors. **Known for:** prime rib; views; wide selection of beers on tap, including local options. $ Average main: $18 ⊠ Merchants Wharf Mall, 2 Marine Way ☎ 907/586–5018 ⊕ www.hangaronthewharf.com.

Heritage Coffee Company

$ | CAFÉ | Established in 1974, Heritage Coffee serves locally roasted coffees, along with gelato, fresh pastries, and a variety of sandwiches. The flagship store sits on the corner of Front and Seward streets, while other locations include a smaller café with limited outdoor seating at 230 South Franklin Street, a branch inside Foodland IGA market, and a kiosk at the University of Alaska Southeast. **Known for:** espresso; lively atmosphere; baked goods. $ Average main: $9 ⊠ 130

Front St. ☎ 907/586–1088 ⊕ www.heritagecoffee.com.

★ **Tracy's King Crab Shack**

$$ | SEAFOOD | Alaskan king crab—a not-to-be-missed Alaskan delicacy—is the specialty of popular Tracy's. There's often a line to place your order, but the wait is entirely worth it. **Known for:** crab bisque; Bristol Bay king crab legs with butter; casual, fun vibe. $ Average main: $15 ⊠ 432 S. Franklin St. ☎ 907/723–1811 ⊕ www.kingcrabshack.com ⊘ Closed Oct.–Apr.

Shopping

Kindred Post

ART GALLERIES | Kindred Post is more than the downtown area's sole post office. The local owner, a poet and artist, has transformed the space into an elegant gallery that features locally made jewelry, ceramics, prints, and other works of art. ⊠ 145 S. Franklin St. ☎ 907/523–5053 ⊕ www.kindredpost.com ⊘ Closed Sun.

Rie Muñoz Gallery

ART GALLERIES | Rie Muñoz, one of Alaska's best-known artists, was the creator of a stylized, simple, and colorful design technique that is much copied but rarely equaled. This gallery run by her son is located in the Mendenhall Valley, a 10-minute walk from the airport. ⊠ *2101 N. Jordan Ave.* ☎ *907/789–7449, 800/247–3151* ⊕ *www.riemunoz.com* ⊘ *Closed Sun. and Mon.*

Sealaska Heritage Store

ART GALLERIES | On the Front Street side of the Walter Soboleff Building, Juneau's regional Alaska Native arts and cultural center, this shop and gallery sells work by Northwest Coast and Alaska Native artists from Seattle to Yakutat and farther north. Here you'll find a wide range of items, from moderately priced earrings and T-shirts to high-end, one-of-a-kind pieces. ⊠ *105 Front St.* ☎ *907/463–4844* ⊕ *www.sealaskaheritage.org.*

Wm. Spear Design

ART GALLERIES | Lawyer-turned-artist Wm. Spear produces fun and colorful enameled pins and zipper pulls. His quirky shop is above the local toy store, through a separate entrance. ⊠ *174 S. Franklin St.* ☎ *907/586–2209* ⊕ *www.wmspear.com.*

 Activities

BIKING
Cycle Alaska

BICYCLING | Rentals from Cycle Alaska include everything from a helmet and minipump to a bottle of water and a granola bar. You can reserve a bike online at their website and also check out Juneau's free new bike map at *juneau-rides.org/juneau-bike-map.* ⊠ *1107 W. 8th St.* ☎ *907/780–2253* ⊕ *www.cycleak.com* ⊜ *From $37.*

BOATING, CANOEING, AND KAYAKING
Above & Beyond Alaska

BOATING | Juneau-based Above & Beyond conducts day and overnight camping trips, ice-climbing adventures, and Mendenhall Glacier and sea-kayaking trips. The owners also run the Alaska Boat & Kayak Shop, which offers kayak and canoe rentals. Both are located in Auke Bay. ⊠ *Auke Bay Harbor, 11521 Glacier Hwy., Auke Bay* ☎ *907/364–2333* ⊕ *www.beyondak. com* ⊜ *Tours from $240.*

★ Adventure Bound Alaska

BOATING | All-day trips to Sawyer Glacier within Tracy Arm in summer are available from Adventure Bound Alaska. ⊠ *76 Egan Dr.* ☎ *907/463–2509, 800/228–3875* ⊕ *www.adventureboundalaska.com* ⊜ *$160.*

FLIGHTSEEING

Several local companies operate helicopter flightseeing trips to the spectacular glaciers flowing from Juneau Icefield. Most have booths along the downtown cruise-ship dock. All include a touchdown on a glacier, providing the opportunity to romp on these rivers of ice. Some also lead trips that include a dogsled ride on the glacier. Note that although we recommend the best companies, even some of the most experienced pilots have had accidents; always ask a carrier about its recent safety record before booking a trip.

Temsco Helicopters

TOUR—SPORTS | The self-proclaimed pioneers of Alaska glacier helicopter touring, Temsco Helicopters offers glacier tours, dogsled adventures, and year-round flightseeing. Book through your cruise line or contact the company for pricing. ⊠ *1650 Maplesden Way* ☎ *907/789–9501, 877/789–9501* ⊕ *www. temscoair.com.*

Ward Air

TOUR—SPORTS | Take flightseeing trips to Glacier Bay, the Juneau Icefield, Elfin Cove, Tracy Arm, and Pack Creek with Ward Air, or charter a floatplane to access one of the area's remote U.S. Forest Service cabins. ⊠ *8991 Yandukin Dr.* ☎ *907/789–9150, 800/478–9150* ⊕ *www. wardair.com.*

★ Wings Airways and Taku Glacier Lodge

TOUR—SPORTS | This Juneau-based company specializes in glacier sightseeing followed by a salmon feast at a remote, historic Alaskan lodge, complete with glacier views in their Taku Lodge Feast & 5 Glacier Discovery Tour—one of the best day trips out of the state capital. The 5 Glacier Discovery Tour is also available as a stand-alone flightseeing trip. ✉ *2 Marine Way, Suite 175* 🕾 *907/586–6275* ⊕ *www.wingsairways.com* 🖃 *$225 for glacier tour, $320 for tour/lodge combo.*

GOLD PANNING

Alaska Travel Adventures

LOCAL SPORTS | FAMILY | Gold panning is fun, especially for children, and Juneau is one of Southeast's best-known gold-panning towns. Sometimes you actually discover a few flecks of the precious metal in the bottom of your pan. You can buy a pan at almost any Alaska hardware or sporting-goods store. Alaska Travel Adventures has gold-panning tours near the famous Alaska-Juneau Mine. ✉ *Juneau* 🕾 *800/323–5757, 907/789–0052* ⊕ *www.alaskatraveladventures.com* 🖃 *From $69.*

HIKING

★ Gastineau Guiding

HIKING/WALKING | This company leads a variety of hikes in the Juneau area. Especially popular are the "Town, Tram, and Timberline Trek" tours, which include a shuttle ride through the historic district in downtown Juneau, a tram ride up Mt. Roberts, a short hike at the top, and a stop at the Alpine Tea house to sample Alaska-made tea. ✉ *1330 Eastaugh Way, Suite 2* 🕾 *907/586–8231* ⊕ *www.stepintoalaska.com* 🖃 *From $49.*

WHALE WATCHING

Alaska Galore Tours

WHALE-WATCHING | This company offers small-group whale-watching excursions of up to 20 guests aboard a luxury yacht with an onboard naturalist, as well as a combination whale-watch-and-flightseeing tour over the Juneau Icefield.

✉ *Juneau* 🕾 *907/321–5859, 888/432–6722* ⊕ *alaska-whale-watching-juneau.com* 🖃 *From $149.*

Harv & Marv's Outback Alaska

WHALE-WATCHING | Experienced local captains lead these whale-watching excursions for groups of up to 6 or up to 18 passengers. Private tours can also be arranged. ✉ *Juneau* 🕾 *907/209–7288, 866/909–7288* ⊕ *www.harvandmarvs-alaska-whale-watching.com* 🖃 *From $145.*

★ Weather Permitting Alaska

WHALE-WATCHING | The small-boat luxury whale-watching trips of Weather Permitting last four hours, including van travel. Visitors get plenty of time to view whales, bears, sea lions, eagles, porpoises, and other animals, all the while enjoying dramatic scenery. With only 10 customers on a trip (excepting single groups of up to 12), this is among the most intimate and comprehensive whale watches anywhere. For a truly unique experience, schedule a customized trip with an "Alaskan celebrity" such as the famous whale photographer and marine biologist Flip Nicklin (if he's available). ✉ *19400 Beardsley Way* 🕾 *907/789–5843* ⊕ *www.weatherpermittingalaska.com* 🖃 *From $189.*

Ketchikan

Ketchikan is famous for its colorful totem poles, rainy skies, steep–as–San Francisco streets, and lush island setting. Some 13,500 people call the town home, and, in the summer, cruise ships crowd the shoreline, floatplanes depart noisily for Misty Fiords National Monument, and salmon-laden commercial fishing boats motor through Tongass Narrows. In the last decade Ketchikan's rowdy, blue-collar heritage of logging and fishing has been softened by the loss of many timber-industry jobs and the dramatic rise of cruise-ship tourism, but visitors can still glimpse the rugged frontier spirit that once permeated this hardscrabble cannery town.

Ketchikan is the first bite of Alaska that many travelers taste. Despite its imposing backdrop, hillside homes, and many staircases, the town is relatively easy to walk through. Favorite downtown stops include Creek Street, a narrow boardwalk filled with locally owned shops, and the Southeast Alaska Discovery Center, where you can learn about the Tongass National Forest from local rangers. A bit farther away you'll find the Totem Heritage Center. Out of town (but included on most bus tours) are two longtime favorites: Totem Bight State Historical Park to the north and Saxman Totem Park to the south.

COMING ASHORE

Most ships dock or tender passengers ashore directly across from the Ketchikan Visitors Bureau on Front and Mission streets, in the center of downtown. A new dock, several blocks north on the other side of the tunnel, is still within easy walking distance of most of the town's sights. Walking-tour signs lead you around the city. For panoramic vistas of the surrounding area—and a wee bit of exercise—climb the stairs leading up several steep hillsides.

To reach sights farther from downtown, rent a car, hire a cab, or ride the local buses. Metered taxis meet the ships right on the docks and also wait across the street. Rates are $3.70 for pickup and $3.50 per mile. Up to six passengers can hire a taxi to tour for $75 per hour. Local buses run along the main route through town and south to Saxman. The fare is $2.

VISITOR INFORMATION

The helpful visitors bureau is right next to the cruise-ship docks. Half the space is occupied by day-tour, flightseeing, and boat-tour operators.

Ketchikan Best Bets

- **Exploring Creek Street.** No visit to Ketchikan would be complete without a stroll along this elevated wooden boulevard, once the site of the town's rip-roaring bordellos.

- **Totem gazing at Saxman Totem Park.** View one of the best totem collections in all of Southeast Alaska at this must-see stop.

- **Rain-forest Canopy Tours.** Zip through the towering trees of Ketchikan's coastal rain forest, experiencing the majesty of this unique ecosystem from a bird's-eye view.

CONTACTS Ketchikan Visitors Bureau ✉ *131 Front St.* ☎ *907/225–6166, 800/770–3300* ⊕ *www.visit-ketchikan. com.*

◉ Sights

Creek Street

HISTORIC SITE | This was once Ketchikan's red-light district. During Prohibition, Creek Street was home to numerous speakeasies, and in the early 1900s more than 30 houses of prostitution operated here. Today the small, colorful houses, built on stilts over the creek waters, have been restored as interesting shops. When the fish are running, the Creek Street footbridge makes a stellar viewing platform for salmon and trout, as well as the sea lions and other animals that eat them. ✉ *Ketchikan* ⊕ *creekstreetketchikan.com.*

The Rock

PUBLIC ART | Ketchikan is known for its public art, and this bronze monument by local artist Dave Rubin provides a striking introduction. *The Rock* (2010) depicts

Common Nautical Terms

Before acquainting yourself with your ship, you should add a few nautical terms to your vocabulary:

Berth. Sleeping space on a ship (literally refers to your bed).

Bow. The pointy end of the ship, also known as forward. Yes, it's also the front of the ship.

Bridge. The navigational control center (where the captain drives the ship).

Bulkhead. A wall or upright partition separating a ship's compartments.

Cabin. Your accommodation on a ship (used interchangeably with *stateroom*).

Course. Measured in degrees, the direction in which a ship is headed.

Debark. To leave a ship (also known as disembarkation).

Draft. The depth of water needed to float a ship; the measurement from a ship's waterline to the lowest point of its keel.

Embark. To go onboard a ship.

Galley. The ship's kitchen.

Gangway. The stairway or ramp used to access the ship from the dock.

Hatch. An opening or door on a ship, either vertical or horizontal.

Head. A bathroom aboard a ship.

Helm. The apparatus for steering a ship.

Muster. To assemble the passengers and/or crew on a ship.

Pitch. Plunging in a longitudinal direction; the up-and-down motion of a ship. (A major cause of seasickness.)

Port. The left side of the ship when you're facing forward.

Promenade. Usually outside, a deck that fully or partially encircles the ship, popular for walking and jogging.

Roll. Side-to-side movement of the ship. (Another seasickness culprit.)

Stabilizers. Operated by gyroscopes, these retractable finlike devices below the waterline extend from a ship's hull to reduce roll and provide stability. (Your best friend if you're prone to motion sickness.)

Starboard. The right side of the ship when you're facing forward.

Stern. The rounded end of the ship, also called aft. It's the back end.

Tender. A boat carried on a ship that's used to take passengers ashore when it's not possible to tie up at a dock.

Thrusters. Fanlike propulsion devices under the waterline that move a ship sideways.

Wake. The ripples left on the water's surface by a moving ship.

seven life-size figures representative of Ketchikan's history: a Tlingit drummer, a logger, a miner, a fisherman, an aviator, a pioneer woman and Tlingit Chief George Johnson (the sculpture's only specific portrayal). The piece is located on the waterfront next to the Ketchikan Visitors Bureau. For a complete listing of Ketchikan's public art, galleries, museums, and cultural organizations, pick up a copy of *Art Lives Here,* the bureau's free guide. ⊠ *Front and Mill Sts., on boardwalk.*

Salmon Ladder

VIEWPOINT | Get out your camera and set it for high speed at the fish ladder, a series of pools arranged like steps that allow fish to travel upstream around a dam or falls. When the salmon start running, from June onward, thousands of fish leap the falls or take the easier fish-ladder route. They spawn in Ketchikan Creek's waters farther upstream. Many can also be seen in the creek's eddies above and below the falls. The falls, fish ladder, and a large carving of a jumping salmon are just off Park Avenue on Married Man's Trail. The trail was once used by married men for discreet access to the red-light district on Creek Street. ⊠ Married Man's Trail, off Park Ave.

Saxman Totem Park

NATIVE SITE | A 2½-mile paved walking path–bike trail parallels the road from Ketchikan to Saxman Native Village, named for a missionary who helped Native Alaskans settle here before 1900. A totem park dominates the center of Saxman, with poles representing human- and animal-inspired figures, including bears, ravens, whales, and eagles. Saxman's Beaver Clan tribal house is said to be the largest in Alaska. Carvers create totem poles and totemic art objects in the adjacent carver's shed. You can get to the park on foot or by taxi, bicycle, or city bus. You can visit the totem park on your own, but to visit the tribal house and theater you must take a tour. ⊠ S. Tongass Hwy., 2 miles south of town ⊕ www.capefoxtours.com/alaskan-native-dancers ⊠ $5.

Southeast Alaska Discovery Center

INFO CENTER | FAMILY | This impressive public lands interpretive center contains exhibits—including one on the rain forest—that focus on the resources, Native cultures, and ecosystems of Southeast. The U.S. Forest Service and other federal agencies provide information on Alaska's public lands, and a large gift shop sells natural-history books, maps, and videos

about the region's sights. America the Beautiful–National Park and Federal Recreational Land Passes are accepted and sold. ⊠ 50 Main St. ☎ 907/228–6220 ⊕ www.alaskacenters.gov/ketchikan. cfm ⊠ $5 May–Sept., free Oct.–Apr. ⊘ Closed Sat.–Thurs. in Oct.–Apr.

Tongass Historical Museum

MUSEUM | Native artifacts and pioneer relics revisit the mining and fishing eras at this museum in the same building as the library. Exhibits include a big, brilliantly polished lens from Tree Point Lighthouse, well-presented Native tools and artwork, and photography collections. Other exhibits are temporary, but always include Tlingit items. ⊠ 629 Dock St. ☎ 907/225–5600 ⊕ www.ktn-ak.us/tongass-historical-museum ⊠ $6 ⊘ Closed Oct.–Apr.

★ Totem Bight State Historical Park

NATIVE SITE | About a quarter of the Ketchikan bus tours include this park that contains many totem poles and has a hand-hewn Native clan house. Totem Bight sits on a scenic spit of land facing the waters of Tongass Narrows. Master Native carvers crafted the first replica poles here as part of a U.S. Forest Services program that began in the late 1930s. The tools the carvers used were handmade in the Native style, and modern paints were used to re-create colors originally made using natural substances from clamshells to lichen. The clan house, open daily in summer, was built to resemble a type that might have held several related families. Note the raven painting on the front: each eye contains a small face. ⊠ N. Tongass Hwy., about 10 miles north of town ☎ 907/247–8574 Ketchikan Ranger Station ⊕ dnr.alaska.gov/parks/units/totembgh.htm ⊠ Free.

Totem Heritage Center

NATIVE SITE | Gathered from Tlingit and Haida village sites, many of the Native totems in the center's collection are well over a century old—a rare age for cedar carvings, which are eventually lost to

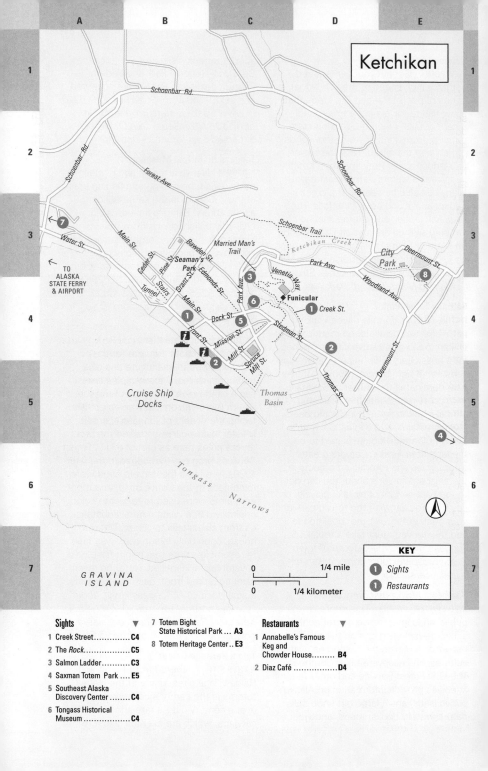

Ketchikan

A | B | C | D | E

Schoenbar Rd.

Forest Ave.

Schoenbar Rd.

Schoenbar Trail

Ketchikan Creek

Water St.

TO
ALASKA
STATE FERRY
& AIRPORT

Main St.

Cedar St.

Pine St.

Bawden St.

Grant St.

Edmonds St.

Stairs

Tunnel

Seaman's
Park

Married Man's
Trail

Park Ave.

Park Ave.

City
Park

Deermount St.

Venetia Way

Woodland Ave.

Deermount St.

Main St.

Dock St.

Mission St.

Mill St.

Spruce
Mill St.

Stedman St.

Funicular

Creek St.

Thomas St.

Cruise Ship
Docks

Thomas
Basin

Tongass   Narrows

GRAVINA
ISLAND

0 — 1/4 mile

0 — 1/4 kilometer

KEY

🔵 Sights

🔴 Restaurants

decay in Southeast's exceedingly wet climate. Crafts of the Tlingit, Haida, and Tsimshian cultures are also on display inside the facility, and outside stand several more poles carved in the three decades since it opened. The center offers guided tours and hosts classes, workshops, and seminars related to Northwest Coast Native art and culture. ✉ *601 Deermount St.* ☎ *907/225–5900* ⊕ *www.ktn-ak.us/totem-heritage-center* 🎫 *$6* ⊙ *Closed weekends in Oct.–Apr.*

🍴 Restaurants

Annabelle's Famous Keg and Chowder House

$$ | SEAFOOD | An unpretentious Victorian-style restaurant on the Gilmore Hotel's ground floor, Annabelle's serves pastas, steamer clams and other seafood dishes, and several kinds of chowder. Prime rib on Friday and Saturday evenings is a favorite, and the lounge, which has a jukebox, has a friendly vibe. **Known for:** seafood chowder; Alaskan crab; relaxed atmosphere. ⑤ *Average main: $20* ✉ *326 Front St.* ☎ *907/225–6009* ⊕ *www.annabellesketchikan.com.*

Diaz Café

$ | ASIAN | Take a break from salmon saturation at this Old Town Ketchikan spot on historic Stedman Street. The café serves hearty Filipino cuisine beloved both of locals and cruise-ship staffers hungry for a taste of home, and the linoleum-and-tile 1950s interior is a wonderful time warp. **Known for:** lumpia; chicken adobo; retro decor. ⑤ *Average main: $10* ✉ *335 Stedman St.* ☎ *907/225–2257* ⊕ *diazcafe.business.site* ⊙ *Closed Mon.*

🛍 Shopping

Scanlon Gallery

ART GALLERIES | In business since 1972, Scanlon carries the prints of well-known Alaska artists, including Byron Birdsall, John Fehringer, Barbara Lavallee, Rie Muñoz, and Jon Van Zyle. The gallery also

exhibits jewelry, glasswork, and pottery. ✉ *318 Mission St.* ☎ *907/247–4730, 888/228–4730* ⊕ *www.scanlongallery.com.*

Soho Coho Art Gallery

ART GALLERIES | Design, art, clothing, and collectibles can all be found at stylish Soho Coho. Also here are T-shirts featuring the work of owner Ray Troll—best known for his wacky fish art—and works by other Southeast artists. ✉ *5 Creek St.* ☎ *907/225–5954, 800/888–4070* ⊕ *www.trollart.com.*

Activities

CANOPY TOURS

Alaska Canopy Adventures

TOUR—SPORTS | Featuring a series of zip lines, aerial boardwalks, and suspension bridges, canopy tours provide an up-close view of the coastal forests. At Alaska Canopy Adventures—a course at the Alaska Rainforest Sanctuary, 8.4 miles south of town—the longest of the tour's eight zip lines stretches more than 800 feet, and whisks you along some 130 feet off the ground. Ketchikan's version of this fast-growing outdoor activity often includes Alaskan wildlife viewing—black bears and eagles are frequently spotted from on high. Book online (discounts available) or through your cruise line. ✉ *116 Wood Rd.* ☎ *907/225–5503* ⊕ *www.alaskacanopy.com* 🎫 *From $189.*

Southeast Exposure

TOUR—SPORTS | A rain-forest zip line and ropes course is offered through Southeast Exposure, a well-known kayaking outfit in the area. ✉ *37 Potter Rd.* ☎ *907/225–8829* ⊕ *www.southeastexposure.com* 🎫 *From $90 (kayaking) and $125 (zip-lining).*

FLIGHTSEEING

Alaska Travel Adventures

TOUR—SPORTS | This company's back-country Jeep trips are fun, as are the 20-person canoe outings perfect for people just dipping their toes into (very)

"On a cool spring day, after walking on glaciers and seeing so much wildlife in the Tundra and sea coast, Ketchikan is comfortable and warm." —Sandy Cook, Fodors.com photo contest participant

soft adventure travel. ⊠ *Ketchikan* ☎ *800/323–5757, 907/247–5295* ⊕ *www. bestofalaskatravel.com* ☒ *$99 (canoe outings), $159 (Jeep trips).*

Allen Marine Tours

TOUR—SPORTS | One of Southeast's best-known tour operators, Allen Marine conducts Misty Fiords National Monument catamaran tours throughout the summer. The company also offers half-day wildlife viewing tours. ⊠ *5 Salmon Landing* ☎ *907/225–8100, 877/686–8100* ⊕ *www. allenmarinetours.com.*

HIKING
Deer Mountain

HIKING/WALKING | The 3-mile trail from downtown to the 3,000-foot summit of Deer Mountain will repay your efforts with a spectacular panorama of the city below and the wilderness behind. The trail officially begins at the corner of Nordstrom Drive and Ketchikan Lake Road, but consider starting on the paved, 1½-mile scenic walk on the corner of Fair and Deermount streets. Pass through dense forests before emerging into the

alpine country. A shelter cabin near the summit provides a place to warm up. ⊠ *Fair and Deermount Sts.* ⊕ *www. seatrails.org/com_ketchikan/trl-deer-mountain.htm.*

LUMBERJACK SHOWS
Great Alaskan Lumberjack Show

LOCAL SPORTS | FAMILY | The show consists of a 60-minute lumberjack competition providing a Disneyesque taste of old-time woodsman skills, including ax throwing, bucksawing, springboard chopping, log-rolling duels, and a 50-foot speed climb. It's a little hokey, but it's good fun (and kids will love it). Shows take place in a covered, heated grandstand directly behind the Salmon Landing Marketplace and are presented rain or shine all summer. ⊠ *420 Spruce Mill Way* ☎ *907/225–9050, 888/320–9049* ⊕ *www. alaskanlumberjackshow.com* ☒ *$37.*

SEA KAYAKING
Southeast Exposure

KAYAKING | This outfit conducts a 3½-hour guided Eagle Islands sea-kayak tour and a 4½-hour Tatoosh Islands sea-kayak tour in

Behm Canal. ⊠ *37 Potter Rd.* ☎ *907/225–8829* ⊕ *www.southeastexposure.com* ⊠ *From $90.*

★ Southeast Sea Kayaks

KAYAKING | Paddle across the Tongass Narrows in this company's 2½-hour introductory tour or venture farther afield on one of its guided multinight trips to Misty Fiords. Travelers with just one day to spend on a Ketchikan adventure should consider the five-hour combination tour of kayaking through Orcas Cove and flightseeing Misty Fiords National Monument. It's hard to beat a day that includes a transfer from a boat to a floatplane. ⊠ *3 Salmon Landing* ☎ *907/225–1258, 800/287–1607* ⊕ *www.kayakketchikan. com* ⊠ *From $93.*

Kodiak Island

On the second-largest island in the United States (Hawaii's Big Island is the largest), the town of Kodiak is the least touristy of all the Alaska port towns. It's an out-of-the-way destination for smaller cruise ships and Alaska state ferries.

Despite its small population (about 6,475 people scattered among the several islands in the Kodiak group), there's a lot of "big" stuff here: Kodiak is home to a very large commercial fishing fleet, with some of the busiest fishing ports in the United States. The harbor is also an important supply point for small communities on the Aleutian Islands and the Alaska Peninsula. It's also home to the country's largest Coast Guard base in the Pacific, and the world-famous Kodiak brown bear, billed as the largest land carnivore in the world.

COMING ASHORE

Most cruise ships dock at Pier 2, a half mile south of downtown Kodiak. Most ships offer shuttles into town (about $7 round-trip), but if yours doesn't, it's a 15-minute walk. Taxis may also be waiting at the pier.

TOURS

CONTACTS Kodiak Adventures Unlimited ⊠ *105 W. Marine Way* ☎ *907/486–8766* ⊕ *www.kodiakadventuresunlimited.com.*

VISITOR INFORMATION

Pick up maps, details on kayaking trips, bear-viewing flights, marine tours, and more from the local visitors center.

CONTACTS Kodiak Island Convention & Visitors Bureau ⊠ *100 Marine Way, Suite 200* ☎ *907/486–4782, 800/789–4782* ⊕ *www. kodiak.org.*

Sights

Alutiiq Museum and Archaeological Repository

MUSEUM | Home to one of the largest collections of Alaska Native materials in the world, the Alutiiq Museum contains archaeological and ethnographic items dating back 7,500 years. The more than 150,000 artifacts include harpoons, masks, dolls, stone tools, seal-gut parkas, grass baskets, and pottery fragments. The museum store sells Alaska Native arts and educational materials. ⊠ *215 Mission Rd., Suite 101* ☎ *844/425–8844* ⊕ *www.alutiiqmuseum.org* ⊠ *$7* ⊗ *Closed Sun. and Mon.*

Baranov Museum

MUSEUM | The museum presents artifacts from the area's Russian past in an 1808 structure built to warehouse sea-otter pelts. On display are samovars, intricate Native basketry, and other relics from the early Native Koniags and the later Russian settlers. Albums of archival photography portray various aspects of the island's history. In the early 1800s, the museum's namesake, Alexander Baranov, was the chief manager for the fur-trading Russian-American Company. Baranov commissioned the building that now houses the museum, which W.J. Erskine, who owned a big cod fishery, made his home in 1911. ⊠ *101 Marine Way* ☎ *907/486–5920* ⊕ *www.*

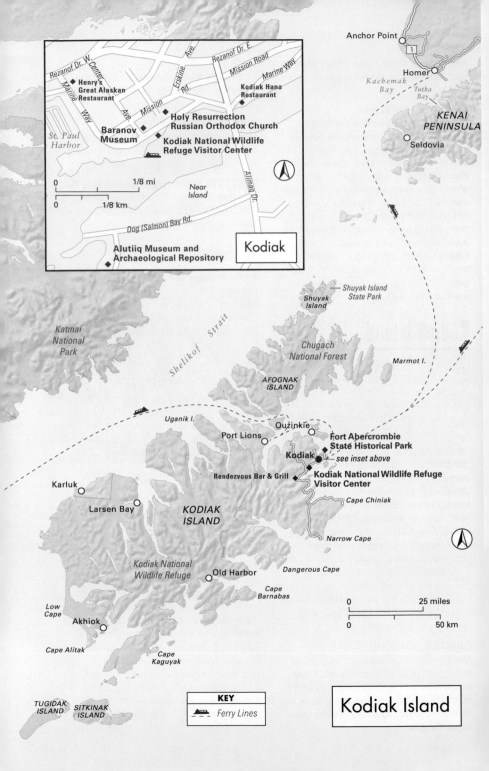

Kodiak

Rezanof Dr. W.

Rezanof Dr. E.

Mission Road

Marine Way

◆ Henry's Great Alaskan Restaurant

Erskine Ave.

Mission Rd.

Kodiak Hana Restaurant ◆

Center Ave.

Marine Way

St. Paul Harbor

Mission Ave.

◆ Holy Resurrection Russian Orthodox Church

Baranov Museum ◆

◆ Kodiak National Wildlife Refuge Visitor Center

Allmaq Dr.

0   1/8 mi
0   1/8 km

Near Island

Dog (Salmon) Bay Rd.

◆ Alutiiq Museum and Archaeological Repository

Anchor Point

1

Homer

Kachemak Bay

Tutka Bay

KENAI PENINSULA

○ Seldovia

Shuyak Island State Park

Shuyak Island

Katmai National Park

Shelikof Strait

Chugach National Forest

Marmot I.

AFOGNAK ISLAND

Uganik I.

Ouzinkie ○

Fort Abercrombie State Historical Park

Port Lions ○

Kodiak ◆ ← *see inset above*

◆ **Kodiak National Wildlife Refuge Visitor Center**

Karluk ○

Rendezvous Bar & Grill ◆

KODIAK ISLAND

Larsen Bay ○

Cape Chiniak

Narrow Cape

Kodiak National Wildlife Refuge

Old Harbor ○

Dangerous Cape

Cape Barnabas

Low Cape

Akhiok ○

0   25 miles
0   50 km

Cape Alitak

Cape Kaguyak

TUGIDAK ISLAND

SITKINAK ISLAND

KEY

⛴ *Ferry Lines*

Kodiak Island

baranovmuseum.org 🏷 *$5* ⊘ *Closed Sun. and Mon.*

Fort Abercrombie State Historical Park
HISTORIC SITE | FAMILY | As part of America's North Pacific defense during World War II, Kodiak was the site of an important naval station, now occupied by the Coast Guard fleet that patrols the surrounding fishing grounds. Part of the old military installation has been incorporated into this park north of town. Self-guided tours take you past concrete bunkers and gun emplacements, and trails wind through moss-draped spruce forest. There's a highly scenic overlook, great for bird and whale watching, and inside a bunker a volunteer group runs the **Kodiak Military History Museum.** ⊠ *Mile 3.7, E. Rezanof Dr.* ☎ *907/486–6339* ⊕ *www.dnr.alaska.gov/parks/units/kodiak/ftaber.htm* 🏷 *$5.*

Holy Resurrection Russian Orthodox Church
RELIGIOUS SITE | The ornate Russian Orthodox church is a visual feast, both inside and out. The cross-shaped building is topped by two onion-shaped blue domes, and the interior contains brass candelabra, distinctive chandeliers, and numerous icons representing Orthodox saints. Three different churches have stood on this site since 1794. The present structure, built in 1945, is on the National Register of Historic Places. ⊠ *385 Kashevaroff Ave.* ☎ *907/486–5532 parish priest* ⊕ *www.oca.org/parishes/oca-ak-kodhrc* 🏷 *Free.*

Kodiak National Wildlife Refuge Visitor Center
INFO CENTER | FAMILY | Indispensable for those exploring the wildlife refuge, this center a block from the downtown ferry dock is an interesting stop on its own. Wander through exhibits about the refuge's flora and fauna, attend an interpretive talk, and marvel at the complete 36-foot hanging skeleton of a male gray whale on the second floor. ⊠ *402 Center Ave.* ☎ *907/487–2626* ⊕ *www.fws.gov/refuge/kodiak.*

🍴 Restaurants

Henry's Great Alaskan Restaurant
$$ | AMERICAN | A big, boisterous, friendly place near the small-boat harbor, Henry's has a menu that's equally big. There's fresh local seafood, of course, but also everything from barbecue and rack of lamb to gourmet salads, pastas, and even some Cajun dishes. **Known for:** great post-fishing dining destination; tasty seafood bowls; very relaxed environment. $ *Average main: $20* ⊠ *512 W. Marine Way* ☎ *907/486–8844* ⊕ *www.henrysgreatalaskan.com* ⊘ *Closed Sun. Oct.–Apr.*

Kodiak Hana Restaurant
$$ | SEAFOOD | This converted powerhouse facility allows a close-up view of Near Island and the channel connecting the boat harbors with the Gulf of Alaska. Enjoy fine steaks and classic seafood dishes, or fresh sushi and sashimi while watching the procession of fishing boats gliding past on their way to catch or deliver your next meal. **Known for:** excellent sushi; great views of marine wildlife; diverse fresh fish dishes. $ *Average main: $20* ⊠ *516 E. Marine Way* ☎ *907/481–1088* ⊕ *www.powerhousekodiak.com* ⊘ *Closed Mon. No lunch Sun.*

Rendezvous Bar & Grill
$$ | AMERICAN | A shanty roadhouse of sorts, Rendezvous serves drinks all night and caters to locals. Every afternoon (except Monday), however, the locals and tourists show up in droves to fill their bellies with the tastiest eats on the island. **Known for:** amazing fish tacos; laid-back ambience; no food (just drinks) after 7:30 pm. $ *Average main: $15* ⊠ *11652 Chiniak Hwy.* ☎ *907/487–2233* ⊘ *No lunch or dinner Mon.*

Did You Know?

Despite their given names, black and brown bears range in color from pure black to nearly blond. Size is the defining characteristic: male brown bears on Kodiak Island—home to the largest browns on Earth—can reach 1,700 pounds and stand 10 feet tall. Male black bears rarely exceed 500 pounds or 6 feet.

⚡ Activities

BEAR WATCHING

Kodiak Adventures Unlimited

TOUR—SPORTS | This outfit with a summer kiosk in St. Paul Harbor (across from Wells Fargo) books charter and tour operators for all of Kodiak. ⊠ *105 W. Marine Way* ☎ *907/486–8766* ⊕ *www.kodiakadventuresunlimited.com.*

FISHING

Memory Makers Tour and Guide Service

TOUR—SPORTS | Guide Dake Schmidt is knowledgeable and passionate about fishing local rivers; his angling half- and full-day trips are a boon for those not flying off to remote lodges. Fishing gear, lunch (on full-day excursions), and a ride in a comfortable van are provided. Memory Makers also conducts sightseeing, wildlife-viewing, and photography tours. ⊠ *1523B Mission Rd.* ☎ *907/486–7000* ⊕ *www.memorymakersinak.com* ☒ *From $150 half-day, $300 full-day.*

Metlakatla

12 miles south of Ketchikan.

The village of Metlakatla—the name translates roughly as "saltwater passage"—is on Annette Island, a dozen miles by sea from busy Ketchikan but a world away culturally. A visit to this quiet community offers the chance to learn about life in a small Inside Passage Native community

In most Southeast Native villages, the people are of Tlingit or Haida heritage, but most residents of Metlakatla are Tsimshian. They moved to the island from British Columbia in 1887 with William Duncan, an Anglican missionary from England. The town grew rapidly and soon contained dozens of buildings, including a cannery, a sawmill, and a church that could seat 1,000 people. Congress declared Annette Island a federal Indian reservation in 1891, and it remains the only reservation in Alaska today. Every year on August 7, locals celebrate Metlakatla's founding with a parade, foot races, food stands, and fireworks.

During World War II the U.S. Army built a major air base 7 miles from Metlakatla that included observation towers to spy on Japanese subs, as well as airplane hangars, gun emplacements, and housing for 10,000 soldiers. After the war it served as Ketchikan's airport for many years, but today the long runways are virtually abandoned save for a few private flights.

COMING ASHORE

Cruise ships dock at the Metlakatla dock adjacent to town. There's free Wi-Fi at the Metlakatla Artists' Village on Airport Road.

TOURS

Run by the Metlakatla community, **Metlakatla Tours** leads local tours that include visits to Duncan Cottage, the cannery, and the longhouse, along with a Tsimshian dance performance. Local taxis can take you to other sights around the island, including Yellow Hill and the old Air Force base.

CONTACTS Metlakatla Tours ☎ *907/886–8687* ⊕ *www.visitmetlakatla.com.*

👁 Sights

Longhouse

NATIVE SITE | Father William Duncan, an Anglican missionary, strove to eliminate some aspects of Tsimshian culture and Christianize the people of Metlakatla, but they have resurrected their past and perform old and new dances in traditional regalia. The best place to catch these performances is at the longhouse that faces Metlakatla's boat harbor. Three totem poles stand in back of the building, and a Tsimshian design covers the front. Inside are displays of Native crafts and a model of fish traps once common throughout the Inside Passage. Next to the longhouse are booths displaying locally made arts and crafts. ⊠ *Metlakatla* ☎ *907/886–4441* ⊕ *www.metlakatla.com.*

William Duncan Memorial Church

RELIGIOUS SITE | This clapboard church is one of tiny Metlakatla's nine churches. The original burned in 1948. The current version, topped with two steeples, was rebuilt several years later. Nearby, **Father Duncan's Cottage,** maintained to appear exactly as it would have in 1891, contains original furnishings, personal items, and a collection of turn-of-the-20th-century music boxes. ⊠ *4th Ave. and Church St.* ☎ *907/886–4441* ⊕ *www.metlakatla.com* 🖃 *$2.*

Yellow Hill

VIEWPOINT | A boardwalk 2 miles from town leads up the 540-foot Yellow Hill. Distinctive yellow sandstone rocks and panoramic vistas make this a worthwhile detour on clear days. ⊠ *West of Airport Rd., 2 miles south of town.*

Misty Fiords National Monument

 Sights

★ **Misty Fiords National Monument**
NATIONAL/STATE PARK | Cliff-faced fjords (or fiords, if you follow the attraction's spelling), tall mountains, waterfalls, and islands with spectacular coastal scenery draw visitors to this wilderness area just east of Ketchikan. Most arrive on day trips via floatplane or aboard a catamaran. Both methods have their advantages: air travel reveals Misty Fiord's enormous scope, while trips by sea afford more intimate vistas. You can also kayak here, but it's a long paddle from Ketchikan. For a more manageable trip, consider having a boat drop you off within the monument. Traveling on these waters can be an almost mystical experience, with

Misty Fiords Best Bets

■ **Flightsee.** The unspoiled wilderness of Misty Fiords from the air is a sight you won't soon forget. Arrange trips from Ketchikan.

■ **Go Fish.** One of Southeast Alaska's most fertile marine ecosystems, Misty is home to healthy runs of all five salmon species and some excellent fishing.

■ **Watch wildlife.** You may catch a glimpse of Southeast regulars (bears and porpoises) or seldom-seen characters (mountain goats, wolves, killer whales, and wolverines).

the green forests reflected in the many fjords' waters. You may find yourself in the company of a whale, see a bear along the shore fishing for salmon, or even pull in your own salmon. The 15 cabins the Forest Service manages here can be booked through the Recreation.gov website. ⊠ *Ketchikan* ☎ *907/225–2148 Ketchikan-Misty Fiords Ranger District* ⊕ *www.recreation.gov.*

Ketchikan Visitors Bureau

INFO CENTER | Most visitors to Misty Fiords arrive on day trips via floatplane from Ketchikan or onboard catamarans. The bureau can provide a list of local providers. ⊠ *Ketchikan* ☎ *800/770–3300* ⊕ *www.visit-ketchikan.com.*

🏃 Activities

FLIGHTSEEING

The dramatic fjords and isolated alpine lakes of the 2.3-million-acre Misty Fiords National Monument don't exactly lend themselves to pedestrian exploration. But thanks to flightseeing services like **Island Wings Air Service** (☎ *907/225–2444* or 888/854–2444 ⊕ www.islandwings. com) and **Southeast Aviation** (☎ 907/225– 2900 or 888/359–6478 ⊕ www.south- eastaviation.com), the sublime splendor of this region doesn't go unseen. Island Wings offers a popular two-hour tour that includes a 35-minute stopover at one of the monument's many lakes or fjords. Southeast Aviation offers transportation from the cruise-ship pier and a 2½-hour tour that includes a water landing for photos. Both companies are based in Ketchikan.

Petersburg

Only ferries and smaller cruise ships can squeak through Wrangell Narrows with the aid of more than 50 buoys and range markers along the 22-mile waterway, which takes almost four hours. But the inaccessibility of Petersburg is also part of its charm: you'll never be overwhelmed here by hordes of cruise passengers.

The Scandinavian heritage is gradually being submerged by the larger American culture, but you can occasionally hear Norwegian spoken, especially during the Little Norway Festival, held here each year on the weekend closest to May 17 (Norwegian Constitution Day). If you're in town during the festival, be sure to take part in one of the fish feeds that highlight Syttende Mai (aka the Norwegian Constitution Day) celebration. You won't find better folk dancing and beer-batter halibut outside Norway.

One of the most pleasant things to do in Petersburg is to roam among the fishing vessels tied up dockside in the harbor. This is one of Alaska's busiest, most prosperous fishing communities, with an enormous variety of seacraft. You'll see small trollers, big halibut vessels, and sleek pleasure craft. By watching shrimp, salmon, or halibut catches being brought ashore (though be prepared for the pungent aroma), you can get a real appreciation for this industry.

On clear days Petersburg's scenery is second to none. Across Frederick Sound the sawlike peaks of the Stikine Ice Cap scrape clouds from the sky, looking every bit as malevolent as their monikers suggest. (Some of the most wickedly named summits include Devil's Thumb, Kate's Needle, and Witches Tits.) LeConte Glacier, Petersburg's biggest draw, lies at the foot of the ice cap, about 25 miles east of town. Accessible only by water or air, the LeConte is the continent's southernmost tidewater glacier and one of its most active, often calving off so many icebergs that the tidewater bay at its face is carpeted shore to shore with floating bergs.

COMING ASHORE
Cruise companies with stops at Petersburg include UnCruise and Lindblad Expeditions. These lines operate smaller, adventure-oriented ships that offer complimentary walking and hiking tours ashore led by an onboard guide or naturalist. The ships dock in the South Harbor, which is about a half-mile walk from downtown.

TOURS
If you want to learn about local history, the commercial fishing industry, and the Tongass National Forest, you can take a guided tour.

VISITOR INFORMATION
Petersburg Visitor Information Center Though small, the center is a good place to pick up maps and learn about tours, charters, and nearby outdoor recreation opportunities. It is open May through September, Monday through Saturday 9 to 5 and Sunday noon to 4 and October through April, weekdays from 10 to 2. ✉ 1st and Fram Sts. ☎ 907/772–4636, 866/484–4700 ⊕ www.petersburg.org.

Did You Know?

Lakes like this one in the Rousseau Range in Misty Fiords National Monument make attractive places to contemplate how an area that was covered in glaciers 17,000 years ago is now filled with saltwater fjords, tidewater estuaries, 3,000-foot mist-shrouded mountains, and miles and miles of pristine solitude.

◉ Sights

Blind Slough Recreation Area

NATIONAL/STATE PARK | This recreation area includes a number of sites scattered along the Mitkof Highway from 15 to 20 miles south of Petersburg. Blind River Rapids Trail is a wheelchair-accessible 1-mile boardwalk that leads to a three-sided shelter overlooking the river—one of Southeast's most popular fishing spots—before looping back through the muskeg. Not far away is a bird-viewing area where several dozen trumpeter swans spend the winter. In summer you're likely to see many ducks and other waterfowl. At Mile 18 the state-run hatchery releases thousands of king and coho salmon each year. The kings return in June and July, the coho in August and September. Nearby is a popular picnic area. Four miles south of the hatchery is a Forest Service campground. ⊠ *Petersburg* ☎ *907/772–3871 USFS Petersburg Ranger District* ⊕ *www.fs.usda.gov/detail/r10/specialplaces/?cid=fsbdev2_038848.*

Clausen Memorial Museum

MUSEUM | The exhibits here explore commercial fishing and the cannery industry, the era of fish traps, the social life of Petersburg, and Tlingit culture. Don't miss the 126½-pound king salmon—the largest ever caught commercially—as well as the Tlingit dugout canoe; the Cape Decision lighthouse station lens; and *Earth, Sea and Sky,* a 3-D wall mural outside. ⊠ *203 Fram St.* ☎ *907/772–3598* ⊠ *$3.*

Eagle's Roost Park

CITY PARK | Just north of the Petersburg Fisheries cannery, this small roadside park is a great place to spot eagles, especially at low tide. On a clear day you will also discover dramatic views of the sharp-edged Coast Range, including the 9,077-foot summit of Devil's Thumb. ⊠ *617 N. Nordic Dr.*

Hammer Slough

BODY OF WATER | Houses on high stilts and the historic Sons of Norway Hall border this creek that floods with each high tide, creating a photogenic reflecting pool. ⊠ *Hammer Slough Trail.*

★ LeConte Glacier

NATURE SITE | Petersburg's biggest draw lies at the foot of the Stikine Ice Cap. Accessible only by air or water, LeConte Glacier is the continent's southernmost tidewater glacier and one of its most active, often calving off so many icebergs that the tidewater bay at its face is carpeted shore to shore with them. ⊠ *25 miles northeast of Petersburg* ☎ *907/772–4636 Petersburg visitor information* ⊕ *www.petersburgak.org.*

Sons of Norway Hall

LOCAL INTEREST | Built in 1912, this large, white, barnlike structure just south of the Hammer Slough is the headquarters of an organization devoted to keeping alive the traditions and culture of Norway. Petersburg's Norwegian roots date back to 1897, when Peter Buschmann arrived and founded the Icy Strait Packing Company cannery. As his business and family flourished, others arrived to join them, many of Norwegian descent. By 1920, they and the area's Tlingit residents had established a year-round community of 600 residents. The hall, its red shutters decorated with colorful Norwegian rosemaling designs, is listed on the National Register of Historic Places. Outside sits a replica of a Viking ship that is a featured attraction in the annual Little Norway Festival each May. On the building's south side is a bronze tribute to deceased local fishermen. ⊠ *23 S. Sing Lee Alley* ☎ *907/772–4575* ⊕ *www.petersburgsons.org.*

⊕ Restaurants

Coastal Cold Storage

$ | SEAFOOD | This busy little seafood deli in the heart of Petersburg is a great

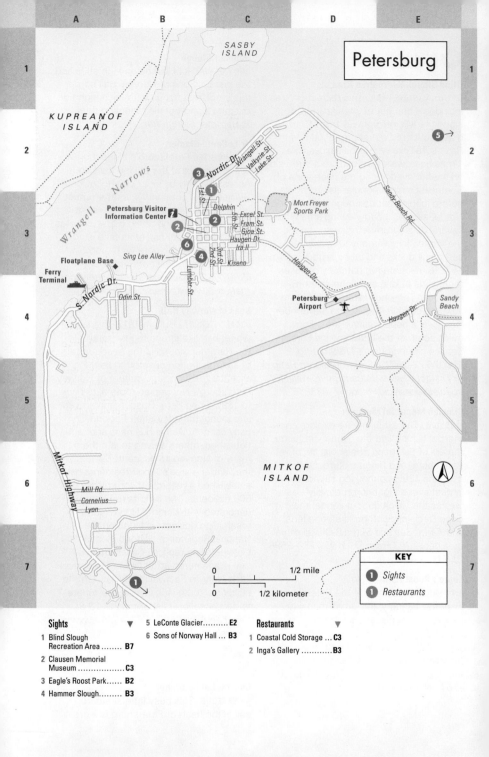

Petersburg

KUPREANOF ISLAND

SASBY ISLAND

Narrows

Wrangell

Nordic Dr.

Wrangell St.
Valkyrie St.
Lake St.

1st St.

Dolphin

Petersburg Visitor Information Center

Excel St.
Fram St.
Gjoa St.
Haugen Dr.
Ira II

5th St.

3rd St.

2nd St.

Kiseno

Mort Freyer Sports Park

Sing Lee Alley

Floatplane Base

Ferry Terminal

S. Nordic Dr.

Odin St.

Lumber St.

Haugen Dr.

Petersburg Airport

Sandy Beach Rd.

Sandy Beach

Haugen Dr.

Mitkof Highway

Mill Rd.
Cornelius
Lyon

MITKOF ISLAND

N

0   1/2 mile
0   1/2 kilometer

KEY

1 Sights
1 Restaurants

Sights ▼

1 Blind Slough
  Recreation Area **B7**
2 Clausen Memorial
  Museum **C3**
3 Eagle's Roost Park **B2**
4 Hammer Slough **B3**
5 LeConte Glacier **E2**
6 Sons of Norway Hall ... **B3**

Restaurants ▼

1 Coastal Cold Storage ... **C3**
2 Inga's Gallery **B3**

place for a quick bite en route to your next adventure. Live or cooked crab is available for takeout, and the shop can process your sport-caught fish. **Known for:** beer-battered halibut bits; outdoor seating; full-service fish processing. $ *Average main: $10* ⊠ *306 N. Nordic Dr.* ☎ *907/772–4177.*

Inga's Galley

$ | **PACIFIC NORTHWEST** | Locally sourced ingredients—including Southeast seafood and organic produce—are at the heart of casual Inga's menu. The dishes at this local favorite, a glorified food cart with picnic tables, change "with season, availability, and mood," and most go superbly well with the Baranof Island Brewery beers poured here (there's also wine). **Known for:** outdoor, picnic-style dining; smoked salmon chowder; vegetarian options. $ *Average main: $12* ⊠ *104 N. Nordic Dr.* ☎ *907/772–2090* ⊙ *Closed mid-Sept.–mid-Apr.*

🛍 Shopping

Northern Lights Smokeries

FOOD/CANDY | Owner Thomas Cumps has made a name for himself with his hot-smoked white king, red king, and sockeye salmon, along with a local favorite, cold smoked black cod. It's best to call ahead to make sure Cumps will be around before you stop by. You can take your fish with you or have it shipped. ⊠ *501 Noseeum St.* ☎ *907/518–1616* ⊕ *www.nlsmokeries.com.*

Tonka Seafoods

FOOD/CANDY | Sample smoked or canned halibut and salmon at Tonka Seafoods, located in the old Mitkof Cannery building. Be sure to taste the white king salmon—an especially flavorful type of chinook that the locals swear by. Tonka will also ship. ⊠ *1200 S. Nordic Dr.* ☎ *888/560–3662* ⊕ *www.tonkaseafoods. com.*

🏃 Activities

HIKING

For an enjoyable loop hike from town, follow Dolphin Street uphill from the center of town. At the intersection with 5th Street, a boardwalk path leads 900 feet through forested wetlands to the baseball fields, where a second boardwalk takes you to 12th Street and Haugen Drive. Turn left on Haugen and follow it past the airport to **Sandy Beach Park,** where picnickers can sit under log shelters and low tide reveals remnants of ancient fish traps and a number of petroglyphs. From here you can return to town via Sandy Beach Road or hike the beach when the tide is out. Along the way is the charming **Outlook Park,** a covered observatory with binoculars to scan for marine life. A pullout at Hungry Point provides views to the Coast Range and Frederick Sound. Across the road the half-mile **Hungry Point Trail** takes you back to the baseball fields—a great spot for panoramic views of the mountains— where you can return downtown on the nature boardwalk. Plan on an hour and a half for this walk.

Raven's Roost Cabin Hike

HIKING/WALKING | A 4.2-mile trail begins at the southern edge of the Petersburg airport's runway and winds 1,800 feet in elevation to Raven's Roost Cabin. Along the way you take in a panorama that reaches from the ice-bound Coast Range to the protected waters and forested islands of the Inside Passage far below. Get details on these and other hikes from the Petersburg Visitor Information Center or the Petersburg Ranger District. The two-story Forest Service cabin is available for rent ($40 per night). ⊠ *Petersburg Ranger District, 12 N. Nordic Dr.* ☎ *907/772–3871* ⊕ *www.fs.usda.gov/ recarea/tongass/recarea/?recid=79036.*

Prince Rupert, British Columbia

Just 66 km (40 miles) south of the Alaskan border, Prince Rupert is the largest community on British Columbia's north coast. On Kaien Island at the mouth of the Skeena River and surrounded by deep green fjords and coastal rain forest, Prince Rupert is rich in the culture of the Tsimshian, First Nations people who have been in the area for thousands of years. As the western terminus of Canada's second transcontinental railroad and blessed with a deep natural harbor, Prince Rupert was, at the time of its incorporation in 1910, poised to rival Vancouver as a center for transpacific trade. This didn't happen, partly because the main visionary behind the scheme, Grand Trunk Pacific Railroad president Charles Hays, went down with the *Titanic* on his way back from a financing trip to England. Prince Rupert turned instead to fishing and forestry. A port of call for both BC and Alaska ferries, but relatively new to cruise ships, this community of 12,000 retains a laid-back, small-town air.

COMING ASHORE

Large cruise ships call at Prince Rupert dock at the **Northland Cruise Terminal,** while smaller ships tie up at **Atlin Terminal** next door. Both terminals are in the city's historic Cow Bay district, steps from the Museum of Northern British Columbia and about five blocks from the central business district. The terminals for both British Columbia and Alaska ferries as well as the VIA Rail station are grouped together about 2 km (1 mile) from town. Most points of interest are within walking distance of the cruise-ship terminals.

TOURS

CONTACTS Skeena Taxi ☎ *250/624–2185.*

Prince Rupert Best Bets

- **Wildlife Viewing.** The area is home to North America's largest concentration of grizzly bears; the nearby waters are alive with seals, humpbacks, and orcas.

- **Local Interest.** Pay a visit to the excellent Museum of Northern British Columbia, followed by a stroll around the funky Cow Bay neighborhood.

- **A Cannery Tour.** If you have a little extra time, hit the North Pacific Cannery National Historic Site, in nearby Port Edward (⊕ *www.northpacificcannery.ca*).

VISITOR INFORMATION

Prince Rupert's Visitor Information Centre is located on the waterfront, within steps of the cruise ship terminals and the Cow Bay neighborhood.

CONTACTS Tourism Prince Rupert ✉ *200-215 Cow Bay Rd.* ☎ *250/624–5637, 800/667–1994* ⊕ *www.visitprincerupert.com.*

Sights

Cow Bay

NEIGHBORHOOD | Home to both of Prince Rupert's cruise ship terminals, Cow Bay is a quaint historic waterfront area of shops, galleries, cafés, seafood restaurants, yachts, and fishing boats—and it takes its name seriously. Lampposts, benches, and anything else that doesn't move is painted Holstein-style. You can stop for a coffee or seafood lunch, or shop for local crafts. ✉ *Prince Rupert* ⊕ *www.bctravel.com/north/princerupert/townsite.html.*

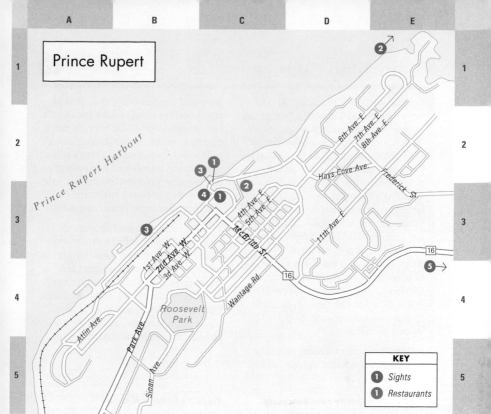

Prince Rupert

Tsimshian Culture

Coastal parts of Canada and Alaska have been inhabited by the Tsimshian people for thousands of years. Prince Rupert's ideal location, at the confluence of the Skeena River with coastal saltwater, made it a highly prized place to establish a fishing village. A wealth of salmon, herring, and hooligan (or, more correctly, eulachon) congregate here annually, and they are accompanied by the seals, whales, and birds that prey on them. These fish are always in top shape as they approach the mouth of the river; farther up the waterway they will cease eating as their energy begins to wane and their terminal quest to spawn continues.

Before the modern fishing industry transformed the coast, plank houses were laid out following the curve of the shoreline, usually with the chief's house in the center. Each house had a name like Moon House, Beaver House, or House Where People Always Want to Go. If the owner was rich enough to commission a frontal totem, this pole was erected between the house and the shore, facing approaching canoes.

The Tsimshian took advantage of seasonal foods by efficiently drying and smoking fish and meat, rendering oil from fish and seals, and preserving berries and wild crab apples in oil. For shelter, they lived in plank houses during the winter, and built smokehouses and lean-tos covered with bark or mats at hunting and fishing sites.

Khutzeymateen Grizzly Bear Sanctuary

NATURE PRESERVE | Jointly administered by the British Columbia provincial government and the Tsimshian First Nation, Canada's only grizzly bear sanctuary, 45 km (28 miles) northeast of Prince Rupert, was established in 1994. It contains one of North America's highest concentrations of grizzlies, protecting a population of about 50 bears, as well as the surrounding wilderness and wetlands that make up their habitat. Eagles, porpoises, and whales may also be spotted in the bay on the approach to the sanctuary. You can visit the sanctuary only with a licensed guide (the website has contact information) and with the proper permits, and access is via boat or floatplane only. Bear viewing is best between mid-May and late July; trips may not be offered in August and September. ⊠ *Prince Rupert* ⊕ *www.env.gov.bc.ca/bcparks/explore/ parkpgs/khutzeymateen.*

Kwinitsa Railway Museum

MUSEUM | Prince Rupert's dream of being the northeast's major port and tourist destination died along with Charles Hays, the town's founder and head of the Grand Trunk Pacific Railway, who went down with the *Titanic* in 1912. The story of his railway empire, and its remnants, can be seen at this small museum, which traces the lives of the linemen, agents, and operators who worked the early railroad. ⊠ *Bill Murray Way* ☎ *250/624–3207* ⊕ *www.museumofnorthernbc.com* ✉ *Donations accepted.*

Museum of Northern British Columbia

MUSEUM | A major attraction in the region, this longhouse-style edifice overlooking the waterfront contains one of the country's finest collections of coastal First Nations artworks, with superb artifacts portraying 10,000 years of Northwest Coast history. You may also have a chance to see artisans working in a nearby carving shed. Along with the permanent exhibit, there is a roster of temporary exhibitions on history and art. You can also purchase unusual local crafts at the museum gift shop. ⊠ *100 1st Ave. W* ☎ *250/624–3207* ⊕ *www. museumofnorthernbc.com* ☷ *C$6.*

North Pacific Cannery National Historic Site
HISTORIC SITE | In the late-19th century, hundreds of cannery villages, built on pilings on the edge of the wilderness, lined the coast between California and Alaska. Most are gone now, but BC's oldest (it dates to 1889) and most complete surviving example is 22 km (14 miles) south of Prince Rupert, via Highway 16 and Port Edward, at the mouth of the Skeena River. Once home to more than 700 people during canning season, the town of 28 buildings, including managers' houses, the company store, and cannery works, is now a national historic site. Staff members lead tours, give demonstrations of the canning process, and represent the unique culture of cannery villages. The site also has a seafood restaurant and overnight accommodations in its European Bunkhouse. ⊠ *1889 Skeena Dr., Port Edward* ☎ *250/628–3538* ⊕ *www. northpacificcannery.ca* ☷ *C$12.*

🍴 Restaurants

Cow Bay Café
$$ | ITALIAN | This lively restaurant is a favorite among locals and visitors alike for its rustic Italian food and charming ambience. Set right on the harbor, the lovely views complement the warm, cozy interior. **Known for:** mocha milkshake; seafood linguine; waterfront location. ⑤ *Average main: C$18* ⊠ *205 Cow Bay Rd.* ☎ *250/627–1212* ⊕ *www.cowbayca-fe.com* ⊙ *Closed Mon.*

Dolly's Fish Market
$$ | SEAFOOD | FAMILY | A local institution, this seafood market and restaurant serves the freshest seafood with a no-frills attitude. Nothing gourmet here, just straightforward, well-prepared fish

and (crispy) fries, along with other deep-fried favorites: halibut, shrimp, scallops, and smoked salmon. **Known for:** crab cakes; chowder; early dinner (closing time is 8 pm). ⑤ *Average main: C$18* ⊠ *7 Cow Bay Rd.* ☎ *250/624–6090* ⊕ *www. dollysfishmarket.com.*

★ **Fukasaku**
$ | SUSHI | The first sushi and seafood restaurant to be 100% certified by Vancouver Aquarium's Ocean Wise (sustainable food) program, this 29-seat upscale diner offers food that is as fresh and creative as it gets in these parts. Even if its location is a bit strange—an adjunct to a souvenir shop—the food artistry delivers. **Known for:** menu highlighting British Columbia; artisan sake; catch of the day. ⑤ *Average main: C$12* ⊠ *215 Cow Bay Rd.* ☎ *250/627–7874* ⊕ *www.fukasaku.ca* ⊙ *Closed Sun. and Mon.*

🛍 Shopping

Prince Rupert has a great selection of locally made crafts and First Nations artwork. Look for items carved in argillite, a kind of slate unique to this region.

Cow Bay Gift Galley
GIFTS/SOUVENIRS | The name says it all: here you'll find a colorful array of gifts, novelty items, souvenirs, housewares, furniture, and local arts and crafts. ⊠ *24 Cow Bay Rd.* ☎ *250/627–1808.*

Homework
CLOTHING | This large, contemporary gift shop offers everything from soap and bath items to decorating, housewares, candles, women's clothing (some locally made), fashion footwear, jewelry, and novelty gift items. ⊠ *145 Cow Bay Rd.* ☎ *250/624–3663* ⊕ *homeworkstore.ca.*

Ice House Gallery
ART GALLERIES | Only the works of more than 80 local artists and artisans are displayed in this gallery run by the North Coast Artists' Cooperative. Items include paintings, jewelry, weaving, beaded

Did You Know?

Real glacier drama happens in Prince William Sound. The area has the highest concentration of calving tidewater glaciers in the state. Columbia Glacier, the world's fastest retreating glacier, is carving a new fjord in the sound.

doeskin slippers, quilts, wood carvings, glass, and pottery. ⊠ *Atlin Cruise Ship Terminal, 190–215 Cow Bay Rd.* ☎ *250/624–4546* ⊕ *www.icehousegallery.ca.*

Prince William Sound

Tucked into the east side of the Kenai Peninsula, the sound is a peaceful escape from the throngs of people congesting the towns and highways. Enhanced with steep fjords, green enshrouded waterfalls, and calving tidewater glaciers, Prince William Sound is a stunning arena. It has a convoluted coastline, in that it is riddled with islands, which makes it hard to discern just how vast the area is. The sound covers almost 15,000 square miles—more than 12 times the size of Rhode Island—and is home to more than 150 glaciers. The sound is vibrantly alive with all manner of marine life, including salmon, halibut, humpback whales, orcas, sea otters, sea lions, and porpoises. Bald eagles are easily seen soaring above, and often brown and black bears, Sitka black-tailed deer, and gray wolves can be spotted on the shore.

Unfortunately, the Exxon Valdez oil spill in 1989 heavily damaged parts of the sound, and oil still washes up on shore after high tides and storms. The original spill was devastating to both animal and human lives. What lasting effect this lurking oil will have on the area is still being studied and remains a topic of much debate.

⊙ Sights

The major attraction in Prince William Sound on most Gulf of Alaska cruises is the day spent in **College Fjord.** This deep finger of water boasts the largest collection of tidewater glaciers in the world, and is ringed by 16 glaciers, each named after one of the colleges that sponsored early exploration of the fjord.

A visit to Columbia Glacier, which flows from the surrounding Chugach Mountains, is included on many Gulf of Alaska cruises (often via Valdez). Its deep aquamarine face is 5 miles across, and it calves new icebergs with resounding cannonades. This glacier is one of the largest and most readily accessible of Alaska's coastal glaciers.

Sitka

Sitka was home to the Kiksádi clan of the Tlingit people for centuries prior to the 18th-century arrival of the Russians under the direction of territorial governor Alexander Baranof. The Tlingits attacked Baranof's people and burned his buildings in 1802, but Baranof returned in 1804 with formidable strength, including shipboard cannons. He attacked the Tlingits at their fort near Indian River (site of the present-day, 105-acre Sitka National Historical Park) and drove them to Chichagof Island, 70 miles northwest of Sitka. The Tlingits and Russians made peace in 1821, and eventually the capital of Russian America was shifted from Kodiak to Sitka.

Today Sitka is known for its beautiful setting and some of Southeast Alaska's most famous landmarks: the onion-dome St. Michael's Cathedral; the Alaska Raptor Center, where you can come up close to ailing and recovering birds of prey; and Sitka National Historical Park, where you can see some of the oldest and most skillfully carved totem poles in the state.

COMING ASHORE

Once able to accommodate only the smallest excursion vessels, Sitka now welcomes medium to large cruise ships at a privately owned dock about 5 miles north of town at Halibut Point. Some large cruise ships must drop anchor in

Continued on page 304

ALASKA'S GLACIERS
NOTORIOUS LANDSCAPE ARCHITECTS

(opposite and above) Facing the Taku Glacier challenge outside Juneau.

Glaciers—those massive, blue-hued tongues of ice that issue forth from Alaska's mountain ranges—perfectly embody the harsh climate, unforgiving terrain, and haunting beauty that make this state one of the world's wildest places. Alaska is home to roughly 100,000 glaciers, which cover almost 5% of the state's land.

FROZEN GIANTS

A glacier occurs where annual snowfall exceeds annual snowmelt. Snow accumulates over thousands of years, forming massive sheets of compacted ice. (Southeast Alaska's **Taku Glacier**, popular with flightseeing devotees, is one of Earth's meatiest: some sections measure over 4,500 feet thick.) Under the pressure of its own weight, the glacier succumbs to gravity and begins to flow downhill. This movement results in sprawling masses of rippled ice (Alaska's **Bering Glacier**, at 127 miles, is North America's longest). When glaciers reach the tidewaters of the coast, icebergs calve, or break off from the glacier's face, plunging dramatically into the sea.

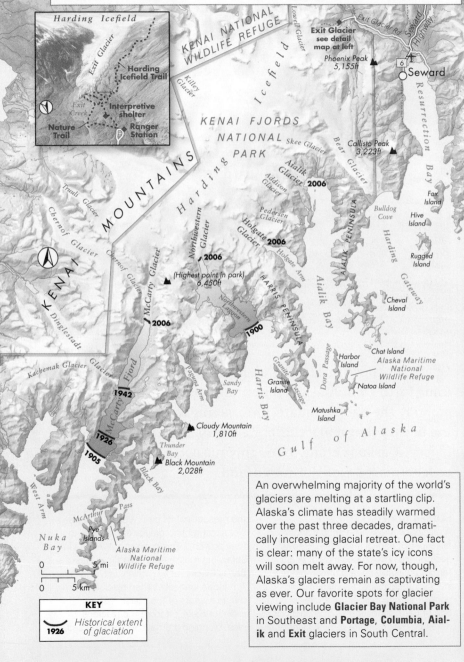

THE RAPIDLY RETREATING GLACIERS IN KENAI FJORDS NATIONAL PARK

Harding Icefield

Exit Glacier

Harding Icefield Trail

Exit Creek

Interpretive shelter

Nature Trail

Ranger Station

KENAI NATIONAL WILDLIFE REFUGE

Lowell Glacier

Exit Glacier see detail map at left

Phoenix Peak 5,155ft

Seward 6

Seward

Resurrection Bay

Exit Glacier Rd.

Seward Highway

Killey Glacier

KENAI FJORDS NATIONAL PARK

Skee Glacier

Bear Glacier

Callisto Peak 3,223ft

Fox Island

Bulldog Cove

Hive Island

Rugged Island

Harding Gateway

Atalik Glacier **2006**

Addison Glacier

Pedersen Glacier

Holgate Glacier **2006**

Holgate Arm

AIALIK PENINSULA

Cheval Island

Truuli Glacier

Chernof Glacier

KENAI MOUNTAINS

Harding

2006 (Highest point in park) 6,450ft

Northwestern Glacier

Northwestern Lagoon

HARRIS PENINSULA

1900

Aialik Bay

Doroshin Passage

Chat Island

Harbor Island

Alaska Maritime National Wildlife Refuge

Natoa Island

Dinglestadt Glacier

McCarty Glacier

2006

McCarty Fiord

Chernof Glacier

Pagunn Arm

Sandy Bay

Harris Bay

Granite Island

Granite Passage

Matushka Island

Kachemak Glacier

Glacier

1942

1926

1905

Thunder Bay

Cloudy Mountain 1,810ft

Black Mountain 2,028ft

Gulf of Alaska

Black Bay

West Arm

McArthur Pass

Pye Islands

Nuka Bay

Alaska Maritime National Wildlife Refuge

0 ——— 5 mi
0 ——— 5 km

An overwhelming majority of the world's glaciers are melting at a startling clip. Alaska's climate has steadily warmed over the past three decades, dramatically increasing glacial retreat. One fact is clear: many of the state's icy icons will soon melt away. For now, though, Alaska's glaciers remain as captivating as ever. Our favorite spots for glacier viewing include **Glacier Bay National Park** in Southeast and **Portage**, **Columbia**, **Aialik** and **Exit** glaciers in South Central.

ICY BLUE HIKES & THUNDEROUS BOATING EXCURSIONS

Glaciers enchant us with their size and astonishing power to shape the landscape. But let's face it: nothing rivals the sheer excitement of watching a bus-size block of ice burst from a glacier's face, creating an unholy thunderclap that resounds across an isolated Alaskan bay.

Most frequently undertaken with a seasoned guide, **glacier trekking** is becoming increasingly popular. Many guides transport visitors to and from glaciers (in some cases by helicopter or small plane), and provide ski excursions, dogsled tours, or guided hikes on the glacier's surface. Striding through the surreal landscape of a glacier, ice crunching underfoot, can be an otherworldly experience. Whether you're whooping it up on a dogsled tour, learning the fundamentals of glacier travel, or simply poking about on a massive field of ice, you're sure to gain an acute appreciation for the massive scale of the state's natural environment.

You can also experience glaciers via boat, such as the Alaska Marine Highway, a cruise ship, a small chartered boat, or even your own bobbing kayak. Our favorite out of Seward is the ride with Kenai Fjords Tours. Don't be discouraged by rainy weather. Glaciers often appear even bluer on overcast days. When piloting your own vessel, be sure to keep your distance from the glacier's face.

Taking in the sights at Mendenhall Glacier

DID YOU KNOW?

What do glaciers and cows have in common? They both *calve*. While bovine calving refers to actual calf-birth, the word is also used to describe a tidewater glacier's stunning habit of rupturing icebergs from its terminus. When glacier ice meets the sea, steady tidal movement and warmer temperatures cause these frequent, booming deposits.

GLACIER-VIEWING TIPS

■ The most important rule of thumb is never to venture onto a glacier without proper training or the help of a guide.

■ Not surprisingly, glaciers have a cooling effect on their surroundings, so wear layers and bring gloves and rain gear.

■ Glaciers can powerfully reflect sunlight, even on cloudy days. Sunscreen, sunglasses, and a brimmed hat are essential.

■ Warm, thick-soled waterproof footwear is a must. Crampons are highly recommended.

■ Don't forget to bring a camera and binoculars (preferably waterproof).

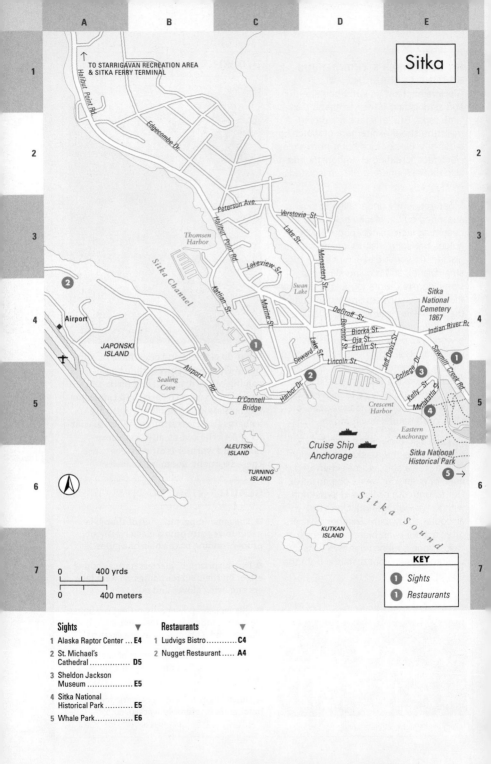

Sitka

TO STARRIGAVAN RECREATION AREA
& SITKA FERRY TERMINAL

Halibut Point Rd.

Edgecombe Dr.

Peterson Ave.

Verstovia St.

Lake St.

Thomsen
Harbor

Halibut Point Rd.

Lakeview St.

Monastery St.

Sitka Channel

Karlian St.

Swan
Lake

Sitka
National
Cemetery
1867

DeGroff St.

Airport

Marine St.

Biorka St.

Indian River Rd.

JAPONSKI
ISLAND

Oja St.

Etolin St.

Baranof St.

Seward St.

Lake St.

Jeff Davis St.

Sawmill Creek Rd.

Sealing
Cove

Airport Rd.

Lincoln St.

College Dr.

Kelly St.

Metlakatla St.

O'Connell
Bridge

Harbor Dr.

Crescent
Harbor

Eastern
Anchorage

ALEUTSKI
ISLAND

Cruise Ship
Anchorage

Sitka National
Historical Park

TURNING
ISLAND

Sitka Sound

KUTKAN
ISLAND

| 0 | 400 yards |
| 0 | 400 meters |

KEY

1 Sights

1 Restaurants

Sitka in wintry late-morning dawn light

the harbor and tender passengers ashore near Harrigan Centennial Hall. You can recognize the hall by the big Tlingit war canoe to the side of the building. Sitka is an extremely walkable town, and the waterfront attractions are all fairly close to the tender landing. Highliner Coffee on Seward Street offers free Wi-Fi with a coffee purchase.

TOURS
Sitka Tours

TOUR—SPORTS | Longtime local business Sitka Tours meets ferries and cruise ships and leads both bus tours and historical walks. ✉ Sitka ☎ 907/747–5800 ⊕ www.sitkatoursalaska.com.

Tribal Tours

TOUR—SPORTS | This company conducts bus and walking tours that emphasize Sitka's rich Tlingit culture and include Naa Kahídi dance performances at the Tribal Community House. ✉ Sitka ☎ 907/747–7137 ⊕ www.sitkatours.com.

VISITOR INFORMATION
CONTACTS Sitka Convention and Visitors Bureau ✉ 104 Lake St. ☎ 907/747–8604 ⊕ www.sitka.org.

 Sights

Alaska Raptor Center

ZOO | FAMILY | Above Indian Creek, a 20-minute walk from downtown, Alaska's only full-service avian hospital rehabilitates from 100 to 200 birds each year. Well-versed guides provide an introduction to the center (there's also a short video), and guests can visit with one of these majestic birds. The primary attraction is an enclosed 20,000-square-foot flight-training center, built to replicate the rain forest, where injured eagles relearn survival skills, including flying and catching salmon. Visitors watch through one-way glass windows. A large deck out back faces an open-air enclosure for eagles and other raptors whose injuries prevent them from returning to the wild. Additional mews with hawks, owls, and other birds lie along a rain-forest path.

The gift shop sells all sorts of eagle paraphernalia, the proceeds from which fund the center's programs. ✉ *1000 Raptor Way, off Sawmill Creek Rd.* ☎ *907/747-8662, 800/643-9425* ⊕ *www.alaskaraptor.org* 🗐 *$13* 🕙 *No tours Oct.–Apr.*

St. Michael's Cathedral

RELIGIOUS SITE | One of Southeast's best-known landmarks, the onion-dome cathedral is so treasured by locals that in 1966, as a fire engulfed the building, townspeople risked their lives and rushed inside to rescue precious Russian icons, religious objects, and vestments. An almost exact replica of St. Michael's was completed in 1976. Today you can view what may well be the largest collection of Russian icons in the United States, among them *Our Lady of Sitka* (also known as the *Sitka Madonna*) and the *Christ Pantocrator* (*Christ the World Judge*), displayed on the altar screen. ✉ *240 Lincoln St.* ☎ *907/747-8120* ⊕ *stmichaelcathedral.org.*

Sheldon Jackson Museum

MUSEUM | This octagonal museum that dates from 1895 contains priceless Alaska Native items collected by Dr. Sheldon Jackson (1834–1909), who traveled the remote regions of Alaska as an educator and missionary. The collection represents every Alaska Native culture. On display are carved masks, Chilkat blankets, dogsleds, kayaks, and even the impressive helmet worn by Chief Katlian during an 1804 battle against the Russians. The museum's small but well-stocked gift shop carries books, paper goods, and handicrafts created by Alaska Native artists. ✉ *104 College Dr.* ☎ *907/747-8981* ⊕ *www.museums.state.ak.us* 🗐 *$7 mid-May–mid-Sept., $5 mid-Sept.–mid-May* 🕙 *Closed Sun. and Mon.*

★ Sitka National Historical Park

MUSEUM | The main building at this 113-acre park houses a small museum with fascinating historical exhibits and photos of Tlingit Native culture. Highlights include a brass peace hat given to the Sitka Kiksádi by Russian traders in the early 1800s and Chilkat robes. Head to the theater to watch a 12-minute video about Russian–Tlingit conflict in the 19th century. Ask a ranger to point you toward the Centennial Totem Pole, installed in 2011 to honor the park's 100th anniversary. Also here is where Native artisans demonstrate silversmithing, weaving, wood carving, and basketry. Make an effort to strike up a conversation with the artists; they're on-site to showcase and discuss their work and Tlingit cultural traditions. At the far end of the building are seven totems (some more than a century old) that have been brought indoors to protect them from decay. Behind the center a wide, 2-mile path winds through the forest and along the shore of Sitka Sound. Scattered along the way are some of the most skillfully carved Native totem poles in Alaska. Keep going on the trail to see spawning salmon from the footbridge over Indian River. In summer, Park Service rangers lead themed walks that focus on the Russian–Tlingit conflict, the area's natural history, and the park's totem poles. ✉ *106 Metlakatla St.* ☎ *907/747-0110 visitor center* ⊕ *www.nps.gov/sitk* 🗐 *Free.*

Whale Park

CITY PARK | FAMILY | This small waterside park sits in the trees 4 miles east of Sitka right off Sawmill Creek Road. Boardwalk paths lead to five viewing platforms and steps lead down to the rocky shoreline. A gazebo next to the parking area contains signs describing the whales that visit Silver Bay, and you can listen to their sounds from recordings and an offshore hydrophone. ✉ *Sawmill Creek Rd.*

🍴 Restaurants

★ Ludvig's Bistro

$$$ | MEDITERRANEAN | Food lovers pack into Ludvig's to sample chef-owner Colette Nelson's remarkably creative cuisine, which means there's often a wait, but rest assured that your meal will

Did You Know?

Individual elements of totem poles can be interpreted with some specificity—the two bottom faces on this Heida house post in Sitka, for example, represent the passing of information between generations—but traditionally, it's thought that no one can fully interpret a single totem's interconnected stories except the carver.

be worth it. The interior evokes an Italian bistro, with rich yellow walls and copper-topped tables. **Known for:** king salmon and scallops; great reputation throughout the region; wine list. $ *Average main: $26* ✉ *256 Katlian St.* ☎ *907/966–3663* ⊕ *www.ludvigsbistro.com* ⊘ *Closed Sun., mid-Sept.–Apr.*

Nugget Restaurant

$ | AMERICAN | Travelers flying out of Sitka's airport repair to the Nugget while hoping their jet will arrive through the pea-soup fog outside. The Nugget serves American classics for breakfast, lunch, and dinner, but the homemade pies are the real attraction. **Known for:** homemade pie; better-than-usual airport dining; Friday night prime rib. $ *Average main: $12* ✉ *Sitka Airport Terminal, 600 Airport Dr.* ☎ *907/966–2480.*

Shopping

Artist Cove Gallery

ART GALLERIES | Works by Alaska Native artists from Sitka and remote villages are the focus at this gallery that carries basketry, jewelry, and dolls. ✉ *241 Lincoln St.* ☎ *907/747–6990.*

Sitka Rose Gallery

ART GALLERIES | In an 1895 Victorian next to the Bishop's House, the gallery, Sitka's most charming shop, sells Alaskan paintings, sculptures, Native art, and jewelry. ✉ *419 Lincoln St.* ☎ *907/747–3030, 888/236–1536* ⊕ *www.sitkarosegallery. com.*

WinterSong Soap Company

GIFTS/SOUVENIRS | The colorful and scented soaps sold at this shop near St. Michael's Cathedral are handcrafted on the premises. ✉ *321 Lincoln St.* ☎ *907/747–8949, 888/819–8949* ⊕ *www. wintersongsoap.com.*

Activities

FISHING

Sitka is home to a fleet of charter boats. The Sitka Convention and Visitors Bureau website ⊕ *visitsitka.org* has descriptions of and links to several dozen sportfishing operators.

The Boat Company

FISHING | This outfitter offers multiday wildlife-watching and fishing trips departing from Sitka and Juneau. ✉ *Sitka* ☎ *360/697–4242, 877/647–8268* ⊕ *www. theboatcompany.org.*

SEA KAYAKING

Sitka Sound Ocean Adventures

BOATING | The guide company's waterfront operation is easy to find: just look for the big blue bus at Crescent Harbor next to Sitka Historical Society. Sitka Sound runs various guided kayak trips through the mysterious and beautiful outer islands off the coast of Sitka. Guides help new-to-the-area paddlers understand Sitka Sound's wonders, and for day trips the company packs a great picnic. Experienced paddlers who want to go it alone can rent gear. ✉ *Harbor Dr., at Centennial Hall* ☎ *907/752–0660* ⊕ *www.kayaksitka. com* From $79.

WHALE WATCHING

Allen Marine Tours

BOATING | One of Southeast's largest and best-known tour operators leads several boat-based Sitka Sound tours throughout the summer. The Wildlife Quest tours provide a fine opportunity to view humpback whales, sea otters, puffins, eagles, and brown bears in a spectacular setting. When seas are calm enough, Allen Marine conducts a tour to the bird sanctuary at St. Lazaria Islands National Wildlife Refuge. Private catamaran tours for up to six guests can also be arranged. ✉ *1512 Sawmill Creek Rd.* ☎ *907/747–8100, 888/747–8101* ⊕ *www.allenmarine-tours.com* Call for rates.

Haines from Skagway

If your cruise ship stops only in Skagway, you can catch a fast catamaran to Haines for a delightful day away from the crowds. **Haines-Skagway Fast Ferry** (☎ 907/766–2100 or 888/766–2103) provides a passenger catamaran ferry between Skagway and Haines ($72 round-trip, and 45 minutes each way), with several runs a day in summer. **Alaska Fjordlines** (☎ 907/766–3395 or 800/320–0146 ⊕ www.alaskafjordlines.com) operates a high-speed catamaran from Skagway and Haines to Juneau and back ($169 round-trip), stopping along the way to watch whales and other marine mammals in Lynn Canal. The morning catamaran leaves Haines at 8:30, and the connecting bus from Auke Bay arrives in Juneau at noon. Passengers are back in Haines by 7:30 pm. Check your itinerary carefully to make sure you'll return before your ship's scheduled departure.

Skagway

Located at the northern terminus of the Inside Passage, Skagway is only a one-hour ferry ride from Haines. The town is an amazingly preserved artifact from North America's biggest, most-storied gold rush. Most of the downtown district forms part of the Klondike Gold Rush National Historical Park, a unit of the National Park System dedicated to commemorating and interpreting the frenzied stampede of 1897 that extended to Dawson City in Canada's Yukon.

Nearly all the historic sights are within a few blocks of the cruiseship and ferry dock, allowing visitors to meander through the town's attractions at whatever pace they choose. Whether you're disembarking from a cruise ship, a ferry, or a dusty automobile fresh from the Golden Circle, you'll quickly discover that tourism is the lifeblood of this town. Unless you're visiting in winter or hiking into the backcountry on the Chilkoot Trail, you aren't likely to find a quiet Alaska experience around Skagway.

COMING ASHORE

Skagway is a major stop for cruise ships in Alaska, and this little town sometimes has four large ships in port at once. Some dock a short stroll from downtown, others a half mile away at the Railroad Dock, where city buses are waiting to provide transportation to the center of town. The charge is $2 one-way or $5 for a day pass.

Virtually all the shops and gold-rush sights are along Broadway, the main strip that leads from the visitor center through the middle of town. It's a nice walk from the docks up through Broadway, but you can also take tours in horse-drawn surreys, antique limousines, and modern vans. Glacial Smoothies on 3rd Avenue has Wi-Fi.

TOURS
Skagway Street Car Company
TOUR—SPORTS | Revisit the gold-rush days in modern restorations of the bright yellow 1920s sightseeing buses with Skagway Street Car Company. Costumed conductors lead these popular 90-minute tours, but advance reservations are recommended for independent travelers, since most seats are sold aboard cruise

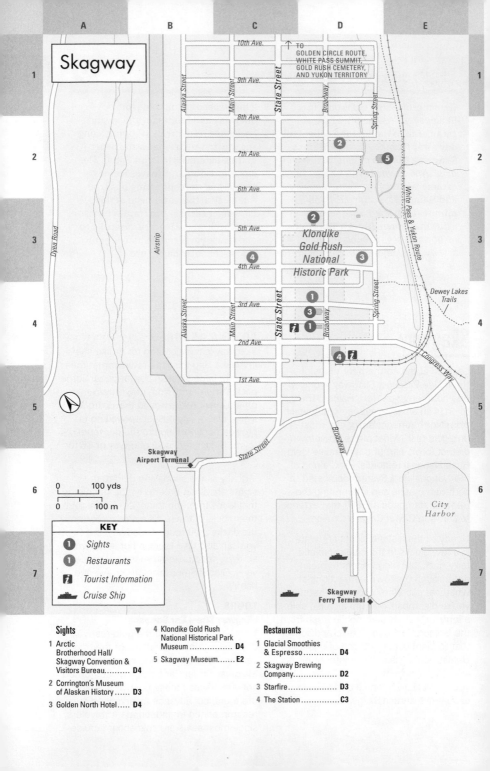

Skagway

ships. Call a week ahead in peak season to reserve a space. ✉ *270 2nd Ave.* ☎ *907/983–2908* ⊕ *www.skagwaystreetcar.com.*

TRAIN EXCURSIONS

Skagway offers one of the few opportunities to drive in the region. Take the Alaska Highway to the Canadian Yukon's Whitehorse and then drive on Klondike Highway to the Alaska Panhandle. Southeast Alaska's only railroad, the White Pass and Yukon Route, operates several different tours departing from Skagway, Fraser, British Columbia, and on some days, Carcross, Yukon. The tracks follow the historic path over the White Pass summit—a mountain-climbing, cliff-hanging route of as far as 67½ miles each way. Bus connections are available at Fraser to Whitehorse, Yukon. While the route is primarily for visitors, some locals use the service for transportation between Skagway and Whitehorse.

CONTACTS White Pass and Yukon Route ☎ *907/983–2217, 800/343–7373* ⊕ *www.wpyr.com.*

VISITOR INFORMATION

CONTACTS Skagway Convention and Visitors Bureau ☎ *907/983–2854, 888/762–1898* ⊕ *www.skagway.com.*

 Sights

Arctic Brotherhood Hall

BUILDING | The local members of the Arctic Brotherhood, a fraternal organization of Alaska and Yukon pioneers, built their hall's (now renovated) false front out of 8,833 pieces of driftwood and flotsam from local beaches. The result: one of the most unusual buildings in all of Alaska. The AB Hall now houses the **Skagway Convention and Visitors Bureau,** along with public restrooms. ✉ *Broadway between 2nd and 3rd Aves.* ☎ *907/983–2854, 888/762–1898 message only* ⊕ *www.skagway.com.*

Skagway Best Bets

■ **Riding the White Pass and Yukon Route.** Winding upward through unparalleled scenery and steep-sided gorges to the breathtaking summit of White Pass, the route remains an engineering marvel.

■ **Klondike Gold Rush National Historical Park.** This marvelous collection of museums and landmarks spread throughout downtown will immerse you in the rough-and-tumble spirit of yesteryear.

■ **Shopping.** From scrimshaw to silver, Skagway's shops offer huge collections of art, jewelry, and crafts.

Corrington's Museum of Alaskan History

MUSEUM | Inside a gift shop, this impressive (and free) scrimshaw museum highlights more than 40 exquisitely carved walrus tusks and other exhibits that detail Alaska's history. Dennis Corrington, a onetime Iditarod Race runner, and the founder of the museum, is often present. A bright flower garden decorates the exterior. ✉ *5th Ave. and Broadway* ☎ *907/983–2579* ✉ *Free.*

Golden North Hotel

HOTEL—SIGHT | Built during the 1898 gold rush, the Golden North Hotel was—until closing in 2002—Alaska's oldest hotel. Despite the closure, the building has been lovingly maintained and still retains its gold rush–era appearance; a golden dome tops the corner cupola. Today the downstairs houses shops. ✉ *3rd Ave. and Broadway.*

Klondike Gold Rush National Historical Park Museum

MUSEUM | Housed in the former White Pass and Yukon Route Depot, this

Travel the White Pass and Yukon route via train out of Skagway.

wonderful museum contains exhibits, photos, and artifacts from the White Pass and Chilkoot trails. It's a must-see for anyone planning on taking a White Pass train ride, driving the nearby Klondike Highway, or hiking the Chilkoot Trail. Films, ranger talks, and walking tours are offered. Special free Robert Service poetry performances by Buckwheat Donahue—a beloved local character and head of the Skagway Convention and Visitors Bureau—occasionally take place at the visitor center next door. ⊠ *2nd Ave., south of Broadway* ☎ *907/983–2921, 907/983–9224* ⊕ *www.nps.gov/klgo* ⊠ *Free.*

Skagway Museum

MUSEUM | This nicely designed museum—also known as the Trail of '98 Museum—occupies the ground floor of the beautiful building that also houses Skagway City Hall. Inside, you'll find a 19th-century Tlingit canoe (one of only two like it on the West Coast), historic photos, a red-and-black sleigh, and other gold rush–era artifacts, along with a healthy collection of contemporary local art and post–gold rush history exhibits. ⊠ *7th Ave. and Spring St.* ☎ *907/983–2420* ⊠ *$2.*

Restaurants

Glacial Smoothies and Espresso

$ | CAFÉ | Prices are steeper at this local hangout than at some coffee shops, but the ingredients are fresh and local, and nearly everything on the menu is made on-site. Customers can cool down with a Mango Madness or Blueberry Blues smoothie, and soft-serve ice cream in summer. **Known for:** fresh fruit smoothies; locally sourced ingredients; soup and sandwich combo. ⑤ *Average main: $7* ⊠ *336 3rd Ave.* ☎ *907/983–3223* ⊕ *www. glacialsmoothies.com* ⊗ *No dinner.*

Skagway Brewing Company

$$ | AMERICAN | Though beer is the primary business of Skagway Brewing, this local pub has a diverse dinner menu that includes burgers, halibut and chips, pasta dishes, hearty salads, and vegetarian options such as falafel. Whatever you

order, sampling the locally made ale is a must; Skagway's five staples are Prospector Pale, Chilkoot Trail IPA, Boom Town Brown, Blue Top Porter, and Spruce Tip Blonde Ale. **Known for:** beer samplers; burger night; crowded with locals. ⑤ *Average main: $17* ✉ *730 Broadway* ☎ *907/983–2739* ⊕ *www.skagwaybrewing.com* ⊙ *No lunch in winter.*

★ **Starfire**

$$ | **THAI** | A popular spot with the locals, and known to attract repeat customers from as far away as Juneau, this Thai restaurant fills up very quickly in the summer around dinner hour; it's best to call ahead. One reason for the crowds is the authenticity of the traditional Thai cuisine; Starfire's American chef learned his recipes during visits to Thailand, where he watched local friends and their grandmothers at work in their kitchens. **Known for:** gang dang red curry; fresh herbs grown on-site; outdoor dining. ⑤ *Average main: $17* ✉ *4th Ave. and Spring St.* ☎ *907/983–3663* ⊕ *www.starfirealaska.com* ⊙ *Closed in winter.*

The Station

$ | **AMERICAN** | Housed in a former gas station, this year-round restaurant is known for its comfort-food specials. The huge calzones are stuffed and served piping hot with sides of house marinara and ranch dressing—build your own or choose one of the chef's creations. **Known for:** build-your-own calzones; cheesy bread; friendly local staff. ⑤ *Average main: $10* ✉ *444 4th St.* ☎ *907/983–2200* ⊕ *skagwayhotelandrestaurant.com/station.*

🛍 Shopping

Alaska Artworks

CRAFTS | For those in search of locally produced silver jewelry, watercolor prints, and other handmade crafts, this artist-owned shop is a good place to start. ✉ *510 Broadway* ☎ *907/983–3443* ⊕ *alaskaartworks.com* ⊙ *Closed Sept.–Apr.*

Skaguay News Depot & Books

BOOKS/STATIONERY | This small but quaint bookstore carries Alaska titles, children's books, magazines, maps, and gifts. Its moniker is a throwback to the town name's former spelling. The owner, Jeff Brady, ran the local newspaper, the *Skagway News,* for more than 30 years. ✉ *264 Broadway* ☎ *907/983–3354* ⊕ *www.skagwaybooks.com.*

🏃 Activities

DOGSLEDDING
Temsco Helicopters

TOUR—SPORTS | This company flies passengers to Denver Glacier for an hour of learning about mushing and riding on a dogsled. Guided tours of other area glaciers are also conducted. ✉ *901 Terminal Way* ☎ *907/983–2900, 866/683–2900* ⊕ *www.temscoair.com* 🖃 *Check with your cruise line or call for prices.*

HIKING
Packer Expeditions

TOUR—SPORTS | This company offers guided hikes on wilderness trails not accessible by road. One trip includes a helicopter flight, a 2-mile hike toward the Laughton Glacier, and a one-hour ride back to town on the White Pass Railroad. A longer hike on the same trail uses the train for access in both directions and includes time hiking on the glacier. They also guide kayaking trips on Lake Bernard, part of the waterways utilized by the gold stampeders in the 1890s. ✉ *4th Ave. and State St.* ☎ *907/983–3005* ⊕ *www.packerexpeditions.com* 🖃 *Check with your cruise line or call for prices.*

Tracy Arm

Tracy Arm and its sister fjord, Endicott Arm, have become staples on many Inside Passage cruises. Ships sail into the arm just before or after a visit to Juneau, 50 miles to the north. A day of scenic cruising in Tracy Arm is a lesson in geology and the forces that shape Alaska. The fjord was carved by a glacier eons ago, leaving behind sheer granite cliffs. Waterfalls continue the process of erosion that the glaciers began. Very small ships may nudge their bows under the waterfalls so crew members can fill pitchers full of glacial runoff. It's a unique Alaska refreshment. Tracy Arm's glaciers haven't disappeared, though; they've just receded, and at the very end of Tracy Arm you'll come to two of them, known as the twin Sawyer Glaciers. Because the glaciers constantly shed enormous blocks of ice, navigating the passage is sometimes difficult, which can prevent ships from reaching the glacier's face.

Valdez

Valdez (pronounced val- *deez*) is the largest of the Prince William Sound communities. This year-round ice-free port was the entry point for people and goods going to the Interior during the gold rush. Today that flow has been reversed, as Valdez Harbor is the southern terminus of the Trans-Alaska Pipeline, which carries crude oil from Prudhoe Bay and surrounding oil fields nearly 800 miles to the north. This region, with its dependence on commercial fishing, is still feeling the aftereffects of the massive oil spill in 1989. Much of Valdez looks modern, because the business area was relocated and rebuilt after its destruction by the 1964 Good Friday earthquake. Even though the town is younger than the rest of developed Alaska, it's acquiring a lived-in look.

COMING ASHORE

Ships tie up at one of the world's largest floating container docks. About 3 miles from the heart of town, the dock is used not only for cruise ships but also for cargo ships loading with timber and other products bound for markets "outside" (that's what Alaskans call the rest of the world). Ship-organized motor coaches meet you on the pier and provide transportation into town. Cabs and car-rental services will also provide transportation from the pier, and individualized tours of the area can be arranged with the cab dispatcher. Several local ground- and adventure-tour operators meet passengers as well. It is also a popular excursion from Anchorage, about 5½ hours away by car.

VISITOR INFORMATION

Once in town, you find that Valdez is a very compact community. Motor coaches generally drop passengers at the Visitor Bureau.

CONTACTS Valdez Visitor's Center ✉ *309 Fairbanks Dr.* ☎ *907/835–2984* ⊕ *www. valdezalaska.org.*

Sights

Columbia Glacier A visit to Columbia Glacier, which flows from the surrounding Chugach Mountains, should definitely be on your Valdez agenda. Its deep aquamarine face is 5 miles across, and it calves icebergs with resounding cannonades. This glacier is one of the largest and most readily accessible of Alaska's coastal glaciers. The state ferry travels past its face, and scheduled tours of the glaciers and the rest of the sound are available by boat and aircraft from Valdez, Cordova, and Whittier. ✉ *Valdez* ⊕ *www.alaska.org/ detail/columbia-glacier.*

Maxine & Jesse Whitney Museum

MUSEUM | This museum contains one of the largest collections of Alaska Native artifacts. Over the course of several decades, Maxine Whitney, a gift-shop owner, amassed the ivory and baleen pieces, masks, dolls, fur garments, and other objects on display. Whitney donated her collection to Prince William Sound Community College in 1998; the museum is adjacent to the college. ✉ *Prince William Community College, 303 Lowe St.*

☎ *907/834–1690* ⊕ *mjwhitneymuseum. org* ✉ *Free* ☽ *Closed Oct.–Apr.*

Valdez Museum & Historical Archive
MUSEUM | FAMILY | The museum has two sections, the Egan and the Hazelet, named after their respective streets. The highlights of the Hazelet include a 35- by 40-foot model of what Old Town looked like before the 1964 earthquake and artifacts of the historic event that registered 9.5 on the Richter scale. An award-winning film that screens often describes the quake. Two blocks away, the Egan explores the lives, livelihoods, and events significant to Valdez and surrounding regions. On display are a restored 1880s Gleason & Baily hand-pump fire engine, a 1907 Ahrens steam fire engine, and a 19th-century saloon, and there are exhibits about local Alaska Native culture, early explorers, bush pilots, and the 1989 oil spill. Every summer the museum hosts an exhibit of quilts and fiber arts made by local and regional artisans, and other exhibits are presented seasonally. ✉ *217 Egan Dr.* ☎ *907/835–2764 Egan Dr., 907/835–407 S. Hazelet Ave.* ⊕ *www. valdezmuseum.org* ✉ *$9.*

🍴 Restaurants

MacMurray's Alaska Halibut House
$$ | SEAFOOD | At this very casual family-owned establishment you order at the counter, sit at the Formica-covered tables, and check out the photos of local fishing boats. The battered halibut is excellent—light and not greasy. **Known for:** old-school fish-and-chips; relaxed atmosphere; amazing fried halibut. ⑤ *Average main: $15* ✉ *208 Meals Ave.* ☎ *907/835–2788* ☽ *Closed Sun.*

🏃 Activities

GLACIER TRIPS
Dean Cummings' H2O Guides
TOUR—SPORTS | Top-notch heli-skiing and snowboarding experiences are H2O's

Valdez Best Bets

5

Ports of Call VALDEZ

■ **Touring the Sound.** Take a tour of Prince William Sound and get a seaside view of the Alyeska Pipeline terminal, where the 800-mile-long Trans-Alaska Pipeline loads oil into huge tanker ships.

■ **Kayaking.** Several local companies offer sea-kayaking tours of varying lengths and degrees of difficulty.

■ **Glacier Hiking.** Worthington Glacier State Park at Thompson Pass is a roadside attraction.

specialty. For more than two decades, this company has been providing access to an amazing 150-square-mile playground. ✉ *Valdez* ☎ *907/835–8418* ⊕ *www.alaskahelicopterskiing.com.*

SEA KAYAKING
Anadyr Adventures
TOUR—SPORTS | For more than a quarter century this company has led sea-kayak trips into Alaska's most spectacular wilderness, Prince William Sound. Guides will escort you on day trips, multiday camping trips, "mother ship" adventures based in a remote anchorage, or lodge-based trips for the ultimate combination of adventure by day and comfort by night. If you're already an experienced kayaker, Anadyr will outfit you and you can travel on your own. Also available are guided hiking and glacier trips, ice caving at Valdez Glacier, soft-adventure charter-boat trips in the sound, and water-taxi service to or from anywhere on the eastern side of the sound. ✉ *225 N. Harbor Dr.* ☎ *907/835–2814, 800/865–2925* ⊕ *www.anadyradventures.com* ✉ *Day trips from $79.*

WILDLIFE VIEWING

Lu-Lu Belle Glacier Wildlife Tours

BOATING | The "Limousine of the Prince William Sound," Valdez-based *Lu-Lu Belle* sets sail on small-group whale-watching and wildlife-viewing cruises that also goes up close to the massive Columbia Glacier. Cruises last about seven hours. There's a snack bar onboard, but it's good to pack a lunch, too. ⊠ *Valdez* ☎ *800/411–0090* ⊕ *www.lulubelletours. com* ⊠ *$140.*

Victoria, British Columbia

Although Victoria isn't in Alaska, it's a port of call for many ships cruising the Inside Passage. Despite its role as the provincial capital, Victoria was largely bypassed, economically, by Vancouver throughout the 20th century. This, as it turns out, was all to the good, helping to preserve Victoria's historic downtown and keeping the city free of freeways. For much of the 20th century Victoria was marketed to tourists as "The Most British City in Canada," and it still has more than its share of Anglo-themed pubs, tea shops, and double-decker buses. These days, however, Victorians prefer to celebrate their combined indigenous, Asian, and European heritage, and the city's stunning wilderness backdrop. Locals do often venture out for afternoon tea, but they're just as likely to nosh on dim sum or tapas. Decades-old shops sell imported linens and tweeds, but newer upstarts offer local designs in hemp and organic cotton. And let's not forget that fabric favored by locals: Gore-Tex. The outdoors is ever present here. You can hike, bike, kayak, sail, or whale-watch straight from the city center, and forests, beaches, offshore islands, and wilderness parklands lie just minutes away.

COMING ASHORE

Only the smallest excursion vessels dock downtown in Victoria's Inner Harbour. Cruise ships tie up at the Ogden Point cruise-ship terminal (⊕ *www.gvha. ca*), 2.4 km (1½ miles) from the Inner Harbour, and a few pocket cruise ships moor at Sidney, 29 km (18 miles) north of Victoria. When ships are in port a shuttle bus makes trips between Ogden Point and downtown Victoria at least every 20 minutes; the last shuttle from downtown leaves one hour prior to scheduled ship departures from the port. The C$12 shuttle fare allows you to make as many return trips as you like. The walk downtown is pleasant and will take 20 to 30 minutes.

GETTING AROUND

Most points of interest are within walking distance of the Inner Harbour. For those that aren't, public and private transportation is readily available. The public bus system is excellent; pick up route maps and schedules at the Victoria Visitor Information Centre. City tours by horse-drawn carriage, pedicab, and double-decker bus, as well as limousine service, are available at the cruise-ship terminal. **If you're coming from Alaska, remember to adjust your watch.** British Columbia is on Pacific Time, one hour ahead of Alaska Time.

Taxis also meet each ship, and fares run about C$1.88 per kilometer; the meter starts at C$3.25. A cab from Ogden Point to the downtown core will cost about C$10–C$12.

CONTACTS Bluebird Cabs ☎ *250/382– 2222* ⊕ *www.taxicab.com* **Yellow Cab** ☎ *250/381–2222* ⊕ *www.yellowcabvictoria.com.*

VISITOR INFORMATION

CONTACTS Victoria Visitor Information Centre ⊠ *812 Wharf St.* ☎ *250/953–2033, 800/663–3883* ⊕ *www.tourismvictoria. com.*

Sights

Victoria's heart is the Inner Harbour, always bustling with ferries, seaplanes, and yachts. In summer the waterfront comes alive with strollers, artists, and street entertainers. But the Saanich Peninsula, home to the BC and Washington State ferry terminals as well as the Victoria International Airport, is the first part of Vancouver Island that most visitors see. Bus tours to the Butchart Gardens run several times a day, and many tours take in other sights in the area such as **Butterfly Gardens**; several companies also offer winery tours. If you're driving or bicycling (Victoria is Canada's cycling capital), be sure to include the picturesque seaside town of Sidney.

Abkhazi Garden and Teahouse

GARDEN | Called "the garden that love built," this once-private garden is as fascinating for its history as for its innovative design. The seeds were planted, figuratively, in Paris in the 1920s, when Englishwoman Peggy Pemberton-Carter met exiled Georgian Prince Nicholas Abkhazi. World War II internment camps (his in Germany, hers near Shanghai) interrupted their romance, but they reunited and married in Victoria in 1946. They spent the next 40 years together cultivating their garden. Rescued from developers and now operated by the Land Conservancy of British Columbia, the 1-acre site is recognized as a leading example of West Coast horticultural design, resplendent with native Garry Oak trees, Japanese maples, and mature rhododendrons. The teahouse (⊕ *www. abkhaziteahouse.com*), in the parlor of the modernist home, serves lunch and afternoon tea daily until 4 pm, with reduced hours in winter. ☒ *1964 Fairfield Rd., Fairfield* ☎ *778/265–6466* ⊕ *www. conservancy.bc.ca* ☒ *C$10* ⊙ *Closed Mon. and Tues. during Oct.–Mar.*

Victoria Best Bets

■ Most cruise ships visit Victoria in the late afternoon and evening, which is an ideal time for a stroll around the city's compact downtown, or the splendid 55-acre Butchart Gardens.

■ Victoria's other main attraction is the city center itself, with its street entertainers, yachts at harbor, cafés, funky little shops, intriguing museums, and illuminated Victorian architecture.

■ A promenade around the Inner Harbour.

★ Butchart Gardens

GARDEN | This stunning 55-acre garden and National Historic Site has been drawing visitors since it was started in a limestone quarry in 1904. Highlights include the dramatic 70-foot Ross Fountain, the formal Japanese garden, and the intricate Italian garden complete with a gelato stand. Kids will love the old-fashioned carousel and will likely enjoy the 45-min uto miniboat tours around Tod Inlet. From mid-June to mid-September the gardens are illuminated at night with hundreds of hidden lights. In July and August, jazz, blues, and classical musicians play at an outdoor stage each evening, and fireworks draw crowds every Saturday night. The wheelchair- and stroller-accessible site is also home to a seed-and-gift shop, a plant identification center, two restaurants (one offering traditional afternoon tea), and a coffee shop; you can even call ahead for a picnic basket on fireworks nights. To avoid crowds, come at opening time, in the late afternoon or evening (except ultrabusy fireworks Saturday evenings), or between September and June, when the gardens are still stunning

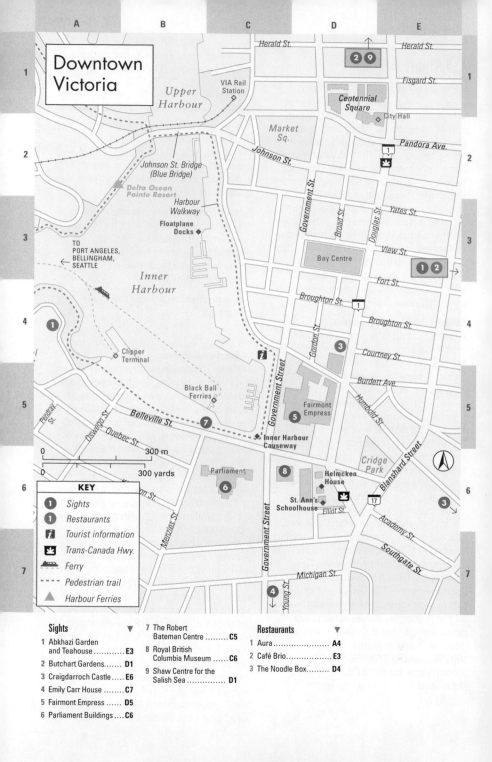

Downtown Victoria

and admission rates are reduced. The grounds are especially magical at Christmas, with themed lighting and an ice rink. The gardens are a 20-minute drive north of Downtown; parking is free but fills up on fireworks Saturdays. You can get here by city Bus #75 from Douglas Street in Downtown Victoria, but service is slow and infrequent. **CVS Tours** (877/578–5552 www.cvstours.com) runs shuttles from Downtown Victoria. ⊠ 800 Benvenuto Ave., Brentwood Bay ☎ 250/652–5256, 866/652–4422 ⊕ www. butchartgardens.com ⌨ C$32 ⌕ Rates are lower between Sept. and mid June.

★ Craigdarroch Castle

CASTLE/PALACE | This magnificent and somewhat imposing mansion, complete with turrets and Gothic rooflines, was built as the home of one of British Columbia's wealthiest men, coal baron Robert Dunsmuir, who died in 1889, just a few months before the castle's completion. It's now a museum depicting life in the late 1800s. The castle's 39 rooms have ornate Victorian furnishings, stained-glass windows, carved woodwork, and a beautifully restored painted ceiling in the drawing room. A winding staircase climbs four floors to a tower overlooking Victoria. Castles run in the family: son James went on to build the more lavish Hatley Castle west of Victoria. The castle is not wheelchair accessible and has no elevators. ⊠ 1050 Joan Crescent, Rockland ☎ 250/592–5323 ⊕ www.thecastle. ca ⌨ C$14.95.

Emily Carr House

LOCAL INTEREST | One of Canada's most celebrated artists and a respected writer, Emily Carr (1871–1945) lived in this extremely proper, wooden Victorian house before she abandoned her middle-class life to live in the wilds of British Columbia. Carr's own descriptions, from her autobiography Book of Small, were used to restore the house. Art on display includes reproductions of Carr's

work—visit the Art Gallery of Greater Victoria or the Vancouver Art Gallery to see the originals. ⊠ 207 Government St., James Bay, Downtown ☎ 250/383–5843 ⊕ www.emilycarr.com ⌨ C$6.75 ⊗ Closed Sun.–Mon. May–Sept; Closed Oct.–Apr.

Fairmont Empress

BUILDING | Opened in 1908 by the Canadian Pacific Railway, the Empress is one of the grand château-style railroad hotels that grace many Canadian cities. Designed by Francis Rattenbury, who also designed the Parliament Buildings across the way, the solid Edwardian grandeur of the Empress has made it a symbol of the city. The elements that made the hotel an attraction for travelers in the past—old-world architecture, ornate decor, and a commanding view of the Inner Harbour—are still here although they exude a fresh, contemporary air. Nonguests can reserve ahead for afternoon tea (the dress code is smart casual) in the chandelier-draped Tea Lobby, meet for Pimm's cocktails or enjoy superb Pacific Northwest cuisine at the Q Lounge and Restaurant, or enjoy a treatment at the hotel's Willow Stream spa. In summer, lunch, snacks, and cocktails are served on the veranda overlooking the Inner Harbour. ⊠ 721 Government St., Downtown ☎ 250/384–8111, 250/389–2727 tea reservations ⊕ www. fairmont.com/empress ⌨ Free; afternoon tea C$63.

Parliament Buildings

BUILDING | Officially the British Columbia Provincial Legislative Assembly Buildings, these massive stone structures are more popularly referred to as the Parliament Buildings. Designed by Francis Rattenbury (who also designed the Fairmont Empress Hotel) when he was just 25 years old, and completed in 1897, they dominate the Inner Harbour. Atop the central dome is a gilded statue of Captain George Vancouver (1757–98), the first

The Butchart Gardens, Victoria, British Columbia

European to sail around Vancouver Island. A statue of Queen Victoria (1819–1901) reigns over the front of the complex. More than 3,300 lights outline the buildings at night. The interior is lavishly done with stained-glass windows, gilt moldings, and historic photographs, and in summer actors play historic figures from British Columbia's past. When the legislature is in session, you can sit in the public gallery and watch British Columbia's democracy at work (custom has the opposing parties sitting 2½ sword lengths apart). Free, informative, 30- to 45-minute tours run every 20 to 30 minutes in summer and several times a day in the off-season (less frequently if school groups or private tours are coming through). Tours are obligatory on summer weekends (mid-May until Labor Day) and optional the rest of the time. Self guided booklets are available online. ⊠ *501 Belleville St., James Bay, Downtown* ☎ *250/387–3046* ⊕ *www.leg.bc.ca* ⊠ *Free.*

★ **The Robert Bateman Centre**
MUSEUM | Opened in 2013 in a historic waterfront structure, this small but impressive gallery displays more than 100 works—from etchings to paintings—spanning seven decades in the career of Canada's best-known wildlife artist. One gallery, where paintings are matched to birdsongs, is especially innovative. The building, Victoria's original steamship terminal, is also home to a waterfront restaurant and a shop selling high-end local art. Proceeds from gallery admissions go to support the Bateman Foundation's conservation work. ⊠ *470 Belleville St., James Bay* ☎ *250/940–3630* ⊕ *batemancentre.org* ⊠ *C$10.*

★ **Royal British Columbia Museum**
MUSEUM | FAMILY | This excellent museum, one of Victoria's leading attractions, traces several thousand years of British Columbian history. Especially strong is its First Peoples Gallery, home to a genuine Kwakwaka'wakw big house, an intriguing exhibit on First Nations languages, and a dramatically displayed

collection of masks and other artifacts. The Natural History Gallery traces British Columbia's landscapes, from prehistory to modern-day climate change, in realistic dioramas. An *Ocean Station* exhibit gets kids involved in running a Jules Verne–style submarine. In the History Gallery, a replica of Captain Vancouver's HMS *Discovery* creaks convincingly, and a re-created frontier town comes to life with cobbled streets, silent movies, and the rumble of an arriving train. An IMAX theater presents films on a six-story-tall screen. Optional one-hour tours, included in the admission price, run roughly twice a day in summer and less frequently in winter. Most focus on a particular gallery, though the 90-minute Highlights Tour touches on all galleries, and the 30-minute Behind the Scenes tour is fascinating. Special exhibits, usually held between mid-May and mid-November, attract crowds despite the higher admission prices. You can skip (sometimes very long) ticket lines by booking online. The museum complex has several more interesting sights, beyond the expected gift shop and café. In front of the museum, at Government and Belleville streets, is the **Netherlands Centennial Carillon.** With 62 bells, it's the largest bell tower in Canada; the Westminster chimes ring out every hour, and free recitals are occasionally held on Sunday afternoon. The Native Plant Garden at the museum's entrance showcases 400 indigenous plant species. Behind the main building, bordering Douglas Street, are the grassy lawns of **Thunderbird Park,** home to 10 totem poles (carved replicas of originals that are preserved in the museum). One of the oldest houses in BC, **Helmcken House** (*open late May–early Sept., daily noon–4*) was built in 1852 for pioneer doctor and statesman John Sebastian Helmcken. Inside are displays of the family's belongings, including the doctor's medical tools. Behind it is **St. Ann's School House,** built in 1858. One of British Columbia's oldest schools, it is thought

to be Victoria's oldest building still standing. Both buildings are part of the Royal British Columbia Museum. ⊠ *675 Belleville St., Downtown* ☎ *250/356–7226, 888/447–7977 museum, 877/480–4887 IMAX theater* ⊕ *www.royalbcmuseum. bc.ca* ⊠ *C$26.95, IMAX theater C$11.95; combination ticket C$36.90.*

Shaw Centre for the Salish Sea

ZOO | FAMILY | A simulated ride underwater in a deep-sea elevator is just the beginning of a visit to this fun and educational marine interpretive center. Devoted entirely to the aquatic life and conservation needs of the Salish Sea—the waters south and east of Vancouver Island—the small but modern center displays local sea life, including luminous jellyfish, bright purple starfish, wolf eels, rockfish, and octopi. Hands-on activities and touch tanks delight kids, who also love the high-tech effects, including a floor projection that ripples when stepped on and a pop-up tank you can poke your head into. ⊠ *9811 Seaport Pl., Sidney* ☎ *250/665–7511* ⊕ *www.salishseacentre.org* ⊠ *C$17.50* ☞ *Last admission 30 mins before closing.*

🍴 Restaurants

The foodie vibe and eat-local ethos here is extraordinary, and although some restaurants along the Inner Harbour lean on views over service, chances are you'll find something to please.

★ Aura

$$$$ | PACIFIC NORTHWEST | When an award-winning chef names "imagination" as his most treasured possession, you know the food here is likely to be creative, if not exquisite. The seasonal menu uses primarily local ingredients, revealing Asian influences. **Known for:** waterfront patio; local wine list; stylish dining room. ⑤ *Average main: C$31* ⊠ *Inn at Laurel Point, 680 Montreal St., James Bay, Downtown* ☎ *250/414–6739* ⊕ *www. aurarestaurant.ca.*

★ Café Brio

$$$$ | MODERN CANADIAN | This intimate yet bustling Italian villa–style room has long been a Victoria favorite, mainly because of its Mediterranean-influenced atmosphere and cuisine, which is prepared primarily with locally raised ingredients. The menu changes almost daily, but you might find local rockfish paired with peperonata (sweet roasted red onion and heirloom tomato syrup), maple-glazed quail, or even an apricot dessert soup. **Known for:** house-made charcuterie; 400-label wine list; seasonal dishes. ⑤ *Average main: C$32* ✉ *944 Fort St., Downtown* ☎ *250/383–0009, 866/270–5461* ⊕ *www.cafe-brio.com* ☾ *No lunch. Closed Jan.*

The Noodle Box

$$ | ASIAN | Noodles, whether Indonesian style with peanut sauce, thick hokkien in teriyaki, or Thai-style chow mein, are scooped straight from the open kitchen's steaming woks into bowls or cardboard take-out boxes. Malaysian-, Singapore-, and Thai-style curries run from mild to scaldingly hot. **Known for:** vegan-friendly menu; gluten-free dining. ⑤ *Average main: C$13* ✉ *818 Douglas St., Downtown* ☎ *250/384–1314* ⊕ *www.thenoodlebox.net.*

Shopping

Shopping in Victoria is easy: virtually everything is in the downtown area on or near Government Street stretching north from the Fairmont Empress Hotel. These include unexpected finds in Trounce Alley, Chinatown, and the Lower Johnson (LoJo) area. Victoria stores specializing in English imports are plentiful, though Canadian-made goods, including BC jade and First Nations work, are usually a better buy.

Artina's

JEWELRY/ACCESSORIES | Canadian-made jewelry—all handmade, one-of-a-kind pieces—fills the display cases at this unique jewelry shop. ✉ *1002 Government St., Downtown* ☎ *250/386–7000* ⊕ *www.artinas.com.*

Lower Johnson Street

SHOPPING NEIGHBORHOODS | This row of candy-color Victorian-era shopfronts in LoJo (Lower Johnson) is Victoria's hub for independent fashion boutiques. Storefronts—some closet size—are filled with local designers' wares, funky boutiques, and shops selling ecologically friendly clothes of hemp and organic cotton. Market Square (⊕ *www.marketsquare.ca*) is especially eclectic, particularly during the summer when the open courtyard fills with local vendors. ✉ *Johnson St., between Government and Store Sts., Downtown.*

Munro's Books

BOOKS/STATIONERY | Move over, Chapters-Indigo: this beautifully restored 1909 former bank now houses one of Canada's best-stocked independent bookstores. Deals abound in the remainders bin. ✉ *1108 Government St., Downtown* ☎ *250/382–2464* ⊕ *www.munrobooks.com.*

★ Silk Road

FOOD/CANDY | Tea aspires to new heights in this chic emporium at the edge of Chinatown. Shelves are stacked with more than 300 intriguing varieties; some you can enjoy in flights at an impressive tasting bar, and others have been restyled into aromatherapy remedies and spa treatments, including a green tea facial, which you can try out in the tiny spa downstairs. Or check out Silk Road's afternoon teas at The Grand Hotel (res: 250/380-4458). ✉ *1624 Government St., Downtown* ☎ *250/704–2688* ⊕ *www.silkroadtea.com.*

Wrangell

An unassuming timber and fishing community, Wrangell sits on the northern tip of Wrangell Island, near the mouth of the fast-flowing Stikine River—North America's largest undammed river. The Stikine plays a large role in the lives of many Wrangell residents, including those who grew up homesteading on the islands that pepper the area. Trips on the river with local guides are highly recommended for the insight they provide into the Stikine and a very Alaskan way of life. Like much of Southeast, Wrangell has suffered in recent years from a declining resource-based economy. But locals are working to build tourism. Bearfest celebrates Wrangell's proximity to the Anan Wildlife Observatory, where you can get a close-up view of brown and black bears.

The rough-around-the-edges town is off the track of the larger cruise ships, so it does not get the same seasonal traffic that Ketchikan and Juneau do. Hence, it is nearly devoid of the souvenir shops that dominate so many other nearby downtown areas. But the gift shops and art galleries that are here do sell locally created work, and the town is very welcoming to visitors.

COMING ASHORE

Cruise ships calling in to Wrangell dock downtown, within walking distance of the museum and gift stores. Greeters welcome you and are available to answer questions. Wrangell's few attractions—the most notable being totem-filled Chief Shakes Island—are within walking distance of the pier. The Nolan Center houses an excellent museum, and Petroglyph Beach, where rocks are imprinted with mysterious prehistoric symbols, is 1 mile from the pier. Most cruise-ship visitors see it on guided shore excursions or by taxi.

TAXIS
CONTACTS Northern Lights Taxi
☎ *907/874–4646.*

TOURS
Sunrise Aviation
TOUR—SPORTS | This charter-only air carrier flies to the Anan Wildlife Observatory, LeConte Glacier, and Forest Service cabins. ✉ *Wrangell Airport, Airport Rd.* ☎ *907/874–2319, 800/874–2311* ⊕ *www.wrangell.com/organization/sunrise-aviation.*

VISITOR INFORMATION
CONTACTS Wrangell Visitor Center
✉ *296 Campbell Dr., in Nolan Center* ☎ *907/874–2829, 800/367–9745* ⊕ *www.wrangellalaska.org.*

 Sights

Anan Wildlife Observatory A prime spot to view brown and black bears, Anan lies within the Tongass National Forest. Each summer as many as 30 or 40 bears gather at Anan Creek to feed on huge runs of pink salmon. On an average visit of about three hours you might spot bears while strolling the half-mile viewing boardwalk. Once on the platform, you will likely see many bears. For 30 minute intervals, five people at a time can slip into a photo blind, accessible from the platform, that provides opportunities to shoot close-up, stream-level images of bears catching salmon. Anan is accessible only by boat or floatplane. Passes are required from July 5 to August 25 for the limited number of visits the Forest Service permits each day. Unless you have experience navigating the Stikine by boat and in walking through bear country, it's best to visit Anan with a local guide. Most guide companies provide passes. ✉ *Wrangell ⚓ About 30 miles southeast of Wrangell* ☎ *907/874–2323 Wrangell Ranger District* ⊕ *www.wrangell.com/visitorservices/anan-bear-and-wildlife-observatory.*

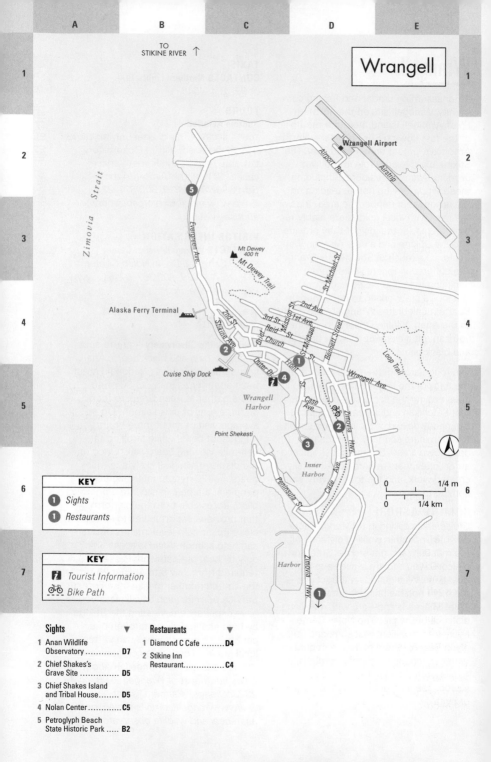

Wrangell

TO
STIKINE RIVER ↑

Wrangell Airport

Airstrip

Airport Rd

Zimovia Strait

Mt Dewey
400 ft
Mt Dewey Trail

Evergreen Ave.

Alaska Ferry Terminal

2nd Ave
St Michaels St.
3rd St.
1st Ave
Reid St.
Church St.
Front St.
2nd St.
Stikine Ave.
Grief St.
Outer Dr.

Cruise Ship Dock

Wrangell
Harbor

Point Shekesti

Case Ave.

Bennett Street
Wrangell Ave.
Loop Trail

Zimovia Hwy.
Case Ave.

Inner
Harbor

Peninsula St.

Zimovia Hwy.

Harbor

KEY

1 Sights

1 Restaurants

KEY

🛈 Tourist Information

🚲 Bike Path

0 ──── 1/4 m
0 ──── 1/4 km

Chief Shakes's Grave Site

NATIVE SITE | Buried here is Shakes V, who led the local Tlingit during the first half of the 19th century. A white picket fence surrounds the grave, and two killer-whale totem poles mark his resting spot, which overlooks the harbor. ⊠ *Case Ave.*

Chief Shakes Island and Tribal House

NATURE PRESERVE | A footbridge from the bottom of Shakes Street provides access to this small island in the center of Wrangell's protected harbor. The Tribal House, constructed in 1940 as a replica of the original 19th-century structure, was completely restored by local carvers in 2012 and 2013, as were the surrounding totem poles. The interior of the building can be viewed for a fee; arrangements should be made through Wrangell Cooperative Association ⊕ *wca-t.com.* ⊠ *Off Shakes St.* ☎ *907/874–4304* ⊕ *www.wrangell.com/visitorservices/ chief-shakes-tribal-house* 💲 *$4.*

Nolan Center

MUSEUM | The nexus of cultural life in Wrangell, the center houses the town's museum, a 200-seat combination movie theater, performance space, and convention facility, and a visitor center. Exhibits at the **Wrangell Museum** chronicle the region's rich history. On display here are the oldest known Tlingit house posts (dating from the late 18th century), decorative posts from Chief Shakes's clan house, petroglyphs, century-old spruce-root and cedar-bark baskets, masks, gold-rush memorabilia, and fascinating photographs. If you're spending any time in town, don't pass this up. The **Wrangell Visitor Center,** staffed when the museum is open, has information about local touring options. ⊠ *296 Campbell Dr.* ☎ *907/874–3699* ⊕ *www.wrangell.com/ cc/welcome-nolan-center.*

Petroglyph Beach State Historic Park

NATIONAL/STATE PARK | Scattered among other rocks at this public beach are three-dozen-or-more large stones bearing designs and pictures chiseled by unknown ancient artists. No one knows why the rocks at this curious site were etched the way they were, or even exactly how old the etchings are. You can access the beach via a boardwalk, where you'll find signs describing the site, along with carved replicas of the petroglyphs. Most of the petroglyphs are to the right between the viewing deck and a large outcropping of rock in the tidal beach area. Because the original petroglyphs can be damaged by physical contact, only photographs are permitted. But you are welcome to use the replicas to make a rubbing from rice paper and charcoal or crayons (available in local stores). ⊠ *½ mile north of ferry terminal, off Evergreen Ave.* ⊕ *dnr.alaska.gov/parks/aspunits/ southeast/wrangpetroshs.*

 Restaurants

Diamond C Cafe

$ | CAFÉ | The breakfasts at the Diamond C are just part of the attraction; the café also serves as the gathering place for locals and, really, it's fun to just sit back and listen. As you dig into the breakfast hash and other goodies, though, there's a chance you'll only have eyes for your plate. **Known for:** biscuits and gravy; casual diner vibe; generous portions. 💲 *Average main: $10* ⊠ *223 Front St.* ☎ *907/874–3677* 🕐 *No dinner.*

Stikine Inn Restaurant

$$ | AMERICAN | With views overlooking the water, the Stikine Inn's restaurant (often called the Stik) is easily the prettiest place to dine in Wrangell. Given the town's scarcity of options, the place could just assemble a get-by menu, but the salads, pizzas, burgers, and hearty soups here are seriously tasty. **Known for:** burgers; oversized desserts; views. 💲 *Average main: $15* ⊠ *107 Stikine Ave.* ☎ *907/874–3388* ⊕ *www.stikineinn.com/ dining* 🕐 *Closed Nov.–Mar.*

Shopping

Angerman's Sporting Goods

GIFTS/SOUVENIRS | This is primarily a place for locals to stock up on practical outdoor clothing and fishing gear, but Angerman's also sells souvenir T-shirts, jewelry, gifts, and other tourist items. ⊠ *2 Front St.* ☎ *907/874–3640.*

Activities

ANAN WILDLIFE VIEWING

The following Wrangell-based guide companies are authorized to run trips to Anan.

Alaska Charters and Adventures

TOUR—SIGHT | This outfit leads small group tours (six guests or fewer) to Anan for day trips of seven or eight hours. Most of the time is spent above Anan Creek on an observation deck reached via a half-mile trail. Reservations are recommended well in advance. The same company also offers whale-watching tours, kayak adventures, and fishing trips. ⊠ *Wrangell* ☎ *888/993–2750* ⊕ *www.alaskaupclose. com* ⊠ *From $328.*

Alaska Vistas

TOUR—SIGHT | Watch bears feeding on salmon at a small waterfall from an observatory deck with this reliable outfitter. Like other Anan tours, this one includes an hour-long boat ride from Wrangell. Alaska Vistas also leads rafting trips down the Stikine River along with jet-boat tours and sea-kayaking adventures. ⊠ *Box 2245* ☎ *907/874–3006, 888/874–3006* ⊕ *www.alaskavistas.com* ⊠ *From $270.*

Alaska Waters

TOUR—SIGHT | This family-owned business leads six-hour tours from late June to August. Cofounder Wilma Stokes-Leslie, who is of Tlingit and Haida descent, was born and raised in Wrangell, as were many of the other members of her team. ⊠ *7 Stikine Ave.* ☎ *907/874–2378, 800/347–4462* ⊕ *www.alaskawaters.com* ⊠ *From $290.*

BOATING

★ Breakaway Adventures

BOATING | This well-established outfitter, in business for nearly three decades, leads a variety of jet-boat trips, including a tour to Chief Shakes Glacier and the nearby hot springs. Tours can be arranged for groups of up to 50 people. You can catch one of its water taxis to Petersburg or Prince of Wales Island, as well as to one of the area's U.S. Forest Service cabins. ⊠ *City dock* ☎ *907/874–2488, 888/385–2488* ⊕ *www.breakawayadventures.com* ⊠ *From $140.*

Chapter 6

INLAND
CRUISE TOUR
DESTINATIONS

Updated by
Joey Besl and
David Cannamore

Alaska's Interior remains the last frontier, even for the Last Frontier state. The northern lights sparkle above a vast, mostly uninhabited landscape that promises adventure for those who choose to traverse it.

Come here for wildlife-rich, pristine land and hardy locals, a rich and quirky history, outdoor activities like rafting and dogsledding, nonstop daylight in the summer, or northern lights in winter. Don't forget to top off the experience with a soak in the hot springs.

The geology of the Interior played a key role in history at the turn of the 20th century. The image of early-1900s Alaska, set to the harsh tunes of countless honky-tonk saloons and the clanging of pans, is rooted around the Interior's goldfields. Gold fever struck in Circle and Eagle in the 1890s, spread into Canada's Yukon Territory in the big Klondike gold rush of 1898, headed as far west as the beaches of Nome in 1900, then came back to Alaska's Interior when Fairbanks hit pay dirt in 1903. Through it all, the broad, swift Yukon River was the rush's main highway. Flowing almost 2,300 miles from Canada to the Bering Sea, just below the Arctic Circle, it carried prospectors across the north in search of instant fortune.

Although Fairbanks has grown into a bustling city with some serious attractions, many towns and communities in the Interior seem little changed from the gold-rush days. Visiting the galleries at the Morris Thompson Cultural and Visitors Center makes it clear how intertwined the Interior's past and present lifestyles remain. When early missionaries set up schools in the Bush, the Alaska Native peoples were sent to regional centers for schooling and "salvation," but that stopped long ago, and today Interior Alaska's Native villages are thriving, with their own schools and a particularly Alaskan blend of modern life and tradition. Fort Yukon, 145 miles northeast of Fairbanks on the Arctic Circle, is the largest Athabascan village in the state, with just under 600 residents.

Alaska's current gold rush—the pipeline carrying (a little less each year) "black gold" from the oil fields in Prudhoe Bay south to the port of Valdez—snakes its way through the Interior. The Richardson Highway, which started as a gold stampeders' trail, parallels the Trans-Alaska Pipeline on its route south of Fairbanks. And gold still glitters in the Interior: Fairbanks, the site of the largest gold production in Alaska in pre–Second World War days, is home to the Fort Knox Gold Mine, which has approximately doubled Alaska's gold production. Throughout the region, with the price of gold down from its highs of a few years ago but still quite lofty, hundreds of tiny mines—from one-man operations to full-scale works—have geared up again, proving that what the poet Robert Service wrote more than a hundred years ago still holds true: "There are strange things done in the midnight sun / by the men who moil for gold."

Planning

When to Go

June and July bring near-constant sun (nothing quite like walking out of a restaurant at 11 pm into broad daylight), sometimes punctuated by afternoon cloudbursts. Like most of Alaska, many of the Interior's main attractions are seasonal, May into mid-September. A trip in May avoids the rush, but it can snow in Fairbanks in spring. Late August brings fall colors, ripe berries, active wildlife, and the start of northern lights season, with marvelous shows if you hit the right night.

Getting Here and Around

AIR TRAVEL

Beyond the highways are many Native villages reached by small airplanes making daily connections out of Fairbanks, which is the regional hub and the thriving commercial center of the Interior. Delta offers seasonal nonstop service from Fairbanks to the Lower 48. Alaska Airlines and ERA Alaska fly the Anchorage–Fairbanks route. There are hotel shuttles, rental cars, and taxis available at the Fairbanks airport.

BUS TRAVELT

The Alaska Park Connection provides regularly scheduled shuttle service between Seward, Anchorage, and Denali National Park from mid-May to mid-September. Denali Overland Transportation serves Anchorage, Talkeetna, and Denali National Park with charter bus and van service. Alaska/Yukon Trails runs between Fairbanks, Denali, Anchorage, Talkeetna, Whitehorse, and Dawson City.

COMMUTER BUSES Alaska/Yukon Trails
☎ *800/770–7275, 907/479–2277* ⊕ *www. alaskashuttle.com.*

CAR TRAVEL

Interior Alaska is sandwiched between two monumental mountain ranges: the Brooks Range to the north and the Alaska Range to the south. In such a vast wilderness many of the region's residents define their area by a limited network of two-lane highways. You really need a car in the Interior, even if you're based in Fairbanks.

Fairbanks is a sprawling city. Things are too spread out for walking; public transportation is good but service is limited. Hotels run shuttle buses to and from the airport, and you can get around by taxi, but that's going to add up fast. Save yourself some frustration and just rent a car.

The Steese Highway, the Dalton Highway, and the Taylor Highway (which is closed in winter) are well-maintained gravel roads. However, summer rain can make them slick and dangerous. ■TIP→ **Rental-car companies have varying policies on whether they allow travel on gravel roads, so check in advance.**

The George Parks Highway runs south to Denali National Park and Preserve and on to Anchorage, the state's largest city, 360 miles away on the coast. The Richardson Highway extends to the southeast to Delta Junction before turning south to Valdez, which is 368 miles from Fairbanks.

Two major routes lead north. You can take the Elliott Highway to the Dalton Highway, following the Trans-Alaska Pipeline to its origins at Prudhoe Bay on Alaska's North Slope (you can't drive all the way to the end, but you can get close). Alternatively, explore the Steese Highway to its termination at the Yukon River and the town of Circle.

TRAIN TRAVEL

Between late May and early September, Alaska Railroad's daily passenger service runs between Seward, Anchorage, and Fairbanks, with stops at Talkeetna and Denali National Park and Preserve.

Standard trains have dining, lounge, and dome cars, plus the only outdoor viewing platform of its kind. Holland America and Princess offer luxurious travel packages as well.

CONTACTS Alaska Railroad 📞 *907/265–2494*, *800/544–0552* ⊕ *www.alaskarailroad.com* **Gray Line Alaska** 📞 *888/425–1737* ⊕ *www.graylinealaska.com.* **Princess Tours** 📞 *800/426–0500* ⊕ *www.princesslodges.com.*

Tours

Especially if you're interested in getting out into the wilderness or out to one of the villages, we recommend a tour—it's far less stressful, particularly if you'd otherwise be faced with tasks that you've never undertaken before, such as driving remote unpaved roads without knowing how to change a tire or, worse, wandering the backcountry with limited previous Alaska experience.

TOUR CONTACTS GoNorth Alaska Travel Center 📞 *907/479-7271*, *855/236-7271* ⊕ *www.gonorth-alaska.com.* **Northern Alaska Tour Company** 📞 *907/474-8600*, *800/474-1986* ⊕ *www.northernalaska. com.*

Restaurants

Even in the most elegant establishments Alaskans sometimes sport sweats or Carhartts. Most restaurants fly in fresh salmon and halibut from the coast. Meat-and-potatoes main courses and the occasional pasta dish fill menus, but most restaurants offer palatable vegetarian choices, too. The food isn't the only thing full of local flavor: walls are usually decked out in some combination of snowshoes, caribou and bear hides, the state flag, and historic photos.

Hotels

You won't find ultraluxury hotels, but you can find a range of bed-and-breakfasts, rustic-chic lodges, and national chains, as well as local spots that will please even the most discriminating travelers. For interaction with Alaskans, choose a B&B, as they're usually locally owned; proprietors tend to be eager to provide travel tips or an unforgettable story. The cheapest options are tents or RVs, and there is no shortage of campgrounds here.

Prices in the reviews are the lowest cost of a standard double room in high season.

What it Costs			
$	$$	$$$	$$$$
RESTAURANTS			
Under $15	$15–$20	$21–$25	over $25
HOTELS			
Under $125	$125–$175	$176–$225	over $225

Health and Safety

To keep yourself from going insane when you're being attacked by a cloud of mosquitoes—and they grow them big in the Interior—DEET, and lots of it, is your best bet. And don't wear blue. Mosquitoes really like blue.

Fairbanks

On a first drive around Fairbanks, the city appears to be a sprawling conglomeration of strip malls, chain stores, and other evidence of suburbia. But look beyond the obvious in the Interior's biggest town and you'll discover why thousands insist that this is the best place to live in Alaska—most citing the incredibly tight and supportive community.

The hardy Alaskans who refuse to leave during the cold and dark winters share a strong camaraderie. The fight to stave off cabin fever leads to creative festivals, from winter solstice celebrations to midnight baseball in summer. Quirky is celebrated in Fairbanks. But so is the ability to take care of business, no matter the obstacles (including seriously cold temperatures). It takes a special kind of confidence to live here, and that adds to the town's attractiveness.

Many old homes and commercial buildings trace their history to the city's early days, especially in the downtown area, with its narrow, winding streets following the contours of the Chena River. Even if each year brings more chain stores, the beautiful hillsides and river valleys remain. And the farmers' market here is a stunner. Of course there is Fairbanks's fall, winter, and spring bonus: being able to see the aurora, or northern lights, an average of 243 nights a year.

As you walk the streets of Fairbanks today, it takes a good imagination to envision the rough-and-tumble gold-mining camp that first took shape along the Chena River in the early 1900s. Although a few older neighborhoods have weathered log cabins, the rest is a Western hodgepodge that reflects the urge to build whatever one wants, wherever one wants—a trait that has long been a community standard (and sometimes leads to really interesting roof angles as the house sinks in permafrost).

The city is making some real efforts to preserve what's left of its gold-rush past, most notably in the 44-acre Pioneer Park, where dozens of cabins and many other relics were moved out of the path of progress. Downtown Fairbanks began to deteriorate in the 1970s, before and after the boom associated with the building of the Trans-Alaska Pipeline. But the downward spiral ended long ago and most of downtown has been rebuilt.

Fairbanks Gold

The gold strike by Felix Pedro in 1902 is commemorated annually in late July with the celebration of Golden Days, marked by a parade and several days of gold rush–inspired activities.

VISITOR INFORMATION

Make the **Morris Thompson Cultural and Visitors Center** your first stop in Fairbanks, where you can plan your whole trip, from a quick visit to a local attraction or a backcountry adventure. This center is also home to the **Fairbanks Convention and Visitors Bureau** and the **Alaska Public Lands Information Center.** While you're here, browse the free exhibits on Interior Alaska's environment and people, as well as the recently opened, fantastic displays of both gold-rush and Native history. In the summer, the center hosts Alaska Native art, music, storytelling, and dance. Don't forget to enjoy the free films, use the Wi-Fi and Internet access, or peruse the literature at the Alaska Geographic Bookstore.

CONTACTS Alaska Department of Fish and Game ⊠ *1300 College Rd.* ☎ *907/459–7207 for sportfishing information, 907/459–7206 for hunting and wildlife-related information* ⊕ *www.adfg. alaska.gov.* **Alaska Public Lands Information Center** ⊠ *101 Dunkel St.* ☎ *907/459–3730* ⊕ *www.alaskacenters.gov/fairbanks. cfm.* **Explore Fairbanks** ⊠ *101 Dunkel St.* ☎ *907/456–5774* ⊕ *www.explorefairbanks.com.* **Morris Thompson Cultural and Visitors Center** ⊠ *101 Dunkel St.* ☎ *907/459–3700* ⊕ *www.morristhompsoncenter.org.*

TOURS
Gray Line Alaska
TOUR—SIGHT | The company conducts scenic and informative tours of the

Fairbanks area. An eight-hour sightseeing package includes a stern-wheeler cruise and tour of a historic goldfield operation. Other tours include visits to Iditarod kennels and ATV treks through the forest under the midnight sun. ⊠ *Fairbanks* ☎ *888/425–1737* ⊕ *www.graylinealaska. com* 🚢 *From $56.*

Sights

★ Fountainhead Antique Automobile Museum

MUSEUM | Among the world's finest auto museums, Fountainhead provides a fascinating survey of history, design, culture, and, of course, cars (specifically ones from 1898 to 1938). Obscure makes—Buckmobiles, Packards, and Hudsons among them—compete for attention with more familiar specimens from Ford, Cadillac, and Chrysler. The museum's holdings include the first car ever made in Alaska, built in Skagway out of sheet metal and old boat parts. Alongside the cars, all but three of them in running condition, are equally remarkable historical photographs and exhibits of vintage clothing that illustrate the era's evolution of style, especially for women. ⊠ *Wedgewood Resort, 212 Wedgewood Dr.* ☎ *907/450–2100* ⊕ *www. fountainheadmuseum.com* 🚢 *$10* ⊗ *Closed Mon., Tues., and Thurs.–Sat. mid-Sept.–mid-May.*

Large Animal Research Station

COLLEGE | FAMILY | On the fringes of the University of Alaska campus is a 134-acre home to dozens of musk ox and domestic reindeer. Resident and visiting scientists study these large ungulates to better understand their physiologies and how they adapt to Arctic conditions. The station also serves as a valuable outreach program. Once nearly eradicated from Alaska, the shaggy, prehistoric-looking beasts known as musk ox are marvels of adaptive physiques and behaviors. Their qiviut, the delicate undercoat of soft hair, is combed out (without harming the animals) and made into yarn for scarves, hats, and gloves. The station has this unprocessed wool and yarn for sale to help fund the care of the animals. On tours you visit the pens for a close-up look at the animals and their young, while learning about the biology and ecology of the animals from a naturalist. Call ahead to arrange tours from mid-September through mid-May; otherwise you can just stop by. ⊠ *2220 Yankovich Rd., off Ballaine Rd.* ☎ *907/474–5724* ⊕ *www.lars. uaf.edu* 🚢 *Grounds free, tours $10.*

★ Morris Thompson Cultural and Visitors Center

INFO CENTER | As with visitor centers elsewhere, you can get help with everything at this multifaceted facility, from taking in local attractions to negotiating a backcountry adventure. But the highlights here are the museum-quality displays about Interior Alaska. A walk-through exhibit re-creates a fish camp, and you can walk through a full-size public-use cabin similar to ones you can rent on your own. Be sure to peer out the cabin window: an artful rendition of the northern lights awaits. Alaska Native artists frequently sell jewelry and other wares at the center; in addition to making a unique purchase you can chat with them about growing up in the villages or, in some cases, at fish camps such as the one the exhibit depicts. Named for a Tanana leader who dedicated his life to building bridges between Native and non-Native cultures, the center hosts summer programs showcasing Alaska Native art, music, storytelling, and dance. On the edge of the center's parking lot is **Antler Arch.** Made from more than 100 moose and caribou antlers, it serves as a gateway to the bike and walking path along the Chena River. ⊠ *101 Dunkel St.* ☎ *907/459–3700* ⊕ *www.morristhompsoncenter.org* 🚢 *Free.*

Did You Know?

The University of Alaska
Museum of the North
is pure Alaska inside
and out: the exterior
was inspired by the
state's alpine ridges,
glaciers, Yukon River, and
northern lights, and the
interior houses thousands
of years of Alaskan art,
culture, and nature.
Don't miss Blue Babe, the
36,000-year-old steppe
bison. Also inside is one
of the best gift shops in
the city.

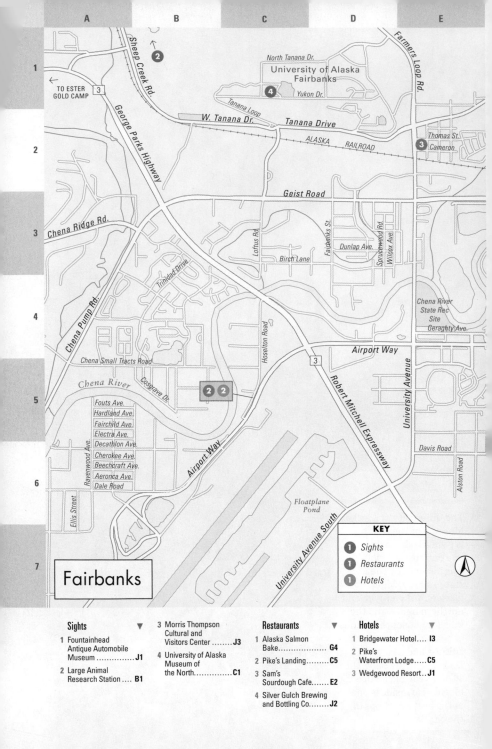

Fairbanks

KEY

- 🔴 Sights
- 🔴 Restaurants
- 🔴 Hotels

Sights ▼

1 Fountainhead Antique Automobile Museum **J1**

2 Large Animal Research Station **B1**

3 Morris Thompson Cultural and Visitors Center **J3**

4 University of Alaska Museum of the North..............**C1**

Restaurants ▼

1 Alaska Salmon Bake...................**G4**

2 Pike's Landing.........**C5**

3 Sam's Sourdough Cafe.......**E2**

4 Silver Gulch Brewing and Bottling Co........**J2**

Hotels ▼

1 Bridgewater Hotel.... **I3**

2 Pike's Waterfront Lodge.....**C5**

3 Wedgewood Resort..**J1**

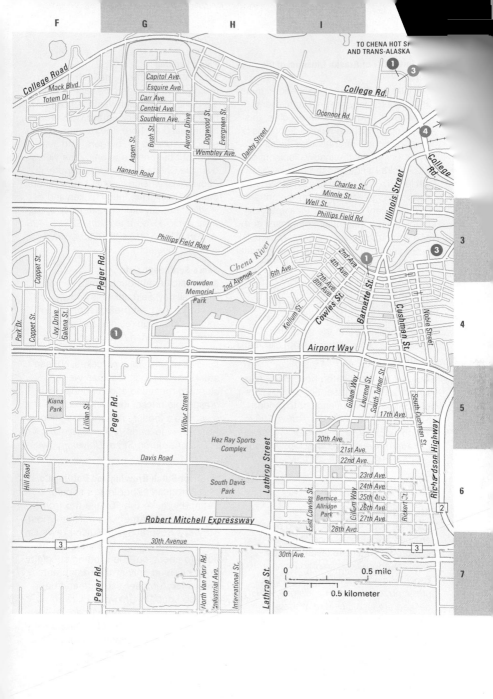

University of Alaska Museum of the North

MUSEUM | With sweeping exterior curves and graceful lines that evoke glaciers, mountains, and the northern lights, this don't-miss museum has some of Alaska's most distinctive architecture. Inside, two-story viewing windows look out on the Alaska Range and the Tanana Valley while Otto, the 8-foot, 9-inch brown bear specimen, greets visitors to the entrance of the Gallery of Alaska. "Please touch" items include the molars of a mammoth and a mastodon, animal pelts, replica petroglyphs, and a massive quartz crystal found in Alaska's Brooks Range. The gallery also contains dioramas showing the state's animals and how they interact, and the fantastic collection of Alaska Native clothes, tools, and boats provide insights into the ways that different groups came to terms with climatic extremes.

Another highlight is the Rose Berry Alaska Art Gallery, representing 2,000 years of Alaska's art, from ancient to modern. ⊠ *University of Alaska Fairbanks, 1962 Yukon Dr.* ☎ *907/474–7505* ⊕ *www. uaf.edu/museum* ⊠ *$14* ⊙ *Closed Sun. Sept.–May.*

🍴 Restaurants

Alaska Salmon Bake

$$$$ | **SEAFOOD** | Salmon cooked over an open fire with a sauce of lemon and brown sugar is a favorite at this indoor-outdoor restaurant in Pioneer Park's Mining Valley. Bering Sea cod, prime rib, a salad bar, beverages, and dessert are also included at the all-you-can-eat dinner. **Known for:** sunny outdoor seating; wood-grilled salmon; cabin dedicated to just desserts. ⑤ *Average main: $36* ⊠ *Airport Way and Peger Rd.* ☎ *907/452–7274, 800/354–7274* ⊕ *www.akvisit.com* ⊙ *Closed mid-Sept.–mid-May.*

Pike's Landing

$$$ | **AMERICAN** | The seats in the dining room of this extended log-cabin building are perfect for cooler weather, but the huge paddle-up deck dotted with firepits is the real draw here. The menu is mostly salads, sandwiches, burgers, and seafood, but the chance to enjoy the views over the Chena River and the landmark "Love Alaska" sign is what keeps diners coming. **Known for:** fried chicken and waffles; Sunday brunch; extensive waterfront deck. ⑤ *Average main: $23* ⊠ *4438 Airport Way* ☎ *907/479–6305* ⊕ *www. pikes-landing.com.*

Sam's Sourdough Cafe

$ | **AMERICAN** | Although Sam's serves meals all day, Fairbanksans know it as one of the best breakfast places in town. Sourdough recipes are a kind of minor religion in Alaska, and Sam's serves an extensive menu of sourdough specialties, including hotcakes, cheese steaks, and French toast, as well as standard meat-and-eggs options, all at reasonable prices. **Known for:** local flair on comfort food; reindeer sausage; long waits on weekends. ⑤ *Average main: $13* ⊠ *3702 Cameron St., at University Ave.* ☎ *907/479–0523.*

★ Silver Gulch Brewing and Bottling Co.

$$$ | **AMERICAN** | Beer lovers should definitely make the 10-mile trip from town to North America's northernmost brewery. Several Silver Gulch brews can be found throughout the state, so be sure to check out the rotating specialty brews served only at the restaurant. **Known for:** reindeer sausage and beer cheese soup; inventive brick oven pizzas; summertime beer garden. ⑤ *Average main: $22* ⊠ *2195 Old Steese Hwy.* ☎ *907/452–2739* ⊕ *www.silvergulch. com* ⊙ *No lunch weekdays.*

Hotels

For expanded hotel reviews, visit Fodors. com.

Bridgewater Hotel

$$ | **HOTEL** | In the heart of downtown Fairbanks, just above the Chena River, the Bridgewater has gone through several incarnations, emerging most recently as a modern, European-style hotel. **Pros:** good location; free airport and train shuttle; the most character of any downtown Fairbanks hotel. **Cons:** small, modest rooms; no refrigerators; restaurant serves breakfast only. $ *Rooms from: $159* ⊠ *723 1st Ave., Downtown* ☎ *907/452–6661, 833/303–4760* ⊕ *www.bridgewaterhotel. net* ⊘ *Closed mid-Sept.–mid-May* ⇨ *93 rooms* ⏺❙ *No meals.*

Pike's Waterfront Lodge

$$$$ | **HOTEL** | Log columns and beams support the high ceiling in the lobby of this hotel and conference center designed to remind guests of the city's gold rush past. **Pros:** location along the Chena River; Pike's Landing next door is a hot spot; close to the airport. **Cons:** small gym; restaurant in a separate building; historic signs everywhere can become information overload. $ *Rooms from: $267* ⊠ *1850 Hoselton Rd.* ☎ *907/456–4500, 877/774–2400* ⊕ *www. pikeslodge.com* ⇨ *180 rooms, 28 cabins* ⏺❙ *Breakfast.*

★ Wedgewood Resort

$$$ | **RESORT** | Wild and cultivated flowers adorn the landscaped grounds of this 105-acre resort bordering the Creamer's Field Migratory Waterfowl Refuge. **Pros:** free shuttle downtown; trails through a wildlife sanctuary; antique automobile museum on-site. **Cons:** away from other Fairbanks attractions; one fitness center for seven buildings; apartment block appearance. $ *Rooms from: $189* ⊠ *212 Wedgewood Dr.* ☎ *907/452-1442, 800/528-4916* ⊕ *www.fountainheadhotels.com/wedgewood* ▭ *No credit cards* ⇨ *463 rooms.*

Nightlife

Check the *Fairbanks Daily News-Miner* website for current nightspots, plays, concerts, and art shows.

Blue Loon

BARS/PUBS | Between Ester and Fairbanks on the Parks Highway, the Blue Loon presents year-round entertainment and serves great grill food and pizzas. Movies screen twice a night, except when there's a special event. National bands and comedians perform here, and there are outdoor concerts in summer and a DJ spins until late on weekends. ⊠ *2999 Parks Hwy., Mile 353.5* ☎ *907/457–5666* ⊕ *www.theblueloon.com* ⊘ *Closed Sun. and Mon.*

★ HooDoo Brewing Co

BARS/PUBS | The go-to spot for locals thirsting for well-crafted beer in Fairbanks is HooDoo. The company sells growlers to go, but its beer is best enjoyed outdoors on a sunny afternoon around the brewery's spool tables—or if the weather gets bad, inside the airy taproom. The beer line is often long, but it moves quickly and it's a good place to meet new friends. The only issue is that it closes at 8 pm. Free brewery tours take place on Saturday at 4 pm. ⊠ *1951 Fox Ave.* ☎ *907/459–2337* ⊕ *www.hoodoobrew. com* ⊘ *Closed Sun. and Mon.*

Howling Dog Saloon

BARS/PUBS | A local institution, the Howling Dog specializes in live blues and rock and roll. A party crowd of college students, airline pilots, tourists, miners, and bikers assembles for the cocktails, bar food, and music. Shows are played on a red-carpet stage acquired after Ronald Reagan and Pope John Paul II's visit to Fairbanks in 1984. ⊠ *2160 Old Steese Hwy. N, Mile 11.5, Fox* ☎ *907/456–4695* ⊕ *www.howlingdogsaloonak.com.*

Senator's Saloon

BARS/PUBS | On a warm summer evening, the saloon at the Pump House

Restaurant is a fine place to listen to music alongside the Chena River. You can also peruse the wine list at the mahogany bar or shoot pool on the billiards table dating from 1898. ⊠ *796 Chena Pump Rd.* ☎ *907/479–8452* ⊕ *www.pumphouse.com* ⊗ *Closed Jan. and Mon. in Sept.–late May.*

Shopping

The Alaska House Art Gallery

ART GALLERIES | Owners Yolande Fejes and Ron Veliz take the "Alaska" in their gallery's name seriously; almost everything here is made in the state (with a few Canadian artists represented). Visit this hand-built log house for fine art and souvenirs made with regional pride. The gallery is also a worthy stop during the monthly First Friday showcase of local artists and their works. ⊠ *1003 Cushman St., Downtown* ☎ *907/456–6449* ⊕ *www.thealaskahouse.com.*

Beads and Things

CRAFTS | This shop sells Alaska Native handicrafts from around the state, along with a world's worth of beads for those who want to design their own pieces. ⊠ *537 2nd Ave., Downtown* ☎ *907/456–2323.*

Great Alaskan Bowl Company

CRAFTS | The big one-stop shop for Alaskan-made gifts and souvenirs, Great Alaskan specializes in lathe-turned bowls made out of Alaskan birch. ⊠ *4630 Old Airport Rd.* ☎ *907/474–9663, 800/770–4222* ⊕ *www.woodbowl.com.*

Judie Gumm Designs

JEWELRY/ACCESSORIES | In her small shop, owner Judie Gumm fashions stunning and moderately priced silver and gold designs best described as sculptural interpretations of Northern images. Gumm, a longtime Ester resident, is a fun person to chat up about life in this small and quirky community tucked just off the highway west of Fairbanks.

⊠ *3600 Main St., Ester* ☎ *907/479–4568, 800/478–4568* ⊕ *www.judiegumm.com.*

A Weaver's Yarn

CRAFTS | Artists Susan and Martin Miller own this shop that will delight knitters both new and experienced. It's the perfect place to buy a gift for that knitter back home or to pick up some qiviut, the pricey but exquisite undercoat wool of the musk ox that is some of the world's softest material. ⊠ *1810 Alaska Way, College* ☎ *907/374–1995* ⊕ *www.aweaversyarn.com.*

Activities

BOATING

★ CanoeAlaska

TOUR—SPORTS | This outfit rents gear and arranges pickups and drop-offs for the Class I waters of the lower Chena River (the only real challenge for canoeists on the lower river is watching out for powerboats), as well as other local rivers. ⊠ *Pioneer Park Boat Dock, 1101 Peger Rd., along Chena River* ☎ *907/457–2453* ⊕ *www.canoealaska.com* ⊠ *From $55 for an 8-hr kayak, canoe, or paddleboard rental.*

★ Riverboat Discovery

TOUR—SPORTS | Relive the city's riverboat history and the Interior's cultural heritage each summer aboard the Riverboat *Discovery*, a three-hour narrated trip by stern-wheeler along the Chena and Tanana rivers to a rustic Alaska Native village on the Tanana. The cruise provides a glimpse of the lifestyle of the dog mushers, subsistence fishermen, traders, and Alaska Natives who populate the Yukon River drainage. Sights along the way include operating fish wheels, a bush airfield, floatplanes, a smokehouse and cache, log cabins, and dog kennels once tended by the late Susan Butcher, the first person to win the Iditarod four times. The Binkley family, with four generations of river pilots, has traveled the great rivers of the north for more than a century. ⊠ *1975 Discovery Dr.* ☎ *907/479–6673, 866/479–6673* ⊕ *www. riverboatdiscovery.com* 🖃 *$65.*

DOG MUSHING

Throughout Alaska, sprint races, freight hauling, and long-distance endurance runs are held throughout the winter, with the majority running in late February and March, when longer days afford more enjoyment of the remaining winter snow. Men and women often compete in the same classes in the major races. For children, various racing classes are based on age, starting with the one-dog category for the youngest. The Interior sees a constant string of sled-dog races from November to March, culminating in the North American Open Sled-Dog Championship, which attracts international competitors.

Paws for Adventure Sled Dog Tours

LOCAL SPORTS | Paws offers everything from a quick ride to mushing immersion courses. Experience the joys of mushing—and snap plenty of photos—on a one-hour ride, or learn how to drive a team at the three-hour mushing school. The multiday trips include mushing school plus overnight mushing, camping, and stays at Tolovana Roadhouse. ⊠ *George Rd., at Herning Rd., on A Taste of Alaska Lodge property* ☎ *907/699–3960* ⊕ *www.pawsforadventure.com* 🖃 *From $75.*

GOLD PANNING

Gold Dredge 8

LOCAL SPORTS | From the comfort of a narrow-gauge railroad, Gold Dredge 8 offers a two-hour tour of a seasonal mining operation. Miners demonstrate classic and modern techniques, after which visitors get to try their luck panning for gold. Many historic elements from the old El Dorado Gold Mine have been transported here, so a tour provides a fairly complete look at how Fairbanks got rich. ⊠ *1803 Old Steese Hwy. N* ☎ *907/479–6673, 866/479–6673* ⊕ *www.golddredge8.com* 🖃 *$40.*

NORTHERN LIGHTS TOURS

Aurora Borealis Lodge

TOUR—SIGHT | This lodge on Cleary Summit that has big picture windows conducts late-night viewing tours from late August to April to see the northern lights sky. The tour fee—from $75 to $85, depending on your Fairbanks pickup point—includes hot drinks and transportation. Visitors driving themselves pay $25. You can extend your northern lights viewing pleasure by spending the night. Each of the four spacious rooms (starting at $209 for two people) in the two-story lodge building has large, north-facing windows, a private bath, and a kitchen. The standalone Logan Chalet ($350 rate for one to four people, three-night minimum) holds up to six people. Both accommodations have free Wi-Fi and offer discounts for multinight stays. ⊠ *1906 Ridge Run Rd., Mile 20.5 Steese Hwy., at Cleary Summit* ☎ *907/389–2812* ⊕ *auroracabin.com.*

Chena Hot Springs Resort

HOT SPRINGS | About 60 miles northeast of Fairbanks, the Chena Hot Springs Resort offers guests winter snow coach rides to a yurt on Charlie Dome with a 360-degree vista of nothing but wilderness—and a good chance of viewing the northern lights. The resort also offers a heated log cabin "aurorium" a short hike away. Guests can even arrange a wake-up call when staff spot the lights. ⊠ *End (Mile 56.5) of Chena Hot Springs Rd., Chena Hot Springs* ☎ *907/451–8104* ⊕ *chenahotsprings.com.*

Mt. Aurora Skiland

SPORTS VENUE | Visitors fill the warm mountaintop lodges at Mt. Aurora from 9 pm to 3 am on winter nights. Images from an aurora webcam are shown on a large-screen TV. The admission fee includes hot drinks. ⊠ *2315 Skiland Rd., Mile 20.5 Steese Hwy., at Cleary Summit* ☎ *907/389–2314* ⊕ *skiland.org* 🖃 *$30* ☉ *Closed April–Sept.*

Denali National Park and Preserve

More than 6 million acres of wilderness, Denali National Park and Preserve is the heart of Alaska: the biggest mountains, the wildest rivers, and so much wildlife, you'll probably end up frying your camera trying to catch it all. One road in, the tallest mountain on the continent, and endless possibilities await you.

Although it isn't technically a port of call, Denali National Park and Preserve is, quite understandably, one of the most popular land extensions to an Alaska cruise. Anchorage, 240 miles south of the park, serves as a point of departure.

GEOLOGY AND TERRAIN

The most prominent geological feature of the park is the Alaska Range, a 600-mile-long crescent of mountains that separates Southcentral Alaska from the Interior. Mt. Hunter (14,573 feet), Mt. Foraker (17,400 feet), and Denali (20,310 feet) itself are the mammoths of the group. Glaciers flow from the entire Alaska Range.

Another, smaller group of mountains—the Outer Range, north of Denali's park road—is a mix of volcanics and heavily metamorphosed sediments. Though not as breathtaking as the Alaska Range, the Outer Range is popular with hikers and backpackers because its summits and ridges are not as technically difficult to reach.

Several of Denali's most spectacular landforms are deep in the park, but are still visible from the park road. The multicolor volcanic rocks at Cathedral Mountain and Polychrome Pass reflect the vivid hues of the American Southwest. The braided channels of glacially fed streams such as the Teklanika, Toklat, and McKinley rivers serve as highway routes for both animals and hikers. The debris- and tundra-covered ice of the Muldrow Glacier, one of the largest glaciers to flow out of Denali National Park's high mountains, is visible from Eielson Visitor Center, at Mile 66 of the park road. Wonder Lake, a dark and narrow kettle pond that's a remnant from Alaska's ice ages, lies at Mile 85, just a few miles from the former gold-boom camp of Kantishna.

Park Basics

Denali Visitor Center

INFO CENTER | Open from mid-May through mid-September, the center is a mile-and-a half beyond the park's entrance, and includes two floors' worth of displays detailing the park's natural and cultural history along with several life-size representations of the park's largest animals. A theater on the main floor plays the 20-minute film *The Heartbeats of Denali* twice an hour. The center is the starting point for most interpretive ranger hikes and several other trails you can explore independently. This is also the place to go for your backcountry camping permits (permits aren't necessary for day hikes). Nearby facilities include the railroad and bus depots, the Morino Grill, and the Alaska Geographic bookstore. ⊠ *Denali National Park Rd., Denali National Park* ☎ *907/683–9532* ⊕ *www.nps.gov/dena* ☉ *Closed mid-Sept.–mid-May.*

Eielson Visitor Center

INFO CENTER | Famous for its views of Denali, the Eielson Visitor Center is found at Mile 66 of the park road. Park rangers are present throughout the day either leading presentations or hikes such as the leisurely Eielson Stroll. While there is a small gallery of Denali-inspired art here, this visitor center is all about the view, dominated, with a little luck, by the mountain itself. The center opens on June 1 and closes on the second Thursday after Labor Day. It's accessible by any of the shuttle buses that pass Mile 66, excluding the Kantishna Experience tour. ⊠ *Mile 66, Park Rd., Denali National*

Park ⊕ www.nps.gov/dena/planyourvisit/ the-eielson-visitor-center.htm ⊗ Closed early Sept.–May.

Murie Science and Learning Center

COLLEGE | Next to the Denali Visitor Center, Murie Science and Learning Center is the foundation of the park's science-based education programs, and also serves as the winter visitor center when the Denali Visitor Center is closed. Hours during the summer vary, and the center usually opens only for special presentations. During off-season camping at the Riley Campground, it's the go-to spot for ranger information and, yes, bathrooms with running water. ⊠ Mile 1.5, Park Rd., Denali National Park ☎ 907/683–6432 ⊕ www.nps.gov/rlc/murie.

Wilderness Access Center

INFO CENTER | Also known as the Bus Depot, this center just inside the park entrance is where you can reserve campgrounds and bus trips into the park. For those that arrive after 7 pm, campground reservations can be made at the Riley Creek Mercantile until 11 pm. There's also a coffee stand—your last chance for a cup of joe unless you bring the makings for campsite coffee with you. ⊠ Mile 0.5, Park Rd., Denali National Park ☎ 907/683–9532 ⊕ www.nps.gov/dena/ planyourvisit/wildernessaccesscenter. htm ⊗ Closed mid-Sept.–mid-May.

Transportation and Tours

Don't be alarmed by the crowded park entrance; that gets left behind very quickly. After the chaos of private businesses that line the George Parks Highway and the throngs at the visitor center, there's pretty much nothing else in the park but wilderness. From the bus you'll have the opportunity to see Denali's wildlife in natural settings, as the animals are habituated to the road and vehicles, and go about their daily routine with little bother. In fact, the animals really like the road:

it's easier for them to walk along it than to work through the tundra and tussocks.

Bus trips take time. The maximum speed limit is 35 mph, and the buses don't hit that very often. Add in rest stops, wildlife sightings, and slowdowns for passing, and it's an 8- to 11-hour day to reach the heart of the park and the best Denali views from Miles 62–85. Buses run from May 20 to September 13, although if you're running up close against one of those dates, call to make sure.

All prices listed below are for adults and include the $10 park admission fee, unless otherwise noted. ■TIP→ If you decide to tour the park by bus, you have two choices: a sightseeing bus tour offered by a park concessionaire or a ride on the shuttle bus. The differences between the two are significant.

Tour buses

NATIONAL/STATE PARK | Guided bus tours offer the most informative introduction to the park. Each trip is led by a trained naturalist who drives the bus and gives a full narration. All tours include rest stops approximately every 90 minutes. Unlike the transit buses, you are not allowed to wander off on your own. The shortest is the five-hour Natural History Tour that travels to Teklanika at Mile 27. Besides moose and the occasional caribou, chances of seeing the park's large mammals are limited on this route, and glimpses of Denali are possible but not probable. The next longest option is the seven to eight-hour Tundra Wilderness Tour that reaches Stony Brook at Mile 62; this is the best choice for wildlife and photography enthusiasts. The longest narrated tour is the Kantishna Experience, a 12-hour extravaganza that runs the full 92 miles of park road to the old mining town of Kantishna. Advance reservations are required for all bus tours, and they can be made starting on December 1, with exact departure times fluctuating depending on demand and time of year. It's best to consult Doyon/Aramark for

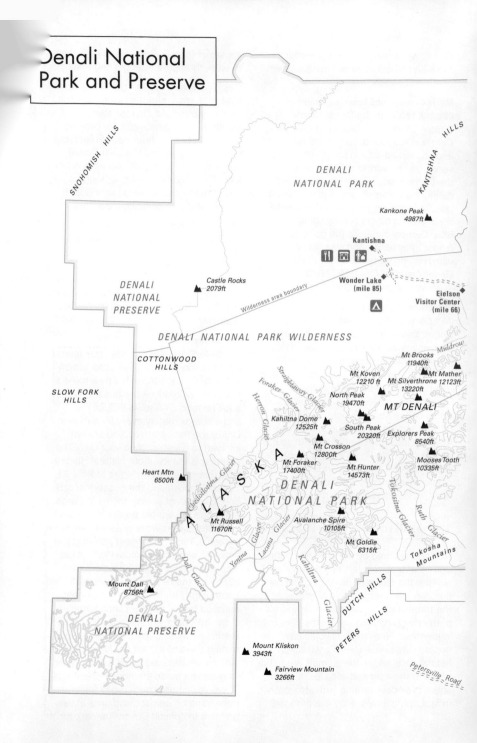

Denali National Park and Preserve

SNOHOMISH HILLS

DENALI NATIONAL PARK

KANTISHNA HILLS

Kankone Peak
4987ft ▲

Kantishna

DENALI NATIONAL PRESERVE

Castle Rocks
2079ft ▲

Wilderness area boundary

Wonder Lake
(mile 85) ◆

Eielson
Visitor Center
(mile 66) ◆

DENALI NATIONAL PARK WILDERNESS

COTTONWOOD HILLS

Muldrow

SLOW FORK HILLS

Straightaway Glacier

Mt Brooks
11940ft ▲

Mt Koven
12210ft ▲

Mt Mather ▲
Mt Silverthrone 12123ft
13220ft ▲

North Peak
19470ft ▲

MT DENALI

Foraker Glacier

Kahiltna Dome
12525ft ▲

South Peak
20320ft ▲

Explorers Peak
8540ft ▲

Herron Glacier

Mt Crosson
12800ft ▲

Heart Mtn
6500ft ▲

Mt Foraker
17400ft ▲

Mt Hunter
14573ft ▲

Mooses Tooth
10335ft ▲

Tokositna Glacier

Ruth Glacier

A L A S K A

Chedotlothna Glacier

DENALI NATIONAL PARK

Mt Russell
11670ft ▲

Avalanche Spire
10105ft ▲

Tokosha Mountains

Yentna Glacier

Lacuna Glacier

Mt Goldie
6315ft ▲

Mount Dall
8756ft ▲

Dall Glacier

Kahiltna Glacier

DUTCH HILLS

DENALI NATIONAL PRESERVE

PETERS HILLS

Mount Kliskon
3943ft ▲

Fairview Mountain
3266ft ▲

Petersville Road

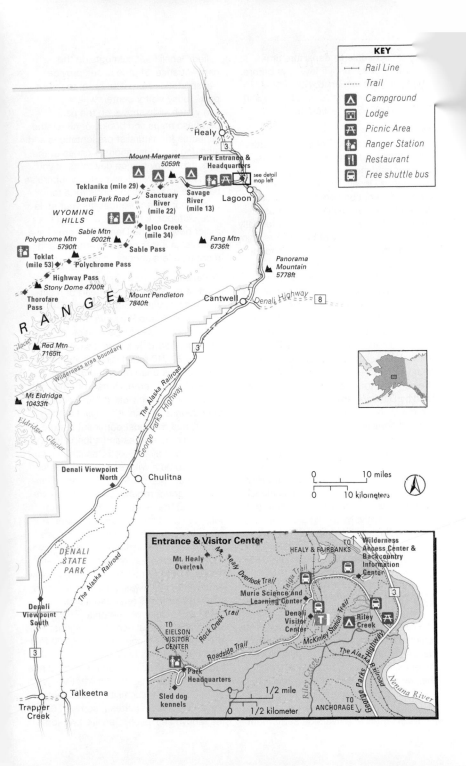

KEY

⊢—⊣	Rail Line
⋯⋯	Trail
⛺	Campground
🏨	Lodge
⛱	Picnic Area
👫	Ranger Station
🍴	Restaurant
🚌	Free shuttle bus

Healy

Mount Margaret
5059ft

Park Entrance &
Headquarters

see detail
map left

Teklanika (mile 29)

Denali Park Road

Savage
River
(mile 13)

Lagoon

Sanctuary
River
(mile 22)

WYOMING
HILLS

Igloo Creek
(mile 34)

Sable Mtn
6002ft

Fang Mtn
6736ft

Polychrome Mtn
5790ft

Sable Pass

Toklat
(mile 53)

Polychrome Pass

Panorama
Mountain
5778ft

Highway Pass

Stony Dome 4700ft

Thorofare
Pass

Mount Pendleton
7840ft

Cantwell

Denali Highway

8

R A N G E

Red Mtn
7165ft

Wilderness area boundary

3

Glacier

Mt Eldridge
10433ft

The Alaska Railroad

George Parks Highway

Eldridge Glacier

Denali Viewpoint
North

Chulitna

0   10 miles

0   10 kilometers

DENALI
STATE
PARK

The Alaska Railroad

Denali
Viewpoint
South

3

Talkeetna

Trapper
Creek

Entrance & Visitor Center

Mt. Healy
Overlook

TO
HEALY & FAIRBANKS

Wilderness
Access Center &
Backcountry
Information
Center

Mt. Healy Overlook Trail

Taiga Trail

Murie Science and
Learning Center

3

Denali
Visitor
Center

McKinley Station Trail

Riley
Creek

Rock Creek Trail

TO
EIELSON
VISITOR
CENTER

Roadside Trail

McKinley Station Trail

Riley Creek

The Alaska Railroad

Park
Headquarters

Sled dog
kennels

TO
ANCHORAGE

George Parks Highway

Nenana River

0   1/2 mile

0   1/2 kilometer

exact schedule as departure times are often not set until a few days before. ✉ Denali National Park 🕾 800/622-7275 🌐 www.reservedenali.com 📧 From $80 🕙 Closed mid-Sept.–mid-May.

Shuttle buses

NATIONAL/STATE PARK | The park's shuttle and transit buses are a more informal, cheaper, and independent way to experience Denali. These buses are green-painted, converted school buses while the formally narrated tour buses are tan. While these trips are not formally narrated, the majority of bus drivers enjoy sharing information with riders, and the buses are equipped with speakers. Transit buses offer the freedom to disembark virtually anywhere along the road system and explore the park for yourself. Catching a ride back is as simple as returning to the road and waiting for the next transit bus to come by. Note that full buses will not stop, so it's possible to wait for an hour or more for your ride back. Like the narrated tours, transit buses are operated by Doyon/Aramark and bookings are made through the concessionaire. Reservations are not required, and about a quarter of the seats are saved for walk-ons. But if you're visiting during peak season, it's best to make reservations ahead of time to ensure availability. Schedules can be found on the National Park Service's Denali website; departure times are relatively reliable although they can fluctuate during the summer. ✉ Denali National Park 🕾 800/622-7275 🌐 www.reservedenali.com 📧 Free–$60 🕙 Closed mid-Sept.–mid-May.

👁 Sights

You can take a tour bus or the Alaskan Railroad from Anchorage to the Denali National Park entrance. Princess, Holland America, and Royal Caribbean attach their own railcars behind the trains for a more luxurious experience. Most cruise passengers stay one or two nights in hotels at a riverside settlement called Denali Park, just outside the park entrance. Shuttle buses provide transportation from your hotel to the park's busy visitor center, where you can watch slide shows on the park, purchase maps and books, or check the schedule for naturalist presentations and sled-dog demonstrations. Access to the park itself is by bus on day tours. If you aren't visiting Denali as part of your cruise package, make reservations for a tour or outdoor adventure that fits your style (see Outdoor Activities, below). All the major hotels in the Denali Park area have good restaurants on the premises, and most travelers choose to dine there.

★ Denali

MOUNTAIN—SIGHT | In the heart of mainland Alaska, within 6-million-acre Denali National Park and Preserve, the continent's most majestic peak rises into the heavens. Formerly known as Mt. McKinley, this 20,310-foot massif of ice, snow, and rock has been renamed to honor its Alaska Native name, Denali, or "the High One." Some simply call it "the Mountain." One thing is certain: it's a giant among giants, and the most dominant feature in a land of extremes and superlatives. Those who have walked Denali's slopes know it to be a wild, desolate place. As the highest peak in North America, Denali is a target of mountaineers who aspire to ascend the "seven summits"—the tallest mountains on each continent. A foreboding and mysterious place, it was terra incognita—unclimbed and unknown to most people—as recently as the late 1890s. Among Athabascan tribes, however, the mountain was a revered landmark; many generations regarded it as a holy place and a point of reference. The mountain's vertical rise is the highest in the world. This means that at 18,000 feet over the lowlands (which are some 2,000 feet above sea level), Denali's vertical rise is even greater than that of Mt. Everest, at 29,035-feet (which sits 12,000 feet above the Tibetan plateau, some 17,000 feet above sea level). Denali's awesome

In 2015, President Obama renamed Mt. McKinley as Denali, its original name, which means "the High One."

height and its subarctic location make it one of the coldest mountains on Earth, if not *the* coldest. Primarily made of granite, Denali undergoes continual shifting and uplift thanks to plate tectonics (the Pacific Plate pushing against the North American Plate); it grows about 1 millimeter per year. ⊠ *Denali National Park.*

🛏 Hotels

★ Camp Denali and North Face Lodge

$$$$ | RESORT | The legendary, family-owned and-operated Camp Denali and North Face Lodge both offer stunning views of Denali and active learning experiences deep within Denali National Park, at Mile 89 on the park road. **Pros:** only in-park lodge with a view of Denali; knowledgeable and attentive staff; strong emphasis on learning. **Cons:** credit cards not accepted; steep rates and three-night minimum stay; alcohol is BYO. ⑤ *Rooms from: $1,280 ⊠ Mile 89, Denali Park Rd., Denali National Park* ☎ *907/683–2290* ⊕ *www.campdenali.com* ▭ *No credit cards* ⊙ *Closed mid-Sept.–late May* ⇌ *18*

cabins (Camp Denali), 15 rooms (North Face Lodge) ¶⊙¶ All-inclusive.*

Denali Park Village

$$$$ | RESORT | This sprawling 20-acre resortlike property operated by one of the National Park Service's largest concessionaires, Aramark, sits just 7 miles south of the park entrance next to the Nenana River. **Pros:** shuttle service for all guests; transfers to railroad depot; close to both park and nearby dining. **Cons.** not the place for quiet or to meet many (or any) locals; draws lots of big tour groups; resort-style complex lacks local flavor. ⑤ *Rooms from: $379 ⊠ Mile 231, Parks Hwy., Denali National Park* ☎ *800/276–7234* ⊕ *www.denaliparkvil-lage.com* ⊙ *Closed mid-Sept.–mid-May* ⇌ *338 rooms, 50 cabins* ¶⊙¶ *No meals.*

McKinley Creekside Cabins

$$$ | HOTEL | These accommodations sit on 10 acres and are bordered on the south side by Carlo Creek, with 14 cabins right along the Creek and 13 rooms in a hotel-style building. **Pros:** great location by the water; nice mountain views;

barbecue and covered pavillion next to the creek available. **Cons:** no TVs in cabins; right off the side of the highway; cabins close together with little privacy. Ⓢ *Rooms from: $239* ✉ *Mile 224, Parks Hwy., Carlo Creek* ☎ *907/683–2277* ⊕ *www.mckinleycabins.com* ☽ *Closed mid-Sept.–mid-May* ⇥ *32 cabins, 13 rooms* ⦵ *No meals.*

Activities

HIKING
GUIDED HIKES
In addition to exploring the park on your own, you can take free ranger-guided discovery hikes and learn more about the park's natural and human history. Rangers lead daily hikes throughout summer. Inquire at the visitor center. You can also tour with privately operated outfitters.

Rangers will talk about the area's plants, animals, and geological features. Before heading into the wilderness, even on a short hike, check in at the Backcountry Information Center located in the visitor center. Rangers will update you on conditions and make route suggestions. Because this is bear country, the Park Service provides backpackers with bear-proof food containers. These containers are mandatory if you're staying overnight in the backcountry.

NATURE TRAILS AND SHORT WALKS
The park offers plenty of options for those who prefer to stay on marked and groomed pathways. The entrance area has more than a half-dozen forest and tundra trails. These range from easy to challenging, so there's something suitable for all ages and hiking abilities. Some, like the **Taiga Loop Trail** and **McKinley Station Loop Trail,** are less than 1½ miles; others, like the **Rock Creek Trail** and **Triple Lakes Trail,** are several miles round-trip, with an altitude gain of hundreds of feet. Along these paths you may see beavers working on their lodges in Horseshoe Lake, red squirrels chattering in trees,

red foxes hunting for rodents, sheep grazing on tundra, golden eagles gliding over alpine ridges, and moose feeding on willow.

The **Savage River Trail,** farthest from the park entrance and as far as private vehicles are allowed, offers a 1¾-mile round-trip hike along a raging river and under rocky cliffs. Be on the lookout for caribou, Dall sheep, foxes, and marmots.

The only relatively long, marked trail for hiking in the park, **Mt. Healy Overlook Trail,** is accessible from the entrance area; it gains 1,700 feet in 2½ miles and takes about four hours round-trip, with outstanding views of the Nenana River below and the Alaska Range, including the upper slopes of Denali.

MULTISPORT OUTFITTERS
★ **Denali Outdoor Center**
TOUR—SPORTS | With two locations, one in Glitter Gulch and another close to Healy, Denali Outdoor Center can take you rafting on Class IV rapids, kayaking, put you on a mountain bike, and then get you a cabin so you can sack out and recover from your day. Prices for white-water rafting and inflatable kayak trips (which include instruction and all equipment) start at $94; bike rentals cost $25 for six hours, $40 for the day, and tours cost $57. Lakefront cabins on Otto Lake near Healy run $106 per night, or just stay at the campground for $12 per person. ✉ *Mile 0.5, Otto Lake Rd., off Mile 247, Parks Hwy., Healy* ☎ *907/683–1925, 888/303–1925* ⊕ *www.denalioutdoorcenter.com* ☽ *Closed mid-May–mid-Sept.*

Fortymile Country

A trip through the Fortymile Country up the Taylor Highway will take you back in time more than a century—when gold was the lure that drew travelers to Interior Alaska. It's one of the few places to see active mining without leaving the road system. In addition, remote

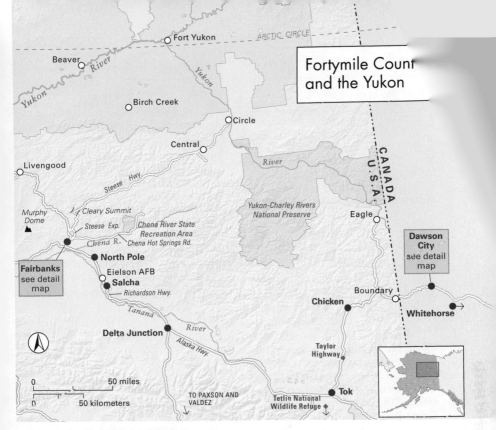

Map: Fortymile Country and the Yukon

Fort Yukon · ARCTIC CIRCLE · Beaver · River · Yukon · Birch Creek · Circle · Central · River · Livengood · Steese Hwy. · Cleary Summit · Murphy Dome · Steese Exp. · Chena R. · Chena River State Recreation Area · Chena Hot Springs Rd. · North Pole · Eielson AFB · Salcha · Richardson Hwy. · Fairbanks see detail map · Tanana · River · Delta Junction · Alaska Hwy. · Yukon-Charley Rivers National Preserve · Eagle · CANADA U.S.A. · Dawson City see detail map · Boundary · Chicken · Whitehorse · Taylor Highway · Tok · TO PAXSON AND VALDEZ · Tetlin National Wildlife Refuge

0 — 50 miles
0 — 50 kilometers

wilderness experiences and float trips abound. If you're headed to Fortymile Country from Fairbanks, you'll drive along the historic Richardson Highway, once a pack-train trail (think mules with bags) and a dogsled route for mail carriers and gold miners in the Interior. As quirky places to turn off a highway go, North Pole, Salcha, and Delta Junction are up there with the best of them.

Taylor Highway

SCENIC DRIVE | The 160-mile Taylor Highway runs north from the Alaska Highway at Tetlin Junction, 12 miles east of Tok. It's a narrow rough-gravel road that winds along mountain ridges and through valleys of the Fortymile River. The road passes the tiny community of Chicken and ends in Eagle at the Yukon River. This is one of only three places in Alaska where the Yukon River can be reached by road.

A cutoff just south of Eagle connects to the Canadian Top of the World Highway leading to Dawson City in the Yukon Territory, which is the route many Alaskans take to Dawson City. That route is far more scenic, and shorter, than the alternative of taking the Alcan to Whitehorse and then turning north, but it's another of those stretches for which it's good to make sure your insurance policy covers towing and windshield replacement. The highway is not plowed in winter, so it is snowed shut from fall to spring. If you're roughing it, know that the Bureau of Land Management also maintains three first-come, first-served campsites (as all BLM campsites are) on the Taylor Highway between Tetlin Junction and Eagle at Miles 49, 82, and 160.

rth Pole and Salcha

North Pole, 14 miles southeast of Fairbanks, may be a featureless suburb, but you'd have to be a Scrooge not to admit that this town's year-round acknowledgment of the December holiday season is at least a little bit fun to take in. The Santa Claus House Gift Shop (on St. Nicholas Drive, of course) is a must-see stop. Sixteen miles farther along in Salcha, the Knotty Shop is a burl-lover's paradise.

Sights

The Knotty Shop

STORE/MALL | This shop has a large selection of Alaskan handicrafts as well as a mounted wildlife display and a yard full of spruce-burl sculptures that photographers find hard to resist. Burls are actually caused by parasites in the living tree, and they create beautiful patterns in the wood. Soft drinks, coffee, and ice cream are served over a spruce-burl counter. ✉ *Mile 332, 6565 Richardson Hwy., Salcha ⊹ 32 miles south of Fairbanks* ☎ *907/488–3014.*

Santa Claus House Gift Shop

STORE/MALL | If you stop in North Pole, don't skip this shop. Look for the world's largest Santa statue and the Christmas murals on the side of the building, as well as the year-round department-store style display windows. Inside, you'll find toys, gifts, Alaskan handicrafts, and, of course, Christmas cookies. Santa is on duty to talk to children in summers and during the holiday season. Also in summers, visit Antler Academy inside the red reindeer barn, where guests can interact with Santa's sleigh team. And yes, you can get your mail sent with a genuine North Pole postmark, a service offered since 1952. ✉ *101 St. Nicholas Dr.* ☎ *907/488–2200, 800/588–4078* ⊕ *www.santaclaushouse.com.*

Delta Junction

100 miles southeast of Fairbanks, 108 miles northwest of Tok.

Delta is not only a handy stop on the Richardson Highway, it's the official western terminus of the Alaska Highway. In summer Delta, the largest agricultural center in Alaska, becomes a bustling rest stop for road-weary travelers. The town is known for its access to good fishing and its proximity to the Delta Bison Range. Don't expect to see the elusive 500-strong bison herd, though, as the animals roam freely and generally avoid people.

GETTING HERE AND AROUND

Delta Junction is at the junction of the Alaska and Richardson highways, a little under two hours' drive from Fairbanks and five to six hours' drive from Valdez.

Sights

Delta Junction Visitor Center

INFO CENTER | In addition to finding out what's up in Delta Junction, you can purchase an "I Drove the Alaska Highway" certificate ($2) here—technically, the Alcan ends in Delta because there was already a road this far from Fairbanks. Across the street is the Sullivan Roadhouse Historical Museum (ask about hours at the visitor center). If you're in town on a Wednesday or Saturday between mid-May and early September, check out the wonderfully named Highway's End Farmer's Market, open both days from 10 to 5. ✉ *2855 Alaska Hwy.* ☎ *907/895–5068* ⊕ *www.deltachamber.org* ◷ *Visitor center closed Sept.–May.*

Rika's Roadhouse

HISTORIC SITE | The landmark Rika's Roadhouse, part of the 10-acre Big Delta State Historical Park, is a good detour for the free tours of the beautifully restored and meticulously maintained grounds, gardens, and historic buildings. In the past, roadhouses were erected at fairly regular intervals in the north, providing everything a traveler might need. Rika's, which operated from 1913 to 1947, is far and away the prettiest and best preserved of the survivors. It's a great place to get out, stretch, and buy homemade sandwiches, pies, and soft-serve ice cream. ⊠ *Mile 275, Richardson Hwy.* ☎ *507/884–9103* ⊕ *www.dnr.alaska. gov/parks/units/deltajct/bigdelta* ⊠ *Free* ⊗ *Closed mid-May–mid-Sept.*

Tok

12 miles west of Tetlin Junction, 175 miles southwest of Dawson City, 200 miles southeast of Fairbanks.

Loggers, miners, old sourdoughs (Alaskan for "colorful local curmudgeons"), and hunting guides who live and work along Tok's streams or in the millions of acres of spruce forest nearby come here for supplies. The population of Tok is 1,250 year-round, but its residents are joined each summer by thousands of travelers, among them adventurers journeying up the Alaska Highway from the Lower 48. Tok is more of a gateway to nearby attractions, such as the Tetlin National Wildlife Refuge, than a destination in itself, but its visitor center is worth a visit. The town also has markets, fueling stops, and some restaurants and hotels.

GETTING HERE AND AROUND

Tok sits at the junction of the Glenn and Alaska highways. 40-Mile Air serves the town from Fairbanks with three flights per week and flies to the Tetlin National Wildlife Refuge and other wilderness locations. The refuge lies south of the Alaska Highway southeast of Tok.

Loop tour: A huge loop driving tour starting in Tok takes in many of Alaska's terrific landscapes. Head down the Tok Cutoff to the Richardson Highway and continue south to Valdez. From there, catch the

Border Crossing

Crossing into Interior Alaska from the Lower 48 or from the ferry terminals in Southeast requires border crossings into Canada and then into Alaska. Be very certain of all the requirements for crossing an international border before you travel, including restrictions on pets and firearms and the need for adequate personal identification for every member of the party. Even citizens of Canada and the United States traveling between Alaska and Canada are required to have a passport—and they will be checked.

ferry to Whittier, Cordova, or Seward. Explore the Kenai and Anchorage, then head north on the Seward Highway to the parks, to Denali, Fairbanks, and beyond. Loop back to Tok and you will have experienced most of what can be seen from the road system.

AIRLINE CONTACT 40-Mile Air ⊠ *Mile 1313, Alaska Hwy.* ☎ *907/883–5191* ⊕ *fortymileair.com.*

⊙ Sights

Tetlin National Wildlife Refuge

NATURE PRESERVE | This 700,000-acre refuge has most of the charismatic megafauna that visitors travel to Alaska to see, including black and grizzly bears, moose, Dall sheep, wolves, caribou, and tons of birds. Just south of the Alaska Highway east of the town of Tok all the way to the U.S.–Canada border, the refuge has a visitor center at Mile 1,229. A large deck here has spotting scopes, and inside are maps, books, and wildlife exhibits, as well as a board with information on current road conditions. At Mile 1,240 you can hike a 1-mile raised-plank boardwalk through lowland forest to scenic Hidden Lake. Basic and seasonal lakefront campgrounds can be found at Miles 1,249 and 1,256. ✉ Visitor Center, Mile 1,229, Alaska Hwy. ☎ 907/883–5312 ⊕ www.fws.gov/refuge/tetlin ✉ Free ⊙ Visitor center closed mid-Sept.–mid-May.

Tok Main Street Visitor Center

INFO CENTER | To help with your planning, stop in at Tok's visitor center, which has travel information covering the entire state, as well as wildlife and natural-history exhibits. This is one of Alaska's largest info centers, and the staff is quite helpful. ✉ Mile 1,314, Alaska Hwy. ☎ 907/883–5775 ⊕ www.tokalaskainfo.com ✉ Free ⊙ Closed Oct.–Apr.

 Restaurants

Fast Eddy's Restaurant

$$ | AMERICAN | Not the greasy fast-food joint its name might suggest, this relaxing place serves surprisingly interesting cuisine. Portions are sizable—that prime rib dinner will induce a nap—and the variety provides welcome relief from the roadhouse burgers served by most Alaska Highway restaurants. **Known for:** deep-fried mushrooms; blueberry milk shakes; massive menu for a tiny town. $ Average main: $15 ✉ Mile 1,313, Alaska Hwy. ☎ 907/883–4411 ⊕ www.fasteddysrestaurant.com.

Hotels

Burnt Paw and Cabins Outback

$$ | B&B/INN | One of Tok's nicer lodgings, Burnt Paw has seven comfortable, sod-roof cabins—each with two beds, a private bath, a microwave, a refrigerator, Wi-Fi, satellite TV, and adorable sled-dog puppies. **Pros:** cozy cabins; good breakfast; best location in town. **Cons:** no kitchenettes; fee for pets; not for those who don't enjoy dogs. $ Rooms from: $149 ✉ Mile 1,314.3, Alaska Hwy. ☎ 907/883–4121 ⊕ www.

burntpawcabins.com ⊙ Closed Dec.–Feb. ⇌ 7 cabins ❍ Breakfast.

Cleft of the Rock Bed & Breakfast

$$ | B&B/INN | This family-run inn has picturesque private cabins and a comfortable apartment in a home. **Pros:** comfortable cabins; close to town; bikes and kayaks available for guests. **Cons:** no guided activities; no kitchenettes in cabins; some cabins not handicap-accessible. $ Rooms from: $140 ✉ 0.5 Sundog Trail, off Alaska Hwy. Mile 1,316.5 ☎ 907/883–4219 ⊕ cleftoftherock.net ⊙ Cabins closed late Sept.–mid-May, apt. available year-round ⇌ 5 cabins, 1 room ❍ Breakfast.

Chicken

78 miles north of Tok, 109 miles west of Dawson City.

Chicken was, and still is, the heart of the southern Fortymile Mining District, and many of these works are visible along the highway. The second town in Alaska to be incorporated (Skagway was the first), the town got its name (or so the story goes) after its residents, who wanted to call it "Ptarmigan," couldn't figure out how to spell that. Chicken has only a handful of permanent residents, mostly miners and trappers, creating an authentic frontier atmosphere.

Chicken is far from a prime shopping stop, but what it lacks in infrastructure, it makes up for in atmosphere. The town is small, so you don't have far to go to find everything you need. If you like bluegrass music, be sure to check out the Chickenstock Music Festival (⊕ www.chickenstockmusicfest.com) if you're passing through in mid-June.

GETTING HERE AND AROUND

Chicken sits off the Taylor Highway, a packed gravel road that closes in winter. The town is accessible only by car or bush plane—or, during winter, dogsled or snowmachine. No major commercial flights come here. Most people fly to Fairbanks and drive the five hours or so to Chicken, or visit as part of a longer road trip.

Overland travel between Chicken and Dawson City winds along a gravel road. Some drivers love it, some white-knuckle it.

◉ Sights

Chicken Creek RV Park & Cabins

TOUR—SIGHT | Free gold panning and in-season tours of a historic schoolhouse (offered daily at 10 am and 2 pm) are among the activities offered through this RV park's gift shop. The shop also has free Wi-Fi and an ATM. The RV park has gas and diesel, hostel rooms, camping sites, and cabins. ⊠ *Mile 66.8, at Chicken Creek Bridge* ☎ *907/505–0231* ⊕ *www.townofchicken.com* ⊗ *Closed mid-Sept.–mid-May.*

Chicken Gold Camp & Outpost

HISTORIC SITE | Finder's keepers is the name of the game at the Gold Camp, where you can pan for gold and tour a historic dredge. The Pedro Dredge scooped up 55,000 ounces of gold from Chicken Creek between 1959 and 1967, but apparently plenty was left behind in the creek and elsewhere. Guests can stay in the Gold Camp's cabins, campground, or RV park, but anyone can roam the associated historic buildings for free. Day trips, kayaking, and other activities can also be arranged. Hungry gold seekers can fill up in the café on wood-fired pizzas, sandwiches, and baked goods, or fuel up with an espresso. Bluegrass lovers appreciate the family-friendly Chickenstock Music Festival, held the second weekend in June. ⊠ *Airport Rd. off Taylor Hwy.* ☎ *907/782–4427 Apr.–Oct., 907/399–0005 in winter* ⊕ *www.chickengold.com* ⊗ *Closed mid-Sept.–mid-May.*

Downtown Chicken

TOWN | The longest-running business in town has classic wooden porches and provides multiple services. A fun place to explore, the complex includes the Chicken Creek Café, an eight-stool saloon, liquor store, and gift emporium. Free camping and overnight RV parking are available, with cabins and wall tents for rent. Gas and diesel are available from 7:30 am until the bar closes. The café serves baked wild Alaskan salmon for lunch and dinner, as well as scratch chicken pot pie and buffalo chili. ⊠ *Airport Rd. off Taylor Hwy.* ⊕ *www.chickenalaska.com.*

🏃 Activities

CANOEING
Fortymile River

CANOEING/ROWING/SKULLING | The beautiful Fortymile River offers everything from a 38-mile run to a lengthy journey to the Yukon and then down to Eagle. Its waters range from easy Class I to serious Class IV (possibly Class V) stretches. Only experienced canoeists should attempt boating on this river, and rapids should be scouted beforehand. Several access points can be found off the Taylor Highway. ⊠ *Chicken* ⊕ *www.rivers.gov/rivers/fortymile.php.*

Yukon Territory

The happy, shining promise of gold is what called Canada's Yukon Territory to the world's attention with the Klondike gold rush of 1897–98. Maybe as many as 100,000 people set off for the confluence of the Yukon and Klondike rivers, on the promise of nuggets the size of basketballs just waiting to be picked up. In the end, roughly only a dozen of them actually went home rich in gold, but all who returned did so rich in memories and stories that are still being told.

Though the international border divides Alaska from Yukon Territory, the Yukon River tends to unify the region. Early prospectors, miners, traders, and camp owers moved readily up and down the er with little regard to national boundies. An earlier Alaska strike preceded the Klondike find by years, yet Circle was all but abandoned in the stampede to the creeks around Dawson City. Later gold discoveries in the Alaskan Fortymile Country, Nome, and Fairbanks reversed that flow across the border into Alaska.

Dawson City

109 miles east of Chicken.

Beautiful Dawson City is the prime specimen of a Yukon gold-rush town. Since the first swell of hopeful migrants more than 100 years ago, many of the original buildings have disappeared, victims of fire, flood, and weathering. But plenty remain, and it's easy to step back in time, by attending a performance at the Palace Theatre, erected in 1899, or stepping into a shop whose building originally served stampeders. In modern Dawson City, street paving is erratic, and the place maintains a serious frontier vibe. But it's also a center for the arts—the town's yearly summer music festival is one of Canada's biggest—and as the last touch of civilization before the deep wild, it's where hikers share tables with hard-core miners at quirky local restaurants.

Today Dawson City is home to about 1,300 people, 360 or so of whom are of First Nations descent. The city itself is now a National Historic Site of Canada. Besides being one of the hippest, funkiest towns in the north, Dawson also serves as a base from which to explore the Tombstone Territorial Park, a natural wonderland with plants and animals found nowhere else, living in the spaces between high, steep mountain ranges.

GETTING HERE AND AROUND
The Alaska Highway starts in Dawson Creek, British Columbia, and stretches almost 1,500 miles to Fairbanks. Numerous bus companies offer package tours

or simple shuttle services (⇨ *see Whitehorse Essentials, below*). Regular air service to Dawson flies from Fairbanks in summer. Air North, Yukon's Airline, in Whitehorse, offers direct service from Whitehorse to Dawson City in summer.

Loop tour: Drivers traveling north- and southbound on the Alaska Highway can make a loop with the Taylor Highway route. This adds 100 miles to the trip but is worth it. Part with the Alaska Highway at Tetlin Junction and wind through the Fortymile Country past the little communities of Chicken and Jack Wade Camp into Canada. The border is open from 8 am to 8 pm in summer. The Canadian section of the Taylor Highway is called Top of the World Highway, and with most of it on a ridgeline between two huge valleys, it really does feel like the top of the world, opening broad views of range after range of tundra-covered mountains stretching in every direction. Join back with the Alaska Highway at Whitehorse.

AIRLINE CONTACTS Air North, Yukon's Airline ☎ *800/661–0407* ⊕ *www.flyairnorth.com.*

VISITOR INFORMATION
CONTACTS Klondike Visitors Association ✉ *1102 Front St.* ☎ *867/993–5575* ⊕ *www.dawsoncity.ca.* **Visitor Information Centre** ✉ *Front and King Sts.* ☎ *867/993–5566 May–Sept., 867/993–5575 Oct.–Apr.* ⊕ *www.dawsoncity.ca/plan-your-trip.*

 Sights

Dänojà Zho Cultural Centre
MUSEUM | Its inviting atmosphere makes the center a good stop to explore the heritage of Tr'ondëk Hwëch'in First Nations people. For countless generations Hän-speaking people lived in the Yukon River drainage of western Yukon and eastern Alaska. This specific language group settled around the mouth of the Klondike River. Through annually rotating displays, as well as tours, cultural activities, films, live radio broadcasts, and

performances, you can learn about the traditional and contemporary life of "the people of the river." Though somewhat sparse, the historical exhibits convey a sense of what the gold rush was like for the people who were here first. Special summer activities include music events and daily workshops in beading, indigenous medicine, and tea- and jelly-making. The gift shop sells fine First Nations art, clothing, and beaded footwear, and stocks music and books. ☒ *1131 Front St.* ☎ *867/993–7100* ⊕ *www.trondekheritage.com* ⬚ *C$7* ☉ *Closed mid-Sept.–late May and Sun.*

Dawson City Museum

MUSEUM | There's a lot going on at this museum with exhibits about the gold rush, the geology and prehistory of the Klondike, and the Yukon region's First Nations peoples. While touring the excellent displays of gold-rush material downstairs, you may find it surprising just how luxurious Dawson was for the lucky few who could call themselves rich. Many visitors zip past the household goods upstairs, but don't miss the piece of mammoth meat on the stairway landing. Four restored locomotives and other railway cars and gear from the Klondike Mines Railway are housed in an adjacent building. The museum also has a library and archives, helpful to those seeking information about gold-rush ancestors, and offers programs and demonstrations daily. ☒ *Old Territorial Administration Bldg., 595 5th Ave.* ☎ *867/993–5291* ⊕ *www.dawsonmuseum.ca* ⬚ *C$9* ☉ *Closed Sept.–mid-May, except by appointment.*

Diamond Tooth Gerties Gambling Hall

CASINO—SIGHT | Adults-only Gerties presents live entertainment and high-energy performances, including a scintillating cancan three times nightly during the summer. This community nonprofit is the only authentic, legal gambling establishment operating in the entire North (it's also the oldest gambling hall in Canada),

though the scene is mostly slots along with a few gaming tables. And there really was a Diamond Tooth Gertie—Gertie Lovejoy, a dance-hall queen who wore a diamond between her two front teeth. ☒ *Queen St. and 4th Ave.* ☎ *867/993–5525* ⊕ *www.diamondtoothgerties. ca* ⬚ *C$12* ☉ *Closed Sun.–Thurs. late Sept.–mid-May.*

Gold Dredge No. 4

MINE | When this massive wooden-hull gold dredge was in operation (1913–59), it ate rivers whole, spitting out gravel and keeping the gold for itself—on one highly productive day it sucked up 800 ounces. These days the dredge—a Canadian National Historic Site—occupies a spot along Bonanza Creek about 10 miles southeast of Dawson. The dredge is still a stop for a look, even on your own, if only to ponder the geology and economics that made it viable to haul this enormous piece of equipment into the middle of nowhere at a time when gold only brought $20 an ounce. Goldbottom Mine Tours offers seven tours a day in summer, and can provide shuttle service from Front Street. You can pan for gold yourself in Bonanza Creek, where the Klondike Visitors Association offers a free claim for visitors. Bring your own supplies (almost every gift shop in town sells pans). ☒ *Mile 8 Bonanza Creek Rd.* ✛ *Exit Klondike Hwy. at Km marker 74* ☎ *867/993–5023* ⊕ *www. goldbottom.com* ⬚ *C$20* ☉ *Closed mid-Sept.–mid-May.*

Jack London Museum

MUSEUM | This reproduction of London's home from 1897 to 1898 is constructed with half the wood from his original wilderness home that was found south of Dawson in the 1930s. The other half was sent to Oakland, California, where a similar structure sits at Jack London Square. The small museum contains photos and documents from London's life and the gold-rush era. Half-hour talks are given twice daily during peak season.

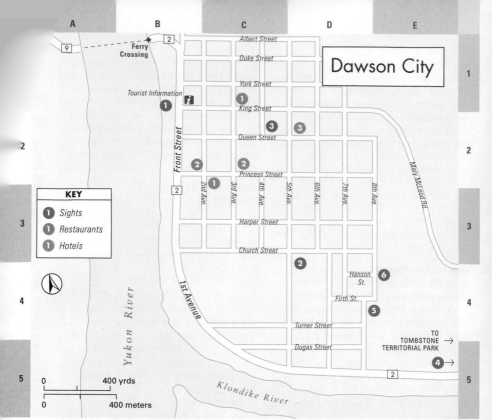

Dawson City

Sights ▼

1 Dänojà Zho Cultural
   Centre.................... **B1**
2 Dawson City Museum.. **D3**
3 Diamond Tooth Gerties
   Gambling Hall **C2**
4 Gold Dredge No. 4 .... **E5**
5 Jack London Museum .. **E4**
6 Robert Service Cabin.... **E4**

Restaurants ▼

1 Klondike Kate's........... **C1**
2 Red Mammoth Bistro... **B2**

Hotels ▼

1 Bombay Peggy's **C2**
2 Eldorado Hotel **C2**
3 Triple J Hotel &
   Cabins.................... **D2**

⊠ *8th Ave. and Firth St.* ☎ *867/993–5575* ⊕ *www.jacklondonmuseum.ca* ⊠ *C\$5* ☉ *Closed Oct.–Apr.*

Robert Service Cabin

HOUSE | The poet Robert Service lived in this Dawson cabin from 1909 to 1912. From late May to early September, enjoy daily readings outside the cabin or learn the region's history on a guided Parks Canada hike up to Crocus Bluffs. Call ahead for the schedule. ⊠ *8th Ave. and Hanson St.* ☎ *867/993–5566* ⊠ *C\$7.*

 ## Activities

HIKING
Tombstone Territorial Park

HIKING/WALKING | Often described as "the Patagonia of the Northern Hemisphere," Tombstone has some of the best hiking and views of granite peaks in the Yukon. About 56 km (36 miles) northeast of Dawson City and bisected by the Dempster Highway, Tombstone occupies 2,200 square km (850 square miles) of wilderness supporting a vast array of wildlife and vegetation. Backcountry mountaineering and wildlife-viewing options abound, though for the most part the terrain is too difficult for hiking novices. The park maintains day-use trails at Km markers 58.5, 71.5 (two here), 74.4, and 78.2. At Km marker 71.5 is the Tombstone Interpretive Centre and Campground. The center has informative displays and great mountain views. Stop here to get a handle on everything the park has to offer, and to learn how animals make it through the winter. Flightseeing trips over the jagged Tombstone Range depart from Dawson City. ⊠ *Dawson City* ☎ *867/993–7714 in Dawson City, 800/661–0408* ⊕ *www.env. gov.yk.ca/tombstone* ⊠ *Free.*

 ## Hotels

Bombay Peggy's

\$\$\$ | B&B/INN | Named and fashioned after one of the last of Dawson's legal

 # Writers' Contribution

Scholars still argue the precise details of the lives of writers Robert Service (1874–1958) and Jack London (1876–1916) in Dawson City, but no one disputes that between Service's poems and London's short stories the two did more than anyone else to popularize and romanticize the Yukon.

madams, Peggy's is done in elaborate Victorian gold-rush style, with heavy, plush draperies and rich color schemes. **Pros:** an engaging step back in time; nice touches such as fresh croissants and "Sherry Hour"; fun on-site pub. **Cons:** no elevator; not all rooms have air-conditioning; three upstairs rooms, known as the Snugs, share a bathroom. ⑤ *Rooms from: C\$185* ⊠ *2nd Ave. and Princess St.* ☎ *867/993–6969* ⊕ *www.bombaypeggys. com* ⤷ *7 rooms* ⦿⧉ *Breakfast.*

Eldorado Hotel

\$\$ | HOTEL | Though this hotel has a pioneer-style facade, its rooms are outfitted with modern amenities such as high-def TVs and Internet connections, and some suites even have Jacuzzis. **Pros:** in-hotel bar and restaurant; kitchenettes in some rooms; good location. **Cons:** no elevator; free Wi-Fi has data limits; no pets. ⑤ *Rooms from: C\$165* ⊠ *902 3rd Ave.* ☎ *867/993–5451, 800/764–3536 from Alaska and the Yukon* ⊕ *www.eldorado-hotel.ca* ☉ *Closed mid-Dec.–mid-Jan.* ⤷ *62 rooms.*

Triple J Hotel & Cabins

\$\$ | HOTEL | With a pretty white-and-blue annex of suites and standard rooms as well as a selection of log cabins, Triple J offers choice for everyone from solo travelers to families. **Pros:** free Wi-Fi; in-room kitchenettes in cabins and annex;

e restaurant on-site. **Cons:** smallish ⌐owers in cabins; kitchenettes lack ⌐vens; some cabin porches face a gravel parking lot. ⑤ *Rooms from: C$149* ✉ *5th Ave. and Queen St.* ☎ *867/993–5323, 800/764–3555* ⊕ *www.triplejhotel.com* ⇆ *39 rooms, 23 cabins.*

Whitehorse

337 miles southeast of Dawson City, 600 miles southeast of Fairbanks, 110 miles north of Skagway.

Near the White Horse Rapids of the Yukon River, Whitehorse began as an encampment in the late 1890s, a logical layover for gold rushers heading north along the Chilkoot Trail toward Dawson. The next great population boom came during the Second World War with the building of the Alcan—the Alaska-Canada Highway. Today this city of about 25,000 residents is Yukon's center of commerce, communication, and transportation, and the seat of the territorial government. It also has the only Tim Hortons café locations for hundreds of miles.

Besides being a great starting point for explorations of other areas of the Yukon, the town has plenty of diversions and recreational opportunities. You can spend a day exploring its museums and cultural displays—research the Yukon's mining and development history, look into the backgrounds of the town's founders, learn about its indigenous First Nations people, and gain an appreciation of the Yukon Territory from prehistoric times up to the present.

GETTING HERE AND AROUND

Air Canada flies to Whitehorse in summer from Anchorage through Vancouver. Air North, Yukon's Whitehorse-based Airline, provides direct, seasonal air service from Whitehorse to several other Canadian cities, including Dawson City, Vancouver, and Calgary. Juneau-based

Alaska Seaplanes also operates a service between Alaska's capital and Whitehorse.

To take in all the scenery along the way, you can drive yourself up the Alcan Highway, or let someone else do the driving on a bus tour. Alaska/Yukon Trails provides tours from Whitehorse to Dawson City to Fairbanks. There are multiple rental-car companies, buses, and taxis in Whitehorse; Whitehorse Transit has a city bus circuit that will get you where you need to go. From Whitehorse you can also make your way to Skagway, at the northern end of the Inside Passage—the drive takes about three hours via the Klondike Highway.

AIRLINE CONTACTS Air North, Yukon's Airline ☎ *800/661–0407* ⊕ *www.flyairnorth. com.*

BUS CONTACTS Alaska/Yukon Trails ☎ *800/770–7275* ⊕ *www.alaskashuttle. com.*

CITY BUS CONTACTS Whitehorse Transit ☎ *867/668–8396* ⊕ *www.whitehorse.ca/ transit.*

TAXI CONTACTS Grizzly Bear Taxi ☎ *867/667–4888.*

VISITOR INFORMATION
CONTACTS Whitehorse Visitor Information Centre ✉ *100 Hanson St.* ☎ *867/667–3084, 800/661–0494* ⊕ *www.travelyukon. com.*

 Sights

Canyon City Historic Site
ARCHAEOLOGICAL SITE | This archaeological dig site provides a glimpse into the past of the local First Nations people. Long before Western civilizations developed the Miles Canyon area, the First Nations people used it as a seasonal fish camp. From mid-June to late August, the Yukon Conservation Society sponsors two-hour, kid-friendly natural and historical hikes here that provide the opportunity to experience the surrounding countryside

with local naturalists. A bookstore in the society's office specializes in the Yukon's history and wilderness and sells souvenirs, maps, and posters. ✉ *302 Hawkins St.* ☎ *867/668–5678* ⊕ *www.yukonconservation.org* ⊠ *Free.*

MacBride Museum of Yukon History

MUSEUM | The exhibits at the MacBride provide a comprehensive view of the colorful characters and groundbreaking events that shaped the Yukon. An old-fashioned confectionery and an 1898 miner's saloon are among the highlights of the Gold to Government Gallery illuminating gold-rush and Whitehorse history. The gold-related exhibits illustrate particularly well what people went through in quest of a little glint of color. Other displays investigate the Yukon's wildlife and geology, and there are fine collections of photography and First Nations beadwork. Outdoor artifacts include the cabin of Sam McGee, who was immortalized in Robert Service's famous poem "The Cremation of Sam McGee." ✉ *1124 Front St.* ☎ *867/667–2709* ⊕ *www.macbridemuseum.com* ⊠ *C$10* ⊙ *Closed Sun. and Mon. early Sept.–mid-May.*

Miles Canyon

NATURE SITE | Both scenic and historic, Miles Canyon is a short drive south of Whitehorse. Although the dam below the canyon makes its waters seem relatively tame, it was this perilous stretch of the Yukon River that determined the location of Whitehorse as the starting point for river travel north. The dam, built in 1958, created a lake that put an end to the infamous White Horse Rapids. Back in 1897, though, Jack London won the admiration—and cash—of fellow stampeders headed north to the Klondike goldfields because of his steady hand as pilot of hand-hewn wooden boats here. You can hike on trails along the canyon or rent a kayak and paddle on through. ✉ *Miles Canyon Rd.*

S.S. *Klondike*

HISTORIC SITE | You can't really understand the scale of the gold rush without touring a riverboat. The SS *Klondike*, a national historic site, is dry-docked on the bank of the Yukon River in central Whitehorse's Rotary Park, just a minute's drive from downtown. The 210-foot stern-wheeler was built in 1929, sank in 1936, and was rebuilt in 1937. In the days when the Yukon River was the transportation link between Whitehorse and Dawson City, the S.S. *Klondike* was the largest boat plying the river. Riverboats were as much a way of life here as on the Mississippi of Mark Twain, and the tour of the *Klondike* is a fascinating way to see how the boats were adapted to the north. In the old days they were among the few places that provided indigenous people paying jobs, so there's a rich First Nations and Alaska Natives history as well. You can obtain a self-guided tour brochure for C$2. Guided tours are available through Parks Canada at 10:30 am and 2:15 pm daily (C$6). ✉ *Robert Service Way at 4th Ave., on bank of Yukon River* ☎ *867/667–4511 mid-May–mid-Sept.,* 800/661–0486 ⊕ *www.pc.gc.ca/ssklondike* ⊠ *Free* ⊙ *Closed early Sept.–mid-May.*

Takhini Hot Pools

HOT SPRINGS | Relax away the driving miles with a dip into Takhini Hot Pools at this complex off the Klondike Highway. Lounge or swim in the two hot spring–warmed pools (suits, towels, and flip-flops are for rent). There's also a campground, with space for both tents and RVs, a restaurant specializing in crepes, and a 20-bed hostel. The pools are open year-round, making for a breathtaking way to take in the wintry outdoors while staying warm and toasty. Private late-night pool rentals give you a good excuse to stay up past your bedtime. There's also a hair-freezing photo contest each February, and discounted admission to the pools on some weeknights in winter. ✉ *Km 10/Mile 6, Takhini Hot Springs Rd.* ⊹ *18 miles north of Whitehorse*

📱 867/456–8000 ⊕ www.takhinihot-springs.com 🖼 C$12.

Waterfront Walkway

PROMENADE | The walkway along the Yukon River passes by a few points of interest. Start along the river just east of the MacBride Museum entrance on Front Street. Traveling upstream (south), you'll see the old White Pass and Yukon Route Building on Main Street. The walk is a good way to get an overview of the old town site, and just stretch your legs if you've been driving all day. ✉ *Whitehorse.*

Whitehorse Fishway

DAM | **FAMILY** | Yukon Energy built this fishway to facilitate the yearly chinook (king) salmon run around the Whitehorse Rapids hydroelectric dam. The salmon hold one of nature's great endurance records, the longest fish migration in the world—more than 2,000 miles from the Bering Sea to Whitehorse. There's a platform for viewing the ladder, and TV monitors display pictures from underwater cameras. Interesting interpretive exhibits, talks by local First Nations elders, and labeled tanks of freshwater fish enhance the experience. The best time to visit is August, when hundreds of salmon use the ladder to bypass the dam. ✉ *Nisutlin Dr.* 📱 *867/633–5965* 🖼 *C$3 suggested donation.*

Yukon Beringia Interpretive Centre

MUSEUM | The story of the Yukon during the last Ice Age comes alive at this center near the Whitehorse Airport. Beringia is the name given to the large subcontinental landmasses of eastern Siberia and Interior Alaska and the Yukon, which stayed ice-free and were linked by the Bering Land Bridge during the latest Ice Age. The area that is now Whitehorse wasn't actually part of this—it was glaciated—but lands farther north, among them what is present-day Dawson City, were in the thick of it, and miners are still turning up mammoth bones. Large dioramas depict the lives of animals in Ice Age Beringia, and there are skeleton replicas. A 26,000-year-old horsehide reveals that horses weren't as big back then as they are now. ✉ *Mile 886, Alaska Hwy.* 📱 *867/667–8855* ⊕ *www.beringia. com* 🖼 *C$6.*

Yukon Permanent Art Collection

MUSEUM | The lobby of the Government of Yukon Main Administration Building displays selections from the Yukon Permanent Art Collection, featuring traditional and contemporary works by Yukon artists. The space also includes a 24-panel mural by artist David MacLagan depicting the historical evolution of the Yukon. In addition to the collection on the premises, the brochure *Art Adventures on Yukon Time,* available at visitor centers throughout the Yukon, guides you to artists' studios as well as galleries, festivals, and public art locations. ✉ *2071 2nd Ave.* 📱 *867/667–5811* ⊕ *www.tc.gov.yk.ca/ ypac* 🖼 *Free* ◷ *Closed weekends.*

Yukon Transportation Museum

MUSEUM | This museum takes a fascinating look at the planes, trains, trucks, and snowmachines that opened up the north. Even if big machines don't interest you, this is a cool place to learn about the innovations and adaptations that transport in the north has inspired. ✉ *30 Electra Crescent* 📱 *867/668–4792* ⊕ *www. goytm.ca* 🖼 *C$10* ◷ *Closed Tues.–Sat. Sept.–May, except by appointment.*

Yukon Wildlife Preserve

NATURE PRESERVE | The preserve provides a fail-safe way to photograph sometimes hard-to-spot animals in a natural setting. Animals roaming freely here include moose, elk, caribou, mountain goats, musk oxen, bison, mule deer, and Dall and Stone sheep. Bus tours take place throughout the day, and self-guided walking maps are available. ✉ *Mile 5, Takhini Hot Springs Rd., Takhini Hot Springs* 📱 *867/456–7300* ⊕ *www.yukonwildlife.ca* 🖼 *C$15 self-guided tour, C$22 bus tour* ◷ *Closed Mon.–Thurs. Oct.–Apr. except by appointment.*

 Activities

DOG MUSHING

Yukon Quest International Sled Dog Race

LOCAL SPORTS | Because the terrain is rougher and there are fewer checkpoints, most dog mushers think this 1,000-mile race between Whitehorse and Fairbanks provides more intense competition than the higher-profile Iditarod. The Yukon Quest takes place in February; the starting line alternates yearly between the two cities. Twenty to 30 mushers participate, with most finishing in 9 to 14 days. ⊠ *Whitehorse* ☎ *867/668–4711* ⊕ *www.yukonquest.com.*

HIKING

Kluane National Park and Reserve

HIKING/WALKING | About 170 km (100 miles) west of Whitehorse, the reserve has millions of acres for hiking. This is a completely roadless wilderness, with hundreds of glaciers and so many mountains over 14,000 feet high that most of them haven't been named yet (one exception: Mt. Logan, Canada's highest peak). Kluane, the neighboring Wrangell–St. Elias National Park in Alaska, and a few smaller parks, constitute the largest protected wilderness in all North America. The staff at the Haines Junction visitor center can provide hiking, flightseeing, and other information. ⊠ *Visitor center, 119 Logan St., Haines Junction* ☎ *867/634–7250* ⊕ *www.pc.gc.ca/kluane.*

Restaurants

The Claim Cafe & Food Co

$$ | CAFÉ | Choose from fresh-baked breads and pastries, homemade soups and sandwiches, and salads and quiches at this charming café and deli. Locals love the chocolate cake, a moist, rich delight. **Known for:** outdoor seating; gluten-free options; chocolate indulgences. ⑤ *Average main: C$15* ⊠ *305 Strickland St.* ☎ *867/667–2202* ⊕ *www.theclaim.ca* ⊙ *Closed Sun.*

★ Klondike Rib & Salmon

$$$$ | AMERICAN | Wild-game dishes such as elk, reindeer, bison, and boar are the Klondike's specialty, but it's also known for halibut, salmon, arctic char, and killer ribs. The restaurant meets vegetarians' needs with pasta and meatless dishes. **Known for:** the best wild game in town; long waits; oldest operating building in Whitehorse. ⑤ *Average main: C$29* ⊠ *2116 2nd Ave.* ☎ *867/667–7554* ⊕ *www.klondikerib.com* ⊙ *Closed mid-Sept.–mid-May.*

★ Midnight Sun Coffee Roasters

$ | CAFÉ | One of the hippest coffee shops you'll ever set foot in—but completely devoid of snobbery—shares space with a bicycle shop, cleverly named Icycle Sport. Service is superfriendly and the coffee is, quite simply, stellar, as are the baked goods. **Known for:** eclectic, family-run energy; small-batch coffee; fantastic flower boxes in summer. ⑤ *Average main: C$5* ⊠ *21 Waterfront Pl.* ☎ *888/633–4563, 867/633–4563* ⊕ *www.yukoncoffee.com* ⊙ *Closed Sun.*

🛏 Hotels

Coast High Country Inn & Convention Centre

$$$ | B&B/INN | At this downtown hotel you'll find modern, comfortably appointed standard rooms and premium ones with Jacuzzis and kitchenettes. **Pros:** free airport shuttle; central location; on-site dining at Morels. **Cons:** some rooms lack air-conditioning and bathtubs; standard rooms are minimally decorated; some rooms are very small. ⑤ *Rooms from: C$210* ⊠ *4051 4th Ave.* ☎ *867/667–4471, 800/554–4471* ⊕ *www.highcountryinn.yk.ca* ➾ *82 rooms* ⏐⊙⏐ *No meals.*

Edgewater Hotel

$$$$ | HOTEL | Thanks to its small size, comfy bedding, and sophisticated style, the Edgewater has the ambience of a boutique hotel. **Pros:** rich history; one block from the Yukon River; free Wi-Fi. **Cons:** no breakfast; some noise from

ain Street; adjacent parking is limited.
⑤ *Rooms from: C$259* ✉ *101 Main St.*
☎ *867/667–2572* ⊕ *www.edgewaterho-telwhitehorse.com* ↩ *32 rooms* ⦿ *No meals.*

Westmark Whitehorse Hotel & Conference Center

$$$ | **HOTEL** | Rooms are standard issue but clean (suites have a little more personality) at this full-service downtown property, the largest hotel in the Yukon. **Pros:** laundry facilities; great restaurant and lounge; breakfast buffet available in summer. **Cons:** can get noisy; fee for Wi-Fi; no air-conditioning. ⑤ *Rooms from: C$199* ✉ *201 Wood St.* ☎ *867/393–9700, 800/544–0970 reservations* ⊕ *www.westmarkhotels.com* ↩ *180 rooms* ⦿ *No meals.*

Index

A

Abkhazi Garden and Teahouse, *317*
Accessibility, *27, 35*
Adventure and scenic tours
  Denali National Park and Preserve, *341, 344*
  Fairbanks, *331–332*
  inland tour destinations, *330*
  Juneau, *271*
  Ketchikan, *281–283*
  Kodiak Island, *283*
  Seward, *217, 219*
  Valdez, *315*
  Wrangell, *323, 326*
Adventure Bound Alaska, *275*
Aialik Glacier, *302*
Alaska Aviation Museum, *198*
Alaska Botanical Garden, *198–199*
Alaska Chilkat Bald Eagle Preserve, *255, 257*
Alaska Fjordlines, *258*
Alaska Heritage Museum at Wells Fargo, *199*
Alaska Indian Arts, *257*
Alaska Marine Highway, *68–71, 240*
Alaska Native Heritage Center, *199*
Alaska Native peoples, *262–265*
Alaska Public Lands Information Center, *199*
Alaska Raptor Center, *305–306*
Alaska SeaLife Center, *219*
Alaska Seaplanes, *253–254*
Alaska State Capital, *269*
Alaska State Library, Archives, and Museum, *269*
Alaskan Dream Cruises, *51–52, 64–67*
Alutiiq Museum and Archeological Repository, *283*
American Cruise Lines, *52, 72–75*
Anan Wildlife Observatory, *323, 326*
Anchorage, *16–17, 197–205*
Anchorage Market and Festival, *205*
Anchorage Museum, *199*
Antler Arch, *332*
Arctic Brotherhood Hall, *311*
Arriving, *40–41, 246–257*
Aura ✕, *321*
Aurora Borealis, *339*

B

Balcony cabins, *35*
Bald eagles, *255, 257*
Baranov Museum, *283, 285*
Bars, pubs, lounges and saloons, *46*
  Anchorage, *204*
  Fairbanks, *337–338*
  Juneau, *273*
  Seattle, *214, 216*
  Vancouver, *232*
Bartlett Cove, *253*

Bear-watching
  Fortymile Country, *349–350*
  Haines, *258*
  Homer, *266–267*
  Kodiak Island, *287*
  Prince Rupert, *296*
  Wrangell, *323*
Bering Glacier, *301*
Bicycling, *275*
Bill Reid Gallery, *226*
Bird-watching
  Fortymile Country, *349–350*
  Haines, *255, 257, 258*
  Homer, *260*
  Petersburg, *291*
  Sitka, *305–306*
Blind Slough Recreation Area, *291*
Blue Water Cafe & Raw Bar ✕, *229*
Boarding, *41*
Boating, *303*
  Fairbanks, *338–339*
  Gustavus, *253, 254*
  Haines, *258*
  Homer, *267*
  Juneau, *275*
  Whittier, *243–244*
  Wrangell, *326*
Booking your cruise, *38–39*
Border crossing, *349*
Breakaway Adventures, *326*
Butchart Gardens, *317, 319*
Butterfly Gardens, *317*

C

Cabins, *26–27, 34–37*
Cafe Brio ✕, *322*
Camp Denali and North Face Lodge 🔢, *345*
Canada Place, *226–227*
Canoeing, *338, 351*
Canopy tours, *281–282*
Canyon City Historic Site, *356–357*
Capilano Suspension Bridge, *227*
Car rentals, *196*
Carnival Cruise Lines, *26, 27, 52, 76–81*
Casinos, *46–47, 353*
Celebrity Cruises, *26, 27, 52, 82–89*
Chief Shakes Island and Tribal House, *325*
Chief Shakes's Grave Site, *325*
Chicken, *350–351*
Chicken Creek RV Park & Cabins, *351*
Chicken Gold Camp & Outpost, *351*
Children, attractions for, *271*
  Alaska Marine Highway, *69*
  Alaskan Dream Cruises, *65*
  American Cruise Lines, *73*
  Carnival Cruise Lines, *78*
  Celebrity Cruises, *84*
  Crystal Cruises, *92–93*
  Disney Cruise Line, *100*
  Holland America Line, *106*
  Lindblad Expeditions, *120*
  Norwegian Cruise Line, *124*
  Oceania Cruises, *134*
  Princess Cruises, *140*

Regent Seven Seas Cru...
Royal Caribbean Interna...
Seabourn Cruise Line, *16...*
Silversea Cruises, *172*
UnCruise Adventures, *179*
Viking Ocean Cruises, *184*
Windstar Cruises, *191*
Chilkoot Charlie's (bar), *204*
Chinatown Night Market, *227*
Clausen Memorial Museum, *291*
Clothing for the trip, *38–40*
College Fjord, *299*
Columbia Glacier, *302, 314*
Communications, *49, 247*
Corrington's Museum of Alaskan History, *311*
Costs, *32–34, 45, 197, 249, 330*
Cow Bay, *294*
Crafts. ⇨ See Native handicrafts
Craigdarroch Castle, *319*
Creek Street (Ketchikan), *277–278*
Crime, *50*
Crocodile, The (club), *216*
Crow's Nest Restaurant ✕, *202*
Cruise ships, reviews of, *62–193*
Cruise tours, *31–32*
Crush Wine Bistro and Cellar ✕, *202*
Crystal Cruises, *52–53, 90–97*
Cuisine, *18–19*
Currency, *247*
Customs and duties, *50–51*

D

Dänojà Zho Cultural Centre, *352–353*
Dawson City, *352–356*
Dawson City Museum, *353*
Deck plans, *36–37*
Delta Junction, *348–349*
Delta Junction Visitor Center, *348*
Denali National Park and Preserve, *17, 340–346*
Denali Outdoor Center, *346*
Denali Visitor Center, *340*
Diamond, The (bar), *232*
Diamond Tooth Gerties Gambling Hall, *353*
Dining on board, *27, 44–45*
  Alaskan Dream Cruises, *64–65*
  Alaska Marine Highway, *69*
  American Cruise Lines, *72–73*
  Carnival Cruise Lines, *76–77, 81*
  Celebrity Cruises, *82–83, 86–87, 89*
  Crystal Cruises, *90–91, 94–95, 97–98*
  Disney Cruise Line, *98–99, 103*
  Holland American Line, *104–105, 109, 111, 113, 114–115, 116–117*
  Lindblad Expeditions, *119*
  Norwegian Cruise Line, *122–123, 127, 128–129, 131*
  Oceania Cruises, *132–133, 134–135, 136–137*
  Princess Cruises, *138–139, 142–143, 144–145, 146–147*
  Regent Seven Seas Cruises, *148–149, 153*
  Royal Caribbean International, *154–155, 158, 161, 162–163*
  Seabourn Cruise Line, *164–165, 168–169*

Credits

...ver: Kevin G Smith / age fotostock [Description: Cruise ship docked at Haines harbor in Portage Cove, Haines, Southeast Alaska]. ...over, from left to right: Can Balcioglu/Shutterstock. Jerryway | Dreamstime.com; David Davis/Shutterstock. Spine: Ruth Peterkin/ ...terstock. Interior, from left to right: alaskarap (1). Atterhorn | Dreamstime.com (2–3). Stephen Frink Collection / Alamy (5). Chapter 1: ...perience an Alaskan Cruise: Papilio / Alamy (6–7). emperorcosar / Shutterstock (8–9). Gleb Tarro / Shutterstock (9). Larjon | Dreamstime. ...om (9). Steve Boice / Shutterstock (10). Mscornelius | Dreamstime.com (10). reisegraf.ch / Shutterstock (10). Russ Heinl / Shutterstock (10). Jeanninebryan Dreamstime.com (11). Dbvirago | Dreamstime.com (11). Paxson Woelber [CC 2.0] / Wikimedia Commons (11). artincamera / Shutterstock (12). Bob Pool / Shutterstock (12). Mikhail Varentsov / Shutterstock (12). Leieng | Dreamsttime.com (13). FloridaStock / Shutterstock (14). takeshi82 / Shutterstock (14). unge255_photostock / Shutterstock (14). Walleyelj | Dreamstime.com (14). Surangaw | Dreamstime.com (15). Carmengabrielafilip | Dreamstime.com (15). Kondor83/Shutterstock (18). Chrisimages | Dreamstime.com (18). LunaseeStudios/Shutterstock (18). hlphoto/Shutterstock (19). Asya Nurullina/Shutterstock (19). Antonov Roman/Shutterstock (20). vitaliy_73/ Shutterstock (20). Khritthithat Weerasirirut/Shutterstock (20). The Kobuk Team (21). Reinhardt | Dreamstime.com (21). Chase Dekker/ Shutterstock (22). Tory Kallman/Shutterstock (22). Major Marine Tours (22). John Coffey (22). Walleyelj | Dreamstime.com (23). Wildnerdpix/ Shutterstock (23). Julien Schroder (23). Anastasiia Vereshchagina/Shutterstock (23). VicPhotoria/Shutterstock (24). Hemuli/Shutterstock (25). American Safari Cruises (28). Chapter 2: Planning your Alaska Cruise: American Safari Cruises (29). Chapter 3: Cruise Lines and Cruise Ships: Visual&Written SL / Alamy (59). Alaska Dream Cruises (64). John_Engelman (64). Alaska Dream Cruises (65). Alaska Dream Cruises (66). Glenn Aronwits/digitalphotos.com/gapanorams.com (66). Alaska Dream Cruises (66). Eli Duke/Flickr, [CC BY-SA 2.0] (68). Jay Galvin/ Flickr, [CC BY 2.0] (68). Mscornelius | Dreamstime.com (69). Sunny K Awazahura- R / age fotostock (70). Eli Duke/Flickr, [CC BY-SA 2.0] (70). Eli Duke/Flickr, [CC BY-SA 2.0] (70). Courtesy of American Cruise Lines (72). Courtesy of American Cruise Lines (72). Courtesy of American Cruise Lines (73). Courtesy of American Cruise Lines (74). Courtesy of American Cruise Lines (74). Courtesy of American Cruise Lines (74). Carnival Cruise Lines (76). Carnival Cruise Lines (76). Carnival Cruise Lines (77). Carnival Cruise Lines (78). Carnival Cruise Lines (78). Andy Newman/Carnival Cruise Lines (78). Andy NEWMAN/CCL (80). ANDY NEWMAN/CCL (80). Andy Newman, 2004 (81). Courtesy Celebrity Cruises (82). Courtesy Celebrity Cruises (82). Courtesy Celebrity Cruises (83). Courtesy Celebrity Cruises (83), Celebrity Cruises (84). Celebrity Cruises (84). 2011 Michel Verdure (86). 2011 Michel Verdure (86). 2011 Michel Verdure (87). Stephen Beaudet (88). Stephen Beaudet (88). Stephen Beaudet (89). Courtesy Crystal Cruises (90). Courtesy Crystal Cruises (90). Courtesy Crystal Cruises (91). Courtesy Crystal Cruises (91). Courtesy Crystal Cruises (92). Ian Schemper (92). Courtesy Crystal Cruises (92). Ian Schemper (94). Courtesy Crystal Cruises (94). Courtesy Crystal Cruises (96). Disney Cruise Line (98). Disney Cruise Line (98). Disney Cruise Line (99). Disney Cruise Line (99). Disney Cruise Line (100). Disney Cruise Line (100). Disney Cruise Line (100). Disney Cruise Line (102). Disney Cruise Line (102). Disney Cruise Line (103). Courtesy Holland America Line (104). Courtesy Holland America Line (104). Courtesy Holland America Line (105). Courtesy Holland America Line (105). Courtesy Holland America Line (106). Andy Newman/Hal (106). Courtesy Holland America Line (106). Courtesy Holland America Line (108). Courtesy Holland America Line (108). Courtesy Holland America Line (109). Courtesy Holland America Line (110). Michel Verdure/Holland America Line (111). Andy Newman/Hal (112). Holland America Line (112). Courtesy Holland America Line (113). Courtesy Holland America Line (114). Courtesy Holland America Line (114). Michel Verdure/Holland America Line (115). Michel Verdure/Holland America Line (116). Holland America Line (116). Holland America Line (117). Michael S. Nolan (118). Michael S. Nolan (118). Sisse Brimberg & Cotton Coulson/Lindblad Expeditions (119). Stewart Cohen (120). Michael S. Nolan (120). 2018 Danny Lehman/Norwegian Cruise Line (122). Courtesy Norwegian Cruise Line (122). 2017 Rick Diaz Photography/Norwegian Cruise Line Unlimited Usage (123). Courtesy Norwegian Cruise Line (124). 2017 Rick Diaz Photography/Norwegian Cruise Line (124). 2018 Rick Diaz Photography/Norwegian Cruise Line (124). Courtesy Norwegian Cruise Line (126). Courtesy Norwegian Cruise Line (126). Courtesy Norwegian Cruise Line (127). Michel Verdure/ Norwegian Cruise Line (128). Michel Verdure/Norwegian Cruise Line (128). Michel Verdure/Norwegian Cruise Line (129). 2017 Norwegian Cruise Line (130). 2018 Tom Roesser.Norwegian Cruise Line Unlimited Usage (130). 2018 Rick Diaz Photography/Norwegian Cruise Line (131). Courtesy of Oceania Cruises, Inc. (132–137). Princess Cruises (138–146). Andy Newman/Princess Cruises (147). Courtesy Regent Seven Seas Cruises (148–150). Courtesy Regent Seven Seas Cruises (152). Michel Verdure (152). Courtesy Regent Seven Seas Cruises (153). Courtesy Royal Caribbean International (154–160). Courtesy Royal Caribbean International (162). Courtesy Royal Caribbean International (162). Courtesy of Seabourn Cruise Line (164–168). Courtesy of Silversea Cruises (170–175). AMOS (176–177). InnerSea Discoveries (178–180). Archimage (182). Courtesy of Viking Cruises (182). Eric Laignel (183). Courtesy of Viking Cruises (184). Archimage (184). Courtesy of Viking Cruises (184). Courtesy of Viking Cruises (186). Courtesy of Windstar (188). Courtesy of Windstar (188). Courtesy of Windstar (189). Courtesy of Windstar (190). Courtesy of Windstar (190). Courtesy of Windstar (190). Courtesy of Windstar (192). Courtesy of Windstar (193). Asterixvs | Dreamstime.com (194). Chapter 4: Ports of Embarkation: Courtesy of Agua Verde Paddle Club (195). Jose Fuste Raga / age fotostock (211). Richard Cummins / age fotostock (215). Mark Newman/age fotostock (221). Chris Cheadle / age fotostock (226). SuperStock / age fotostock (231). Steve Rosset/iStockphoto (234–235). Hannamariah/Shutterstock (237). Stephen Frink Collection / Alamy (239). ImageState / Alamy (239). Andoni Canela/age fotostock (240). Michael S. Nolan/age fotostock (242). Chapter 5: Ports of Call: Alaska Stock LLC / Alamy (245). Bryan Busovicki/Shutterstock (251). Bryan & Cherry Alexander Photography / Alamy (261). Walleyelj | Dreamstime.com (262). Sitka National Historical Park (263). Tracy Ferrero / Alamy (263). Tracy Ferrero / Alamy (264–265). crmarlow (274). Sandy1122 (282). FLPA/Mark Newman / age fotostock (286). Chip Porter / age fotostock (290). True North Images/age fotostock (298). Alyssaand | Dreamstime.com (300). Rolf Hicker / age fotostock (301). Renaud Visage/age fotostock (303). Alaska Stock LLC / Alamy (303). Brandon Laufenberg/iStockphoto (305). Nancy Nehring/iStockphoto (307). Tammy Wolfe/iStockphoto (312). Xuanlu Wang/Shutterstock (320). Chapter 6: Island Cruise Tour Destinations: crmarlow (327). Patricia Fisher/Fisher Photography (333). PhotoDisc (345). About Our Writers: All photos are courtesy of the writers except for the following: Linda Coffman, Courtesy of Mel Coffman.

Fodor's THE COMPLETE GUIDE TO ALASKA CRUISES

Editorial: Douglas Stallings, *Editorial Director*; Margaret Kelly, Jacinta O'Halloran, *Senior Editors*; Kayla Becker, Alexis Kelly, Amanda Sadlowski, *Editors*; Teddy Minford, *Content Editor*; Rachael Roth, *Content Manager*

Design: Tina Malaney, *Design and Production Director*; Jessica Gonzalez, *Production Designer*

Photography: Jill Krueger, *Senior Photo Editor*

Maps: Rebecca Baer, *Senior Map Editor*; Mark Stroud (Moon Street Cartography), David Lindroth, *Cartographers*

Production: Jennifer DePrima, *Editorial Production Manager*; Carrie Parker, *Senior Production Editor*; Elyse Rozelle, *Production Editor*

Business & Operations: Chuck Hoover, *Chief Marketing Officer*; Joy Lai, *Vice President and General Manager*; Stephen Horowitz, *Director of Business Development and Revenue Operations*; Tara McCrillis, *Director of Publishing Operations*

Public Relations and Marketing: Joe Ewaskiw, *Manager*; Esther Su, *Marketing Manager*

Writers: Teeka Ballas, Joey Besl, David Cannamore, Linda Coffman, Alexander Deedy, Amy Fletcher, Chris McBeath

Editor: Kayla Becker

Production Editor: Carrie Parker

Production Design: Liliana Guia

3rd Edition

ISBN 978-1-64097-121-9

ISSN 2330-4421

Library of Congress Control Number 2018950613

All details in this book are based on information supplied to us at press time. Always confirm information when it matters, especially if you're making a detour to visit a specific place. Fodor's expressly disclaims any liability, loss, or risk, personal or otherwise, that is incurred as a consequence of the use of any of the contents of this book.

SPECIAL SALES
This book is available at special discounts for bulk purchases for sales promotions or premiums. For more information, e-mail SpecialMarkets@fodors.com.

PRINTED IN THE UNITED STATES OF AMERICA

10 9 8 7 6 5 4 3 2 1

About Our Writers

Based in Anchorage, **Teeka Ballas** is the publisher/editor of F Magazine, Alaska's only independent statewide arts magazine. For 13 years, she has worked as a freelance writer, staffer and stringer for newspapers, international wire services, travel publications and radio. In addition, Ballas is the director and events coordinator for four statewide arts and media competitions, and directs teen musicals for Alaska Theatre of Youth. She worked on the Kenai Peninsula and Southcentral Alaska chapter this edition.

Joey Besl is a Cincinnati native (and unabashed Ohio-phile) now based in Anchorage, where he plans to continue exploring the North from the state's largest base camp. He works as a staff writer at University of Alaska Anchorage and can be found at the bus stops and bike lanes of the city. He updated the Anchorage, Fairbanks, and Yukon sections of this guide.

A lifelong Alaskan, **David Cannamore** makes his home in the tiny town of Gustavus on the footsteps of Glacier Bay National Park. After updating the Denali National Park and Preserve chapter this edition, David returned to his cabin, wife, cats, and summer occupation as a kayak guide. When not paddling, David can be found freelance writing, cobbling together a novel, or trying to make his tiny cabin more insulated.

Linda Coffman, our resident Cruise Diva, updated all the Alaska cruising content (both Planning and the Cruise Lines and Cruise Ships). She is a freelance travel writer who has been dishing out cruise-related advice and information for more than two decades.

Her articles have appeared online and in national magazines and newspapers, including *Porthole*, *Consumer's Digest*, the *Chicago Sun Times*, and *USA Today*. An avid cruiser, she spends most of her time cruising in the Caribbean when she's not at home in Augusta, Georgia.

Alexander Deedy is a freelance writer who wrote parts of the Experience chapter this edition.

The catalyst for **Amy Fletcher's** initial visit to Alaska in 1992 was an enticing two-line description of Juneau's stunning natural beauty in a travel guide. She arrived to find the writer had not exaggerated, and two decades later she still calls the city home. She currently works as the arts editor for the Juneau Empire. She updated Juneau, the Inside Passage, and Southeast Alaska and Travel Smart for this guide.

Award-winning freelance travel writer **Chris McBeath** spent more than 25 years in the tourism industry, years that have given her an insider's eye about what makes a great vacation. British Columbia is her home, and she updated coverage of Vancouver, Victoria, Prince Rupert, and Seattle for this book.